BIRMINGHAM-SOUTHERN COLLEGE
5 0553 01079915 0

D0966278

LIBERTY AND EQUALITY

1920–1994

ALSO BY OSCAR AND LILIAN HANDLIN

Liberty in Peril 1850–1920 (1992)
Liberty in Expansion 1760–1850 (1989)
Liberty and Power 1600–1760 (1986)
A Restless People (1982)
John Dewey: The Middle Works (1982)
Abraham Lincoln and the Union (1980)

ALSO BY OSCAR HANDLIN

The Distortion of America (1981)
Truth in History (1979)
Occasions for Love (1977)
Pictorial History of Immigration (1972)
The Statue of Liberty (1971)
Children of the Uprooted (1966)
Fire-Bell in the Night: The Crisis in Civil Rights (1964)
The Americans (1963)
American Principles and Issues: The National Purpose (1961)
The Newcomers: Negroes and Puerto Ricans in a Changing Metropolis (1959)
John Dewey's Challenge to American Education (1959)
Immigration as a Factor in American History (1959)
Al Smith and His America (1958)
Readings in American History (1957)
Race and Nationality in American Life (1957)
Chance or Destiny (1955)
American People in the Twentieth Century (1954)
Harvard Guide to American History (1954)
Adventure in Freedom (1954)
The Uprooted (1951)
This Was America (1949)
Boston's Immigrants: A Study in Acculturation (1941)

ALSO BY LILIAN HANDLIN

George Bancroft: The Intellectual as Democrat (1984)

BY OSCAR AND MARY F. HANDLIN

The Wealth of the American People (1975)
Facing Life: Youth and the Family in American History (1971)
The American College and American Culture (1970)
The Popular Sources of Political Authority (1966)
The Dimensions of Liberty (1961)
Commonwealth: A Study of the Role of Government in the American Economy (1947)

LIBERTY IN AMERICA
1600 TO THE PRESENT

VOLUME FOUR

Liberty and Equality
1920-1994

Oscar and Lilian Handlin

HarperCollins*Publishers*

In the preparation of this volume we enjoyed the assistance of Kathleen Marotta.

HarperCollins books may be purchased for educational, business, or sales promotional use. For information please write: Special Markets Department, HarperCollins Publishers, Inc., 10 East 53rd Street, New York, NY 10022.

FIRST EDITION

Designed by Sidney Feinberg

Library of Congress Cataloging-in-Publication Data
(Revised for volume 4)

Handlin, Oscar, 1915–
Liberty in America, 1600 to the present.

Includes bibliographical references and indexes.
Contents: v. 1. Liberty and power, 1600–1760—
v. 2. Liberty in expansion, 1760–1850—[etc.]—
v. 3. Liberty in peril, 1850–1920—
v. 4. Liberty and equality, 1920–1994.
1. United States—Politics and government. 2. United States—History. I. Handlin, Lilian. II. Title.
E183.H32 1986 973 85-45997
ISBN 0-06-015617-1 (v. 1)
ISBN 0-06-039059-X (v. 1 : jacket)
ISBN 0-06-039092-1 (v. 2)
ISBN 0-06-039143-X (v. 3)
ISBN 0-06-017153-7 (v. 4)

---

94 95 96 97 98 cc/HC 10 9 8 7 6 5 4 3 2 1

For

Martin and Mary Ellen Wohl

CONTENTS

PREFACE

Liberty and Equality examines the troubled era that transformed the United States after 1920. The pages that follow do not pretend to trace the entire history of the nation in the period examined. Nor do they attempt to describe the evolving ideas about, or concepts of, liberty and equality as reflected in law, philosophy, or metaphysics. A large and provocative literature assembled by social scientists, philosophers, legal scholars, and some historians has treated the complex meanings of both terms and their relationship to various theories of justice. Abstract debates about the viability and desirability of a society dedicated to liberty and equality have concerned generations of thinkers. We chose, however, to examine the unfolding of a simple theme, albeit one central to the American experience: the forces that narrowed or expanded people's ability to act—that is, their freedom in their private and public lives. We therefore emphasized the conditions of life of ordinary men and women and the structures of their society, not the theories of either liberty or equality elaborated by thoughtful scholars.

We ask what kind of persons, leading what lives, joined the Klan or the Christian Front, followed the lead of Father Coughlin or Father Divine, of F.D.R. or J.F.K. in an effort to broaden their capacity to act, as members of families, as workers and voters, as worshipers and as neighbors.

Liberty remained in peril in the United States after 1920. Shackles on free expression and on other rights imposed in the heat of battle did not end with the peace, but became more intense if less visible. The crisis of wartime repression ended, but restraints on the people's ability to act did not fade away; freedom, no more secure after the end of the fighting than before, faced threats not only from acts of government but also from bands of citizens who had lost patience with conventional means of regulating society and sought other violent forms of doing so—as regulators had in the past, as Europeans did in the 1920s. Scientific theories of race generated the belief that the indiscriminate bestowal of the capacity to act on all men and women endangered society; some Americans resolved their fears by clamping down on liberty, in the belief that not everyone could equally enjoy it, that only the state's power could keep in line weak-willed people deficient in self-control who needed restrictive legislation to compel them to do what they could not do autonomously. Prohibition most visibly manifested the effort to impose uniformity upon an increasingly diverse society that sustained regional and local variations but paradoxically, at the same time, became more truly national. As in the past, so in the early part of the twentieth century Americans tried to bring order to the chaos of their lives through regimentation. Pining for a return to an imaginary normalcy, millions of citizens joined secret proto-fascist organizations (the Ku Klux Klan the best-known), held together by fear and hatred—of blacks, Jews, Catholics, and foreigners—as well as by suspicion of modernity deemed an insidious threat to the orderly way of life. The greater the future difficulties society faced, the greater the temptation to resolve them by abrogating some people's liberty.

Toward the end of the twentieth century, furious debates about the relationship between liberty and equality and about equality of opportunity and equality of results reflected the same tendency. The assumption that limiting some people's capacity to act would ultimately benefit the commonweal tempted social manipulators in the 1920s and later to exploit coercion by government to shape the contours of liberty.

The Great Depression of the 1930s therefore struck an already vulnerable society. Its massive personal dislocations and drastic contractions of economic opportunity spread despair that shadowed American life for decades. We ask what happened then to expectations of progress—of steady personal and social improvement. But the Depression did not generate a repressive regime of the type evolved elsewhere, even when the country slipped into a renewed war, global in character and culminating in the traumatic explosion of the atomic bomb. While other nations chose bread over freedom, most often getting neither, the United States entered an era of enormous transformations without meaningful shrinkage in popular ability to act. On the contrary, it then laid the foundation for the spread of freedom to ever-wider circles of the population, significantly expanding both liberty and equality, granting ever more people a meaningful capacity to act and an equality of opportunities previous generations would have envied.

Efforts to harness government to cure the nation's economic ills failed, as unemployment remained high. Though faddish theories, buttressed by impassioned self-righteousness that aimed to alleviate the Depression by restricting liberty, soon evaporated, the vogue for planning survived in spite of its failures. And the Depression crisis legitimized a restructuring of the relation of government to the productive system that affected Americans' ability to act in unintended ways. Though the Second World War supplied unity and discipline to overcome bitter social divisions, to cure a creaky economy and create a more relaxed political order, the experience left people shaken, still in despair about the future of liberty.

Unexpected dangers did not emanate only from government coerciveness. Once state-imposed wartime repression eased, men and women discovered that economic deprivation, racial prejudices, and gender differences forged restrictions on liberty earlier accepted as inescapable aspects of human experience. After 1950 unprecedented abundance exposed those limitations as arbitrary, unnecessary burdens on those who wished to advance beyond the New Frontier to the Great Society. By then unfair limitations of the equality of opportunity called for redress, in order to expand everyone's ability to act.

In response an untried experiment aimed to widen the scope of liberty to include the previously excluded. Past political handicaps had limited the underprivilegeds' access to power. In the flush of optimism fueled by an expanding economy, Americans embarked on a program of redress for women and for some ethnic groups that, for vastly different reasons and in different contexts, considered themselves disadvantaged minorities. The new agenda aimed to widen the capacity to act for those previously handicapped because of color or sex. No other society in history had tried to do the same on such a massive scale. And none succeeded so well in eradicating entrenched prejudices and double standards and also in broadening the equality of opportunity for all. That achievement seemed all the more impressive in 1994 when ethnic and tribal violence pockmarked the globe from Ulster to Corsica, Bosnia, Kurdistan, India, Sri Lanka, and West Irian, and almost every part of Africa.

But the process of endowing all people with the same ability to act and easing everyone's access to opportunity stirred up a new challenge in the linkage between liberty and equality. Americans then confronted difficulties that ironically stemmed from their very success in extending everyone's freedom. The tension between an egalitarian political system and a less-than-egalitarian economic system had troubled only a few during most of the nation's history. But in the second half of the twentieth century ever more influential segments of society sought redress of imbalances by redefining equality of opportunity in terms of equality of results, thereby endangering everyone's liberty.

Equality of results aimed to even out advantages among people who possessed unequal means for self-advancement. Its advocates denounced equality of opportunity as a meaningless sham lulling society's victims into acquiescence in their unjust inferiority. Only equality of results could remedy victimhood since the inherent inequalities among human beings otherwise led to unequal results. Different capacities to act, deemed the outcome of factors beyond individual control, could thus be manipulated out of existence.

Advocates of drastic measures to redress historic inequalities forgot that the antithesis of liberty was privilege, not inequality. Americans held equality of opportunity the corollary of the capacity to act, aiming thereby to combat unjustly derived advantages some people enjoyed through brute force, through discriminatory laws, and through values that arbitrarily favored them over others. In the United States the state historically was not the private preserve of a few, exploited on their own behalf. Government exercised power by the consent of the governed and, representing all citizens, could not favor some to the detriment of others.

The exercise of the capacity to act assumed the absence of artificial constraints upon the individual. And power limited by consent did not justify misuse through state intervention as by preferential treatment to correct the unwelcome results of equality of opportunity. A society in which coercion rather than the capacity to act determined fundamental choices of everyday life was one in which people were not free even if well-educated and fed, as were slaves whose masters cared prudently for their chattels.

We began this history four volumes ago with reflections upon the nineteenth-century dream of the Grand Inquisitor that also considered the attitudes of men and women to liberty. The eloquent words we paraphrased juxtaposed in opposition—bread and freedom—the demands of the belly and of the autonomous human spirit seeking to assert itself in the ability to act. From the seventeenth century onward, that polarity endured in the American experience as millions of newcomers entered a continent they considered empty, as they slowly brought it under modern cultivation, and as in time they fashioned a productive system that yielded them, and the rest of the world, abundance.

Yet for generations, for reasons embodied in their cultures, Americans also sought to develop and preserve decent communities they could transmit as a heritage to their successors. Success in doing so depended upon the use of power that balanced assurances of the ability of each to act and yet also controlled behavior to assure others also the ability to act. Americans rejected the merely negative understanding of liberty as the absence of restraint, knowing that the human condition demanded positive aids to assertion of the self. The quest for balance between the one and the many, between the individual and the group, led to the creation of political institutions for governing by consent expressed through law. Those efforts occupied the seventeenth, eighteenth, and nineteenth centuries, and much of the twentieth as well. For generations, therefore, the conception of the role of the state remained fluid, even as historic definitions of the ability to act and of equality of opportunity changed.

In those centuries Americans also learned how to govern themselves and created the multiple structures and symbols of civil society. They transmitted those skills to millions of newcomers who in turn passed similar skills on to their children. Liberty and equality of opportunity defined the contours of those skills, which never hardened into a rigid ideology. Their elasticity and flexibility facilitated gigantic readjustments. The United States escaped the arrogant destructive ideologies masked with cosmic slogans that provided alibis for twentieth-century tyrannical experiments in utopianism, with their murderous outcomes. In the face of great changes, Americans clung to the historically defined versions of liberty and equality that had served many of them well.

The capacity to act they presumed to be inherent in every moral human being within limits defined by rules agreed to by all who played the same game. The uniqueness of each person produced inequalities of rewards, subject to numerous forces beyond the control of either individual or society. But unequal outcomes within limits were acceptable; wealth disparities in the United States always bothered foreign visitors more than natives. The fact that a few had vastly more than most did not for many people reflect an unjust natural order in need of manipulation, although voices of protest tried unsuccessfully to make Americans less accepting of the realities of their lives.

The twentieth century tested the durability of the laborious achievements of earlier generations. Balances earlier deemed sufficient seemed increasingly less relevant. Inherited conceptions of the capacity to act and of the equality of opportunities failed to satisfy many who demanded broader versions of both. Discontent stemmed in part from the heritage of the New Deal and the Second World War, which provided the momentum for economic expansion along with the necessary government machinery. Those changes also legitimized new social priorities sustaining the social safety net and expanding personal security, to guard citizens against some of the hazards of modern life. Americans still insisted upon a political system of limited authority, exercising power based on consent, and they resented unwarranted extensions of that power by unauthorized bodies and pressure groups. But they no longer regarded the state simply as a mechanism for the procedural settlement of communal conflicts. Instead, government became crucial in expanding people's capacity to act. Increasingly also some people regarded it as a means of obliterating inequalities among citizens.

Earlier generations had relied on self-generated local organizations to deal with the exigencies of disasters. Spontaneous committees took charge when other resources failed. But in the twentieth century voluntarism would no longer do; government bore the brunt of those functions and underwrote citizens' capacity to act, during earthquakes, floods, or hurricanes. That shift involved a compromise between national needs and individual aspirations—a compromise achieved so successfully that the old European question—"Liberty—can we eat liberty?"—for most Americans seemed an irrelevancy.

After 1950, therefore, the historical imperatives of a choice between bread and liberty receded in importance—so much so that one historian in the 1970s could not even understand the relevance of Dostoyevsky's problem to the United States. Abundance ended the want of bread and social change sanctioned the pursuit of personal gratification. But gratified desires proved unsatisfying; suddenly liberated from conventions, people found themselves adrift and discovered the steep cost of pursuing their ambitions. To be utterly free then actually meant to be totally enslaved.

Being a Superwoman did not prove liberating, merely exhausting. Easy divorce penalized women by freeing men to shirk their responsibilities—not what reform legislation intended. And the happiness of free-spirited parents often cost their offspring dearly, to remedy which another rights movement took form—children's rights, part of a social trend that defined individual happiness through socially sustained privileges rather than through mutual obligations. Not all children thereupon embarked on complicated judicial proceedings to divorce their parents but a few did, or, like the Menendez brothers, simply murdered them. The dissolution of familial bonds with the help of the judicial system revealed how blurred the contours of liberty had become since the days when the only debate concerned the size of the stick with which a father could chastise his child.

These changes occurred amidst unprecedented material abundance that permitted a social revolution to eradicate all differences stemming from unequal capacities to take advantage of the opportunities available to all. This change in orientation survived periodic economic contractions that tested the system's ability to accommodate novel demands. Meanwhile developments in the last quarter of the century transformed the ways in which people lived, learned, worked, raised children, sickened, aged, and died. The incapacity of many to meet these changes successfully refueled the debate on the relationship between equality and liberty, between the capacity to act and the unequal results of the ways in which people exploited opportunities.

A vast advice industry tried to satisfy the need for guidance, with government bureaucrats often in the lead. Varied media, in support, joined on a new information superhighway that actually left people more ignorant than before. And since nothing achieved measured up to the need, occasional periods of gloom, buttressed by pseudoscientific decline theories, made people feel that they had lost liberty—precisely when the choices enjoyed should have made them feel more liberated. But the more choices they confronted, the greater the confusion, and the worse the sense of being trapped, that is, unfree. The growing emphasis on the power of the state to remedy personal shortcomings aimed by limiting some people's capacity to act to expand that of others. Coercion was thus proposed to end the conflict between the needs of liberty and the needs of equality by sacrificing the former to the latter, in view of the difficulty of sustaining both.

Stratagems in the Great Society programs that reconciled liberty and promised equality of outcomes left Americans no more satisfied than before. The achievements of the 1960s did not lessen tensions between individual and social needs, between the desire to be free and communal yearnings. Nor did they fully reconcile liberty and equality. Deep fears and disappointments did not subside for a person told that he or she was merely victim of an "individual as central sensibility." Cultural and political revolutions also led to dead ends, since none evolved quite as expected. Most met Andy Warhol's standard for durability in the modern world—anyone could be famous for fifteen minutes. Meanwhile giant universities, foundations, and philanthropic agencies abandoned their former objectives to provide remedies for the perplexed citizenry. Simply Living Programs urged everyone to take charge of their lives, by eating organic foods, joining cooperatives, thinking globally while acting locally, recycling, doing with less, and supporting insurgencies the world over in places most people could not locate on a map. The slogans along the route traveled in pursuit of American liberty changed each decade, but the dilemmas remained the same. From Henry Ford to Lee Iaccoca, from Upton Sinclair to Tom Hayden, from "Leave it to Beaver" via "Ozzie and Harriet," to "All in the Family" and finally to "Archie's Place," none of the answers were wholly persuasive.

Ultimately the issues remained the same—how to live freely without the guidance of external restraints and how to compensate for human variations that determined unequal outcomes. The persistent gap between aspirations and achievements, between dreams and reality, renewed tensions and miseries. Irrelevancies that diverted attention from genuine difficulties offered some relief. But the focus on multiculturalism and bilingual education, the quest for role models and self-esteem along with pathetic naming and renaming enterprises, merely papered over the lack of a will to confront deep social problems.

Fashionable reinventions of the self aimed to cope with such challenges. Self-conscious attempts by people to recast themselves and gain greater liberty through a new self-assurance more in tune with the times included varieties of color power and other forms of liberation. New and presumably more satisfying identities would provide the capacity to act in the modern world. Though most reinventors of the self actually enjoyed more liberty than their predecessors, they felt powerless, in part because they lacked their parents' certainties. The slogan "The personal is political," which transformed private maladies into public issues, compensated for individual shortcomings by turning them into social grievances. The success of many in doing just that produced a crowded social agenda, within which the serious and the trivial received equal time.

A multiplicity of new politics expressed the confusion, yearning, like "the politics of meaning," to quiet the fears of individuals standing alone, confronting the transitory nature of life. But efforts to translate mushy feelings and controversial humanisms into concrete programs floundered. Such efforts resembled the religious awakenings that had erupted in American history in times of change and stress, seeking to remodel society and the individual for the sake of a higher goal, never attaining the moral utopia. At the end of the twentieth century the disappointed zealots took to jogging to relieve their stress while an ever flexible consumer industry cashed in on their need to test the limits of physical endurance in order to feel truly free. Meanwhile earnest types tried to fuel the discontent essential to rekindle the engine of social progress, which, however, carried advocates in unwelcome directions.

Antiauthoritarian trends corroded the structure of civility on which everyone's capacity to act ultimately depended. The relentless intrusion of violence into many aspects of life, the decriminalization of behaviors once deemed deviant, and delegitimization campaigns ostensibly in the name of liberty undermined community structures and diminished everyone's capacity to act. The declining influence of parties and the intrusion of forces difficult to reconcile with the nation's founding documents weakened the political process while the aggrieved, unable to attain their goals democratically, subverted the judiciary to institutionalize private visions of paradise few others shared. The Bill of Rights could not accommodate all the emanations from the country's more progressive law schools.

But those who despaired of the nation's future—a common American malady that cropped up periodically in the nation's history—failed to reckon with the millions whose lives belied the dark forecasts. The alienation, discontent, unbelief, and deep unhappiness that infused the articulate and the underclass left the vast middle class far less affected. Most of them made peace with their existence and contended with surrounding tempests largely by ignoring them. In the face of many challenges, their core values remained constant. Those included honesty, sociability, responsibility, the work ethic, and expectation of a measure of equality of opportunity. Perhaps these values no longer fitted the reality of their lives, but most people, not as farsighted as social scientists, seemed mired in an emotional and valuational universe misaligned, academics told them, with the world they actually inhabited. Blank incomprehension or outright hostility therefore often greeted proposals, articulated in terms foreign to ordinary experiences, to change the situation. The mass of people regarded neither cross-dressing, blurred sexual identities, nor bearing children out of wedlock as forms of liberation. But the fact that such issues were even debated measured the distance the nation had traveled since the seventeenth century, when John Winthrop attempted to define the nature of liberty in the New World.

Most citizens also rebelled against the idea that the public sphere took primacy over the private, from within which they derived their deepest satisfactions and pleasures. Critics regarded the general apathy toward the political system and the low voter turnout as proof that American society lacked legitimacy—a sham democracy without a moral basis, merely satisfying rapacious consumers. But most people disagreed and resented efforts to widen the public sphere, which they suspected correctly aimed to obliterate the private one entirely, since that yearned-for equality of outcomes could only be reached in the public arena where all individuals were controllable. But equality of opportunities paid the handsomest dividends precisely in the private sphere where equality of outcome was irrelevant, and where the inequalities of life were ironed out, usually to everyone's satisfaction. Hence the popular resistance also to attempts to transform the state into an instrument that administered all human affairs, rather than only the justice essential to coexistence. People instinctively remembered Thomas Paine's judgment that government was the badge of lost innocence, designed to keep immoral and sinful people in line, a dangerous instrument whose ultimate reliance on coercion, rather than on freely bestowed loyalty and consent, could just as easily take away what it freely bestowed.

The nation born in the chaotic disorder of seventeenth-century settlement had learned to curb power by consent and embarked on a never-ending process of assuring its citizens' capacity to act. It did so in 1776 by assuming everyone's fitness for freedom, at first abstractly, but in the course of the nineteenth century ever more concretely. It was a testament to the elasticity of Americans' versions of equality and liberty that they accommodated to all these and other pressures and still sustained themselves. Whether the capacity to act will remain as central to the American experience as it has hitherto been, and whether equality of opportunity rather than equality of outcome will prevail, are among the questions that Americans will confront in the new millennium. Perhaps they will profit from learning about the distance traveled since 1600.

PART I

THE WORLD MADE SAFE—
FOR DESPAIR:
1920–1950

CHAPTER 1

THE NORMALCY SLOPE

ALL OF A SUDDEN, the proud structure of Progressivism collapsed. High hopes of a New Freedom that would restore to everyone opportunity and the ability to act, that would indeed expand liberty to a world made safe for democracy—all that turned to nothingness. Americans had too complacently accepted as an inheritance institutions wartime intolerance put in peril. They could not forget they had branded as a traitor the senator who had voted against the war. Amidst the ashes of fine aspirations, only the awkward interval of normalcy seemed appropriate—the wished-for return to something previous, to a pristine state in which the nation set a quiet, orderly course safely away from the idealistic aspirations of turbulent intellectual dreamers.

When that idyllic state soon proved unattainable, those who pinned their hopes on reaching it collapsed in despair. A tempest of gloomy books prophesied that a revolution would sweep away the traditional foundations of western civilization—personal liberty, independent property, and governments accountable to free people. Black veterans returned with few illusions about prospective gains in status, and a general skepticism about progress spread. Men did not long for liberty, H. L. Mencken concluded, but wanted something wholly different, security, which required a mystical surrender of individuality to deified politicians and superhuman engineers.[1]

The closing scene of the Progressive drama, lugubriously played out in the invalid's darkened White House room, revealed a determined wife, a loyal secretary, and an indecisive physician, agreed on the necessity of keeping the full truth from the public. The irresolute Vice President did not know what action to take; the Secretary of State, who alone of the

Cabinet spoke out, earned dismissal by doing so. The Republic floundered, leaderless, while in the gloom of the Executive Mansion's empty East Room a shrunken figure in a wheelchair watched William S. Hart, Tom Mix, and other western movie heroes. Senate rejection of the Treaty of Versailles and defeat of the League of Nations left the country without a peace and set it adrift to the normalcy that finally lowered the curtain on the Progressive vision. The bleak White House gates stood chained and locked, emblems of general frustration and unhappiness.

Woodrow Wilson, stricken, hardly knew what happened and did not stay the trend. He had overlooked the possibility that the Senate might fail to ratify the Treaty of Versailles, assuming that he could control his own party and expecting little opposition from Republicans. He had, however, blundered when he had called for a Democratic Congress in the election of 1918, hoping to capitalize on wartime unity sentiment for his own purposes. The partisanship he thus stirred hurt in the treaty fight. Furthermore, censorship and the stifling of dissenting opinion had closed off the information that might have warned him of the approaching danger. As it was, defeat caught him completely unprepared.

The failure extended beyond the fate of the treaty to the loss of presidential control and a drift toward isolation from the outer world. The United States sloped down from the old idealism to an unreal normalcy, epitomized in Senators William E. Borah and Henry Cabot Lodge, who led the rejectionist forces, calling for Americanism and nationalism, denouncing internationalism. Borah, an erratic old-time progressive, had never traveled outside the United States and saw no reason for involvement in alien affairs; the President, he charged, had betrayed the troops in the field. Lodge, who termed the League "the evil thing with the holy name," capped his triumph over Wilson by securing the presidential nomination for Warren G. Harding, who promised the nation "Not heroics but healing; not nostrums but normalcy; not revolution but restoration."[2]

In 1920 the United States had solved none of the great problems that had beset it at the opening of the twentieth century. For political leadership during the next decade the nation reached back to men suitable for the 1890s, types who had thrived before the national stir Theodore Roosevelt had created.

Normalcy implied that nothing in the structure of government had changed, or at least seemed to have changed, and the electorate preferred it thus. Divided among federal, state, and local jurisdictions, the forms already in place remained much as they had been, or seemed to do so.

In Washington the Chief Executive presided over an enlarged bureaucracy, essentially as before, confronting Congress under the benevolent oversight of the judiciary in a balance that persisted because no one pushed too hard. The average Southern congressman, "a knavish and preposterous nonentity, halfway between a kleagle of the Ku Klux and a grand worthy bow-wow of the Knights of Zoroaster," dominated the legislative process.

The executive departments changed only slightly. A new budget bureau and a General Accounting Office aimed to systematize and control finances, and a growing number of independent agencies, run by experts, operated by codes of administrative law impervious to popular wishes. The Rogers Act (1924) thus organized the professional Foreign Service composed of career diplomats. But the Joint Congressional Committee on Reorganization to study the Executive Branch floundered in the face of "barricades and stumbling blocks in every direction"—except when it came to demands for agricultural credits and for aid to business. The District of Columbia remained a cozy Southern town, not yet air-conditioned and therefore all but empty in the summer.[3]

The political mechanism still operated through the inherited two-party system—with a periodic contest for office every four years. The conventions, the electoral campaigns, and the transitions between Democrats and Republicans proceeded as uneventfully as the cycle of the seasons. The "difficult but dirty game" called for "qualities of low cunning, audacity, unscrupulousness and hypocrisy," but gave the voters an illusion of choice. Meanwhile hundreds of associations and groups lobbied on behalf of their own agendas.

Dissident socialist and progressive organizations faded away except in the West, where the Nonpartisan League and the Farmer Labor Party retained footholds. The Progressive Party of 1924, largely a creation of Robert M. La Follette, secured the support of the American Federation of Labor, tempted by the example of England, where a labor party actually came to power. But the Progressives had no effect on the outcome. The Democrats snatched defeat from the jaws of victory by nominating a conservative Eastern lawyer and a Western radical; the voters preferred Coolidge to chaos—a good thing, according to a political scientist, because it prevented confrontation on clear-cut issues.[4]

Some states indulged in experiment as local conditions permitted; occasionally, forceful governors like Al Smith in New York and Huey P. Long in Louisiana made a difference, the one to sponsor welfare legislation that aided the neglected masses, the other to create a brutal despotism for his own advantage. On Bloody Monday (1929), the Long followers forced the Louisiana House to adjourn so that it could not hear charges that he had ordered the assassination of one of its members. Representatives screamed that the electric tabulating devices had miscalculated the votes, then threw inkpots and punched one another with brass knuckles. Long, like other bosses, claimed credit for building improvements—roads, bridges, schools, an airport, and an unneeded new capital, all of which made jobs for followers and enriched contractors; he therefore never lacked funds to finance his campaigns. Such picaresque characters and spectacular outbreaks only rarely attracted attention; more characteristically, inertia ruled the state capitals in the 1920s.[5]

Government in the great cities hardly changed. Antique machines functioned unchallenged under the likes of Edward H. Crump, Frank Hague, James Michael Curley, Edward J. Kelly, and Jimmy Walker, who dispensed patronage and favors with feudal benevolence and made a good thing of it. There was a Golden Rule in politics: never hesitate to go around the corner for a friend. Guaranteed the support of loyal ethnic groups, the mayors had working arrangements with local labor leaders and sometimes operated in tacit alliance with bootlegging, gambling, and prostitution gangs. New York's great sewer scandal impoverished widows and workers, but enabled Jack Phillips, the pipe king, to dine from a $200,000 dinner service. Frank Hague ("I am the law in Jersey City") ruled from a plush Park Avenue penthouse in Manhattan. They despised the reformer—"a guy who rides through a sewer in a glass-bottomed boat." Yet proposals to create an American Scotland Yard insulated from political influence got nowhere; citizens already resented federal agents who enforced Prohibition laws.[6]

Paradoxically, soaring numbers compelled reformers in the postwar decade to give more thought to city planning than earlier. Some, inclined to write the metropolis off as politically hopeless, dreamed of breaking it up into smaller communities. Others sought to bypass existing municipalities by quasi-governmental authorities charged with specific functions, appointed by the states and isolated from local control. The Port of New York Authority, for instance, created in 1921 in imitation of its counterpart in London, received the power to build and operate harbor facilities. Independent of tax support, financed by bonds, its intricate machinery called for disinterested administration by experts able to offset the conflicting pressure of rival interests. In the corridors of scores of city halls, as in Washington, D.C., and in the state capitals, energetic lobbyists urged the causes of industry, labor, agriculture, and reform. Often off the target, they fired into the rarefied air of their own little circles. Only the trained bureaucrat could precisely appraise these pressures, and, free of popular interference, could make the choice that would provide the maximum satisfaction. Quasi-governmental agencies, usually created for limited terms, acquired permanence—their ideal, administration as a science—but they widened the gap between the people and the government. The specific, laudable design—to place important functions beyond public, and thus potentially corrupting, reach—curtailed citizens' ability to act and thereby impacted negatively on liberty.[7]

In the 1920s the state and federal governments felt the impact of similar influences. In Washington career assistant secretaries supplanted political Cabinet officers in operations. New York, Massachusetts, and other states, on the basis of recommendations from reconstruction commissions, reorganized and streamlined departments, centralizing responsibility in the governor and aiming for nonpartisan efficiency in every aspect of their activities. Even Huey Long's Louisiana imported out-of-state experts, engineers, draftsmen, and inspectors to design its highway program, thereby subtly curtailing the freedom of the citizens while seeming to broaden their liberty. By 1924 government payrolls supported one in ten American employees. Rural political machines, moreover, gained strength from road-building contracts and from alliances with friendly neighborhood gamblers and bootleggers. Despite the effects of the New Deal and the war, these patterns of control would endure through the 1940s.[8]

Broader reforms followed. In some states, statutes regulating conditions of industrial labor surmounted the constitutional hurdles set up by the courts. Improved workmen's compensation laws and more adequate provision for the care of dependents guarded against the hazards of modern society. New York in 1926 expanded low-income housing by granting tax concessions and the power of condemnation to cooperative and limited-dividend corporations. Worries about forest, wildlife, and water power resources strengthened conservation measures and revealed increased concern for the environment; wanton destruction and exfoliation gave way to more control over the way in which humans related to nature. Support for public education increased, and higher outlays did more than accommodate a larger number of pupils; the amount spent on each child multiplied almost as fast. To provide the necessary funds, the states raised taxes, some of them on income. Higher budgets and tighter controls thus seemed both to expand and yet contract the scope of liberty, no longer regarded as the antithesis of social control, but as its product, secured by obedience to the law, identical with the interests of all the people. The relationship to organized labor, however, remained especially unclear, particularly during great nationwide strikes in the coal fields and railroads.[9]

Nothing mattered, not even political ambivalence. In the popular view, politicians less often played sinister than comic roles. H. L. Mencken described the average congressman as an ignoramus quite without the average decencies. Harding's speeches, said William Gibbs McAdoo, "left the impression of an army of pompous phrases moving over the landscape in search of an idea. Sometimes the meandering words would actually capture a straggling thought and bear it triumphantly, a prisoner in their midst, until it died of servitude and overwork." The poet hailed "the only man, woman, or child who wrote a simple declarative sentence with seven grammatical errors." Of a candidate who sought to make honesty his policy, Will Rogers commented that it was not an issue in politics, but a miracle. In *Of Thee I Sing,* a successful musical mockery of the system (1931), the friendless Vice President spends his years in office seeking the two personal references needed for a library card. Fred Allen's Senator Claghorn articulated popular cynicism when he explained that the army, having spent two billion dollars to send fly swatters to Alaska only to discover that no flies existed there, then spent four billion dollars more to raise flies "so's they could use them fly swatters." The vast expansion in governmental authority did not quell age-old hostilities and suspicions. With the concept of liberty "quite beyond the reach of the inferior man's mind," few embraced wholeheartedly the state apparatus as an instrument of expanding citizens' ability to act.[10]

Normalcy conceded the futility of all positive governmental endeavor, whether under the nominal leadership of the fun-loving Warren G. Harding, who opened the White House to tourists, or of the dour Calvin Coolidge, "weaned on a dill pickle," who had never visited Washington before his nomination, or of the latter-day progressive, Herbert Hoover. Even many reformers lost heart. They could "talk for hours on everything from Marxism to the modern novel," but joined no movements—none any good; every man his own Jesus. In 1920 twenty-five million citizens eligible to vote stayed away from the polls, and participation levels remained low through the decade. Calvin Coolidge, urged to speak out, commented, "I don't recall any candidate for President that ever injured himself very much by not talking." Radio, the great postwar innovation, did not significantly alter campaign practice before 1929. The country had turned its back upon excessive idealism at home and abroad and allowed liberty to serve in the slogans of fringe groups.[11]

* * *

The United States rejected the lofty vision of Wilson's New Freedom and of Theodore Roosevelt's Square Deal. Corruption in the Veterans Bureau and in the Cabinet, and the Teapot Dome Scandal, spoiled enjoyment of the fun and games Harding considered among the rewards of office. His successors Coolidge and Hoover yielded to no similar temptations. But all three Presidents espoused economic policies oriented toward business. They believed that the citizens' capacity to act depended on the nation's material well-being, which favorable programs would enhance.

More than nostalgia animated the yearning for normalcy. Americans aimed not to restore imaginary nineteenth-century patterns of life but rather to achieve a static society that had never existed in actuality, one that expressed the inchoate desires for order of people fearful of losing themselves in the maelstrom of rapid change in a botched civilization. They had no desire, by reaching out, to sink "to the level of the coolie in a breech clout, the peon in a coffee sack, and the peasant in rags." Their ideal remained a white-steepled church on a small town's Main Street where neighbors helped each other and the doctor made house calls, a world of Kiwanians or Rotarians or knights and ladies of some sort, respectful of law, with all in place unthreatened by change, enhancing their liberty.[12]

For decades the memory of the war and of the peace, both failures, remained a standing reproof to any who wished to draw the nation into conflicts beyond strictly defined self-interest. Painful frustrations freshened feelings of ideological betrayal and defeat. Selfish pursuit of narrow concerns by the victorious allies in the 1920s convinced Americans of the merits of aloofness. "Let the internationalist dream and the Bolshevist" be destroyed, declared Harding. "In the spirit of the Republic we proclaim Americanism and acclaim America." Europe had not improved; the collapse of monarchs brought worse regimes to power. The new East European states, except for Czechoslovakia, proved no more worthy of support than the empires they had replaced. The specter of revolution everywhere stalked the Continent. Communist disrespect for legality unleashed a fearful force; Fascists seized power in Italy; and the German Republic floundered, its economic and social problems unsolved. Unable to reform it, Americans abandoned the Old World to the grim alternatives of Communism and fascism, while the professional diplomats who controlled the State Department arranged the terms of peaceful coexistence by settling war debts and by negotiating disarmament agreements.[13]

Disillusioned citizens sought the refuge of isolation, demanded total—one hundred percent—Americanism. Unable to understand why their great crusade had failed, they hid behind conspiracy theories applied at home as well as abroad. Confronting daily the harsh need to work in order to get by, often they perceived the long arms of secret manipulators behind their frustration. Whatever did not conform they wished to exclude from their folk community. Vice President Coolidge (1921) thus denounced Eastern women's colleges as hotbeds of radicalism and Bolshevism. Henry Ford gloried in his ignorance of American history, and President Harding's Commissioner of Education proclaimed that if he had the power he "would not only imprison, but would expatriate all" Communists, anarchists, and socialists. Billy Sunday wished to stand wild-eyed socialists before a firing squad; America was "not a country for a dissenter to live in." In vain Senator Borah denounced efforts to control opinion by law and insisted that Americanism depended on the right of free agents to express their views without restraint. Nevertheless Attorney General Daughtery managed to suppress a book purporting to reveal the black blood in the Harding genealogy, and Will Hays, once postmaster, as Hollywood's czar blocked the filming of Nan Britton's fanciful account of her romance with the President. Babylon seemed to William Allen White the setting for a Sunday school story compared with Washington from 1921 to July 1923. In the confused democracy, the many seemed about to fall—"still to be wrangling in a noisy grave."[14]

Economic nationalism meanwhile built a defensive barrier against the outer world. Rising tariffs protected Americans from tempting imports, although the United States sought to export as much as possible and dumped its agricultural surpluses where it could. Alas, the war had turned the country into an international creditor so that potential foreign customers lacked the dollars with which to close the gap between what they bought and what they sold. No matter; a steady flow of loans and investment capital made up the deficiency. Meanwhile the higher prices for foreign goods limited the American consumers' freedom to buy what they wished.[15]

Immigration policy revealed the isolationist trend and the contraction of liberty. Normalcy rejected the openness that for three centuries had welcomed newcomers in the confident expectation that all would contribute to New World expansion. The confidence that the nation of the future would blend diverse strains, each with something to contribute, still sustained traditional policy. But increasingly the more strident advocates of normalcy sought to slam shut the gate by stiff physical, mental, and genetic tests, redefining liberty along racial and ethnic lines.[16]

The immigrants and their offspring after 1920 seemed an ominous presence. The long tradition of inclusiveness did not offset dread of the damaging consequences of easy entry. Laws to bar the diseased, polygamists, and anarchists (codified in 1917) had failed to limit total admissions. Nor had the literacy test enacted over President Wilson's veto (1917). Astonished restrictionists confronted newcomers who learned to read and write. During the war, the Americanization movement had aimed to obliterate recollections of alien birthplaces and cultures. Not good enough! The newcomers threatened to introduce into this country "the European political system whereby government" became a mere balancing of class-conscious groups, each seeking its own advantage at the expense of all the rest—a sort of perpetual civil war.

The antiimmigration movement gained strength from popular racism, buttressed by geneticists, sociologists, and historians. Lothrop Stoddard blanched when he contemplated (1920) the handful of slow-breeding Harvard men who would confront the numerous offspring of fast-breeding Poles at the end of the century. A survey counted twenty-five different languages and dialects spoken at a single Pittsburgh factory. When an Albanian murdered a Greek in the same city, he spent the first night in jail singing his tribal war songs and cursing the ancient enemies of his race. Immigrants not only undermined America's cultural values, they brought to the New World their destructive hatreds and conflicts. The presumed racial inferiority of Malays had earlier justified denial of citizenship to Filipinos; and in 1917 Congress excluded all natives of an Asian "barred zone"—a first step to a more general restrictive policy, aimed at preventing "the hybridizing of races," a future source of friction and danger to democracy,

> O liberty, white goddess . . . with
> . . . hands of steel
> Stay those who to thy sacred portals come
> To waste the gifts of freedom.[17]

Color and other biological features divided human beings and made Slavs, Latins, and Jews—rat men tearing down America—inferior to the more desirable Nordics and Anglo-Saxons, therefore unworthy additions to the national stock. These racial components in the definition of liberty gained force when peace in 1918 brought a revival in immigration. The number of entries rose rapidly until 1924, when hostile American legislation arbitrarily cut it short. The national origins quota system, first embodied in the Johnson Act of 1921, then made permanent in 1924 and amended in 1929, admitted 150,000 applicants each year. Every nation received a quota which bore the same relation to the total as the number of Americans derived from it bore to the whole population of the United States. Great Britain, Ireland, and Germany got more than two-thirds of the spaces. By contrast, Southern Europe received niggardly treatment: Italy only 5,802 and Greece but 307. The presumed linkage among race, nationality, and fitness for freedom provided the justification for restriction.[18]

After 1924 few immigrants arrived, and those were largely members of reunited families. Restrictive legislation made entry difficult, the cost of crossing mounted, and illiberal regimes in Italy, Germany, and Russia held their residents at home. Europe's population having ceased to grow, pressure for departure eased, and the Great Depression of the 1930s fixed people where they were. Universal unemployment made movement pointless except for the northward drift from Mexico, where numbers continued to rise. Wartime labor shortages in the United States attracted about a million legal entrants into the country between 1917 and 1920, in addition to those who simply slipped across the border.

The restrictionists blamed the melting pot for destroying national unity and for lowering standards of living. In addition to halting any further influx, the nation needed to purify itself of the foreign elements already present. To that end, the national government sought to deport dissident radicals, assuming them all aliens, while criminal syndicalist laws hounded into jails troublemakers who, surprisingly, proved to be citizens. The American Protective League, the American Legion, and the Daughters of the American Revolution hunted unpatriotic elements and sniffed out disloyalty in textbooks, while Mayor "Big Bill" Thompson, "a buffoon in a tommyrot factory," prepared for the benefit of the Irish to repulse any effort by King George to invade Chicago. Few bemoaned the negative impact of these repressions on liberty. Nor did many consider the potentially devastating effects of these vain attempts at utter conformity on the liberty of those already American citizens. Illinois in 1923 proclaimed English the state's official language. The expulsion of five elected socialist members by the New York State legislature troubled some civil libertarians, but not enough to halt the measure.

Vigilance against un-American activities stretched into the 1930s. Congressman Martin Dies of Texas in 1935 proposed to relieve unemployment by expelling the three and a half million foreigners he believed illegally in the country. Colonel Robert R. McCormick insistently informed his *Chicago Tribune* readers of worldwide threats to self-government, emanating from fascist and Communist conspiracies of which local dupes acted as tools. Ironically, at a time when liberty abroad seemed more threatened than ever, many Americans wished to sacrifice its inclusiveness at home to protect the chosen few able to enjoy a good parceled out to others by a cautious policy of feel and fumble.[19]

For the sake of normalcy people tightened up, and not only in restrictive immigration policy. Eagerness for order at any cost and by whatever means infused the era. Mob violence subsided but left a lynching habit of the mind, expressed in the determination of zealots to enforce their own type of goodness. God called men and women to prevent their great free nation from being foreignized. Patriotism knew no constraints, and attitudes hardened against any who questioned the dominant political and social views. Shocked at the absence of any previous regulation, the National Flag Conference (1923) created a complete code for civilian use. Jurists praised "responsible citizens" who sought the general good, thereby giving a legal stamp of approval to the conformist mentality that raised few questions and spared society fratricidal battles. But insidious appeals for revival of the ethical will amounted to demands for uniformity that stifled dissent, and particularly challenges to morality and family cohesion, defined in a handbook of 1925 as the cornerstone of citizenship.

New Jersey and other states by law regulated school books, to prevent erosion of national unity—a tricky concept, as manufacturers discovered in an effort to develop the widest market for their products; Procter and Gamble had to advertise kosher Crisco, and Wrigley targeted "Juicy Fruit" and "Sweet 16" at the South. Efforts to free speech after the war became tangled in opinions not only on politics but also on obscenity, pornography, birth control, and religion. Progressive anthropologists and Freudian psychoanalysts became targets of concerted attack for their unconventional theories, which if translated into action would undermine the nation's moral fiber and the ability to maintain its way of life. Personal liberty, argued a work on democratic marriage, encompassed a woman's right to have children or not, just as she chose. Yet not everyone agreed; University of California administrators prevented even a debate on birth control, regarded as but a contemporary manifestation of that ever-present threat—free love.

Many Americans regarded with dismay the relaxed codes of behavior that permitted their neighbors to pursue success and yet enjoy fun and leisure. The naughty, rebellious young disobeyed their parents and drank, shimmied, and petted, evidence of altered sexual mores and weakened families. In the suburbs the clerk and the foreman, in the small towns the druggist and the lawyer, in the country the farmer and the minister, witnessed with disapproval the disintegration of the stable way of life for which they labored; and they wondered about the validity of the nineteenth-century democratic assumption that all people could apply correct reason to solve their own problems. The old debate about the relationship between mind and matter, reason and emotion, thought and instinct, gained new prominence in light of data purporting to prove that animal propensities more often guided human beings than their God-given logical power. During the war army intelligence tests had revealed wide disparities in personal competence. William McDougall, concerned about the relationship of these performances to heredity and eugenics, argued (1921) that men and women behaved less in response to logical precepts than by instincts needing control. Heredity and eugenics, not free choice, determined citizens' capacity to act; current racist assumptions thereupon acquired new prominence in the hands of scientists purporting to reflect a value-free, neutral knowledge.[20]

The new generation measured everything in terms of money, substituted amusement for self-control, and threatened cherished values. Mothers who raised children "to glorify personal liberties and individual rights" too late discovered the result—"total irresponsibility in the matters of moral obligation to society." Communal duties often invoked in times of general disquiet, greater regimentation, and less choice were now to still the forces that seemed to tear the community apart. The old fear that the effort to rise would jeopardize stability grew more oppressive in a society all void, without form. Not only did children leave home, go off to face corruption by the corrosive outer world, but city habits engulfed the entire nation. Earlier the family had provided individuals a needed haven from a heartless world; in the 1920s that institution also seemed too weak to withstand the assaults of change.

New uses of leisure, strange clothing styles, smoking in public, bobbed hair, and cosmetics defied conventions and threatened social order. By abandoning the natural, men and women imprisoned themselves in molds made by advertising. The cereal warned that faulty elimination, the greatest enemy of beauty, played havoc with the complexion and led to sallow skin and listless eyes.

Motor cars raced through the resentful countryside; the phonograph and radio brought profane chants into the home; and in every county seat the dark interior of the movie theater beckoned the unwary. Babylon had indeed conquered when "America's sweetheart" slipped into a hasty marriage after a quick divorce, while Fatty Arbuckle, after getting away with murder, entered a director's career under the name of Will B. Good. Heightened by lurid accounts of the white slave traffic, fury mounted at the betrayal, with the dramatic shifts in family life and in the role of women portents of doom.[21]

Those who would not yield fought back against alien threats to the style of life they wished to preserve. Fundamentalists sought a return to the old-time religion, battling it out over evolution in Dayton, Tennessee. Others spoke wistfully of dictatorship to master a society so complex that it had outrun the capacity of anyone to comprehend it. But Americans overwhelmingly rejected the designation "fascist," with its foreign connotations, although mass direct action bearing other labels tempted many. Discrimination, formal or informal, marked out a racial difference that defined the established group, protected it against outsiders, and gave it pride in its superiority. Jim Crow segregation persisted in the South; and as a sign of their own worth, the hundred-percent Americans determined to exclude from college fraternities and social clubs all targets of prejudice—no longer the blacks alone, but also Catholics and Jews, Italians, Japanese, and Poles, visible threats subject to control, whatever the cost to abstract liberty. Discrimination freed from competition those worried by foreign challenges. It enhanced the life's chances of favored children of proper birth, those of the right sort, who would no longer have to race against the grubby slum kids. It also prevented alien tastes and habits from gaining ascendancy.[22]

Police power, already extended to health, morals, and personal habits, could also apply collective intelligence to regulate corrupting foreign behavior epitomized in intemperance. Later, Alcoholics Anonymous would suggest more effective noncoercive methods of dealing with the problem—easy does it, one day at a time, there but for the grace of God. . . . But in the 1920s legislation remained the preferred means. Earlier temperance agitators had launched their crusade as a refuge from frustration, an outlet for anger, that sanctioned manipulativeness and self-righteous assertiveness, legitimizing coercive means to control others. Similar sentiments motivated twentieth-century reformers who sought to curtail the liberties of undesirable types. The Prohibition movement became the rallying point of those who wished to save the Republic from the corrupting effects of booze, the saloon, machine politics, jazz, and the movies—all the interlocking sins that robbed the nation of its purity. Against the movie world in which viewers absorbed "the corruptly glamorous values" of the exploiting class (1927), Prohibition ensured "better use of wages, better income, better school attendance, less coming home drunk," confirming "the scientific method of estimating social worth." Indeed, Prohibition took "a very real step towards freedom because it set free human personality—personality previously degraded by drink, personality that never had the opportunity to know itself."

Alcohol interfered with true individual liberty, just as did opium, morphine, chloral, or any other habit-forming drugs. The "vast process of national purification" would also hasten "the sublimation of the sex instinct upon which the next stage of progress for the human race" depended. The survival of liberty in the public domain therefore required its ever-greater constriction in private lives.

Despite complaints against invasions of personal liberty by governmental authority—clear limitations on the ability to act—the law correctly frowned upon narcotics and the linked crimes of pornography and contraception. Reproduction and the commercial use of female bodies merged as the targets of male lusts in need of control. In the confusion attendant upon the question of women's control over their reproductive capacities, one item remained constant: the fear of the irresponsible male about to be granted even greater liberty than before. For if the threat of pregnancy disappeared, what else could compel their constancy? Men would be free to satisfy their beastly propensities without fear of retribution. Women's greater liberty meant immeasurably more liberty for males.[23]

Frustration pushed the angry ones to violence. Private slaughter had become a casual American activity—"Almost as many homicides in Erie in an hour as in England in an era" (1925). In 1920 konklaves of the Klan had already spread out of the South, where the order had formed anew in imitation of the Reconstruction bands. In the next few years membership soared in the North as well, with deep pockets of strength in Indiana, Colorado, and Oregon but also in New York and New England. In the Midwest and on the Pacific Coast, as in the South, hooded figures solemnly burned fiery crosses to exorcise the strangers. Despite similarity in tactics to its predecessor, the Klan broadened its objectives, from controlling blacks through violence to political organization aimed at curtailing the power of alien labor agitators, Catholics, and Jews. The Klan also embarked on a general morality crusade, targeting wife-beaters, prostitutes, and other criminals. In addition, the blanket of secrecy hid unrelated acts of violence, as in the Mer Rouge, Louisiana, murders (1923) that grew out of the rivalry of two neighboring towns. The organization enlisted well-intentioned but heedless and politically ambitious men like Hugo L. Black of Alabama, later justice of the U.S. Supreme Court. Despite some state laws against masked assemblies, membership soared; at its peak in 1924 the Klan may have enrolled as many as four million concerned citizens. Its pressure that year blocked a Catholic's nomination for the presidency by the Democratic Party in a bitter battle that ran through 102 ballots. The Klan's strength reflected national frustrations that found relief in secret conclaves, childish masquerades, and murderous outrages designed to intimidate and harass.[24]

The secret order's influence also spread through the *Dearborn Independent,* the weekly published by Henry Ford that circulated to a quarter-million readers, mostly in the Midwest. From 1920 to 1922, its "Chronicler of the Neglected Truth" expounded an anti-Semitic message: an international conspiracy led by Jewish bankers plotted to conquer America by subverting its moral standards. A people without civilization, without any great achievements in any realm but the realm of "get," a people expelled from every land that gave them hospitality, dared to dictate to the sons of Saxons how "to make the world what it ought to be." Ford himself in June 1927 disclaimed responsibility for the series and suspended publication of the *Dearborn Independent,* but millions of copies of the inflammatory articles circulated for years thereafter. Though its power subsided after 1924, the Klan still played a part in Al Smith's defeat in the presidential election of 1928, and traces of its influence persisted for a half-century more in various covert bands.[25]

Klan membership dwindled after criminal prosecution exposed some of its leaders as swindlers. But numerous smaller groups thereafter assumed the task of fending off disruptive foreign changes, as did Harry Jung's National Vigilant Intelligence Federation. In the 1930s, the Depression and fear of renewed involvement in Europe's recurrent wars deepened defensive impulses. In that decade, hardships drew desperate people into angry associations, some in pursuit of an economic nostrum that would cure unemployment, others to battle insidious actual or imagined enemies within the country. Detroit's Black Legion, the United Brotherhood of America (1935–36), held its members in line by frightful initiation rites and by murder and arson in defense of one-hundred-percent Americanism. Other people carried their fears into political rifle and pistol clubs, churches, national guard organizations, and labor unions, doggedly resisting economic innovations or espousing an isolationist foreign policy. *Life* magazine's lurid exaggeration in its lead article for July 26, 1937, "Headlines Proclaim the Rise of Fascism and Communism in America," reflected widespread unease. Many literary figures and the propertyless middle class then drifted toward extremes. Herbert Hoover in 1934 foresaw the end of liberty, which the American people under horrendous pressures prepared to sacrifice on the altar of the machine age.[26]

The frantic bands offered floundering members a purpose in life but lacked coherence and discipline. Any barker who dreamed up a scheme or a grievance attracted joiners, some or many, at least for a while. Victor McLaglen, the movie actor, thus recruited his own private army. However, to hold large numbers together required organizational skill—to convey the gospel, to manage mailing lists, to collect contributions, and to fight off rivals. Mobilizing the efforts of thousands of individuals in a vast country demanded exceptional diplomatic and managerial talent.

Each aspiring leader pursued a personal vision, attracting apostles from among the hordes of aggrieved and placeless, some former Klansmen, others veterans or out of work or bankrupt or lonely victims of personal misfortune. In a field ripe for the harvest, the demagogue and the crank did the reaping, drawing on yearnings "towards a vague community ideal and toward freedom from insecurity and misery." The uniform garb of sheets or shirts bestowed a semblance of security upon those who had wandered up from the hills to Detroit or Chicago or those whose familiar rustic setting had slipped out from under them in industrializing Alabama and Louisiana. In the traditional rural South, an old-fashioned demagogue like Theodore "The Man" Bilbo sopped up the emotions of his audience with meaningless local eloquence. "Friends, fellow citizens, brothers and sisters—hallelujah, my opponent—yea, this opponent of mine who has the dastardly, dewlapped, brazen, sneering, insulting and sinful effrontery to ask you for your votes . . . this opponent of mine says he don't need a platform." Other orators purveyed a novel gospel to offset loneliness, through comradeship, the discipline, and even the uniform of an army and a brotherhood based on national and often racial unity. Not fun and pleasure but sorrow and pathos lay behind what they preached. They abandoned individualism and addressed "aching backs and blistered hands, discouraged souls and broken hearts, hungry women and crying children . . . men able and willing to work walking our streets trying to get work with which to obtain food for their loved ones," while waste, extravagance, and graft pervaded the Capitol.

Schemes for social redemption and economic reform attracted followers, especially when stoked by strident expressions of anti-Semitism and race hatred. William Dudley Pelley, attuned to the cosmic sense of order, considered democracy a Jewish plot to impose industrial slavery on the masses and wished to lead Americans toward a government held together by spiritual restraints. His Silver Shirts aimed to restore Aryan power under one dictator, the Chief, counterpart of the one God. Decked out in brightly polished high leather boots and a Sam Browne belt, Pelley strove to convey a military impression. His rival, Gerald B. Winrod, disagreed on the number of Jews who would achieve salvation on the Last Day. "Too damn many!" said Pelley of Winrod's estimates. Winrod unsuccessfully sought the Republican nomination for a Senate seat in competition against John R. Brinkley, the Kansas doctor who used goat glands to restore sexual powers. George E. Deatherage of the Knights of the White Camelia; George W. Christians of the White Church; James True, inventor of the "kike-killer" bludgeon; Robert E. Edmundson and Dennis Healey of the Khaki Shirts—all fished the same waters.[27]

A few acquired great, sometimes national, followings. Down South, Louisiana's Huey P. Long summoned the poor to a millennial barbecue; in 1934 his Share the Wealth Society claimed three million members; a year later, seven and a half million. No one counted. "Every Man a King, but No Man Wears a Crown"—a mighty slogan. Furnish every family a homestead allowance of five or six thousand dollars by imposing annual capital levies on all fortunes above $1.5 million. In California, Upton Sinclair, veteran utopian and muckraker, galvanized by fear of the Californazis about him, in a fiery race for the governorship promised to End Poverty in California (EPIC). Dr. Francis Townsend enlisted the elderly in support of a plan to bring back prosperity by giving two hundred dollars monthly to each person over the age of sixty not to save but to spend—like trying to make gold out of sea water, according to Walter Lippmann, though not to the members of the three thousand clubs nationwide. And up in Michigan, the radio priest Father Charles Coughlin revived the free-silver cry in fulminations, laced with strands of Catholic theology, against the money changers who battened upon popular misery. His crystal-clear, mellifluous radio messages, inflected with a hint of Irish brogue, conveyed on a nationwide hookup, reached an enormous audience estimated at forty million; one attack on President Hoover evoked 1.2 million letters.[28]

Successful mass organizations depended on fiery oratory to steam up the audience and upon the compilation of mailing lists for solicitation and for enrolling members. Gerald L. K. Smith commanded both techniques. An impassioned preacher, in person and on the radio, he left some parishioners doubtful that he knew what he was talking about. "But it sounded right." Brandishing the Bible, he whipped audiences to feverish excitement with the demand for "a real job, not a little sow belly, black-eyed-pea job, but a real spending money, beefsteak and gravy, Chevrolet, Ford in the garage, new suit, Thomas Jefferson, Jesus Christ, red-white-and-blue job for every man." An alliance with Huey Long, whom he outlived, gave him command of massive Addressograph files.[29]

Other dissidents sought no mass following. Lawrence Dennis, a Harvard-educated Foreign Service officer, thoughtful and well-read, concluded that the era of capitalism, liberalism, and individualism approached its end; only American fascism could lead to national salvation. Formulas of national solidarity within spiritual bonds, devised by a suitable elite, had to end fragmentation, alienation, and the brute struggle for existence. Well-to-do intellectuals like Seward Collins and Philip Johnson also sought firm leadership that could take command; the *American Review* (1934) expressed their hopes and fears. Dorothy Day inspired a band of Catholic Workers who sought to blend socialism and Christianity. Or like Irving Babbitt, Ralph Adams Cram, T. S. Eliot, and George Santayana, such people sought the security of self-reform in an organic society, without, however, taking overt action to attain the homogeneous population and the religious unity they deemed essential. Paradox: the intellectual assaults that aimed to abrogate the liberty of those deemed undeserving actually ended by expanding its scope.

Franklin Roosevelt's overwhelming victory in 1936 over Republican governor Alfred M. Landon and over the Coughlin-supported congressman William Lemke (who garnered 892,378 votes) infuriated the hostile minority by the crushing proof of their estrangement. They shared the bitterness of conservatives enlisted in the Liberty League, of the Chambers of Commerce, of the Hearst press, and of the National Association of Manufacturers. The protesters could not mobilize for action, however. Thousands joined such uniformed bands as the Silver Shirts, but General Smedley Butler failed to unite them all into a single movement (1937). Their fleeting moments in the sun as well as their final demise revealed the resilience of a society able to resist numerous challenges.[30]

Although Pelley sometimes referred to himself as the American Hitler and European mass organizations attracted considerable attention, they had only a slight direct influence on the United States. Fascist Italy tried unavailingly to exploit the Italian Historical Society, the Italian Disabled Soldiers clubs, and many a *circolo* named after various war heroes. The Ministry of Popular Culture formed unions of immigrants residing abroad who swore to serve the Fascist social ideas faithfully, but also to obey and exalt the United States of America and respect its Constitution and its laws. Some Italian language newspapers became pro-Fascist, while the few anti-Fascist and anarchist journals faced rough sledding. However, no Fascist organization acquired a mass following or matched in influence the Dante Alighieri Society (founded in 1890) or the Order of the Sons of Italy in America, which enlisted some 200,000 members in social, fraternal, and cultural activities. The short-lived Khaki Shirts of America, which gathered up remnants of the veterans' Bonus March of 1932, had purely indigenous roots. The American Fascisti Association and

Order of Black Shirts, founded in Georgia in 1930, lacked transatlantic links, but cloaked an employment agency whose leaders soon fell to squabbling among themselves.

Mussolini appealed less to ideology than to group pride, which he hoped would enable four million Italian-Americans branded undesirable by the quota law to hold up their heads. For the sake of Italy's noble traditions, A. H. Giannini of the Bank of America, president of the Italian Chamber of Commerce, criticized anti-Fascists. Even New York City's outspoken congressman Fiorello H. La Guardia for a time refrained from denouncing the regime in Rome; and Governor James M. Curley of Massachusetts, in Faneuil Hall (1936), spoke of Il Duce as a lover of peace and the savior of Christianity, who had rescued Europe from Bolshevism.[31]

In this explosive atmosphere, anti-Fascist protests generated fights, along with complaints against consular officials and cultural agents who pressured residents not to take United States citizenship. Sixty policemen had to protect the eight hundred Sons of Italy who sailed in 1929 to visit the homeland. Despite encouragement from Rome, Italo-Americans by no means flocked into Fascist organizations, and those in the organized labor movement remained hostile. Moreover, suspicion that Mussolini opposed emigration, which decreased Italy's population and the potential fighting forces to support his invasion of Ethiopia, deepened the general disinterest.[32]

In the 1930s, attention shifted to the Third Reich's quest for popular support in the United States. The Nazis drew upon the sentimental reluctance of German-Americans to become "mongrels who do not know where they belong" and upon resentment against wartime prejudice. Various local and regional groups had long aimed to keep cultural identity alive. The Friends of New Germany, for instance, stood for "liberty, loyalty, honesty, patriotism, fellowship, duty, truth and real freedom of the press."[33]

The German-American Bund (Amerika-Deutscher Volksbund) sought the intellectual and spiritual reform of Americans of German extraction whose influence, politically activated, would tip the balance in the struggle against Communism and Jews and in favor of an "independent Aryan-governed United States of America." Loyalty to the fatherland extended beyond those born on German soil according to Ernst Wilhelm Bohle, head of the Auslandsorganisation (Foreign Organization) of the Nazi Party. "We look on Germans abroad as Germans not by accident but by the will of God, chosen to cooperate in the work that

Adolf Hitler began," he proclaimed. These convictions meshed in with a streak of anti-Semitism, with a disdain for democracy, and with an overwhelming desire for firm leadership, according to the Fuehrer-Prinzip.[34]

Stories of the Nazi ability to soften up other nations by skillful propaganda and by manipulating fifth-columnists gave currency to the belief, sustained by its boasting, that the Bund consisted of an army of trained spies and propagandists. Congressman Martin Dies explained that the enemies within a country constituted a peril as great as any external foe. Treason from within, aided by invasion from without, explained the speedy collapse of modern governments under totalitarian assaults. But actually only a few German Americans became involved. Figures of total Bund membership ranged between 20,000 and 25,000, with 100,000 affiliates and sympathizers. A congressional investigator warned (1938) that the Bund had from 18,000 to 50,000 uniformed men nationwide. But the Justice Department, after exhaustive investigation, placed the figure at between 6,500 and 8,500. Sensational journalists, however, got the number up to 200,000.[35]

The Bund's notoriety completely overshadowed the larger and more influential neutral or anti-Nazi German-American societies—the German-American League for Culture, the Turner Alliance, the German-American National Alliance, the Steuben Society, and the Carl Schurz Foundation. Only a dozen of the 178 German-language newspapers in the United States took outright pro-Nazi positions. Victor and Bernard Ridder, publishers of the influential New York *Staats-Zeitung,* stood totally apart, hostile.

Bund speeches, editorials, and articles extolled Hitler, attacked the Reich's European enemies, particularly England, urged new members to fight Communism, and criticized the shortcomings of the United States and of democracy—money-grubbing, crass, selfish individualism, waste and dirt—all revealing the influence of Jewish Reds. The Bund declared war on atheistic teachings, on all racial intermixture between Aryans and non-Aryans, on Communism, and on the dictatorship of the Jewish international minority. Organizers established units in forty-seven states (with Louisiana the sole exception), and also a German-American Business Men's League; an Order Service; the A-V Publishing Company; twelve Prospective Citizens' Leagues, open to those who had resided in the United States for two years and who had taken out first papers; several youth groups; and seven camps for para-military exercises in Nazi regalia. Annual dues and frequent special assessments along with occasional deliveries of cash by couriers from Germany supplied the income.[36]

The Bund newspaper, the *Deutscher Weckruf und Beobachter,* appeared in four editions and claimed a circulation of 250,000, although the Post Office Department noted that New York's version, under second-class privileges, reached merely 1,800. Negligible sales compelled the paper to appeal frequently for financial support, and regular advertisements of the German tourist offices provided a subsidy. Nevertheless Fritz Kuhn, as leader, repeatedly proclaimed the hundred-percent-Americanism of his society and disclaimed any foreign connections. Alterations made the Bund uniform look less like that of a storm trooper and more like that of the American Legion. Genuflections toward Americanism also included performance of the "Star-Spangled Banner" and displays of George Washington posters alongside the swastika symbol. However, denunciation and sustained invective provided speakers at Bund meetings their chief stock-in-trade. Orators often deliberately mispronounced F.D.R.'s name *Rosenfelt* and attacked his alliance with the perfidious English and the unspeakable Communist Jews. Vote Gentile, buy Gentile, employ Gentile—the simple slogan established the theme. The resemblance to a Nazi rally grew out of more than the marching, the uniforms, the boots, and the banners, extended also to the atmosphere and the spirit. Bundists shouted their slogan, "Free America," in a cadence like that of *"Heil Hitler."* One of the largest rallies, in Madison Square Garden, New York City, in February 1939, attracted an audience of 19,000. Kuhn had by then already proclaimed that the time approached for resort to the law of action.[37]

The Bund and its counterparts gained strength among men and women adrift in turbulent times, free as never before of all ties and restraints, but therefore fearfully insecure, ready to say farewell to gradual social reform, to risk all on radical change. Widespread concern about the threat of foreign involvement added to the anxiety that drove them to close ranks against strangers. War, "agitated to the point of wholesale murder by colossal advertising," created the Jews' harvests. Conniving and predatory "Judaists," having "gained ascendancy over the press, over the radio, over the screen," instigated most of the conflicts among Christian nations. Anxiety also stoked hatreds in the temptation to blame other aliens—immigrants, Catholics, blacks. Many of the aggrieved united in the Christian Front and also joined the Union Party during the presidential campaign of 1936. Louisiana under the Long regime offered a foretaste of thuggery concealed by professions of concern for the people's welfare.[38]

A persistent strain of racism extended on through the 1930s, kept alive by the genteel anti-Semitism wafted across the Atlantic from Hilaire Belloc and other literary types. Widespread circulation of the *Conspiracy of the Elders of Zion* and hostile images of Jews, blacks, Slavs, and Latins found support among respectable poets, psychologists, anthropologists, and sociologists. Conventional invective crept into the lines of T. S. Eliot, Ezra Pound, Theodore Dreiser, and E. E. Cummings. Thomas Wolfe went further in his admiration for Hitler, as did H. L. Mencken, ever devoted to the survival of the fittest and offended by American Jews, "very loud and brassy fellows." The universities as a matter of course limited the number of "Hebrews" admitted as students or hired as teachers. An ominous tone infused discussions of genetics, in which manipulative preferences overrode considerations of personal liberty. On the floor of Congress, Louis T. McFadden of Pennsylvania, Jacob Thorkelson of Montana, and John Rankin of Mississippi unabashedly expressed their prejudices. African Americans remained victims not only of verbal assaults but also of social and economic discrimination and of violence: "One drop of Negro blood placed in the veins of the purest Caucasian destroys the inventive genius of his mind and strikes palsied his creative faculty."[39]

In the 1930s bitterness toward the New Deal and fear of the approaching war stirred anxiety among politically conservative and isolationist groups, some of which blamed Jews and foreigners. The America First Committee, the National Civic Federation, and the American Liberty League occasionally heard such views, as did Coughlin's National Union for Social Justice and patriotic societies like the Sentinels of the Republic and the Paul Reveres. Quite incidentally the Daughters of the American Revolution launched a campaign in 1931 to compel teachers to take loyalty oaths, which fifteen states soon made compulsory, in the kind of expectation, derided by Walter Lippmann, that a nation could think and feel with one mind and one heart.[40]

Communist organizations took a somewhat different form and until 1939 evoked a different response. They, too, attracted disoriented, rootless people. Affiliated with the Third International and dominated by leaders who followed a line set in Moscow, the party operated on one level as a political entity that nominated candidates for office and conducted open electoral campaigns. But it also maintained a network of cultural, educational, fraternal, and benevolent associations, while covert factions bored from within labor unions and ethnic groups, thus enlisting the support of stray fellow travelers persuaded that it acted in accord with the "laws of historic development." By 1939 the American League Against War and Fascism had 20,000 members paying dues and 1,023 affiliated organizations with a membership in excess of seven million people. It published a monthly magazine, distributed millions of pamphlets and releases, sponsored congresses, and formed an important instrument for spreading propaganda in support of Soviet foreign policy. Tough veterans of labor strife like Mother Jones understood the danger from "Cominist freaks," but united-front tactics swayed many less knowledgeable "useful idiots." On still another level, undercover, believers formed a pool from which the Soviet Union recruited agents like Steve Nelson for espionage. Often their stated concern for fulfilling the promises of American liberty masked a covert agenda.

Conspiratorial methods exposed the Communists to bitter controversy with socialists and liberals into whose organizations they filtrated and also with dissidents who splintered away. Furthermore the Reds presented an easy target for reactionaries and labor spies like Joseph P. Kamp, Mervin K. Hart, and Allen Zoll, whose wild charges of un-American activity to convert the country from individualism to collectivism obscured the genuine threats posed by the conspirators. Representative John Rankin of Mississippi thought Communism had "got control of a large part of the metropolitan press" to spread alien propaganda under the guise of democracy, "using 'stooges' who can speak 'perfect English.' " Elizabeth Dilling's *The Red Network* typically jumbled together various associations and affiliations in a fashion that made discrimination impossible among the innocent, the worthy, the naïve, the gullible, and the sinister.[41]

The Communists set themselves apart from fascists, however similar in totalitarian tactics and ideology. The Bolsheviks regarded themselves, and others regarded them, as polar opposites of the Klan, the Bund, and the Silver Shirts, whose vociferous anti-Semitism alienated the party, which contained a large percentage of Jewish adherents and which did not bear the odium of racism, as did many fascist groups. Furthermore, the Communists profited, in the United States as in Europe, from the prevailing tendency to range political alignments along a left–right spectrum, with the Leninists located at an extreme that extended over to the socialists, liberals, and democrats. The "united front" line often obscured earlier attacks on liberals as "social fascists." The Communists did not hesitate to take on hazardous causes—leadership of the textile strike in Gastonia, North Carolina, biracial education in the South, and defense of the Scottsboro boys accused of rape, for instance. Often they legitimately presented their actions as fulfillments of American liberty, extended to previously excluded groups.

Hence boring from within and pleas for a united front against fascism made sense when convenient to Moscow. The Communists thus rigorously defended the Loyalists during the Spanish Civil War and helped found a party in Mexico. The FBI and the Military Intelligence Division kept track of activities that verged on espionage or subversion. But the postwar reaction against the excesses of the Red Scare sheltered all dissidents behind the shield of civil liberties as potential victims of intolerance. Wild charges like those of William Wirt against Bolshevik New Dealers boomeranged and earned sympathy for all radicals in search of alternative utopias—resembling other disillusioned Americans who "wanted one thing above all others—to believe." Vladimir Nabokov's anti-Leninism raised suspicion among *New Yorker* editors and proved troublesome when he sought a position at Wellesley, and Charles Yale Harrison, for criticizing the Soviets, gained a reputation as one of "many procurers to Wall Street imperialism."

Inspired by a revolution that tore down an ancient tyranny to liberate the individual, John Reed, Big Bill Heywood, Lincoln Steffens, Edmund Wilson, and others interested in scientific planning perceived in the Soviet Union a model for a reordered society. Theodore Dreiser found plenty of individualism in Russia, and Malcolm Cowley, out of "abiding faith," announced that "the day of mass executions had passed." Eugene V. Debs, Meta Berger, and other socialists concurred. Emma Goldman and Alexander Berkman, less bemused by theory, believed the evidence of their own eyes and dissented. But falsified news reports from Moscow obscured reality, discredited accurate accounts, and sustained illusions, hiding the millions dead in famine and in Stalin's infamous purges. Faith survived even the Nazi pact in 1939. Soviet-style liberty seemed the model for the future.[42]

Various congressional or state legislative committees probed disloyal or subversive organizations deemed unworthy of the blessings of liberty. Suspicion long focused on the fascist mass movements, suspected like the Bund of links to foreign governments. Major Julius Hochfelder, frenetically involved in veterans' and civic organizations, churned out denunciatory letters to newspapers and petitioned managers of public meeting places to deny the Bund use of their premises. In the spring of 1937, Congressmen Samuel Dickstein of New York, who had earlier worried about Communists, and Martin Dies of Texas unavailingly introduced bills calling for the mandatory deportation of criminal aliens. Demands for a congressional investigation also failed, although ample precedents for such fact-finding enquiries, as a means of attracting public attention, went back to the Civil War and became more frequent in the twentieth century. For the moment, however, the targets remained unclear, categorized by the general designation "un-American activities." Representative J. Parnell Thomas of New Jersey argued sarcastically against Dickstein's misplaced ardor—more Communists infested the New Yorker's home district than did fascists the whole of the United States. Conflicting definitions of liberty and of threats to it enlivened the rhetoric of the 1930s.

In July 1937, Dickstein read into the *Congressional Record* the names of forty-six Nazi spies or agents in America. In August, Attorney General Homer Cummings instructed the Federal Bureau of Investigation to determine whether or not the Bund camps violated federal statutes forbidding the shipment of unregistered firearms across state lines. A massive Justice Department report held that although Bund teachings tended to subversion, they did not violate existing federal law.

The Nazi spy trial in the summer of 1938 marked a turning point. Guenther Gustave Rumrich's career in espionage began simply when he wrote a letter of application from New York to the *Völkischer Beobachter* in Berlin (1936). He supplied shipping, industrial, and aviation information, gleaned from newspaper and magazine articles, to the German armed forces. Apprehended in an effort to steal thirty-five American passport blanks and indicted for espionage, he confessed and identified among the ringleaders Dr. Ignatz Griebl, a reserve officer in the U.S. Army. At the trial, Rumrich, Johanna (Jenni) Hoffman, Erich Glaser, and Otto Voss testified to a far-flung network that had smuggled to Germany blueprints of Seversky plane floats and an experimental bomber, as well as specifications of other aircraft. The defendants, found guilty, received short prison terms.

The case raised awareness of the Nazi threat. Although the President urged Americans to distinguish between propaganda and espionage, he also alerted the intelligence agencies to the need for vigilance. In New York and Massachusetts, legislative committees turned up incriminating information on fascist activities, and other states considered more stringent sedition legislation along with teachers' oaths. Congress in 1938 enacted the Foreign Agents Registration Act. It also formed a special House Committee on Un-American Activities under Martin Dies of Texas, despite the warning by Congressman Hamilton Fish of New York that "this bill would set up an American Cheka, nothing more or less," amounting to a witch hunt aiming at thought control. Dies, in the House since 1930 and the nativist son of a nativist former congressman, remained chairman until 1944 and ran a one-man show. Concentrating at first on the German-American Bund, the committee developed information that hinted at plans for sabotage and spying in the event of war between Germany and the United States. Roosevelt, however, worried when Dies attacked members of the administration as Communists or fellow travelers and in 1939 had Jerry Voorhis of California assigned to the Committee to speak up for civil liberties.

The Dies charges contained nuggets of truth; Communists had crept into key positions in certain labor unions and in some government agencies. Gullible fellow travelers attacked the profit system, ridiculed democracy, and rejected American liberty; others marched under a flag they associated with those great humanitarians, Lenin and Stalin. But the truth lay buried beneath the enormous mass of miscellaneous charges witnesses tossed about. Dies embodied a familiar array of attitudes: against heterodoxy, against the foreigner and the naturalized American, against the intellectual, for the old virtues and old ways. Unable to cope with the complexities and subtleties of Communist doctrine or with the fierce cross-currents of political extremism that surfaced during the Spanish Civil War, he seized upon Georgi Dimitroff's metaphor during the Moscow Seventh World Congress of a Trojan horse that would penetrate the impregnable walls of capitalism. Dies thereupon conjured up American fifth-column organizations, camouflaged, working in stealth, bamboozling gullible country bumpkins, behind respectable fronts like Harold Ickes, Eleanor Roosevelt, or Bishop Francis J. McConnell. Indiscriminate trivialities obscured truly important revelations, such as those of the defector General W. G. Krivitsky. Like his colleague J. Parnell Thomas, Dies's absolute hatred of the New Deal and of Roosevelt generated bias responsible for egregious errors and for the inability to distinguish between liberalism and Communism. The use by his enemies of forged documents to discredit him and flippant answers to some of his questions seemed however to validate his accusations.[43]

Ample precedents justified the absence of restraints on probes by congressional committees, which in the past had ultimately broadened the contours of liberty. The danger after 1930 lay in a quarter-century's erosion of the regard for personal freedom.[44]

The end of the fighting in 1918 did not still the vociferous incantations to liberty that had swelled during the war, and that antiradical complaints of the American Legion and other patriotic organizations heightened. The New York State Assembly refused to seat elected socialists, forbade seditious teaching in the public schools, and revoked the license of the radical Rand School. Despite criticism by the American

Civil Liberties Union, restrictions on the press in Pennsylvania stifled accurate accounts of labor conflicts in the coal fields. Panicky exaggeration obscured the situation. An article in *Harper's* (1922) explained that liberty had become "a mere rhetorical figure," with America no longer free in the old sense. The world had become too complicated for human understanding, Walter Lippmann explained; thought had become hazardous and rights insecure. True, the Red disorders predicted by A. Mitchell Palmer never materialized, perhaps because of Justice Department vigilance, perhaps because they had existed only in fevered imaginations. Still, panicky citizens ascribed the wreck of the *Morro Castle* (1934) to arson by Reds and suspected that liberal propaganda in the name of justice masked excuses for vulgarization, usurpation, tyranny, and repression.[45]

The infinitely adaptable word "liberty" spilled ubiquitously forth, serving any programmatic purpose to which politicians and publicists wished to put it—Liberty bonds, engines, bells, statues, League—no pretense to precision. Americans found it as hard to escape the term as to approach the reality. The Supreme Court gingerly asserted that some restraints on personal liberty violated the Fourteenth Amendment, and Justice Brandeis argued eloquently in *Whitney* v. *California* (1927) that the spread of political truth depended on freedom to think and to speak. The open airing of views made discussion meaningful; otherwise an inert people would lack protection against noxious doctrine. But he spoke in dissent against a majority deaf to his plea, and he addressed citizens bewildered about the very meaning of the term, citizens divided bitterly over whether the Ku Klux Klan and advocates of birth control deserved the right to speak or to use the mail. Under these conditions, dissent often seemed an illegitimate exploitation of freedom.

The Prohibition debate revealed similar troubling questions. Freedom, yes! But to drink? Or from the demon rum? Immigration policy? "A specious humanitarianism" amounted to a "flagrant violation of the spirit of liberalism." Every well-developed nationality, a priceless product of social evolution, had had its peculiar contribution to make to future progress; the American contribution was the upward movement of the masses. Any superficial and specious humanitarianism that threatened the standards of the average American violated the national trust. Much better to control human reproduction by eugenics to prevent the procreation of the defective—liabilities, not assets, to society. Religious freedom required an exception for sacramental wine, but did it allow rabbis to sell permits to all comers? And drugs? Seamen signed up on voyages to Cuba for the chance to bring in powder. So, too, policemen had liberty to shoot escaping offenders, and district attorneys to torture suspects from whom they wished to extort confessions; newspapers to publish falsehoods; some states to prescribe the language of instruction in schools, others to chain convicts in brutal gangs, and Southern whites to hold blacks in peonage and to impose a humiliating code of behavior in daily life.[46]

Freedom of assembly, but not parades in masks! The ACLU upheld the liberty to show *The Birth of a Nation;* the NAACP demanded a ban. The FBI did the President's bidding as Governor Long's thugs did his. Sunday, purity, and obscenity laws intruded upon privacy, prevented physicians from dispensing contraceptive information, and forbade residents to possess so much as the picture of a red flag—at least until 1931, when reinterpretation of the Fourteenth Amendment provided a refuge. The licensing power, however, protected padlock laws that enabled municipal authorities to shut down obscene plays, but did not enable them to require permits to distribute religious handbills, and they could recognize, even provide sanctions for, kashrut regulations. However, local governments could not infringe upon freedom of assembly by control of outdoor meetings even in parks, unless the gatherings slipped into anarchic riots. On the other hand, imbeciles had no right to object to compulsory sterilization. Sadly a learned judge noted how frequently "one kind of liberty may cancel and destroy another." The ACLU therefore divided on the extent to which it could rely on the law.[47]

The long-drawn-out international agitation of the Sacco-Vanzetti case (1920–27) evoked shrill protests against the inability to assure a fair trial to the accused, as did the incarceration of the labor leaders Thomas J. Mooney and Warren Billings for bombing a Preparedness Day parade in 1916. Antipicketing laws and injunctions in labor disputes raised other thorny issues, as did the freedom of women and children to contract the terms of their employment despite state minimum-wage laws. An elderly Canadian-born theologian who claimed the liberty of selective conscientious objection thereby proved his unfitness for citizenship. Liberals debated the desirability of charging fascists like Edmonson, Gerald L. K. Smith, and Winrod with conspiracy, and the FBI compiled a list of people for "custodial detention" in a national emergency. Meanwhile scores of voluntary associations insisted that liberty demanded legislation to safeguard labor, children, the family, and the needy. But whether women required sex-based protection or equal treatment became a subject of dispute. The Customs Service on its own decided what obscene books to exclude from the country. Freedom of association became a subject for contention when the WPA barred Bundists from its rolls, and when municipalities denied relief to foreign-born Communists. Or academic freedom, as when Governors Bilbo of Mississippi and Long of Louisiana fired hundreds from state college faculties. Up North, too, the Illinois legislature proposed to tax private institutions like the University of Chicago—hotbeds of sedition. The modern age, dense with people, Professor William McDougall decided, required "increasing restriction of individual liberty of choice and action."[48]

Intimate communities in the past had set standards on these issues. In their absence, no consensus appeared. Clean-book crusaders thrashed about in the effort to suppress indecent publications, to the horror of the American Civil Liberties Union. A Chicago police officer, on his own, banned the movie version of *The Scarlet Letter* (1915) because he could not explain the letter *A* to his daughter. The Legion of Decency, municipal censors, and any one of scores of pressure groups could veto the contents of movies or broadcasts. Since those who controlled the media hoped to placate everyone, their messages usually lacked relevance. Moreover, Brandeis remained in a minority on the Supreme Court, confused like a majority of citizens about the very meaning of liberty. The press escaped previous restraint, although the *New Republic* argued (1938) that a liberal regime could legitimately maintain a more drastic censorship than a conservative one.[49]

A lack of concern and even at times a cynical contempt for liberty troubled observers who noted the willingess to permit governments to exert increasing control of society. Personal and corporate selfishness merged incongruously with tendencies to stamp everyone with a uniform likeness. The chimera of social and economic equality undermined the individual's moral responsibility; such equality became a pretext for lowering standards and made democracy incompatible with civilization (1924).[50]

The states, responsible for most measures affecting the ability to speak and act, defined individual rights inconsistently, as did the Congress and successive Presidents. And the Supreme Court dragged its feet. In the nineteenth century it had asserted that the protection afforded by the Bill of Rights did not bind the individual states. Toward the end of that century, the Court had conceded that the Fourteenth Amendment shielded not only blacks but all property rights. But it had gone no further. Dissenting opinions in the *Gitlow* (1925) and *Whitney* cases (1927) maintained that the Amendment's restraint on state impairment of personal liberty applied to speech and assembly in the absence of imminent danger. But the majority had shied away from the suggestion that the same amendment transferred to the states the guarantees of freedom of speech, press, and religion, by which the Bill of Rights protected individuals against federal action. On the contrary, the wartime cases had drastically curtailed personal freedom. Decisions in the 1920s also upheld some convictions under criminal syndicalism statutes.[51]

However, the Fourteenth Amendment remained a problem, for it left open the inference that its guarantees of due process incorporated the whole Bill of Rights as limits on state action. The argument cropped up, though inconsistently, in unexpected contexts, appearing, for instance, in *Pierce* v. *Society of Sisters* (1925) as an objection to an Oregon law regulating parochial schools. Nevertheless, as late as 1937 in the *Palko* case, the Court rejected the view that some fundamental elements implicit in the concept of ordered liberty deserved incorporation in the Bill of Rights as restraints upon any government interference. Instead the justices ruled on such issues case by case, juggling vague, unexpressed considerations of fairness and prudence and providing inadequate precedents. The Smith Act of 1940 could therefore make mere advocacy of the overthrow of the government illegal.[52]

Despite the uncertainty of constitutional guarantees, the mass organizations, shirted or hooded, failed to flare up although they smoldered amidst abundant flammable material. Anxiety about earning a living and making good, hardly new to the 1920s, deepened as competition increased. The society dedicated to normalcy assured only a few individuals the full ability to act, left others discontent. Indeed, the times raised personal insecurity for many, thereby narrowing their liberty; yet often they washed their hands of politics—too dirty, too rotten, too full of bunk. Hence the willingness to tolerate increased control over private life by "a huge cumbrous and incompetent bureaucracy," justified by the enlarged relation to the public welfare.[53]

Calvin Coolidge came to the White House from the governorship of an urban industrial state, but remained rooted in rural Vermont, a symbol of the old America. Whether in Boston or in Washington, he resisted change, a small-town Yankee who stayed behind his own fence, bought no suit until the old one wore out, acquired a new pair of shoes every two years, and admitted to but one vice—the crossword puzzle. He performed his official duties competently, valued as an anachronism like Norman Rockwell's neat but unreal covers for the *Saturday Evening Post.* The government had to refuse "to exercise authority over the people, that the people might exercise authority over themselves."[54]

* * *

However much Americans longed for such normalcy, stability proved unattainable. In the new postwar world, precipitous alterations substituted compulsion, uniformity, and conformity for diversity and local initiative. Diminished liberty expressed itself in an acute sense of inability to cope successfully with a new environment.[55]

After 1920, the country changed almost beyond recognition, even Yankee New England. Wartime prosperity faded once demand subsided; the old farm problem returned; falling prices and mechanization squeezed small, marginal family enterprises. The drift to the cities resumed, especially when factories spread to regions of the West and the South once entirely agricultural. The Ford, the new network of roads, and occasional telephones opened escapes from isolation for those who stayed and prospered from crops or investments. With the market town or county seat just a short drive away, the husbandman became a familiar element of Main Street life, not so much as the lawyer or doctor, minister or editor, but subject to the same influences.

Continental proportions forced diversity upon American farming, differentiated by variations in climate, soil, and available labor supply. The tobacco regions of Connecticut and North Carolina differed from the fruit and vegetable areas of California and Florida and also from the grain-growing, cotton, rice, sugar, and livestock producers of Louisiana and Texas. In addition the presence of blacks shaped the Southern economy, just as did dependence upon Mexican and Filipino migratory labor in the Southwest.

Everywhere, modernizing trends affected agriculture. While marketing cooperatives by 1929 enrolled two million members, the total number of tillers of the soil shrank as old-timers retired, as young people drifted off to urban employment, and as less efficient producers dropped out. The rhetoric lavished on the old homestead ever more often paid tribute to the past rather than described a present reality. Rural population declined steadily after 1920. Definitions of liberty dependent upon landownership had become as outdated as the one-room schoolhouse.[56]

Uncertainties also plagued manufacturing. Corporations gained in size and in power, in particular in such new industries as autos and aluminum. The old-time entrepreneurs like Carnegie, Rockefeller, and Ford shuffled off to retirement, and leadership passed to promoters and engineers who came up through marketing, pragmatic about labor relations and sensitive to changes in consumer demand. Government now defined its role as mediator and source of information. Emphasis shifted from heavy industries like steel or textiles to entertainment and consumer durables like movies, automobiles, radios, and refrigerators—items that bore a heavy unit cost yet targeted a mass market. Advertising attracted potential buyers, as did liberal credit terms and installment sales. By 1929, purchasers had incurred well over three billion dollars in loans, mostly for automobiles. In that year, seventy percent of the cars sold in the United States carried finance charges. But in addition to wider access to funds, prospective purchasers had to learn that they needed what they did not know they needed—through planned obsolescence and model changes in response to swift shifts in taste. Business psychology helped advertisers exploit the irrational aspects of personality, working through conditioning and imitation rather than through logical processes. The ethical issues of such manipulations remained unresolved, as did the consequences of imposing uniformity on everyone.

As a result, seasonal anxiety infected the firm at every level, from the executive suite to the factory floor, part of the price for the millions of autos, radios, telephones, and new homes sold in the 1920s. Large-scale production subordinated individuals to the job, left them at the mercy of forces over which they had no control. While reformers and social workers focused on ameliorative legislation to regulate the labor of women and children, the people most affected worried about the mysterious alternations of good times and bad that determined levels of employment and of wages.[57]

Anxiety inflated the importance of the ability to communicate. Book clubs and the *Reader's Digest* along with movies and the radio spread similar tastes and ideas, particularly among youth responsive to glittering fashions and unable to express their own feelings, articulate their own meanings. Radio wrapped its soothing message in a neat, compact package garnished with music that eased the tensions in millions of passive and receptive minds. Modern risk-taking proved insidiously tempting to people under stress. William Jennings Bryan, who bore the brunt of the burden of defending Prohibition and attacking evolution, also speculated and lost in Florida real estate, an endeavor in which salesmanship counted heavily. The strain that sociologists discovered in Muncie, Indiana, in the 1920s had antecedents in the nineteenth century, but the pace of activity quickened dramatically. Startling headlines reported one crime-of-the-century murder after another, and not only in the wicked cities. Intrusive roadhouses, bold moonshiners, and weak-willed good citizens ignored the ban on liquor; defiant wives whiled the time away at mah-jongg; and everywhere unease simmered as youth flamed.[58]

The crust of custom still held many in place, devoted to ancestral pieties, firmly clutching inherited verities. People there insisted upon restraint in behavior and in belief, upon a government immune to flux, with emphasis upon cooperation rather than force. The high mark of their crusade was the conviction of John T. Scopes, a country high school instructor, for teaching the doctrine of evolution, contrary to Tennessee law (1925). In his trial, the Rock of Ages interested jurors more than the age of rocks; H. L. Mencken condemned them as morons and hillbillies, bigoted fanatics opposed to modern science and education. The case, however, proved a bonanza for the American Civil Liberties Union, which had defined the issue as one of free speech and gained widespread support as a result.[59]

Increasingly writers and educated readers of the *American Mercury* and the *New Yorker* regarded the ordinary booboisie as a nonpublic—bedlamites speeding out of some subway scuttle, cell, or loft, trudging through the mournful amusement parks in search of fun, willingly deceived and stupidly responsible for their own deception. Or suburbanites, their only monuments thousands of lost golf balls, their dominant concern to make money from each other—all manipulable by public relations. The enormous sale of etiquette books revealed the anxiety about what to eat, drink, and read, and when to sleep. Mencken consoled himself by comparing democracy to a self-limiting disease, like the measles. Any honest man could see, proclaimed Theodore Dreiser, that a Wall Street oligarchy ruled America, where people voted idiotically—unlike the Soviet Union, where Stalin governed for the ultimate benefit of all.[60]

He had spent the best years of his life helping people have a good time, complained Al Capone, and all he got for it was abuse.

A letter left by Two-Gun Crowley, the cop killer, before the police gunned him down (1931): "Under my coat is a weary heart, but a kind one—one that would do nobody any harm."

Americans feared more the trouble they might have than what they already had, clinging to what they were used to before risking change. Too much happened, with life often but a cheat and a disappointment. Men engendered so much more than they could bear or should have to bear, and thus discovered that they could bear anything. That's what was so terrible. They could bear anything. Anything.[61]

Normalcy, a supposed state of equilibrium, proved unattainable in the towns as in the country. In vain the Iron Puddler called work a blessing, not a curse, and praised old-time discipline. The cities could not keep up with expansion. The end of overseas immigration by no means eased the problems of employing, housing, feeding, and educating thousands of native newcomers who crowded in. Calls for social justice and regulation for the common good evoked only hollow echoes, as did contrary cries for liberty with restraint. Reality had its own imperatives. Even to maintain order presented insurmountable difficulties, no matter what size the police department. The thirty-six justices of the First District of the New York State Supreme Court, which embraced Manhattan and the Bronx, annually disposed of some nine thousand of the sixteen thousand new cases that came before them; as a result, in 1923 they confronted a backlog of twenty-two thousand—and rapidly growing. Law enforcement acquired a novel meaning under such circumstances. Invited to head Philadelphia's police, General Smedley D. Butler of the Marine Corps determined to dispose of bootleggers, prostitutes, and thugs in a war on vice, promising a promotion to the first cop who killed a bandit. But his forty-eight-hour sweeps evoked concern about property and civil rights. The crusade against crime lapsed, in the face of reluctance to use force even for reform.[62]

Expansion thrust massive organization upon all expressions of culture that sought control by means other than physical coercion. Insidious attacks upon accepted values in best-selling novels, plays, and poetry condoned deviance and assailed "uplifting tendencies"—Pollyanna optimism, Prohibition, blue laws, sexual inhibitions, exaggerated reverence for women, and home and foreign missions—all products of timidity, fear, and ignorance. To discuss personal liberty in the United States, wrote Clarence Darrow, was like talking about the snakes in Ireland—there were none. Iconoclastic publishers printed whatever sold and used the same merchandising methods as patent-medicine makers, while censorship proved futile. Calvin Coolidge believed that efforts to enlarge state activities masked the untenable theory of some shortcut to perfection.

Publicity took over in politics, too: the candidate with the best story and most money won. Herbert Hoover thus used public relations techniques to define himself as Master of Emergencies in the election of 1928. Walter Lippmann's *Public Opinion* (1922) challenged the view that free debate produced wise national policy and explained that people could cope with remote and inaccessible government only as explored, reported, and imagined by intermediaries.[63]

Influential psychologists also cast doubt on the old democratic assumption that any citizen could apply correct reason to solve any problem. On the contrary, asserted Madison Grant, *vox populi,* far from being *vox dei,* "was an unending wail for rights and never a chant for duty." Wartime army intelligence tests had shown wide disparities in personal competence; William McDougall, concerned about their relationship to heredity and eugenics, therefore argued (1921) that democracy presented hazards for the United States. Theories that reason exerted only a limited influence on human action deepened doubts. In *Behavior* (1914), John B. Watson had explained that unreflective responses to predetermined stimuli conditioned reactions, a suggestion exploited by the advertising of the 1920s. McDougall's *The Group Mind* (1920) also questioned rational behavior by explaining that people responded less often to logical precepts than to instincts, a view that gained force from Freudian influences, "the greatest advance ever made toward the understanding and control of human character," according to Lippmann. Puritan repression of natural desires, explained Waldo Frank's *Our America* (1919), produced fundamental defects in the American character.

Skeptics therefore sneered at

Mr. Do
-nothing the wellknown parvenu
who . . .

studied with Freud a year or two
and when Freud got through
with Do-

nothing Do-
nothing could do
nothing . . . (1926)

Skillful promotion could sell any product—patriotic as well as debunking biographies, lost causes as well as success stories. The 1926 Sesquicentennial celebrated the Declaration of Independence as the sound of the tolling Liberty Bell sped through the air to a radio audience, some of which had learned to question the altruism of the Founding Fathers, for subjectivity had by then filtered into the writing of history. The assertion, in the 1920s, that all written history, "merely relative to time and circumstance," amounted to no more than "a passing shadow, an illusion" licensed a free revaluation of the past in terms of present needs. Social scientists, swayed by relativism, also manipulated evidence to support their views, as Margaret Mead did. Edward L. Bernays, hired by the American Tobacco Company to promote smoking among women (1929), treated cigarettes as phallic symbols to serve "as torches of freedom" for liberated ladies. In vain Robert Hutchins insisted that truth remained everywhere the same; the theory of evolution became a popular means of disowning the past.[64]

Ominously, the press grew bigger, more remote, livelier, and ever less restrained in disseminating rumors. Competently edited, visually appealing through photographs, it steadily gained strength, although the circulation of old-line newspapers like the Boston *Transcript* and the New York *Sun* dwindled. Pulitzer's *World* began to seek the respectability that would ultimately kill it, while Scripps-Howard, Hearst, and other chains widened the distance between editors and community. Few journals showed any scruples in pursuit of a scoop. William Randolph Hearst's empire, firmly planted in every major city, briskly fought off local competitors and held its readers by sensation—that is, by an accurate though lurid depiction of the brutal world in which they lived. The secret of success, explained Ralph Ingersoll, a *Time* editor, lay in converting news into fiction, a formula that helped explain that weekly's displacement of the *Literary Digest* in popularity. The tabloid form, imported from England, further strengthened popular journalism, supplying scandal and human interest stories in a package manageable by straphangers in a crowded subway or trolley car.[65]

After 1920, the Hollywood movie industry grew lustily, its extravagant Oriental palaces reaching from Broadway to Main Street, some seating five thousand customers. Great profits depended on substantial capital and planned production, as in other corporate enterprises, but also provoked accusations of sinister Jewish control. However, the desire to attract increasingly heterogeneous audiences from every part of the country and from every social group created pressures toward uniformity, and made the relationship of actors and directors to viewers impersonal, with performances pitched to the taste of the mythical eleven-year-old girl in Des Moines. Increasingly, success depended on stars, as familiar in the magazine or newspaper as on the screen, their personal and projected lives confused in a common identity, shadowy in outlines yet filtering into the reveries of millions. The audience wished to regard fields, flowers, and white picket fences, not drab city streets. They laughed at *Safety Last* (1923), in which Harold Lloyd scaled the skyscraper for publicity, fending off pigeons, disentangling his foot from a giant clock, and shaking out the mouse that investigated his trousers. Spectacles thrilled—*Ben Hur* (1925), $6 million; or Mae West's corseted seductiveness. Rudolph Valentino seemed to the usually skeptical H. L. Mencken a civilized man of "obvious fineness." At the passionate Sheik's funeral, thousands waited hours for a glimpse while Paula Negri fainted photogenically at the coffin. Nothing more serious intruded on the silver screen: "If you got a message, send it by Western Union"—attributed to Sam Goldwyn.[66]

Sports, too, became part of organized popular culture, even golf (though not a team activity). Ghostwriters busily churned out copy for big-name reporters who "covered" these events in the press. The contests evoked daydreams, with hours of immediate involvement in the ballpark only the start; memories of the turn of fate that saved the day, of the adventure and the emotion, made the weeks of labor bearable; imaginary homers enlivened the youth's dreary days. With events perceived in the mind's eye quite detached from external reality, more often than not men and women emerged hugging comforting illusions, however slightly linked to their own lives. A hundred thousand spectators from all over the country came to Columbus for Red Grange's final game for Illinois against Ohio State. Even after depression struck, a disgusted observer noted that empty bellies could not cure the American addiction to make-believe (1936). The daydreaming would drag them down helplessly in fatuous and unnecessary chaos.[67]

Urban residents accepted disorder, within limits, insofar as it provided anonymity and forestalled the stifling conformity of small-town or rural life. Choices abounded; for as little as five cents to a top of $2.20, the movies, vaudeville, burlesque, or the theater offered a wide range of diversions, although no counterpart of the German political drama. Cheap fares eased travel to parks and waterfront, and the streets themselves, animated by constant movement, provided nonstop entertainment. Critics deplored the sheepishness of Americans who did everything in the mass, swayed by booms, crazes, fads, and revivals. Fashions in clothing, like the length of ladies' skirts and the style of men's trenchcoats, aped the movie characters. And entrepreneurs like Henry Ford manipulated the news to boost sales. In *The Crowd* (1928), King Vidor's film, Mr. Anyman, engulfed in a mass society, loses his identity under the pressure of soul-destroying labor. City people became mob-minded because to go along provided the thrifty, speedy means of getting from one place to another. Only thus could they respond to questions they did not understand and in which they lacked interest. And why run the risk of nervous B.O., which a bar of Lifebuoy could forestall.[68]

Besides, the mass consisted of many heterogeneous elements arranged in numerous shifting groups, among the interstices of which everyone sought a place in which to achieve separateness—individuality. Thirty million people, enrolled in eight hundred fraternal societies, owned a fez, a scimitar, a secret code, or a pair of Anatolian breeches as evidence of their identity. Yankees and Southerners insisted vigorously on the preservation of regional values, as did some heirs of immigrant cultures. Trained, taut, eager common people would thus make themselves worthy to rule and build, to set aside modes of customary behavior. Indeed, the belief endured that the whole national experience involved the rejection by each generation of its predecessor; thus the sons of poor peasants and laborers became physicians and philosophers.[69]

Individualism dominated liberal thinking in the 1920s and repelled communal encroachments on personal freedom. Furious critics attacked "an age gone mad with materialism, intolerance and false standards." A comfortable obliviousness, an ignorant pretense, marked the Babbittry of those who governed. "This the best of all possible worlds. Rah Rah Rah Rotary." Prohibition therefore became the central political issue of the 1920s, more important than the civil liberties that occupied the American Association of University Professors (1914) and the American Civil Liberties Union (1920). Alice Roosevelt Longworth's butler concocted very passable gin from oranges in her small still. Communities might tolerate such deviant behavior by closet rebels, but the desire to preserve stability fenced the alienated apart.[70]

Women who rejected earlier models of domesticity outdistanced men in throwing off restraint. Daisy and Lady Brett left behind the goals defined years before at Seneca Falls; education, the ballot, public office and jobs, the cigarette, the highball, and the golf course became almost as accessible to them as to men. The double standard loosened along with burdensome subjection to frequent childbirth. Easy marriage and easy divorce, small families and plenty of leisure, became the ideals. With their hair cut short and their legs unswathed, free and equal—and separate—they were nobody's babies now, but persons with their own identities and their own desires to satisfy.

But the new status entailed new anxieties. The model all-American girls moved through life self-contained, giving when they received, taking what they needed, individuals like the dancing partners with whom they shared moments of intimacy in the solitude of the crowded ballroom. Although attention focused on Clara Bow, "the 'It' girl," women also made their marks as novelists, painters, and athletes. Hostile tirades did not trouble them: "Spend less on dope and cold cream and get down on your knees and pray," thundered the Reverend Billy Sunday. "You doll women, you parasites, you toys of men, you silken-wrapped geisha girls, you painted, idle purring cats, you parody of the females of your species—find brains enough if you can to see the doom hanging over you and revolt before it is too late!" Members of the younger generation of both sexes gave revolt their own and different meanings.[71]

Their desire for identity took form in rebellion—against the King Tut craze for things Egyptian, against Brush Your Teeth Week, against parents, against beauty pageants, against the queens of Hosiery and Petrolia. The city and town, the factory and office, crowded people in, made them cogs, consumers, all alike, mass-produced, numbered and not named. The past, and the family that linked them to it, tied them down when they wished to fly. Unless they had their fling, spread their wings, they would waste something within them. Fearing the crush of restraints, they revolted more often than had their predecessors.

Alas, the freedom of individuality lay beyond the reach of those who lacked the inner resources to strike out without guide or companion. Many dreamed of flight from the ugly, phony crap about them; few could take off, find the purity, innocence, they desired. Mostly they made do with second-hand experiences, went along with snappy dressers, talkers like Jimmy Walker. In mirrors young girls sought distinctive reflections of unique personalities, but saw only identical copies of slick advertisements, garbed in dresses factories sewed up by the thousands. In the dark at the movie, they sought the feeling of bliss from the thought of the kiss that made the moment sublime, but got no fun from being alone. Every girl needed her love-nest and tried to capture in marriage the equivalent of the romance the dream factories purveyed. A few turned to the healing analyst's couch. Or, like Ring Lardner's Celia Rigg—alone, all alone—they and men like them helped themselves to sips of bourbon.[72]

They formed the rank and file of the unhappy searchers for stability. They had voted for progressivism, which had assured them that the nation—the great group of which all were parts—really cared for them. But political reform had not restored order to their lives. Exposed by the weakness of community and family, they needed love to protect their individuality; searching for it they established connections beneath the hoods or in the crowds that submerged the very individuality they wished to protect. And good, decent men and women who kept their faith and who chanced it alone feared the unpredictable consequences. Like pawns on the chessboard, moved here and there by an unknown player who, unpredictably and without reason, altered the rules, they could not fathom the course their lives took. They found intense, perverse enjoyment in their hopeless despair. Proud like the sandy desert that gloried in its glitter, they could not appraise their own unhappiness.[73]

Men and women who yearned for some sense of order in the encompassing wasteland but did not wish to join the hooded, shirted marchers tried homesteading away from town. Impatiently, they observed the eagerness to communicate with Mars, to converse with spirits, to evoke biography from the wrinkles of the palm or to riddle the inevitable with playing cards. They could not understand why science produced poison gases as its end-product and why scientists who explored the womb, or tomb, or dreams did not set themselves to apprehend now, the point of intersection of the timeless with time.[74]

Their heritage in 1920 left them so: adrift in the mass, susceptible to whim and fashion except insofar as they could cling to traditional values and tastes transposed from elsewhere. The high culture of high society, anchored in Europe and self-consciously elitist, had nothing to say to most Americans. Its effort to rally conservative forces from within entrenched institutions faltered when Europe betrayed it, and the Depression buried it. After 1918 Old World titles lost value; nobility ceased to command respect when Russian dukes drove taxis in Paris. Meanwhile a new art revealed more to painting than the old masters and their imitators; the stock market crash eroded support for the opera houses; and the New Deal's WPA, which dotted the country with Georgian post offices, permissively encouraged every kind of painter and writer.

In the 1920s, the avant-garde that rejected the official culture had fled, either by expatriation to France or England or to such self-contained enclaves as Greenwich Village. There they hoped to find some coherence beneath the world's disordered surface, but they could not hope to know again the infirm glory of the positive hour, could not drink there where trees flowered and springs flowed. And they, too, ignored the men and women among whom they lived except as occasional picturesque background elements. Surrounded by the wreckage of a "botched civilization," with liberty as chimerical as peace, they found as little explanatory power in science as in religion, myth, or magic. By contrast, in the working class and immigrant quarters, the sensitive young exiles saw life as real; there idealized residents dealt with the serious problems of bread, love, and death. Through contact with that more vital world, literature and painting could break through sterile, inherited formulae. "Go to jail," the poet advised young writers, aspiring revolutionaries, and inquiring roughnecks. "You've got to go to jail sometime if you're going to be any good." The tramps knew better.[75]

Plunging into experiment, the rebels, an advance guard in the revolt against official culture, struggled to develop new forms in poetry, painting, architecture, and music, just as they sought new forms of work. The "smart, sophisticated, sensitive yet hard-boiled, art-loving frequenters of the little theatres" set their own standards, disdained the marketplace and best-seller lists, and directed their magazines and shows at small, self-contained audiences. As detached observers, they rarely wished entanglements with popular culture or more intimate relationships with other Americans. They flirted with Communism or with Southern Agrarianism, or Thomism, less out of positive identification with those causes than as further rebellion against a restrictive environment.

Above all, therefore, they resisted impediments to self-expression. They had now gotten to read Melville and gave their own meaning to the pursuit of the white whale, which they took to be that self-designated goal within themselves. However little faith they had, they trusted in the worthiness of that pursuit. They did not go forth because they accepted the existence of the whale; they accepted the existence of the whale because it justified their urge to go forth.[76]

"I wish to believe in God at any price," cried Nina, "a heap of stones, a mud image, a drawing on the wall, a bird, a fish, a snake, a baboon—or even a good man preaching the simple platitudes of truth. I want to believe in something! I want to believe so I can feel." God Himself had thus become an instrument for exercise of the sovereign human personality. T. S. Eliot also reached for faith because he did not choose to despair. The more sensitive, with Wallace Stevens, simply sat on the dump and beat an old tin can for that which they believed. Or else they recalled all the gods that failed. Randolph Bourne in 1917 had yearned for that "vividest kind of poetic vision" and had taken Dewey's philosophy as American religion. It never occurred to him that values could be subordinate to technique. Other questers for purity drifted like Holden toward madness or embraced suicide like Hart Crane.[77]

The crevice between elite and popular culture already apparent in 1920 widened into a yawning chasm across which voices did not travel. Questions about purpose, meaning, and the direction of national development scarcely heard across the gap received no meaningful answers. Liberty in that context meant accepting the universe and feeling normal and inevitable parts of the whole. Academic philosophers drifted away from the issues that had interested the generation of James and Dewey toward problems of logic and epistemology incomprehensible to the uninitiated. Sociologists, preoccupied with control, tinkered with reform schemes. Freud, popularized, denied vice and interpreted evil as illness, calling not for morality but for hygiene. Nor did it help Americans to hear that civilization, in ruins, moved inexorably to collectivism, while the abstruse, rational, socially oriented ideas of the theological seminaries said little to ordinary worshipers who wanted to know why and for what.

Such people remained in the old traditional churches or responded to evangelists who confirmed the strain of normalcy.[78]

Men and women coasting individually down to normalcy found the slope pleasant, even exhilarating, so long as they rode in unrestrained comfort.

Then economic depression after 1929 stripped the ease away and the jolt tossed them about in a mess. Thereafter the belief spread that only intervention by an activist state would restore their ability to act and redeem their liberty.[79]

CHAPTER 2

THE LIMITS OF RATIONAL PLANNING

THE MEN AND WOMEN who marched or wore shirts or hoods wanted such order in their lives as they imagined had assured their ancestors liberty, that is, the ability to act. Otherwise, an expanding, ever-more-complex universe would toss everyone adrift. Hope that humans would use reason scientifically to plan economic and social development survived as a legacy from Progressivism, sustaining entrepreneurial optimists in the 1920s and political reformers in the 1930s. A "newer liberalism" demanded the extension, not the restriction, of government to cope with the practical problems of the good life. The sense of potential power stimulated imagination and daring, and bred an eagerness for general improvement, which became an ingrained conviction. "An abiding faith in the intelligence, the initiative, the character, the courage, and the divine touch in the individual," expressed through organized effort, would guarantee progress and restrain the lust for power, the ever-lurking enemy of popular liberty.[1]

However, Americans painfully discovered the limits of achievement until war for a time made everything possible.

The appearance of prosperity after 1920 deceived those focused on a narrow segment of society, content with enchanting numbers that confirmed what they wished to believe. The illusion extended also to journalists and social scientists more usually inclined to skepticism.[2]

Of course, the stock market! With here and there a correction, security prices soared, created millions in paper profits for investors large and small. But other statistics in the 1920s also measured the nation's permanent prosperity—of bushels of wheat, of tons of steel, of millions of autos produced annually. A striking increase in productivity per man-hour permitted a corresponding increase in consuming power. Street traffic soared: New York City's 125,000 motor vehicles of 1918 became 790,000 in 1932. Every auto that edged onto the clogged highways added to the insatiable demand for gasoline; wildcat prospectors and corporate geologists poked at the earth's surface, coaxing wealth to gush forth. And archaic laws kept the lid off; any agreement to control production might bring on an antitrust prosecution. Therefore American corporations could not combine as the German I. G. Farben and the British Imperial Chemical did in the burgeoning petrochemical industry. Instead Dupont, Union Carbide, and smaller competitors went each their own way. Furthermore, the ancient English rule of capture, applied in twentieth-century America, treated petroleum like game birds, the property not of the owner of the land over which they flew or beneath which it flowed, but of whoever grabbed it first—an incentive to the speediest possible exploitation. Near Long Beach, California, the Signal Hill boom (1921) drew thirty-seven companies into the field; in ten months their hundred and eight wells pumped up fourteen thousand barrels a day. Yet every scheme of proration or control contravened the Sherman and Clayton Acts, with the result uninhibited frenzied exploration. Chaos therefore followed discovery of the great East Texas fields in 1930.[3]

No one manned the brakes or slowed down speculation. Savoring the immediacy of experience, Americans waived the questions of why, for how long, for what purpose, and at what cost—content to accept even the freedom to starve so long as the outcome emanated from their own decisions. Herbert Hoover and other engineers attacked the vicious speculators and called for cooperation. But with professors and journalists mostly back at their desks after 1918, businessmen and lawyers took charge. The Secretary of the Treasury, himself a banker, sought to lower the income tax; and the federal government, operating on a budget after 1921, balanced its books as everyone else did, thus reassuring securities investors.[4]

By 1920 the United States had become an international creditor. Allied debts incurred during the war remained unpaid. Instead, additional amounts flowed eastward across the Atlantic through loans to governments, through investments in foreign enterprises, and through the erection of American branch plants overseas. An excess of exports over imports added to the total due the United States. The historic capital shortage had ended and a mature economy generated surpluses, especially after Wilson's reforms in effect shifted the currency base from government bonds to commercial paper, inflating the money supply in periods of expansion.

Speculation continued. Values spiraled upward, buoyed by pressure from unbounded faith that everyone could get rich. True, average savers increased their holdings by only eleven dollars between 1914 and 1927; but the number of millionaires soared from seven thousand to thirty-five thousand in that interval. The gross national product rose by fifty percent between 1920 and 1929. Meanwhile, real estate boomed; volatile values in Florida and California suffered occasional relapses but not enough to dampen optimism, nurtured by pictures of yacht basins and bathing beauties beneath the palms. The stock markets attained levels unjustified by earnings or dividends. Loose credit practices permitted speculators to deal on margin, to invest in short-term turnovers of large blocks of securities with little cash. Brokers' loans for such accounts climbed from $2.8 billion at the beginning of 1927 to $3.5 billion at the end of that year and rocketed to $6 billion by the summer of 1929.

Banks, made lax by the lure of high interest rates, encouraged expansion, particularly those selling shares through affiliates. The sky seemed the limit! Shrewd as he was, Justice Brandeis could not understand where all the money came from. The nation certainly did not earn it.[5]

Excessive expectations about the capacity of American industry to expand fed the boom. Advertising inflated markets by informing consumers of needs they did not know they had; the campaign to popularize orange juice eased overproduction in California. Low taxes and easy money made government a friend of business.

The modern corporation, remote from its nineteenth-century antecedents in size and in character, autonomous, controlled by bureaucratic managers rather than by stockholders, pursued growth. The grasping individual entrepreneur survived in movies or in memories as a quaint figure of the past. More representative, Alfred P. Sloan guided General Motors to primacy. Educated as an engineer, he decentralized management, gave purchasers choices of styles and prices, installment credit, trade-ins, and annual model changes—the new industrial administrator, an educated professional concerned with service like any other. So ran the comforting assumptions.[6]

The old trust-busting days had ended, with few prosecutions under the Clayton Act, despite its framers' intent. The Supreme Court in 1920 refused to order the dissolution of the United States Steel Corporation, holding that mere size or command of a large part of the market was not evidence of restraint of trade. The dominance of a few large firms in communication by telephone and radio did not in itself cause concern.

Chain stores continued to spread. The number of A&P's climbed from 5,000 in 1922 to 17,500 in 1928, while the managers had to learn to imbue the merchandise "with values of heart, mind and spirit" unreflected in the sale price. John D. Rockefeller and other capitalists, sensitive to currents of popular opinion, employed public relations experts to gain popularity—their concern expressive of a new sense of accountability. From the Ludlow Massacre (1914) they learned the need for better labor relations in their own self-interest. Corporations, flush with profits, could afford measures of concern for their employees and thus fend off union organizers.

John Maurice Clark's influential *Social Control of Business* (1926) argued that monopoly presented no danger. Laissez-faire had indeed ended, but control ought not slip into the state's clumsy hands. Herbert Hoover in 1928 agreed. The planning possible within the firm ought not to extend to the whole society, but the large organized interests of the country could balance one another for the general welfare. The Federal Trade Commission preferred not to police corporations; instead by conferences and stipulations it sponsored practices that evaded possible charges of conspiracy. Liberty gained because government expanded rather than limited the ability to act. Critics who argued that "never before in American history were the forces of reaction so completely in control of our political and economic life" proved poor historians and even worse observers of the social scene.[7]

Thriving new industries justified confidence in the future. The consumption of electricity expanded rapidly, drawing upon both coal and water to generate power. The number of customers climbed, the use by each doubled, and the total output mounted more than five-fold between 1912 and 1929. The expansion promised fortunes to investors. Samuel Insull assembled vast holding companies to tie operations together, and in the process created ample opportunities for manipulating stock values.[8]

Aluminum output climbed dramatically. Primary production rose about six-fold between 1912 and 1929 under a virtual monopoly that promised one dominant firm unlimited future profits. George Eastman in Rochester presided over Kodak's phenomenal growth, made stock available to employees, and donated millions for education. A variety of electrical products dangled signs of progress before consumers. The 100,000 radios produced in 1922 increased to 3,250,000 in 1929, by which time ten million families owned sets; thousands of homes also boasted refrigerators, toasters, clocks, and oil burners. Extensive advertising made product names familiar and sustained demand. In 1930 American factories turned out just over 4.5 million automobiles. Vehicle miles traveled increased about four-fold between 1921 and 1929. Car registrations rose to more than 27 million in 1930, representing the need for highways on which to move, rubber for tires, glass for windows, and steel for bodies. The cost of roads and streets laid out each year tripled between 1915 and 1929, covered in part by federal grants-in-aid. Manufacturing operated on a mammoth scale. In 1929 Ford's River Rouge plant employed more than 103,000 workers, spilled out over 1,115 acres, and contained ninety-three separate structures, ninety-three miles of railroad track, and twenty-seven miles of conveyors.[9]

Construction boomed to meet public and private demand. The total value of new building, in constant dollars, doubled between 1915 and 1929. Much of the urban housing erected in the late nineteenth century had become obsolete either through original deficiencies or through urban changes and population shifts from one neighborhood to another. Replacement added to the boom. The rise in the standard of living of some and the pent-up demand of the low-construction war years increased starts in the 1920s and nurtured exaggerated hopes of profit. Transit facilities, public utilities, and schools as well as new residences absorbed tons of lumber, steel, and concrete, employing thousands. Economic expansion encouraged belief in the development of an associational order that would "act as a whole only in and through harmoniously acting members," thus permitting adequate control without creating a welfare, regulatory, or military state, all deemed ultimate threats to liberty.[10]

Ominous clouds shadowed these sunny prospects. Farmers demanded aid as prices fell from wartime peaks, while debts and fixed interest payments remained high. And factory workers did not thrive. Real earnings lagged behind the rise in productivity and the unskilled did not gain at all. Union membership fell and recurrent strikes won few victories. Although measured by no reliable data, unemployment rose and periodic layoffs reduced annual incomes. Traditional stratagems enabled the jobless to get by for a while: families doubled up and took in lodgers; they cut down on food, used up savings, and borrowed; or the men went out peddling until their fortunes turned. Even the fellow trying to hold down the fifty-buck job with one foot while rocking the cradle with the other got no fun out of it (1926). Miners and lumbermen also found little in which to rejoice as the good times receded after the peace. In the coal fields and steel mills, accidents, black lung disease, long hours, and meager pay packets added to the misery. Even with pie on the counter the poor devils lost the ability to digest it (1921), as

. . . red blistered hands ever stuck
deep down in the foul indescribable muck
where dishes are plunged seventeen at a time
and washed in a tubful of sickening slime.

Years of toil led many only to the disastrous dependency of old age.[11]

Deep pockets of poverty defaced the economy; out of the way, they troubled only a few philanthropists and ministers who recalled the millennial promises of the social gospel. The North Carolina tenants living in primitive isolation and sharecroppers in Georgia, Alabama, and Mississippi caught no glimmer of hope in the alternation of seasons; black and white, they never got ahead in their accounts during the best of times and had no margin for the worst. Among the fruit and vegetable crops of Florida and the Southwest and in the sugar beet fields of Michigan, the migrants seasonally appeared up from Mexico or across from the Caribbean, then receded with the harvest in. In the Appalachian highlands—deforested, game gone—jobs ran out when seams of coal were depleted. Here and there were textile mills, down from the North for the cheap labor; plenty of hands lined up there for the meager wages that soon disappeared in the company store or in rent for the company shack. Their families knew the feel of deprivation, month in, month out; and the slightest disturbance pushed over the brink to disaster those who never even tasted the prosperity of the 1920s.[12]

A far-from-slight disturbance overwhelmed them and many others in 1929. Abuse of the resources of nature and of the pearls of science cast before them yielded slums as well as millionaires, while the dispossessed rallied blindly to the defense of property. The same disaster dragged them all down.

The collapse of speculative security values in 1929 should have surprised no one familiar with past gyrations of stock prices. For a century the cycles followed their mysterious but predictable course with a collapse every twenty years or so. Such ups and downs increased efficiency by eliminating marginal producers and thus strengthened the whole economy. So ran the soothing theory. Warnings of a correction and revelations of corrupt practices on Wall Street and Main Street had punctuated even the frenzied celebrations of normalcy. Yet the number of shares traded soared, as did the prices. Then collapse; and the downturn touched off a panic that fed off itself, snowballed, grew ever worse. On September 3, 1929, General Electric sold for 396¼ and Radio Corporation for 101; on November 13, they went for 168½ and 28.

A sign of the fearful loss of confidence: an enterprising circus publicity man elbowed his way into the hearing room and planted a midget on the knees of the once redoubtable J. P. Morgan, who had appeared to testify before a congressional committee. The banker accepted the intrusion as a normal feature of the strange new world into which the country had drifted.[13]

Fortunes vanished overnight; the once wealthy counted pennies to get by, drastically cutting back expenditures. Families no longer even moderately well-off reduced all expenses. For more than a decade, Americans had acquired homes with mortgages and bought everything on the installment plan—furniture, automobiles, radios, vacuum cleaners, and washing machines. In 1929 a mountain of consumer debt hung over the economy, and when payments stopped so did purchases. Death by design—suicides in depression, like the first leaves that dropped from a tree in autumn. The bewildered gave up, unable to locate the causes of ruin:

> . . . add,
> Subtract, and put ourselves in pawn;
> For all our scratching on the pad,
> We cannot trace the error down.[14]

Sales declined, inventories piled up. No orders reached the factories, where halted production meant layoffs. Unemployment mounted, further reducing consumption. No help came from agriculture; between 1929 and 1932, per-capita cash net income of farmers dropped from $162 to $48 a year—no margin for big spending. Meanwhile, unpaid loans put pressure on banks; the number of failures rose; and the spiral plunged downward. As expected—except that there seemed no bottom.

Of course, the learned and the sophisticated knew the ways of the business cycle. In the nature of the case, what went down would in time go up. But when? And meanwhile? Even before the crash, a committee on Recent Social Trends had predicted drastic reorganizations; and President Hoover, forewarned, had approved creation of the Reconstruction Finance Corporation as a lender of last resort to forestall excessive credit stringencies. It could not, however, stay the increase in bank failures. In February 1931, Hoover called for the ordered liberty of individualism, not government action. In the closing months of 1932, the economy collapsed; unemployment soared, local charity proved inadequate, and starvation threatened families, helpless without the wages spent for food and fuel. Triumphant Communists announced the "approaching old age, senility and collapse of capitalism." Commentators less enamored by Soviet achievements but deeply affected by the moral crisis of the Depression also gave up and dreamed of alternative social models.

In Chicago Al Capone supported a free soup kitchen in a huge South Side building. For eleven days in 1932, with no relief funds available, Philadelphians lived off spoiled vegetables and dandelions—or starved. Food and rent riots erupted. The number of tramps increased—among them now whole families. The damn fool hunted for work—there was no work. But he could not leave the wife and kids to starve alone, so he brought them with him. Now he could watch hunger draw their life away. In the countryside, debt evictions drove tenants onto the roads, to drift away without resources. On the flats in Washington several thousand veterans camped in a "bonus army" until dispersed by the military. Despair! Although politicians close to urban conditions, like Robert Wagner, perceived the long-range downward trend in industry, Hoover in December 1929 anticipated an imminent return to normalcy. Joke: Prosperity? Just around the coroner.[15]

The election of a new President in 1932 did not restore confidence or end joblessness, for while Franklin Delano Roosevelt, former governor of New York, determined to do something, he had no clear idea of what to do. A pleasant man who, Walter Lippmann said, wished very much to be President, he did not reassure the needy on the farms or streets by public emphasis on economy and budget-cutting. Nor did his unwillingness to share responsibility with the outgoing President in the months between the election and the inauguration. But the disease that left him unable to walk without help made him an insistent optimist, the only alternative to permanent helplessness. The experience also endowed him with a resolute and sometimes ruthless determination to use others as needed. Roosevelt's support, solidly grounded in new voters who had flocked to the polls in 1928 and returned thereafter—urban, immigrants or their children, laborers—made him President and made the Democrats masters of Congress. With only occasional lapses he could get done what he wished, if only he knew what that was. He sensed that government had lost contact with the people, while citizens had lost faith in its capacities. The intimacy of the colonial town meeting had given way in the modern age to a situation in which men and women became mere statistical items, a situation not conducive to the preservation of liberty.[16]

Once in office, Roosevelt's appearance of action heartened many who had no other hope. *Happy days are here again*—the contemporary theme—voiced assurance. True, the chaotic and incoherent New Deal resounded with echoes of Wilson's New Freedom and T.R.'s Square

Deal, and jumbled together disparate views; but F.D.R. exuded confidence "because it never occurred to him that he really didn't understand what's wrong with things any more than anybody else did" (1938). Free government required only "the maintenance of a balance within which every individual may have a place if he will take it; in which every individual may find safety if he wishes it; in which every individual may attain such power as his ability permits, consistent with his assuming the accompanying responsibility" (1932).[17]

His administrative staff offered no clue to future policy. The appointment to the Cabinet of three Southern Democrats paid political debts and gained support in Congress. At the Treasury, a businessman aimed to placate financial interests and in Agriculture and Interior progressive Republicans reached out toward the Midwest. Two New Yorkers served Roosevelt in Washington as they had in Albany; one, Frances Perkins, provided links to women and reformers; the other, James A. Farley, managed patronage. But the Cabinet did not shape policy.[18]

As important as the politicians, clusters of philanthropists, social workers, and academics drifted to the President as their counterparts had to T.R. and to Wilson. The entourage included trust-builders and trust-busters, advocates of national planning and of free competition, monetary quacks and sober lawyers. Lacking the binding commitments of professionals and imperfectly acquainted with the rules of the game, the brain trust, heady with responsibility, gaily crossed bureaucratic lines to act vigorously but often abrasively. The sudden taste of power electrified those who had formerly ruled only the classroom. And in the background, but far from unobtrusive, "My Missus" pursued her own agenda. Washington therefore hummed with schemes for remaking the government and the country.

The administration's first hundred days accomplished a lot. The President's vibrant personality inspired his followers with a sense of the importance of their jobs. And his fireside chats sustained enthusiastic public support. Assailed by critics on the left for not doing enough, and by critics on the right for concentrating too much power in his own hands, and swamping freedom by an intrusive federal government, Roosevelt argued that New Deal legislation protected rather than subverted rights, fulfilling old American ideals. When Roosevelt asked (1934), "Are you better off than you were last year?" many answered—yes. Had they lost any constitutional freedom? They answered no.

Believing anything possible, the New Dealers gave scant consideration to formal liberty; hunger, they thought, destroyed the worth of the abstract ability to act. For a decade, unsavory forces had monopolized the word "liberty," restricting its meanings and its benefits to the chosen few, while the "abject, inarticulate and unintelligent" Congress "responded solely to two factors too powerful and prevalent in politics and government—fear and selfishness." The President envisioned himself as renovator of an august building somewhat the worse for wear, neither erecting a new structure nor tearing down the old, but blending the two.[19]

Harry L. Hopkins, the most durable and most influential of the advisers, had come to New York from Iowa, held various private social welfare posts, and knew the suffering that suffused the slums. In 1931, when the Depression deepened unemployment, Governor Roosevelt appointed him director of the New York State Temporary Emergency Relief Administration to stave off mass hunger. Two years later, Hopkins moved on to head the Federal Emergency Relief Administration. To these assignments he brought a commitment to positive action nurtured by a generation of humanitarian reformers convinced of the necessity of doing good "*with* people, not *to* people." The United States, he believed, had built its industrial plant in the nineteenth century, at a price of low wages and low welfare standards. In the twentieth century government intervention to maintain purchasing power would be a permanent feature of American life, manipulating consumption and production to ensure a rising national income and enough taxes to cover federal expenditures. Relief, in his view, therefore meant not a dole to keep recipients from starving, but jobs to preserve their spirits. As Works Project Administrator between 1935 and 1938 he built thousands of schools, bridges, and public buildings and gave meaningful employment to millions, without a taint of scandal; during the Second World War, he would become the President's closest adviser. Opponents regarded him as a menace, a brash and irresponsible bureaucrat. "The trouble with Harry," an observer commented, "was that he never spent his own money." He symbolized a new ethic that would be very hard to restrain. "Thousands of Arkansans come here during the year begging, begging, begging. It is going to be very difficult to ever get away from the habit of giving out federal favors. You cannot imagine how persistent are the forces of plunder," one congressman noted.[20]

Roosevelt's soothing assurance that the nation had nothing to fear but fear itself did not get at the source of disorder. Nor did his inaugural's inflammatory attack on the money changers or his suggestion about moving people from the cities to farms. A shrewd politician, F.D.R. knew that he had no cause to worry either about his own hold on office or about Democratic control of Congress. Although he lacked a consistent political or economic philosophy, a vision of long-term goals, he and many of his collaborators remembered the heady World War days when Washington managed the whole economy and won; they could do the same in the struggle with depression. Crisis justified the power to act. The government would never deprive any minority of liberty unless it abused its liberty to harm the majority. But desperate people in other lands had surrendered their freedom when it came to mean merely humiliation and starvation.[21]

The New Deal aimed first at practical problems—relief of the needy millions and industrial and agricultural recovery—and then social reform. It attained none of its objectives, but it continued the Progressive process of rethinking the relationship of government to the productive system and to individual freedom. It would not abridge the liberty of people to carry on their business unless in the larger interests of the majority. Political leaders could no longer stand aside while industry operated of its own accord or count on the earth unaided to yield its abundance to the husbandman. Only the state could regulate these processes rationally, thereby extending liberty to all. Roosevelt quoted the conservative Elihu Root: the inadequacy of "the old reliance upon the free action of individual wills" called for the intervention of that organized control of government to produce justice and right conduct, earlier left to the decisions of each individual. The change in outlook imbued people with enough hope to survive without succumbing to despair, an achievement in a decade when gloomy observers made out the "gradual extirpation from the public mind" of the ideal of freedom, and when other countries lost faith in democracy. Almost everyone concurred when the President rejected a "return to that definition of liberty" that for many years gradually regimented a free people into the service of the privileged few. He preferred a broader definition that would assure "a greater freedom, a greater security, for the average man than he has ever known before in the history of America."[22]

Through the winter of 1932–33 evidence piled up: men, women, and children in all parts of the country starved, literally went without food. The number of families Boston aided leaped from 7,463 in 1929 to more than 40,000 in 1932; and those helped amounted to only one-fourth of the unemployed. Meager work or none at all! Desperately clinging to respectability, the jobless sold apples at street corners and struggled to preserve their so-American optimism, even the woman who in fourteen hours with the scrub brush earned not one day of security by it. Pitiful heaps of possessions along the sidewalks marked evictions for lack of rent money; the poor clutched the sticks of furniture, evidence of their once and future identity. Informal aid from family and neighbors dried up; welfare agencies—even those supported by community chests (1918)—exhausted those funds. The fruitless search for work at any pay exhausted the strongest men, who confronted defeat as hope flickered and then vanished. A stray dime might as well go for a movie, where the show, though repeated five times over, brought at least shelter. And some—male and female, young and old—as earlier wandered about, found comradeship among the tramps on the road, merged in the heaps of human junk, with still-beating arteries huddled in doorways—such the scope of their liberty.[23]

Like everyone else, Roosevelt considered poverty a responsibility of the states and of local communities. But as governor of New York he had perceived the inadequacy of conventional resources for confronting the armies of the needy; and sadly, the depression hit the poorest hardest. Strikes turned violent, by Philadelphia taxi drivers, by Milwaukee transit workers, by Minneapolis truckers, and by Southern textile hands. In the clash of contending interests, the victorious crippled themselves; and the desire for fuller lives turned self-destructive. Humanitarianism without a sound economic basis proved a cheat and a delusion. No government could afford to rule by sympathy and sentiment. A grave menace faced the country. Yet the "painful process of race betterment" called for leadership in maintaining an equilibrium between the claims of liberty and equality, maintained according to custom, self-help, and self-control—"the essence of the American tradition" (1934).[24]

Only the national government, through its power to tax and borrow, commanded the resources to help. Social workers like Mary van Kleeck, Edith Abbott, and Donald Richberg (who praised Soviet planning) insisted on a right to assistance, but persuaded few because constitutional inhibitions prevented direct action. President Roosevelt nevertheless authorized the Federal Emergency Relief Administration to provide grants to the states for aid. Furthermore, to avoid the odium of a dole, a federal agency hired workers for deserving public projects at the minimum wage. By the end of 1934, more than twenty million Americans, one out of every six, received temporary assistance.[25]

Relief, direct or indirect, left untouched the causes of depression and the number of people without permanent employment. Of course, increased consumption would stimulate manufacturing and put people back to work. Henry Ford and William Green of the American Federation of Labor thus agreed on the need for higher wages. Some New Dealers urged the government to create jobs by pump-priming, as private industry could not, restore purchasing power by putting new funds into the economy. The business cycle did not determine the demand for roads, bridges, and schools as it did for automobiles or coats; socially useful projects, kept to a minimum in times of prosperity, but expanding rapidly during depression, would absorb the unemployed, whose wages spent on food, clothing, and shelter would stimulate production and recovery. So ran the theory. Despite the negative evidence from European experiments, Roosevelt pressed for an increase of opportunities. The Works Progress Administration (1935) provided jobs to three and a half million unemployed, among them writers, artists, and musicians as well as manual laborers. The tasks mattered little so long as the pay went to consumers. The New Deal thus pragmatically anticipated John Maynard Keynes's general theory published later. To spare the country insidious demoralization—"the greatest menace to our social order"—the President determined that no American would remain permanently on the relief rolls. We must "arrange our national economy to end our present unemployment" by a step-by-step approach to meet concrete needs in the "courageous recognition of change."

Pump-priming failed, perhaps because of its faulty assumptions, or inconsistent application. The massive generation of purchasing power raised the output of cars and radios by 1937 above the level of 1930 without restoring health to the economy. Lowered prices achieved through improved technology accounted for increased sales. The employed labor force remained static. Only a halfhearted convert, the President himself longed for reduced expenditures and a balanced budget, and therefore failed to follow through. Cutbacks in 1937 renewed the depression. When spending resumed in 1938, the economy picked up; yet Roosevelt remained a fiscal conservative.[26]

The worldwide depression struck when structural changes in society and in agriculture and industry exposed problems long unresolved. While Americans wrestled with recovery, they jabbed away also at the need—not always recognized—to realign the whole productive system. They did so in neither a radical nor a conservative fashion, but in "a primitive attempt to attain order" through the "collective public responsibility" for running the economy so that mass unemployment would not occur. "The Fourth of July," Roosevelt declared, "commemorates political freedom which without economic freedom was meaningless." Labor Day symbolized the determination to achieve an economic freedom for the average man that would give his political freedom reality. The government, seeking to protect democracy, would prove that it was stronger than the forces of business depression. A majority now accepted the principle that every American had a right to a job and to the necessities of life. Government, merely self-help writ large, by majority rule, could secure "a life of greater opportunity, of greater security, of greater happiness." That end required an adjustment of democracy, to assure "the only sure bulwark of continuing liberty . . . a government strong enough to protect the interests of the people and a people strong enough and well enough informed to maintain its sovereign control over its government" (1937). Transfer of power from the legislature to the executive and increasing restraints upon citizens simply extended the idea of not hurting neighbors and did not infringe on the guarantee of personal liberty to the individual. Applying the ideal of community to the nation at large did not amount to regimentation; communal rugged individualism encouraged cooperation so that everyone could improve their lot in life. Laws to compel employers to pay adequate wages and to forbid the hiring of children did not restrict the individual.[27]

For almost a half century, scholars, publicists, and politicians had noted the end of historic expansion in the United States. The dynamic forces that had fueled past economic development no longer existed. The territorial frontier had disappeared; the country rejected imperial acquisitions; immigration ended; and in the 1920s the rate of population growth slackened. No flow of new settlers appeared in the 1930s, as they had in the past, to buy mortgaged farms so that debtors could start anew in a farther West. Citizens laid off at the factories and construction sites did not go back where they came from, as immigrants had, but festered on the spot. And a steady increase in the number of consumers no longer sustained producers. Meanwhile private enterprise, "masking itself as a system of free enterprise after the American model," in fact became "a concealed cartel system."[28]

Less visible but equally drastic changes profoundly influenced the whole economy. Times were tough in agriculture for years before the crash of 1929. During the war, American farms had fed the world, acreage had expanded, and profits had soared. But by 1920 decreased foreign demand and surpluses depressed prices and incomes. Farmers faced a long, hard season, especially when modernization ruined marginal operators. Southwestern cotton culture, free of the encumbrances left by slavery, exposed the anachronism of Old South tenantry. Falling prices squeezed out croppers unable to earn an alternative livelihood. In 1930 an absolute majority of Mississippi's population lacked gainful employment.

The situation elsewhere created hardships only slightly less harsh.

Americans ate less wheat and corn, more dairy products, fresh vegetables, and fruit; shifting tastes further upset established agricultural patterns. Accelerated mechanization and replacement of the horse by the tractor increased the advantages of more efficient producers and bore harshly upon little family holdings. Despite government efforts to ease credit, debt rose in the 1920s and became intolerable during the Depression; falling prices and land values left more than half the farm mortgages in default in 1932. Foreclosures and evictions then imposed the additional penalty—no place to go. To top off the misery, dust storms and drought blew away the topsoil of large areas in the Great Plains.[29]

The owner then came out to the land in a closed car and felt the dry earth with his fingers as tenants watched uneasily from the sun-beaten dooryard.

The owner man explained, *You know the land is poor. You've scrabbled at it long enough God knows. The tenant system won't work no more—one man in a tractor can take the place of fourteen families. You'll have to get off the land.*

But grampa took up the land, and he had to kill the Indians. And Pa killed weeds and snakes. It's our land.

And where'll we go? How'll we go?[30]

Many small farmers abandoned their plots, yet monstrous efficiency kept production high. The index of output for each person measured thirty-nine in 1909, seventy-eight in 1929, and one hundred in 1939. Too much of a good thing! Prices fell. American agriculture choked on its own abundance, not what Providence had intended when, as Roosevelt thought, it prepared the continent for mankind's second chance. Agriculture remained essential to the welfare of all in "a nation of interdependence." Yet frantic political action brought momentary relief but no cure, at best laws establishing compulsory moratoria in some states to prevent foreclosure.[31]

Soft spots appeared in industry also, left mill towns brutally bare. Aging plants weakened New England textile manufacturers, and the merchant marine collapsed after wartime expansion. Railroads no longer presented attractive investment opportunities, and neither electrification nor diesel locomotives restored confidence in their profitability. Although income from freight haulage remained constant, mileage in operation and passenger revenues declined.[32]

Intermittent gropings for order rarely succeeded. In 1933 Roosevelt might have nationalized the banking system. He wished, however, to maintain it in private hands, under conditions that would prevent renewed collapse, and spare depositors from becoming victims of unscrupulous speculations. Though government could not protect individuals from making erroneous judgments, it could prevent misstatements and chicanery, chase money changers out of their seats in the temples. An act of June 1933 created a federal insurance corporation that guaranteed deposits; and other regulations separated commercial and investment functions to eliminate the abuses of the 1920s. So, too, changes in the Federal Reserve System, new laws empowering a Securities and Exchange Commission to maintain general oversight over investment markets, and restraints upon public utility holding companies, aimed at greater efficiency without stifling the freedom to act. A semi-paternalistic government could thus protect the nation against the selfish forces that had ruined it in the past.

Relief for desperate farmers threatened with loss of land and livelihood became entangled with the desire for reform. Pare Lorenz's films and John Steinbeck's sentimental novels evoked widespread sympathy but no effective action; hopes focused on cooperative organization and subsistence homesteads quickly faded. A stab at inflation tested the populist belief that easy money would raise prices and give potential consumers purchasing power. Professors James H. Rogers and George F. Warren supplied the intellectual justification, and the radio priest, the Reverend Charles Coughlin, mobilized wide public support. In April 1933, responding to a presidential decision to abandon the gold standard, and disregarding clear constitutional restraints, Congress invalidated all public and private contracts for payments in the precious metal. Monetary speculation then lowered the dollar's value in specie to about half of its former worth. Roosevelt, eager for support from Western mining interests, also approved a Silver Purchase Act in June 1934. However, the desired effect, a rise in commodity values, never materialized.[33]

The alternative, crop control, defined the agricultural problem as simply overproduction—the country produced too much corn and cotton, although millions remained hungry and unclothed. The President proposed to replace the old familiar cycles of glut and scarcity, booms and busts, with a sustained increase in production, while assuring a fair exchange of goods between the city and the country. The Agricultural Adjustment Administration (1933) aimed to set prices at a level that would give farmers purchasing power equivalent to that in the base period August 1909–July 1914. That principle of parity, in practice, favored great landowners, who withdrew some acreage from cultivation, invested the government payments in mechanization, and gradually squeezed out small producers. The unexpected result of the acres plowed under and the little pigs slaughtered increased output and diminished the number of family farms, hastening rural depopulation. Furthermore, the neediest—migratory workers, tenants, and croppers—not being landowners, received no aid at all. During the expansive 1920s some twenty million people had left the countryside. After 1930 the trend continued. The New Deal, which aimed at social justice for farmers, in the end could not halt the depopulation of the farmlands. Somberly, demographers predicted that the shift, combined with the end of immigration and the falling birth rate, would yield a steadily aging population and an eventual decline in total growth.[34]

The New Deal, experimental and indiscriminate, encouraged reform ideas, some old, others fostered by the prolonged crisis, some long canvassed by theorists, others dreamed up for the occasion. Seeking protection from "the overlords of the State" as well as "from the overlords of industry and finance," Americans at first defined the scope of political action narrowly. Government fulfilled its entire purpose by ensuring fair play. Operating with "a reasonable efficiency" and providing "far reaching protection of individual rights as against arbitrary administrative abuses," it could expand liberty by broadening everyone's ability to act, thus taking the edge off potential demands for equality.[35]

How? Responses differed, while questions about the future character of the economy remained unanswered. Debates of the general principles divided those who feared that the state would obliterate individual freedom from the more sanguine who expected increased social control to transmute authority into justice and enable people to do what they really pleased, therefore remain as free and equal as before. New Deal measures pursued neither line of logic consistently, though the President agreed to broaden the scope of state action, for example by making health an object of government concern. Anyone unable to meet the requirements of modern civilization exerted a drag on the nation's economic life; it was the government's duty therefore to aid the handicapped and enable them to live independently. Dissenters, Roosevelt suggested, resembled ostriches burying their heads in the sand. And, as everyone knew, it was not good for the ultimate "health of ostriches to bury their heads in the sand."

The clamor for change blurred distinctions between the desire for equality attained by political force and the wish for harmony through mutual submission to common, agreed-on rules. A philosopher argued that a powerful state alone could insure the exercise of popular rights and thereby nurture strong individuals. A historian agreed that a government exercising wider executive power for the common good would act in defense of disciplined liberty. Others denied the duty to serve some intangible "common good" and sought a voluntary Christian democracy. Liberty, the President believed, rose out of the "confusion of many voices," which together created "an understanding of the dominant public need." Political leadership in turn voiced those common ideals and aided their realization. Only thus would the American government be what it was truly meant to be—"a government with a soul." The well-intentioned rhetoric calmed no doubts.[36]

In 1938 the general level of production remained below that of 1929. For many Americans, the Depression killed the dream of self-sufficiency and success. The accumulated savings of lifetimes of restraint disappeared, and men proud of the ability to make good joined the same relief lines as the despised industrial workers. Propertied farmers sullenly broke the law to prevent foreclosures while demanding public aid. The Home Owners Loan Act saved some and the Civilian Conservation Corps gave thousands of youths jobs. Self-help associations of the unemployed and neighborhood rent parties helped out. But critics from the right and the left attacked the President and advocated more drastic change. The American Liberty League trumpeted individualism, while the American Labor Party (1937) believed more planning inevitable. New millennial schemes generated support for Upton Sinclair's Epic Party and for Dr. Townsend's plan to give pensions to all. Huey Long and Theodore Bilbo—the Bilbonic Plague—inimitably garbed in loud check suits and red suspenders, clamorously hawked their own agendas, as did the Communists, the Silver Shirts, and lesser fascist groups. A pious divine condemned capitalism as an expression of a dying civilization dragged down by the stupidity of business oligarchies; he therefore opposed the New Deal, while admiring the Soviet Union. But most Americans shied away from extreme views, preferred Roosevelt's focus on specific issues without broad ideological overtones.[37]

In a later (1944) State of the Union address, F.D.R. enunciated the rights he considered universal—to security, to work, and also to leisure. But his unfolding program showed no such consistency, despite pressure from the influential women prominent in his administration. Social Security, long agitated, arrived in 1935, though not in a form universally approved by its advocates. Unemployment insurance, which Senator Robert Wagner, its sponsor, considered but an extension of workmen's compensation—necessary in an unpredictable economy—also became law, although opposed by employers who bore the cost. A housing act financed local agencies to build 150,000 homes in three years; and the fair labor standards law (1938) set minimum wages and maximum hours. New statutes to regulate the work of women and children encouraged optimists to discern an emergent community and a new morality grounded in comradeship. Although health insurance failed of enactment in the face of intractable opposition, the welfare measures that became law profoundly altered the relationship of government to individuals and to families. They met some immediate needs, skirted constitutional scruples, and evaded the broader implications of creating an activist state. The President believed that they gave the individual liberty of action to make the most of himself but did not permit a few powerful interests "to make industrial cannon fodder of the lives of half the population." The ambition to obtain proper security, a reasonable leisure, and a decent living throughout life took priority over the appetite for great wealth and great power.[38]

Some New Dealers, and occasionally the President, perceived a more general problem: only intelligent planning could stave off "the paralyzing grasp of complete collectivism," because the nation could no longer depend on expansion to resolve its difficulties. Americans had lost the shelter of their favorable historic situation. Free immigration and relatively free trade no longer provided them unlimited access to Old World pools of goods, markets, manpower, and capital. Workers and money from Europe had fueled expansion when needed and had stayed home when not. In the 1930s capital ceased to flow westward. The law ended immigration, and prohibitive tariffs excluded imports so that foreigners could neither purchase products from the United States nor pay their debts. Moreover, a decline in population threatened to follow a falling native birth rate. The country had crossed its last frontier. Earlier in the century, Herbert Croly and Theodore Roosevelt had assumed that careful planning would sustain life amidst limited resources. A mature economy and subdued continent called for reappraised values. America's mission had changed; with the end of the era of production and the exploitation of natural resources, the sober, less dramatic task of administering assets already in hand remained.[39]

Changes in manufacturing and the Depression's impact necessitated sweeping reorganizations by the application of intelligence through social science. William James, Lester Ward, C. H. Cooley, and Thorstein Veblen had argued that evolution, far from a blind, purposeless process, left room for the exercise of human will. John Dewey therefore asserted that citizens, by no means helpless victims of the environment, could act rationally and particularly in the United States, "the fortunate laboratory of the modern world." Engineers, conscious of their status as a professional group and impatient with self-regulating free-market mechanisms, believed that the systematic thinking with which they solved particular problems could equally well apply to the economy as a whole. They considered themselves a "thin red line of experts" protecting labor and consumers against reactionary profiteers and shared Edward Bellamy's utopianism, their faith in a great communal productive unit bolstered by changing concepts of law and psychology. Louis D. Brandeis and Oliver Wendell Holmes regarded law as an instrument of change if only judges and legislators liberated themselves from immutable principles such as the right to property and contract, and devised rules meeting contemporary needs. Meanwhile John B. Watson and others insisted that human behavior and opinion depended on manipulations of external stimuli. The First World War had also shown the utility of planning. The War Industries Board had transformed the productive system, and standardization had created measurable economies. Exaggerated impressions of the success of Soviet planning suggested analogous measures for the United States. In the future, trade associations within a single overall national design would organize whole industries to eliminate waste, to encourage conservation, and to generate massive purchasing power. Those worried about the individual's ability to act could take comfort from Rexford Tugwell, who preferred to call the process democratic "social management" rather than autocratic planning—a "tyrant state," his critics called it. But as the President reminded them in 1937, individualism had caused the Depression, perverted freedom and opportunity to mean a license to climb upwards by pushing others down. And his administration had in the end saved business from the pit into which its licentiousness had thrust the nation.[40]

Interest in technocracy encouraged the new trends. The 1932 reports of a small group of unemployed scientists, engineers, and architects at Columbia University exploited the popular respect for science and expertise. Their authoritative answers appeared amidst general bewilderment. Specific, concrete, factual data emphasized the conflict between producer-engineers, interested in output, and businessmen-entrepreneurs-financiers, interested in prices, profits, and scarcity. Members of a young profession, "a civil general staff" composed "of technicians and administrators" able to plan politically would resolve the world-shaking struggle and build up a philosophy to satisfy practical social needs. Experts would end the unemployment and suffering of boom-bust cycles. Technocracy clubs sprang up nationwide and the planning faith filtered into New Deal policy.[41]

Roosevelt's Commonwealth Club speech in San Francisco (1932) had noted the end of the expansive frontier, conducive to the individualistic methods of the past. The new era called for assertion of government's power to direct the economy. Under public supervision and control, concentration presented no danger. *The Modern Corporation and Private Property,* by A. A. Berle and G. C. Means (1932), argued that efficient great combinations served useful social purposes. Various trade associations suggested abrogation of the antitrust laws to permit self-regulation, price-fixing, and planned production in return for protection of labor and consumers. Local experience demonstrated the value of such products of planning as urban zoning laws. The long-drawn-out controversy over how to operate the dams built during the war at Muscle Shoals gave planners the basis for a development extending across Alabama, Kentucky, and Tennessee. An autonomous Tennessee Valley Authority used public power there to stimulate economic growth and also provided recreational resources in the Great Smoky Mountains National Forest. Other massive dams in the Pacific Northwest (1937–42) aimed to do the same. The more civilized society became, explained the President, the more it called upon government to assume added obligations. In modern times, with wealth no longer the mere product of individual efforts but the result of the manifold uses to which the community put that effort, everyone's capacity to act depended on the quality of that combination. Many hard lessons revealed the human waste that resulted from lack of planning. By extending planning to a wider field, the nation could return to the spirit and vision of the pioneer.[42]

Environmental concern, supported by several forces, strengthened the faith in planning. Some Americans, out of aesthetic anxiety about the landscape, wished the government to preserve the wilderness. Here and there a "ritzy biological survey" cloaked the desire to protect the wild ducks that wealthy Wall Street speculators shot in the tidal marshes. Best-buy consumerism nurtured the fashion for less, for a return to unspoiled nature. More utilitarian citizens, worried by depletion of petroleum, coal, and timber supplies, demanded a larger public role in the economy. In the 1920s the varied conservationists formed a potent political force. Forty states and the federal government had acted through agencies that decided whether to withhold resources for the future or exploit them at once. In 1935 a distinguished National Resources Committee called for long-term research, and *America in Midpassage* (1939), by Charles and Mary Beard, proclaimed the virtues of national management. Whenever the federal government inaugurated yet another gigantic dam, Roosevelt proudly pointed out that these vast efforts, all voluntary undertakings, had cost no one their liberties, but stood as monuments to what a democracy could do when its people united against waste and insecurity.[43]

Yet the best intentioned blueprints failed. Neither in the 1930s nor for many decades later, until computers replaced punched cards, did the technical means exist for assembling and ordering the vast quantities of data on which to base comprehensive plans. The *McKesson-Robbins* case (1938) demonstrated the inadequacy of accounting techniques as instruments of control within large enterprises. A nationwide organization would be even more vulnerable. Furthermore, economic theory rested on a shaky statistical basis. The Census Bureau, the Departments of Commerce and of Agriculture, the Temporary National Economic Committee, numerous administrative agencies and private groups like Dow Jones and F. W. Dodge, along with the Brookings Institution (1928) and the National Bureau of Economic Research (1919), produced reams of numbers—not always compatible; and administrators and congressmen lacked the skill to evaluate them. Nor had adequate conceptual formulae for handling them yet taken shape.[44]

International experience showed that plans locked the economy into a static, even regressive, pattern. By 1930, the great powers had discarded nineteenth-century free-trade doctrines in order to protect their domestic producers. Import quotas and tariffs excluded foreign goods as agriculture, like industry, sought shelter against competition, and as labor sought to save jobs. Autarchy prevailed as the desire for a self-contained national economic order magnified the role of the state. The London Conference (1933) failed; and totalitarian regimes in Japan, Germany, Italy, and the Soviet Union and closed systems in France and Britain hampered economic recovery.

In the United States also, planning required self-sufficiency and surrender of the prospect of future growth. "America must choose!" proclaimed Secretary of Agriculture Henry A. Wallace (1934), himself an advocate of the diminished ambitions of a stable society. In support of his views Wallace drew upon the Old Testament, whose prophets he pictured as New Dealers struggling against "the standpatters worshipping Baal." Individual or corporate preferences could no longer determine commercial decisions; bilateral barter arrangements would shape future exchanges. The new measures required, Wallace believed, a revival of deep religious feelings and a new social discipline. Since he could predict the future from markings on the Great Pyramid, he always believed "that if you envision something that hasn't been, that can be, and bring it into being, that is a tremendously worthwhile thing to do." Hence he assumed that the same activism that improved corn, strawberries, and agricultural prices could apply to society in general through centralized planning under the leadership of a new "flaming one," for a time identified with Roosevelt, a secular messiah whose first apostle would be Wallace.[45]

Blinded to the potentialities of the unexpected, the blueprinters failed to see changes already taking form in the depressed 1930s. They also failed to present their case to voters whose eyes glazed over when long strings of figures materialized to bolster an argument. "All that high-falutin' talk about economic theories does not always soak in with us ordinary folks," though they could well understand a higher price for cotton. The planners also misread the evidence on industrial concentration, which had peaked in the mid-1920s; and they discounted the potentialities of new ownership and dynamic entrepreneurship. Nor did the planners guess that the economy might develop in ways incomprehensible in the terms of the old progressivism. The equivalent of the bygone physical frontier lay at hand scarcely noticed in the eagerness for "a greatly raised standard of living" for all—at once.[46]

The initial planning effort formulated in the National Industrial Recovery Act (June 1933) failed. The ill-conceived NIRA responded to pressures from the AFL for a compulsory thirty-hour week and from businessmen who wished suspension of the antitrust laws to permit price fixing. The law gave trade associations power to govern themselves in return for wages and hours regulation, while a large-scale public-works spending program aimed to restore consumer purchasing power. To liquidate surpluses that had halted manufacturing, councils in each industry, representing government, management, labor, and consumers, could adopt enforceable codes for all the conditions of production—hours, wages, and prices. The councils could also allocate quotas to each firm, thus ending "cutthroat competition." Modern guilds, the President called them. The systematic organization within the plant that had made mass production possible applied industry-wide rationality upon the whole economy. The National Recovery Administration under General Hugh Johnson promptly approved more than five hundred such codes and launched an immense publicity program to popularize the Blue Eagle that signified adherence to the plan.

However, factionalism prevented agreement in many councils and encouraged violations. Important individuals like Henry Ford successfully resisted, and the central authority failed to reconcile differences. Above all, Americans lacked the political will for rigid controls, however much they favored a social service state. Suspicion of a single, all-encompassing government outweighed fears of economic collapse. Vague talk about "spiritual reintegration around a new set of values" did not offset insistence upon preserving "the individualism of the many." The codes contributed little either to recovery or to long-term planning, and sometimes masked strategies for avoiding competition and cutting back output to raise prices. Probably to Roosevelt's secret relief, the Supreme Court, in the *Schechter* case (May 1935), declared the law unconstitutional on the ground that it transferred legislative functions to the executive. The Court also struck down a similar plan for the bituminous coal industry, to the relief of traditionally oriented civil libertarians who feared the New Deal's expansion of governmental power.[47]

Incidental features of the NRA, however, guaranteed labor the right to collective bargaining and established a minimum wage of twenty-five cents an hour and a forty-hour work week—precedents for later regulations. After peaking at more than five million in 1920, union membership had dropped steadily in the face of bitter employer opposition. Although in many towns labor organizations alone helped desperate people grope toward brotherhood, only the Communists seemed to care. Under the New Deal, union membership rose dramatically. The Norris–La Guardia bill had already excluded the use of injunctions in disputes (1932), and in 1935 the National Labor Relations Act permanently codified the protected position of unions, setting up a powerful administrative board to enforce fair practices. Strikes in textiles, steel, and automobiles testified to the penetration of formerly nonunionized industries. The Committee for Industrial Organization signed up the unskilled and theretofore neglected workers, even in the laggard South. The old AFL craft organizations had become "pie-counter," bureaucratic operations willing to cooperate with reasonable employers. By contrast, thousands until then overlooked joined the militant industrial unions. The culmination came on Memorial Day 1937, when employees occupied auto plants in Flint, Michigan, despite conservative protests and without incurring government disapproval. Labor unions then seemed critical to the workers' capacity to act, the right to organize and to strike their "only resource of power and liberty."[48]

For President Roosevelt, recovery from the Depression mattered more than planning and economic reorganization, and recovery proved singularly elusive. The remedies he adopted reflected not the assertion of a single forceful politician but compromises required by the process of enactment. Conferences under the auspices of the Federal Trade Commission made modest efforts at cooperation, and oversight by aggressive interest groups kept maverick enterprises in line. At best, New Deal measures had anodyne effects, rectified manifest abuses, and facilitated later reconstruction. Others proved damaging or altogether ineffective. The depression in agriculture persisted as subsidy payments enabled marginal producers to remain on the land while raising consumer prices and constricting demand. Manufacturing limped along. The frantically devised reforms fitted into no coherent restructuring of the economy and failed to provide a sense of social order to people who desperately longed for it. The New Deal made work—as an earthquake would have, or the construction of pyramids. But unemployment scarcely subsided, the farm problem remained unsolved, and the NRA planning adventure collapsed. Only increased income and inheritance taxes began an unintended redistribution of wealth that reduced some inequalities. The steady growth of the national debt—from $16 billion in 1930 to $48 billion in 1940—also had unexpected consequences.

Government ownership, the radical solution espoused by some workers and intellectuals, attracted little popular support. Writers and artists who resented the tone of the Big Business era—materialism crowding out every spiritual value—considered capitalism moribund, condemned to death because it failed to share equally the wealth modern technology created. The dramas of Erskine Caldwell, of Clifford Odets, of the Federal Theater and the Living Newspaper, conveyed the message. Exhilarated journalists, ministers, and academics, delighted in their own ability to carry on while bankers took a beating, "had some neat blueprint labeled socialism or communism or . . . planned collectivism or cooperative commonwealth" tucked back in their minds. The solution: transfer the means of production to the people so that men of the mind would sit at the managerial desks benignly spreading equal benefits to all. Thus it was that the Soviet Union averted poverty and crises. Formal liberty would ultimately take care of itself. As it was, the insidious forces that produced inequality also destroyed freedom, as the press, corrupted by advertising and the interests, made nothing of dictators like Mayor Hague who disowned the word fascist but denied the Constitution's legitimacy in Jersey City.[49]

But most Americans preferred not to put politicians in charge of the economy; the likelihood of a gain in efficiency seemed as slim as that for a decline in corruption. Roger Baldwin and the American Civil Liberties

Union, worried about the already massive increase in federal power, attacked some NRA provisions. Other critics warned that the urge to pass burdens on to government contained the seeds of dictatorship, with the populace clothed, housed, and fed like slaves. The feeble enthusiasm municipal socialism earlier commanded faded in the 1920s and 1930s. As it was, jaundiced critics (1935) labeled New Deal America "some sort of YMCA show. Starry-eyed bastards spending money that somebody will have to pay. Everybody in our town quit work to go on relief." "Not love of humanity but hate" animated reformers, whose class consciousness only revived the devil cult of the Middle Ages. New Dealers, aware of public sentiment, disavowed intentions of having the state take over and they assumed that enterprise would remain private, though subject to greater oversight.[50]

Attention therefore shifted to developing effective regulation to further fair competition and protect consumers. Old-line agencies like the Maritime, Federal Trade, and Interstate Commerce Commissions, and new ones like the Civil Aeronautics Authority, edged in to govern, subsidize, or control the rates and output of shipping, power, communications, security and commodity markets, and much of agriculture. As a result, the federal bureaucracy almost tripled from 588,000 in 1931 to 1,370,000 in 1941, without effective means of general coordination as against the special pressures that brought each office into being.

Administrative agencies operated within vague guidelines set by legislative intent as interpreted by judges. But cases that involved conspiracy or fairness called for delicate decisions, balancing the wishes of competitors, consumers, and investors, within requirements of due process and reasonableness. Since wrong moves might lead to years of litigation and possible reversal in the courts, officials preferred pragmatic, *ad hoc* arrangements sealed in consent decrees that mediated particular conflicts and established general principle by inference. Lawyers for both sides engaged in a bargaining process and developed a sense of limits beyond which neither government nor enterprise would push. The pressure of affected interests set limits to decisions, as did public opinion, which concerned parties learned to sway by manipulating the news. Moreover, the exchange of personnel between federal agencies and business created an informal structure of mutual understanding about what would get by without reprisal and what would not.[51]

The threat of intervention from some uncontrolled political force remained; but day-to-day operations proceeded under the assumption that business leaders could plan their own affairs with some margin of security within terms set by administrative agencies. In some cases, like railroads and urban transit systems, narrow constraints stifled growth, but most industries bore the burden lightly and even profited from it. The search for means of centralized planning had developed a mechanism for decentralized order that widened the ability to act.

The New Deal's battle with the Depression also unintentionally created the foundation for economic control through monetary policy. The banking crisis of the spring of 1933 and the President's venture in inflation encouraged bold calls for radical fiscal manipulations. Those maneuvers had little effect upon the Depression, but gradually defined the politics of managing credit. Abandonment of the gold standard freed the government to raise or lower the amount of currency in circulation and thus indirectly to affect the pace of business. The mounting public debt held in bonds expanded the pool of available credit. And the power of the Board of Governors of the Federal Reserve system to set the rediscount rate and of the Federal Open Market Committee to alter bank reserve requirements influenced the flow of funds to borrowers.[52]

As his first term drew to a close, Roosevelt knew that the Depression had not ended, and having discovered the limits of his power, knew also that to carry through future great reforms required the removal of formal constitutional obstacles whatever the effect on the liberties to which his opponents appealed.

Buoyed up by his smashing reelection victory over a nondescript Kansas governor in 1936, Roosevelt in a misconceived effort to reshape the Supreme Court (1937) unleashed a wave of hostile propaganda against the "nine old men" who stubbornly impeded progress by striking down the Agricultural Adjustment Act (AAA) and the National Industrial Recovery Act (NIRA). The Court's opponents complained that five unelected men ruled 120 million people; scholars asked whether, given the Court's decisions, the American government remained viable, and others proposed eliminating the power of judicial review. Roosevelt put little store in the procedural liberty that had by then become a term of invective, used by his enemies who trotted out objections even to Ferdinand Pecora's interrogations of bankers; perhaps he shared the views of critics who doubted the Court's significance in sustaining civil liberties.

Although Harold Ickes, among others, considered it an "adroit move," the President's flimsy plan for restructuring the judiciary collapsed. The endeavor antagonized some loyal supporters and roused the resistance of foes fearful for the Republic's safety. Thereafter an alliance of Southern and Western conservatives and some Republicans put the New Dealers on the defensive. In 1938 Roosevelt's shortsighted effort to purge senators who had opposed his Supreme Court bill backfired when voters in the Democratic primaries nominated most of those he opposed. Heavy party losses in the November election gave Republicans six Senate seats, eleven governorships, and more than eighty places in the House, evidence that F.D.R. could not transfer his personal popularity to others.[53]

Ironically, retirements and new appointments had by then already transformed the Court's character. To avoid such self-inflicted wounds as the Dred Scott Case had delivered, Chief Justice Charles Evans Hughes sought stable majorities in accord with popular views. After 1938 the judiciary upheld a new AAA and also the Fair Labor Standards Act of 1938 in decisions that explicitly repudiated earlier narrow judgments and gave Congress almost unlimited power to bar from interstate commerce any articles judged injurious to the public health, morals, or welfare. In *DeJonge* and other cases, the Supreme Court extended the First Amendment protection of Communists, suggesting a new attitude toward civil liberties. A concern for political and civil rights was about to replace scrutiny of economic regulations, which had led the Court to ally itself in early New Deal days with the party of the past.[54]

The planning impulse left a few monuments, largely by indirection. Although the Supreme Court threw out agreements under the NRA Code to limit petroleum output, an interstate oil compact, with congressional approval, did as well (1935). Justices Brandeis and Frankfurter and their followers still resisted bigness and concentration; and acts of 1936 and 1937 protected small shopkeepers by forbidding rebates to chain and department stores. At Roosevelt's request, a Temporary National Economic Committee produced a detailed report on concentration in the American economy, and Thurman Arnold as head of the Justice Department's Antitrust Division after 1938 instituted a massive though ineffective campaign of prosecutions. None of these developments conformed to the planning impulse.[55]

The New Deal struggles drained away the capacity to use power through familiar political channels. Profligate spending that wrecked municipal budgets in the 1920s had depleted resources to fight the Depression, while deadlocked interests shifted large, extraordinary projects into the hands of extrapolitical individuals or agencies able to get things done by circumventing usual procedures. Public authorities and corporations to build bridges or turnpikes already existed in 1932; their spread thereafter revealed the waning faith in politics, as did the growing influence of unelected planning agencies.

Congress and the legislatures, stiffened by routine and by rigid forms, became strongholds of intransigent interests. Some states had not redistricted for half a century. Their lawmakers had long ceased to represent the actual population. Seniority, a cumbersome committee system, and the right to filibuster gave strategic minorities permanent powers of obstruction. Lacking the votes to defeat objectionable proposals, they could maneuver a measure to death or stifle it by crippling amendments. The stubbornness of a single senator from Alabama or Arizona could delay indefinitely measures the majority considered vital. The President and governors lost the capacity to establish policies that commanded assent. Even competent executives with patronage at their disposal worked only through laborious compromises.

The informal anti-Roosevelt alliance in Congress (1937) endured. Northern Republicans hostile to further welfare legislation, Southerners like Walter George of Georgia, fearful of civil rights, and conservative Democrats joined in a mutual assistance pact that kept the President on the defensive. Since those legislators in effect enjoyed uninterrupted tenure and retained control of the decisive committees, voters could not loosen the grip of the alliance on the congressional machinery. Popular elections ceased to resolve disputes. Honest common men, perennial gulls of the greed of others, could not translate their wishes into action through the system, which in part still reflected its rural origins, and even its eighteenth-century social assumptions. Minor variations in platforms and campaign rhetoric convinced few Americans that the choice of one candidate rather than another mattered. Nominating conventions blurred rather than defined differences, preferring candidates who drew support from every sector of the population. Against the forces entrenched on Capitol Hill, therefore, the President enjoyed neither a positive mandate from his own election nor a strong party organization committed to the line he established as leader.

New Deal public works programs complicated matters. However welcome in transferring the unemployed from the breadline to the building site, they functioned through a complex array of entrenched intermediaries—local labor leaders, bureaucrats, contractors, construction companies, insurance agencies, and bankers, all with links to politics and therefore to power. Key individuals—unelected and outside the political system—acquired control through the ability to manage the traffic, as did Robert M. Moses in New York and William F. Callahan in Massachusetts.[56]

* * *

The Depression precipitated a wearisome, unintentional, and often pointless debate about the meaning of liberty. The New Dealers, like the President, rarely considered abstract intellectual issues; work in government had inured politicians to the arts of compromise and accommodation. But the prolonged economic crisis and the repeated insistence on doing something about it, as well as Roosevelt's appearance of indomitable optimism, generated a succession of drastic measures counter to longstanding assumptions about the relationship of the state to the society and the economy. The air then turned blue with the rhetoric of controversy.[57]

Apart from general consideration of the relation of liberty to security, discussion most often centered on the feasibility of national centralized planning, that is, on whether or not decisions in Washington could set the course of the productive system. That fundamental dispute remained unresolved, for the inability to end the Depression revealed the limits of the planning potential. Faith persisted in an "integral state" run by career civil servants, drawing upon "the motivation of a powerful, unifying ideology to implement the decisions of a central planning agency." But experience in the 1930s left Americans dubious about such proposals, fearful of political panderers who turned government into a system of charities, and enlisted individuals as privates in an army, rather than as unique contributors to democratic society.[58]

The long succession of reform and relief efforts raised awareness of issues bearing upon the relationship of the individual to the community, which in turn directed attention to the meaning of liberty as the ability to act, which existing institutions seemed too feeble to protect.[59]

Every crisis generated proposals to turn additional important economic powers over to the government in an "automatic drift toward state capitalism." New Dealers argued that preservation of the potentialities of individual initiative and personal liberty required concessions to meet the elemental needs of the underprivileged and to satisfy the demand for economic security for which impatient citizens might agree to sacrifice political liberty. Reassurances that the country possessed all the physical materials it needed ceased to soothe the angry already disposed to despair. Nor did the unemployed take satisfaction in statements that determination would create an industrial system to generate abundance. Genuine problems created profound differences of opinion that would not dissolve in honeyed optimism about decentralization and teamwork.[60] Under these circumstances, it no longer made sense to define freedom simply as the lack of any restraint, "the chance to do what you want to do."[61]

* * *

As the 1930s drew to a close, Franklin Roosevelt understood the gravity of the situation. The Depression did not dissolve of its own accord, and he held power within a narrow orbit.

He was not a man given to despair; otherwise he would not have come through his illness as he had. But now time ran out. Approaching the end of his second term in office, and his sixtieth year, he feared that he would leave the White House a failure. Pride prevented him from contemplating a return to the life of a country squire in Hyde Park. Conscious of his place in history, he resolved to triumph, although a formidable tradition ruled out a third term. All the great ghosts of the American past from Washington to Theodore Roosevelt sounded the same warning against the presumption of the indispensable Caesar. In a conversation with Harold Ickes, F.D.R. reviewed the full roster of his possible successors. None would do. And shortly a major catastrophe, war, threw new light upon the experience in planning, upon the faith in rationality, and upon the relation of the individual to the community.[62]

Roosevelt believed that his generation had "a rendezvous with destiny." Insofar as it concerned the role of government, the phrase meant "Better the occasional faults of a government that lives in a spirit of charity than the consistent omissions of a government frozen in the ice of its own indifference." Though Republicans, the Liberty League, and other opponents of the New Deal charged that its entire agenda was inimical to liberty, that its reforms had come too fast, and that Roosevelt had dictatorial ambitions, the New Deal had preserved older versions of American liberty while at the same time endowing citizens with new capacities to act.

The legislation Roosevelt sponsored failed to satisfy those who wished to go even further. For the Supreme Court judges, it had gone too far, and as one critic argued, they set out to destroy "laws providing for a better life, more liberty and equality, social justice and the pursuit of happiness of 130 million people." Such intransigence tempted visionaries to call for the abolition of the Court and the weaning of the nation away from its idolatrous worship of the Constitution. Roosevelt would have none of it and, though tempted, by and large failed to remodel the infrastructures of the federal government, partly because of conservative congressional opposition but more important because he believed the system pliable and flexible enough to accommodate drastic changes, while preserving its outward structure intact.

In the end, rational planning floundered, unemployment remained high, and the basic forces that fueled rising consumer demands remained intact. Nor had government by privilege vanished, although Roosevelt claimed to have rooted it out. He, too, remained wedded to an outdated terminology, as much as to outdated economic theories. But the New Deal did recast the role of the state; and it fostered a sense that life had become more equitable, a lasting boon to American liberty because it raised the sense of national community, with the accompanying feeling of mutual responsibility and interdependence, in the belief that everyone's welfare depended upon insuring each his or her sphere of freedom.

The enlarged population pool upon which the New Deal drew made that sense of greater inclusiveness visible. A government always partial to lawyers became even more so when the vast amount of new legislation and the accompanying increase in litigation enhanced the role of the legal profession. Women, minorities, people of different religious backgrounds—and not only white Anglo-Saxon males—now staffed government offices and political positions. Many outsiders became insiders as Roosevelt, deemed a traitor by his class, looked elsewhere for support and advice—to Jews and ethnics among others. At the same time, the changing role of women revealed the growing popularity of a new type of Hollywood leading lady, personified by Katharine Hepburn—self-assured, independent, and professional. The fact that more women entered the labor force reflected economic debacles, not rising feminist consciousness, while the influence of Molly Dewson and the growing importance of gender issues testified to the ways in which the New Deal broke old barriers.

Edmund Wilson had complained that "money-making . . . and . . . a money-making society" were not enough to satisfy humanity. Neither was a devil-take-the-hindmost social system. The New Deal attempted to remedy the deficiency by creating what the *New Republic* called "genuine economic liberty by planning and organizing industry for the general welfare." The Fair Labor Standards Act, which fixed minimum wages and maximum working hours, formed a fitting summation of what the New Deal tried to accomplish. Though the New Deal discovered the limits of national planning, the concept itself acquired respectability as the nation and private enterprise adjusted to greater government involvement in the day-to-day running of the economy. But since "planning" acquired the odium of terms associated with fascist and Communist experiments, public policy analysis became a more acceptable euphemism.

Neither limited structural reforms nor the meager measures of economic redistribution lifted the United States out of the Depression. But they started a process that, in its successful preservation of liberty, spared the nation the need for later upheavals to adjust society to further changes. Neither Roosevelt nor his economic advisers realized that the very sectors they tried to bolster or realign—labor, agriculture, and heavy industry, which had remained politically powerful and monopolized a lion's share of the government's assistance, actually sank into decline. Even before the outbreak of war, new forces, in high technology, service, and consumer goods, prepared to take the lead. That their eventual emergence occurred with less upheaval than would have been the case without the New Deal further testified to its crucial role in ensuring the continuation of American freedoms. Though its political failures continued to plague the nation for decades to come, Roosevelt's Janus-like agenda, facing the future while squinting toward the past, sustained its beneficial consequences.

The national government acquired an outlook more in tune with the times. A rudimentary welfare state, on which future generations would expand, gave the rights to life, liberty, and the pursuit of happiness greater substantive meaning. The government assumed an affirmative responsibility to spare citizens economic deprivation. In place of a potentially restrictive and liberty-destroying policy, based on direct control of productive resources, or, obversely, calling for a destruction of large-scale enterprise, the New Deal opted for a different path. It guaranteed and expanded citizens' capacities to act by helping to provide them greater equality in access to goods and services.[63]

CHAPTER 3

AT THE CRATER'S EDGE

YEAR AFTER YEAR, the intractable depression rejected every cure ingenious New Dealers devised. Unemployment remained high, farming unrewarding, and manufacturing resisted artificial stimuli. Hopes for a rational, planned economy glimmered with no sign of imminent fulfillment. Democratic collectivists who hoped to replace fear by affirmation glumly witnessed the spread of social pessimism. Despair deepened as control slipped into conservative hands.[1]

Then the unpredictable calamity of world war altered all previous calculations, brought the United States to the verge of disaster, until a startling reversal of expectations made society whole again. The men and women who suffered through the experience rarely understood unfolding events. Nor did they perceive the reconstruction of the economy or foresee how their brutal use of force affected liberty.

The war into which the United States slipped edgewise in 1941 imposed planning on the whole society. On the eve of the conflict, A. A. Berle had speculated "that the driving quality" that a great cataclysm might elicit could create a common will, "available for continuous and steady action," pose the danger of a dictatorship. For a time at least, Pearl Harbor justified government by limitless power and supplied the answer to some though not all uncertainties.[2]

Few Americans had sympathized with the fascists. The attack on Ethiopia (1935) alienated those who had earlier approved of Mussolini's social reforms, and only right-wing fanatics approved of the Nazis and the Japanese warlords. Widespread assent greeted Roosevelt's statement (1937) that mere isolation offered no escape from international anarchy; without positive endeavors to preserve peace, the contagion of war would spread. But neither he nor the citizens agreed on the appropriate action.[3]

Attitudes on foreign policy issues rested on no ideological preference. Americans, shielded as Europeans were not from "the callous cruelty, the pitilessness, the dreadful senselessness" of German barbarism after 1933, failed to recognize its difference in kind from other barbarisms. The democratic virtues, battered by the prevailing insecurity, by unavailing faith and by corrosive fear, disintegrated under stress and left the desire to stand apart the country's declared posture in 1939. During the Spanish Civil War, the United States amended its neutrality laws to forbid the sale of arms to combatants in an internal conflict. It thereupon denied the Loyalist request for the right to purchase supplies, although it continued to send oil and scrap iron to Japan for use against China well into 1941. But Hitler and Mussolini had no scruples about aiding their ally, who marched victoriously into Madrid in 1939, teaching the fascists that they had nothing to fear from further adventures. They picked off Austria with no trouble; the settlement at Munich gave them parts of Czechoslovakia; and before long they took the rest of that unhappy country, and prepared to move on in the quest for *Lebensraum*—living space—in an Eastern empire.[4]

Roosevelt no doubt desired the defeat of the Axis, but he deceived himself in the expectation that the world would achieve that outcome without American intervention. In 1940 he won reelection on a peace platform and in the spring of 1941 argued for the Lend-Lease program, on the ground that aid to the Allies would suffice for victory without altering the stringent neutrality laws. Few perceived any general interest in preserving international law, or understood that the French and English in 1938 had become appeasers out of the same aversion to involvement in other nations' quarrels that made the United States isolationist in 1941. From Boston to San Francisco, of course, peace-loving citizens wholeheartedly approved the final Allied determination in 1939 to resist German designs on Poland. Time that the democracies showed their strength—the other democracies! Americans would give moral support while the oceans cut them safely off from the obligation to fight in Asia, Europe, and Africa. In clutching the illusion of being a little nation on the frontiers of the civilized world, they forgot that the sea in the past had always served as a mode of access rather than as a moat. Japanese aircraft carriers in the Pacific reminded them of that.

Roosevelt had shied away from bolder steps, fearful of a divisive political contest. Few of his countrymen then still believed in war's beneficence—God's way to thin out the population. But the confrontation with evil rendered them ambivalent. People wanted it both ways.

They learned from *Bury the Dead* (1936) of combat's malign consequences but took satisfaction in the brutal beating of the same author's *Sailor Off the Bremen* (1939). Political leaders in the democracies sought a less decisive course. The President preferred to believe therefore that Britain and France could stifle the fascist threat without direct American intervention, and he assured everyone that aid to the Allies would not involve the United States in foreign war. The magazine *Look* told its readers that the country's heart was too big, too easily touched, so that it had too long acted as "a sucker nation"—how could it solve difficult international problems while unable to do anything about its own unemployment?[5]

Hence the blank incomprehension with which men and women greeted Pearl Harbor. A misguided U.S. naval policy had concentrated the fleet in Hawaii, prepared to snap Japan's trade links in a single decisive battle, then stifle the islands by a relatively costless blockade. Instead, a target of opportunity took form; the daring raid destroyed the American navy's fighting capacity.

At one stroke, the situation changed. Hostilities began not in a decision from Washington but in a Japanese surprise attack and in declarations of war from Berlin and Rome, signs not of U.S. ability to act but of helplessness. "A rip-roaring, galloping good-old-fashioned, one hundred percent American boom" followed, undertaking to set the whole world free. Appropriately, New York's archbishop, also the military vicar of the armed forces, dedicated his book, *The Road to Victory* (1942), to the sweet land of liberty that would not allow its God-given rights to be bombed or wrenched away. He defined liberty as the freedom to do what was right to do. In stressing the need to keep God in Americanism, he echoed the President, who identified the national cause with the cause of all mankind—"our hope and their hope for liberty under God."

All who fought the same evil—including the Russians—united in pursuit of the same good. To pretend that the war aims of the Soviet Union coincided with his own, Roosevelt chose to ignore the troublesome freedoms in which he believed and Stalin did not. To have acknowledged those differences might have breeched the alliance. Yet by concealing them, the President hopelessly complicated the ultimate problems of making peace and of deciding the scope of liberty in the postwar world.[6]

Well before Pearl Harbor, ordinary people sensed approaching disaster. A decade of horror films prepared them for man's monstrous creation that escaped the laboratory to destroy humanity—*Bride of. . . , Son of. . . , Ghost of . . . , House of . . .* No surprise in whatever disaster followed.

In October 1938, Sylvia Holmes, a black housewife in Newark, New

Jersey, grew more and more excited as she listened to the radio. When she heard, "Get the gas masks," that part convinced her. She dashed out to tell her neighbors, "Don't you know New Jersey is destroyed by the Germans?" She remembered that Hitler had not appreciated President Roosevelt's telegram a few weeks before. The smart Germans came down in something like a balloon—that's when there was the explosion. The world was coming to an end. She went home, her knees shaking so that she could hardly walk up the stairs. She looked in the ice box and saw some chicken left from Sunday dinner that she had been saving for Monday night and said, "We may as well eat this chicken—we won't be here in the morning."

Good Christians assumed that the end of the world had come but that God would take care of His own. Others rejoiced that, should the Martians really take over, they would not have to pay their butchers' bills. And the prospect of scaring ten years of life out of their mothers-in-law delighted still others.

The newspapers the next day announced however that Mrs. Holmes, like millions of other Americans, had erred. They had heard no news broadcast but a radio play, *The War of the Worlds.* And the invaders said to have landed in the Jersey meadows were Martians, not Germans.

But after all, Mrs. Holmes was correct. The danger did come from the Germans, and her world approached an end, not in New Jersey but over Hiroshima where it neared the crater's edge. In 1950 Americans still perched on the brink.[7]

The United States and the Western powers operated under an insane delusion about their enemies' weakness. The optimistic theories of 1939 judged the French fortifications along the Maginot Line impregnable and considered the Nazi army scarcely trained. The Germans lacked oil and rubber. A firm stand and a naval blockade would bring them to their knees. When the Soviet Union moved wantonly into the Baltic states of Estonia, Lithuania, and Latvia, and launched an unprovoked attack upon Finland, the French and English seriously considered sending an expeditionary force to fight the Russians. Only Swedish and Norwegian neutrality closed off that foolhardy option. But that season, the gallant Finns appeared on Broadway in *There Shall Be No Night* (1940), by Robert Sherwood, whose *Idiot's Delight* a few years earlier had exposed the futility of all wars. American policy also labored under the serious misapprehension that the English and French could easily win once they set themselves to the job.[8]

In May 1940 these fanciful assumptions collapsed with the invasions of Denmark, Norway, Holland, Belgium, and France. While the Germans moved toward Paris, the United States cautiously winked at evasions of the neutrality laws. For many now *The Watch on the Rhine* marked the battle line. In March 1941 Congress made the United States the arsenal of democracy by permitting the President to lend or lease supplies to England. Meanwhile a selective service act introduced the draft, and proclamation of a state of unlimited national emergency brought wide-ranging contingency powers into play. But while he assured the British of continued support, Roosevelt in the election campaign of 1940 still promised voters that he would not send American boys to fight overseas. In November 1941, however, an amendment to the neutrality act permitted the arming of merchant ships and opened an undeclared war with Germany and Italy in the Atlantic.

Oswald Garrison Villard concluded his autobiography (1939) certain that his world drew to an end. The United States had come to resemble rotten Europe, having wasted its natural resources, having needlessly invited class strife engendered by unequal economic conditions and by unfair government favoritism. He foresaw a future when crass materialism would destroy democracy and civilization. Rearmament spelled bankruptcy and lower standards of life for vast multitudes, leaving the road open to "the regimented, totalitarian states." He felt certain that much that occurred under Adolf Hitler in Germany paralleled official misconduct in this country during the Red Decade.[9]

Pearl Harbor dissolved opposition to involvement. Secretary of War Henry L. Stimson noted the feeling of relief that the Japanese had fired the first shot. A general resolve to win fueled American society. And the long count of casualties thereafter deepened determination into a willingness to pay the price.[10]

The poet who only a few years earlier had saluted a "Perishing Republic" settling into the mold of vulgarity, heavily thickening to empire, now sang "Shine, Republic," reminding people that

> the love of freedom has been the quality of Western man.
> There is a stubborn torch that flames from Marathon to Concord.
> And you, America, that passion made you.
> You were not born to prosperity, you were born to love freedom.
> You did not say "en masse," you said, "independence."
> But we cannot have all the luxuries and freedom also.
>
> Freedom is poor and laborious, that torch is not safe
> But hungry and often requires blood for its fuel.

Unprepared, the United States confronted the immense tasks of raising and maintaining armed forces, which grew from a few hundred thousand in 1939 to more than fifteen million in 1945, of assuring supplies for distant fronts, and of meeting domestic needs. Vital commodities became scarce—gasoline and rubber, as well as food and numerous manufactured goods. Interstate pipelines got the power of eminent domain (1941), while conversion to military production required elaborate rationing and price and wage controls. The exigencies of war sharply increased government power and limited individual ability to act. Dictates from the War Production Board, the Office of Price Administration, and the War Labor Board allowed no appeal. Suddenly fumbling New Deal controls gave way to the iron rule of a command economy. Abstract discussions of liberty came to a halt. To win the country would do what it had to do in "a time of great turmoil and transition."[11]

No vested rights or privileges stood in the way of satisfying government needs. Between 1940 and 1945 the United States built almost three hundred thousand aircraft, more than eight million tons of naval and fifty-five million tons of merchant shipping, more than eighty-five thousand tanks and about three million machine guns. It did so while fifteen million men and women stepped into the armed services.

Civilians acquiesced when tires and new automobiles disappeared and when ration coupons governed the distribution of food, cigarettes, and gasoline. A black market showed that some individuals still put self-interest first, but most Americans accepted controls on prices, wages, and profits, accepted also the rules of the War Food Administration and the Office of Economic Stabilization. The struggle made life "consciously purposeful again." Labor and capital collaborated willingly. Unions gained membership; their leaders filled important positions in the government, and Walter Reuther of the United Auto Workers helped convert existing automobile plants to warplane production. A cumbersome, intricate, and flawed bureaucracy sprouted in the absence of advance preparation, hastily transmitting to factories nationwide decisions fashioned in Washington. Ironically that community, only dreamed of in peacetime, materialized in response to war. And though the constraints imposed by the needs of fighting constricted citizens' liberties, many felt more free than they had in years. The sense of shared sacrifices and of an uncertain future gave Americans a feeling of power such as no government measures had provided in the past.[12]

Around the globe, unceasing destruction shattered lives and consumed goods. A world scarce recovered from a lesser conflict two decades earlier and still reeling in depression could ill afford the price. The decline of the West seemed to set in; the shattered landscape where cities once stood appeared to validate Spengler's warning of the 1920s.[13] In that world, fewer landmarks oriented people; and expertise counted for less than ever before, when conflicting spokesmen drowned each other out, each hawking a different panacea. People's lives no longer seemed under their own control; and the utterly unpredictable future heightened anxieties, gloom, and insecurity. In the turmoil anything might happen. When it finally did happen, the war provided relief of sorts.

Some citizens found relief because they believed that insane delusions vanished and also because they expected the immediate restraints on liberty to bear beneficial fruits. "The essence of civilization is Restraint" upon the instincts of man, imposed either by divine law or by reason, requiring but the discipline and the standards with which to judge the values of acts and thoughts and passions. In the past excessive emphasis on economic improvement as the measure of progress had led to neglect of spiritual factors. Many believed that "if a man's soul is sick, raise his income and let him add another bathroom to his cottage." The resulting spiritual emptiness would yield to the struggle of war that would "foster freedom and self-dependence and the other moral aims of our American life." None of this denied the truth of Maury Maverick's claim that "you cannot fill the baby's bottle with liberty," but suggested that such thinking reduced the nation's power to combat evil. The war would rededicate the nation to Woodrow Wilson's ideal of 1918. This "final war for human liberty" would reassert the historic values of Western civilization. People would fight for an idea that would assure humans of their dignity and their chance for self-improvement within the contours of liberty.

Bill Mauldin's GI Joes moved in stoic silence. More than three hundred thousand of them lost their lives, about a million suffered casualties. Stubble-faced, they crouched in the mud and asked few questions. Rosey the Riveter and the millions working at home waited, similarly mute. The zoot-suit riots in Los Angeles and a black outbreak in Harlem exposed some uneasiness, but the country experienced only inconsequential antiwar protests and dealt with fewer discipline problems at the front or behind the lines than in earlier conflicts. Americans fought because attacked—life or death, them or us. We are over here, wrote Private First Class Donald Harkness from New Caledonia, to prevent our homes from ever feeling a first-class bombing raid.

But the men in foxholes and factories who knew what they fought against remained hard-put to say what they fought *for.* The turmoil through which they had just lived had already left them bewildered and insecure, regarding life as a series of occurrences in the outside world beyond their control or comprehension. In the heat of crisis, they refused to think beyond the next moment and grew tough, belligerent. A worried soldier, dismayed by events, wrote in a battlefield newspaper:

> Across the world, the retrogressive waves
> Force back on Man his ancient love of caves.

Liberty bore a strange, abstract guise for those in uniform who lacked any ability to act on their own.

A new instrument of destruction developed by scientists spared Americans a costly invasion of Japan. On August 6, 1945, over Hiroshima and on August 9 over Nagasaki, great mushroom clouds left by the blast of atomic bombs marked the death of thousands and the total leveling of whole cities. This awesome power—the greatest invention since leprosy, said H. L. Mencken—compelled the Japanese to surrender on August 14, 1945.[14]

The culminating act of devastation over Hiroshima became the symbol of global conflagration. The line between soldiers and civilians vanished. The German Stukas above Rotterdam, the American Flying Fortresses over Hamburg, the Nazi extermination camps, and the Soviet secret police who massacred thousands of suspected opponents at Katyn and elsewhere respected neither the young nor the aged, neither women nor children. And much of Europe and Asia lingered but degrees removed from the havoc left by the atom bomb. In London, Dresden, Warsaw, and Tokyo, tottering walls enclosed the burned-out spaces left by air attacks.

The leaders offered only stammering explanations of why disaster approached. Franklin Roosevelt bore the greatest burden. He had dimly perceived the enemy—not Germany or Japan, but totalitarianism, the massive deployment of power that reduced the human personality to absolute state service, and then found its supreme outlet in aggressive war. Apolitical constraints, conflicting advice, the difficulty of predicting the future, affected Roosevelt's exposition of the nation's foreign responsibilities to the electorate, which did not understand what the trouble was all about and why it should concern the United States. Though critics would charge Roosevelt and his advisers with horrendous shortsightedness, the United States attained a level of stability and order entirely out of tune with the uncertain, tumultuous developments in the rest of the world. The nation's achievements in 1945 soon overshadowed temporary limitations on citizens' capacity to act.

In January 1941, Roosevelt enunciated his faith in the Four Freedoms—of speech, of religion, from want, and from fear. That summer he and Winston Churchill in the Atlantic Charter disclaimed any desire for territorial aggrandizement, called for open trade and for the rights of all people to self-determination. Americans who refused to accept the lash of terror wielded by the impervious bureaucracies of a coercive state rejected an alien, malignant collectivism in favor of the stimulus of clashing ideas. Whether or not those aims lay within reach, they remained the President's goals until his death in April 1945.[15]

Desolation marked an end but also a beginning. The ashes nurtured years of economic growth, though few as yet understood the change.

In 1939 the United States became again supplier to the combatants. Demands upon its productive capacity took up the previous slack, ended unemployment, and raised incomes. More important ultimately, slowly unfolding but radical structural changes decisively altered the old order.

Between September 1939 and December 1941, a flood of orders from England and France got American assembly lines moving. Workers found jobs and brought home wages. They became buyers and their demands revived lethargic industrial production. Pearl Harbor propelled Americans into the thick of the fighting and shifted the costs to the United States. All-out war then stimulated the economy. The desire for goods soared; farms and factories worked at full speed; employment rose, and women, in ever greater numbers, entered the factories as men's equals; output increased; and good times returned. The gross national product—the total output of goods and services—in 1940 had just about regained its level of 1929; in 1945 it had more than doubled. In the same five years, the paid labor force swelled from forty-five to sixty-four million. Every other index measured similar changes. The issues of security, of freedom from want, debated through the 1930s, acquired a new aspect. The preservation of liberty had then involved regimentation; but once home and out of uniform, men and women would regard the issues of personal freedom and communal responsibility not as antitheses but as complementing each other. One troubling doubt did not go away: would the good times last beyond the peace?

War supplied what the New Deal lacked, a sense of common purpose and the political will to act. Pearl Harbor obliterated all questions about whether to fight; it left only the question of how to win. National defense made the unthinkable necessary. The character of the enemies, their brutal assaults upon civilized values, and their genuine threat to civilization united every sector of the society. Pacifists remained discreetly silent, right-wing extremists subsided, and even the Communists became patriots after Germany attacked the Soviet Union. Although thousands of American families felt the pain of the casualty lists, the United States escaped the physical destruction visited upon other areas. Meanwhile war enlisted energies that left the economy stronger than ever.[16]

Willingness to share political power among all economic and social groups strengthened unity. The government, hesitant to expand its decision-making base in the 1930s, did so after 1941 by involving the formerly passive or hostile. Labor unions, representing far wider constituencies than those of 1917, joined the effort. Unanimity disposed of institutional and political obstacles to action, and eliminated dithering over choices. People who worked together toward a common end learned to agree; the imperatives of war softened conflict. Many sensed that the pillars of society trembled while all that seemed of permanent value disintegrated. The worship of Mammon and Moloch bestialized humanity, depersonalized individuals and made them subservient to an almighty state, extinguishing all liberty, reducing everyone to the rank of coolies. The enormity of power Hitler and Mussolini commanded set the whole world aflame. The process of extinguishing the blaze would set the United States right with itself, restoring the "original American concepts of liberty, freedom and democracy."

Key officials moved easily among corporate, military, and civil government offices, in the process raising mutual understanding. The intermingling of personnel, different from the situation in Japan and Europe, changed the character of business leadership. The individual entrepreneur, already old-fashioned in 1939, became anachronistic in 1945. A few table-thumping dinosaurs fumed at Washington's interference in their affairs. But newer, more adaptable types gradually filtered into the boardrooms and assumed influential executive positions. The process of separating ownership from management in the great corporations accelerated. Founders' sons rarely replaced their fathers; more often professional administrators took over—engineers trained to deal with the technical aspects of production, experts in sales, and lawyers able to negotiate with the government. To do well, the administrator navigated intricate bureaucratic labyrinths, mastered sophisticated statistical data, understood changes in science, and knew enough law to handle complex tax, financial, and contract problems. Familiarity with foreign countries and languages also helped. Such people took the top posts in industry, government, and law, and they willingly shared power with labor's representatives in the interest of efficiency. To offset racism in war plants, an executive order in 1941 created a Fair Employment Practices Commission to monitor discrimination.

Opportunities for women also expanded, and even the peace did not bring a full return to the "pink collar ghetto" of the past. The employment of women on an unprecedented scale helped resolve the manpower crisis. Six million joined the labor force, more than one million in government work. By 1945 they were thirty-eight percent of all federal employees, more than twice the percentage of the last prewar year. Such jobs provided many families not only a welcome second paycheck, but also a sinecure unavailable in any other way. Women were the main beneficiaries of the trend toward greater bureaucratization, their skills particularly suitable to wartime and peacetime needs. Industry also came to rely on them to an unprecedented extent. Many entered the job market married and older than their counterparts earlier in the century. Only two years before, most Americans disapproved of wives working outside the home; by 1942 sixty percent approved, although other traditional social assumptions persisted, like the belief that mothers should raise their own children.

The old issues of job security and individual freedom lost relevance in the crisis, but they never obliterated most Americans' distaste for regimentation and government involvement in ever-wider aspects of life. Although Washington did not always exercise direct control, its guidance, favors, and money exerted substantial influence. Yet all the manifestations of big government, created by war needs, effected relatively little restraint on liberty.

The productive system, lethargic for more than a decade, acquired a momentum that lasted well after the peace. The emergency touched off dramatic reorganization. All indicators of growth—the number of jobs, personal income, and volume of commodities produced—showed the same upward trend. To enlist science, a research council organized under the auspices of the National Academy of Sciences undertook investigations that developed weapons but also refined techniques useful in peacetime. Orderly planning became essential. The navy could not shop for carriers or bombers; it had to collaborate with producers on mutually acceptable terms. Allocation of priorities spared the armed services competition among themselves and with civilian needs. Manpower controls tightened up production and established precedents for future government intervention. Automation further modernized existing facilities so that the output per man-hour rose steadily. The war also stimulated other technological innovations. Advances in electronics and aviation, financed by the military, expanded civilian manufacturing. Heavy taxes on undistributed profits stimulated investment.

Rationing, price-fixing, and other controls disappeared soon after the peace; and several antitrust suits appeared to revive the adversary relationship between government and business. The formal machinery of wartime collaboration vanished. But the interdependence of the polity and the economy endured, along with the apparatus for measuring and diffusing information that bureaucratized and politicized private enterprise. Many Americans discovered in civilian life restraints of personal freedom analogous to those in military service. But opportunity drove workers on. Symptomatically, more than twenty million Americans changed their county of residence between 1940 and 1945.

In vain critics objected to the jackasses, particularly to those in uniform, who exploited the war to extend control and to condition citizens into docile servility. Those doubtful that Western civilization could survive foresaw more radical changes but took comfort from a renewed "concern for the common welfare" evidenced in the way rich and poor rallied to the war effort. Fear of the destructive potential of individual and national selfishness led some one to suggest that maintenance of democratic liberty might in the future require that "the power of individual and collective egoism be . . . broken or at least greatly weakened." Those worried about the deleterious effects of individualism counseled greater stress on communal rather than competitive values, those that united rather than divided people. Fear of military organization with rigid lines of authority from top to bottom and totalitarian controls adopted in order to fight effectively dominated basic policy-making. In the face of vast economic and technological changes, the political system never had time to catch up, leaving open the question whether American democracy could meet the challenge while preserving liberty. The promise of unlimited future improvement justified a mélange of methods for coordinating behavior, neither Hamiltonian nor Jeffersonian, certainly not fascist, Communist, or rugged individualist, but rather pragmatic and unideological. Votes in Congress and executive decisions reflected the trend, which rested on Roosevelt's judgment that the best way to line up labor, business, and the farming interests was to allow each as high a profit as possible while gaining the support of consumers by making rationing and restriction as painless as possible. When Henry Wallace suggested more drastic measures, such as a governmental guarantee of sixty million jobs, far above the prewar employment level, widespread ridicule led to his political demise and showed the limits to the New Deal's adventuresomeness. Its programs aimed less at servicing the lower classes than at building a middle class.[17]

* * *

The war also affected fiscal policy and therefore credit, prices, and the ability to act. What the Depression President did hesitantly, inadequately, and inconsistently, the Commander-in-Chief out of necessity did boldly and unrestrainedly. When it came to military requirements, F.D.R. accepted no limit. The needs of survival made budgets irrelevant. Total federal expenditures soared and created a galloping annual deficit that rose from $3 billion in 1940 to a peak of $55 billion in 1943. Since taxes met only part of the staggering expense, the total national debt climbed from $48 billion in 1940 to $252 billion in 1945, with few complaints and little debate. The levies on incomes and on excess and undistributed profits nevertheless mounted from $2.1 billion in 1940 to $35.1 billion in 1945, restraining inflation and redistributing wealth, since taxes affected increased wages less than increased dividends. The sale of savings bonds directly to the public and to banks also limited inflation. The $45.5 billion in bonds outstanding in 1945 withdrew from circulation funds that, if spent, might otherwise have raised prices; the savings also created resources for expenditures deferred until peace made goods available. Investment patterns achieved more balance than before 1929. Speculators still roamed the exchanges and gamblers still gained or lost, but their activities caused less damage than formerly. Large philanthropic institutions and mutual funds generally managed their great blocks of securities to avoid sharp fluctuations, and the increase in the total number of shareholders also exerted a stabilizing influence.

By 1944 government revenues amounted to one-quarter of the gross national product, as opposed to the four percent of 1930. A steeply progressive tax structure drew upon a wide spectrum, from top to bottom, of the social scale, but the exemptions for dependents meant that a married man with a wife and three children paid no taxes unless his income exceeded $2,500, about the median family income in 1944. The result produced a major shift in income distribution. One-fifth of American families with the highest incomes received fifty-four percent of the total in 1929, and forty-six percent in 1944. The share of total income received by the bottom three-fifths rose from twenty-six percent in 1929 to thirty-two percent in 1944, a modest but significant leveling.

Americans entered this war without the illusions of easy victory that had lulled them in 1917 or 1898. They expected the worst, knowing that battle dissipated resources and destroyed goods and people, diverting energies into unproductive channels; tanks, bombers, and submarines consumed rather than generated wealth. Nor did outrageous bungling and errors of judgment as well as occasional corruption surprise anyone.

SNAFU, the usual term for it, expressed both acceptance and the determination to surmount such hurdles.

Furthermore, people mobilized and removed from the labor force became a drain upon the rest of society; the work of others sustained the millions in uniform. Accepting the need to fight, Americans understood that they would have to pay for the economic disaster that they believed would necessarily follow. The boom touched off in 1939 at first seemed the frenzied activity of people caught in a hurricane—working harder, doing more for dear life, knowing that the luckiest who survived would still have to clean up in the aftermath. Although fatuous social engineers "set out to redress the balance" between rich and poor by taxation and to redistribute income by political pressure, all those men and women, dashing about, learned to behave in an organized way. War, irrational and wasteful, for a time at least imposed obligations of rationality, prudence, and order. It thereby exemplified that "creative destruction" Joseph Schumpeter considered the essence of capitalism.[18]

Government became the largest single consumer. Its expenditures, which even during the New Deal never exceeded $8 billion annually, zoomed to $100 billion. Planning and scheduling to allocate scarce materials improved efficiency. Furthermore, American manufacturing in 1945 inherited a modernized plant and new equipment, the cost often underwritten by the United States, or aided by loans or tax adjustments. The imperceptible long-term effects diverted the economy away from its nineteenth-century course, dissolving the inertial forces of habit, interest, and law. Unshackled, the productive system then veered decisively off in the new direction toward which it had turned only hesitantly in the 1920s.[19]

Rising demand for foods and fibers restored purchasing power at home, and urgent needs abroad expanded the market for American staples. The United States supplied its overseas forces and also those of its allies, and through the United Nations Relief and Rehabilitation Administration (1943) aided civilians in the war-torn countries. The volume of exports grew, as for a time did the size of the merchant fleet. Improved prices and output enriched wheat and cotton growers, stock raisers and dairymen. Manpower shortages and available capital encouraged mechanization and efficient processing. The government still stored surpluses to forestall supply fluctuations, but markets seemed limitless to people shaped by the constricting conditions of the preceding two decades.

In 1944 Roosevelt had announced a second Bill of Rights, expanding liberty by promising security and prosperity for all regardless of station, race, or creed. These rights included assurance of a useful and remunerative job, and earnings for adequate food, clothing, and recreation. Farmers guaranteed a fair return for their toil would make a decent living. Businessmen would earn respectable profits. Every family, assured of a good home, adequate medical care, education, and protection from the fears of old age, sickness, accident, and unemployment, would live without strain.[20]

For the time being the second bill of rights liberated no one. Long-term change in the meaning of liberty emanated not from such pie-in-the-sky pronouncements but from the imperatives of war. Total mobilization blurred the line between public and private. The government underwrote the cost of modernized plants and new equipment, and accumulated stockpiles of strategic materials to secure necessary production. It entered upon joint ventures with independent firms, as when it agreed with Freeport Sulphur to operate a nickel plant in Cuba. In 1945 the United States owned more than fifty percent of the capacity for making synthetic rubber, aircraft, aluminum, and machine tools, and more than three thousand miles of oil pipelines. Political decisions would necessarily guide the economy.

Yet the government did not take over—not even the industries in which it held title to most of the plants. The busy factories, operated by profit-making companies even when publicly owned, restored entrepreneurial confidence, dissolved the defensive frustrations of the 1930s, and eliminated fears of a stagnant economy. Manufacturers, aware of the pent-up spending power of consumers who had long postponed purchases, looked forward to a waiting civilian market once military requirements eased. People who had, of necessity, ridden in car pools had saved the means for new purchases. A sudden inexplicable reversal in the trend of the birth rate also caused cautious optimism. The steady decline stopped in 1942 and the rise of the next eight years promised larger consumer markets. Opportunity awaited.

The assurance of full employment in the act of 1946 therefore proved unnecessary. Manpower demands in the armed forces, in the factories, and in the fields gave each body worth. People long without work found themselves courted. Those once stuck in lowly jobs perceived chances as foremen or superintendents. Expectations soared—for education, for careers in the professions, for management positions. Visionaries like Henry Wallace foresaw a "capitalism of abundance," achieved through redistributive income and welfare payments though consistent with free enterprise. Others like Norman Thomas doubted whether the system could change its spots so easily, but assumed that war had proved the success of planning, which, extended into peacetime, would bring the nation untold, mainly socialist, benefits.

Euphoria spread after the long season of hardship. As a result, the country swarmed with subjects for satire: "the rich radical, the bogus expert, the numbskull newspaper proprietor or editor . . . , the crooked or more usually idiotic labor leaders." But all the loads had lightened and all lives had gained in interest, variety, and time for recreation. The United States, the most prosperous and powerful country in the world, had survived the war not only without the devastation that left much of the rest of the globe in shambles, but with liberties largely intact. Although Senator Bilbo still preached white supremacy and the mandate of the Fair Employment Practices Commission ended on June 30, 1946, the crust of racial prejudice had cracked and the old patterns of discrimination seemed increasingly pointless, nay contradictory of the objectives for which the nation had fought.[21]

Yet the Depression and the war had conditioned citizens to look to the government for solutions of their economic and social problems. Skeptics pointed out that war posters reminding Americans they fought for liberty were already fading, and that the passion for freedom was intermittent and qualified. In the coming era the primary concern for security to escape joblessness might mean the curtailment of liberty.

Preoccupation with military and diplomatic matters after 1939 left Roosevelt obsessed with the certainty that he alone could guide the nation through the extended crisis. The quest for an unprecedented third term in 1940, like the effort to reform the Supreme Court, alienated influential followers. And a split with James A. Farley in 1942 cost the Democrats dearly; they lost most of the gubernatorial contests that year and their strength in Congress shrank. Their narrow fourth-term victory in 1944 boded ill for the future.

For the time being, organized labor's loyalty sustained the Democratic Party in the North. Sheltered by Section 7A of the NIRA, then by the Wagner Act and by the National Labor Relations Board, the CIO advanced in autos, coal, and steel, despite hostile entrepreneurs and outright resistance from old-line craft unions. Even the Taft-Hartley Act's antilabor bias proved harmless. Above all, the common wartime endeavors took the edge off the acerbity, particularly after the U.A.W. and others purged the Communists boring from within. The choice of Harry S Truman as Vice Presidential candidate in 1944, with the agreement of Sidney Hillman of the Garment Workers, signaled rapprochement.[22]

The modes of behavior developed under war conditions influenced the ways in which Americans dealt with the old difficulties of agriculture, of international trade, and of an industrial labor force perennially victimized by unemployment. "A managed economy, founded on private enterprise, and democratically controlled and oriented," enabled them to cope with the problems of the past. Roosevelt's 1944 State of the Union address had called for the means necessary to structure a managed economy toward a higher standard of living in the belief that individual freedom depended on economic security and independence. His promise of a vastly more activist government failed to secure congressional approval in the months that followed, but hinted at the politics of income redistribution submerged during the war. To garner the necessary political support the President encouraged the creation of voting blocs with a significant impact on the political future.[23]

Those blocs evened out the strength of the two major political parties and affected the milieu in which citizens would debate the issues of liberty in the years to come. The Democratic Party became wedded to the coalition that had elected Roosevelt four times, the New Deal its definitive outlook, its voting strength combining Southern support and big-city ethnic enclaves. Republicans also acquiesced in much that the New Deal represented, but their strength lay in rural areas and small towns, whose views on many issues seemed to represent the American consensus yet did not always prevail at the national level.

No speculative orgy, financial panic, or collapse followed the postwar boom. Memories of 1929, still fresh, left even optimistic investors wary. Moreover, the war offered the occasion for reform of the world's disorderly monetary system. A conference at Bretton Woods (1944) laid the foundation for the International Monetary Fund, which freed commerce from dependence either on specie as before 1932, or on barter as in the 1930s. A constant relationship between gold and the dollar (at thirty-five dollars an ounce) liberated international trade by enabling all nations to settle their accounts with one medium or the other.

Widened markets created jobs for a growing American labor force. Doubts about finding places for returning veterans had inspired the Employment Act of 1946 that created a Council of Economic Advisers to monitor trends. The goal of sixty million positions seemed fanciful when enunciated in 1945; the United States soon surpassed it. Both labor and big business misread the economic forces at work in 1945 and prepared to resume their internecine warfare, each side assuming the war had left it in a weakened position and also certain that with the size of the economic pie fixed, what one side gained would be the other's loss. However, joblessness, fluctuating from year to year, did not rise to ten percent, much less to the twenty-five percent of the 1930s. Citizens assumed that society became responsible for assuring work to all who wished it through democratic planning; hence the Council of Economic Advisers regularly mobilized information, appraised the situation and suggested measures to sustain the required level of productive activity. But President Truman's proposal in September 1945 to continue price controls, raise the minimum wage, cut taxes, and later to provide national health insurance, failed to win congressional approval.[24]

Efforts to devise a gradual demobilization plan in 1944 had also failed, despite concern lest returning veterans create vast unemployment. Pressure to bring the boys home mounted when the fighting ended. By December 1946 fewer than two million men remained in the army, and other services also shrank. Nor did production, price, or pay controls long endure. Wage earners wanted relief from irksome wartime ceilings, and manufacturers eagerly sought to exploit civilian opportunities. The disappearance of rationing destroyed the pattern of fixed prices, which thereupon soared, whatever the law said; sellers marked goods up to black-market levels. In the first two weeks of July 1946, the cost of basic commodities jumped twenty-five percent. Yet business resisted demands for higher wages while a succession of strikes in 1946 made labor's wishes known. Controls speedily unraveled. But the government remained the mediator between big business and big labor. The sizable benefits won by CIO unions from the auto and steel companies set the pattern for the rest of the economy, leading to ever-greater federal intervention. Corporate demands for price increases and for relaxation of regulations went hand-in-hand with worker unrest.

Nevertheless depression did not come. Nor did serious inflation. Instead of a collapse into stagnation, peace brought a period of rapid growth. Consumers able to absorb the output of industry fueled expansion, responding favorably to the 1946 Republican slogan—"Had enough?"—of price fixing, of meat rationing, of all sorts of restrictions on the capacity to act. Changes scarcely noticed during the war had created conditions favorable to growth. By 1950 the country boomed. Adjusting for the effects of inflation, the gross national product of the United States on the eve of the war stood at about $170 billion, having edged upward since the depth of the Depression. In 1950, on this scale, the GNP had risen to $355 billion. Productivity, employment, and incomes also climbed, belying the pessimistic expectations of 1945. Year by year the economy served up an ever bigger pie, with always more to share, widening popular ability to act.

The GI Bill of Rights provided returning veterans a sizable array of social services, in addition to loan guarantees and employment and educational opportunities. The program revolutionized American higher education. All at once, thousands of soldiers who had never before considered college an option found themselves in classrooms providing the United States in the immediate future with one of the world's best trained work forces. The bill also transformed the nation from a country of renters to a country of homeowners. The result provided incentives to upwardly mobile behavior. The returning veterans proved fully capable of taking advantage of the opportunity.

Expansion lowered barriers to change. Wartime needs sanctioned planning, which required a perception of common goals. Even at the staid Ford Motor Company, decisions less often turned upon entrepreneurial hunches than upon market surveys. The rapprochement with organized labor brought a glimmer of insight into the relationship between a pleasant workplace and rising output, as the Hawthorne studies (1927–32) had shown. Plastics and other raw materials altered the character of many products; and electronic advances and improved information management created altogether new industries. Concerns about energy supplies eased as continuous mining machines and super-giant shovels exploited abandoned coal sites and overlooked deposits, and improved methods increased the yield of oil. A restructured distribution system also contributed to efficiency when self-service supermarkets replaced neighborhood independent stores or branches of chains.[25]

Only slowly did Americans perceive the effects of a rising population and of an increasingly rational economy. For more than three hundred years, they had worried about the management of scarcities within relatively stable, relatively closed systems. The labor movement also took for granted the fixed size of the available economic cake. Union members learned to march under the banner of solidarity, to submerge individual dreams within the larger concerns defined by union bosses. Power depended on the threat of a strike, which demanded that all unite for the greater good. Many Americans therefore assumed that they could improve their lot only by joining alliances that would fight on their behalf. Disoriented by too many little pigs, too much cotton, they had reacted to surpluses by restoring scarcity, although thousands of potential consumers then lacked food and clothing. "I came to a country," said a wind-bitten vagabond, "where I saw shoemakers barefoot saying they had made too many shoes. I met carpenters living outdoors saying they had built too many houses. Clothing workers I talked with, bushel men and armhole-basters, said their coats were on a ragged edge because they had made too many coats. Farmers were near starvation because they had raised too much wheat and corn, too many hogs, sheep, cattle." No more! After 1945, the unexpected capacity for generating abundance conjured up prospects of unlimited growth, of wealth increasing so rapidly as to satisfy everyone's wants.[26]

Americans then learned the bitter taste of success: after the long struggle toward it, aridity at the destination. Because its attainment once seemed hopeless, success acquired fanciful, dreamlike features. If it be only pie in the sky, let it be perfect, people thought; but then when the dream came true, dismaying imperfections appeared.

Senator Robert Wagner understood the folly of extremists—both those who rejected all changes, and those who wished to get there in one great leap. Perfect liberty or none at all. The country's new economic structures required some corresponding adjustment in government, he believed. But "the terrific urge to prevent another person from making a mistake" led to insistence that freedom demanded state protection of the weak from the strong. That attitude prepared millions to trade liberty for a slavery that promised material security. Hence the danger from impatient utopians, their eyes riveted solely upon distant visions, who pined for a Napoleon to provide the spurious efficiency of despotism instead of relying upon voluntary action.[27]

Roosevelt's third Vice President, kept largely uninformed about the grave decisions made in the spring of 1945, took office three weeks before Germany surrendered. He confronted the unsolved diplomatic problems of relations with the Soviet Union, along with several domestic issues his predecessor had evaded. The war had revealed the tragic paradox embedded in any use of state power, even when employed in defense of liberty. Weapons, never before so destructive, laid waste the whole civilized landscape, made victims of blameless millions. The sheer magnitude of the disaster emptied the issues of fault, guilt, or meaning. But amidst the desolation, something sprouted, unrecognized for a time, then incompletely understood. Disaster mobilized human energies, long flaccid, challenged people to respond, created order, and gave work meaning. The consequences would unfold fully after 1950. The end of the war experience shaped Truman's response to the post-1945 world.

The President, ill-prepared for the succession, confronted at home the postponed problems of labor, immigration, and loyalty, and abroad, Soviet aggression, Korea, and the Bomb. And nothing about the little man from Independence, Missouri (who lacked even a full middle name), inspired confidence among citizens still aware of the crater from which they edged away. His initially high approval rating—eighty-seven percent, according to one Gallup poll—reflected general satisfaction at his decision to rescind many wartime emergency governmental powers by declaring an end to hostilities. But when the new administration could not satisfy the myriad conflicting demands upon it, the President's popularity shrank to thirty-five percent by the end of 1946. Labor policy evoked sharp disagreement. With almost twenty-seven percent of the civilian work force unionized in 1944, some union leaders anticipated the enlistment of most of the rest. Walter Reuther and others regarded the labor union as the crucial countervailing power the modern world needed to balance the overwhelming influence of business, thus presenting the employees some ability to act. The capacity to deliver votes to the Democratic Party demonstrated one way in which labor could show its political muscle.

Some New Deal legislation had tried to hobble management's unfair practices; partly to forestall similar abuses by unions, the new Taft-Hartley Act (1947) gave the President the right to intervene when strikes impacted the national economy. These, among other provisions, evoked union hostility as abrogation of the liberty gained after decades of bloody strife. Passed over Truman's veto, the law provided material for decades of debate. It discouraged labor organization, though far from the only force to do so. Neither the difference between union shop and closed shop, nor various state right-to-work laws, impressed many prospective members. More important industrial changes after 1950 altered the composition of the labor force. As in the past, the American workers' capacity to act, their essential liberty, depended on forces other than the unions. Since the Taft-Hartley Act came at the beginning of a period of enormous expansion, for the time being it brought no untoward upheavals. It thereby assured the rest of the country a level of stability and industrial peace upon which everyone's capacity to act hinged.

Foreign policy issues soon overshadowed the domestic agenda, settled in an atmosphere of fundamental consensus grounded in the nation's ever-expanding gross national product.

War and its aftereffects dominated immigration policy. Down to 1950, travel remained difficult for millions of displaced and homeless persons who desperately sought fresh starts in new countries. Yet rigid American laws remained racially restrictive. Roosevelt did nothing, and Senator Robert Wagner even failed to pry open places for twenty thousand German refugee children (1939). The plight of the 907 passengers on the S.S. *St. Louis* in May 1939 elicited no sympathy as the ship crisscrossed the Atlantic unable to find a port in which to discharge its human cargo. International conferences at Evian and Nassau fumbled helplessly with the subject, and prejudiced bureaucrats in the State Department thereafter stubbornly resisted the slightest concession. Admissions remained at a minimum. The United States, in all, accepted only two hundred thousand fugitives from Hitler's tyranny, about one-half of them Jews.[28]

Postwar immigration filtered through loopholes in the quota system. Americans who acquired wives and families while stationed overseas brought back about 125,000 "war brides." An agreement with the Mexican government temporarily permitted entry of some 220,000 contract laborers between 1942 and 1947, and many illegal aliens crossed and recrossed the border thereafter. Since restrictions did not apply to the independent countries of the Western hemisphere, about twenty thousand Canadians and ten thousand Latin Americans entered annually. Such admissions totaled about a hundred thousand a year. Expediencies elicited by humanitarian concerns only slightly eased the stringencies of the national origins quota system. The Displaced Persons Act of 1948 admitted four hundred thousand in four years, without altering the dominant negative view. "We are pouring billions of dollars into the rehabilitation of [other] countries. Must we also take all of the individuals who live in those countries but do not want to live there anymore?" "The present and the future of America" demanded exclusion of all manner of subversive elements, according to the American Legion. The very people causing all the nation's trouble were slipping through the inadequately enforced immigration laws.[29]

Wartime passions left a mean-spirited residue directed initially at the enemies but, stoked by old hatreds, diffused in time against all strange-seeming people. The differential birth rate still alarmed Americans worried about the reproductive capacity of "such fine old stocks as the Mayflower descendants, the first families of Virginia," and the Daughters of the American Revolution. Gerald L. K. Smith denied that Hitler had killed six million Jews. Illegally admitted to the United States and naturalized to keep Roosevelt in power, he explained, they already walked the streets in pursuit of supremacy for the Jew machine. In fact, wrote one publicist, they were not Jews at all but "Judaized Khazars"—lawbreakers and subversives. Organizations to combat such ideas gained strength, but not enough to extirpate hatred of the foreign, expressed in the desire to freeze the nation's ethnic mix through a selection process that restricted the influx of those deemed most different and thus presumably most threatening to the capacity to act of other Americans.[30]

In this setting, the total of newcomers received after the war proved far less significant than the internal migration by Southern blacks and by Puerto Ricans to the industrial cities, by Easterners to the Pacific Coast and the Gulf states, and by urban residents to the suburbs. Americans remained reluctant to share their liberty with strangers until prosperity, the labor movement's more liberal viewpoint, and the growing political prominence of the children of the "new" immigrants, later revived demands for change. But the judiciary committees, dominated in the Senate by Patrick McCarran and in the House by Francis Walter, remained hostile. As a result, the McCarran-Walter Act, enacted in 1952 over President Truman's veto, merely recodified the old law and made some provisions more stringent, although it eliminated the barriers to admission from Asian countries, to each of which it gave a derisive token quota of one hundred.

Congressional conservatives, patriotic organizations, and nativist groups feared that further immigration would worsen an already bad housing shortage, that urban slums would grow even bigger, that the compassion for Europeans would open the floodgates to even greater migrations from India and China, where living conditions were even more horrendous. The proposed alteration of the immigration laws put the whole form of American life and the national ideals at risk, said Senator Eastland. In the past immigration may indeed have impacted positively on the country, but the current newcomers brought with them alien philosophies and biological incompatibility with America's parent stocks. Radicalism, socialism, Communism, labor troubles, subversive tendencies—all entered the United States with migrants from Eastern Europe. More of them would take America and its liberty away from those who made it great by exposing the country to a biological conquest as lethal as a military one. The new version of Emma Lazarus's sentences inscribed on the Statue of Liberty ought to read "Give me your energetic and your solvent, your educated and healthy, the cream of the crop of your teeming shore. Exclude the undesirable, the illiterate, the poor, the uneducated, the sick to whom is closed the golden door."[31]

The end of fighting in 1945 did not open into an era of peace, either in international relations or within the United States. Roosevelt and Churchill had long ignored the question of the world's appearance after the fighting ended, a subject on which the Soviet Union held ideas out of accord with their own. Neither freedom nor self-determination interested Stalin. A decade of terror had given him power; he wished nothing to diminish his control. Furthermore, his Communist faith envisioned an international revolution that would follow the war—the death struggle of capitalism. He therefore rejected any limits on his future freedom of action, and thereby blocked off the worldwide spread of liberty Americans envisioned. Roosevelt caught glimmers of these intentions but, pretending that they did not exist, induced himself to believe that the Communists, really friends, would respond to kindness. His Annual Message in 1944 denied, not quite candidly, that his conversations with Stalin involved any secret political or financial commitments, when in fact they did.[32]

To deal with the ruthless antagonist who sat beside him at Teheran and Yalta, the President would have had to consider questions he had trained himself not to ask, for instance about the meaning of *governments of their own choice* in Poland and China. Moving from emergency to emergency, making fateful decisions that involved millions, he minimized the Soviet problem, hoping for a compromise. Some Americans went further. Vice President Henry Wallace, hailing the approaching century of the common man, asserted that Russia was as committed to freedom as the United States. (In 1947 Senator Wagner would attack his deafening silence on the Soviets' aggressions, their falsehoods, and their repression of even minimal civil rights.) Two million copies of Wendell Willkie's *One World* argued that Western imperialism posed the great danger to future peace. Willkie anticipated no problems in relations with the Soviet Union, which Stalin had assured him sought only democratic liberties and the right of every nation to manage its own affairs. After years of war, the President refused to concede that earlier mistakes might blight the fruits of victory. The urgencies of survival justified collaboration with the Communists, while rhetorical urgencies fostered the tragic illusion of their democratic intentions.[33]

Roosevelt and Churchill approached reality in February 1945 at a meeting of the heads of state in Yalta. Already then, Lord Moran, the British physician, observed the President's behavior as that of a very sick man. Assuaged by the promise of future free elections in every liberated territory, the English and American leaders admitted to the Polish and Yugoslav governments the very forces that turned those countries into Russian puppets. Hoping against hope to reason with the Communists, Roosevelt secretly agreed to an unbalanced voting formula for the United Nations, to deadly repatriation of fugitives from the Soviet Union, and to the concessions Stalin demanded in Mongolia, Manchuria, and the Kurile Islands, which ran counter to promises given China. The President even then could not recognize or admit to the public his Russian ally's true colors.[34]

In March 1945, word of Stalin's treachery in Eastern Europe came through. Lassitude overcame the President. "We can't do business with Stalin," he concluded—too late. The intimates in whom he could confide and who had kept his spirits up had died or were dying: Missy LeHand, Pa Watson, Louis Howe, Harry Hopkins. Virtually alone, he may have felt the pangs of despair when a cerebral hemorrhage took him off; his attending physician noted the effects of "mental strains and emotional influences."[35]

At Potsdam in July 1945, his successor learned that the Soviet Union, intent on dominating Eastern Europe, did not propose to conduct free elections. Nor did it follow the example of the United States in disarming. And it made no serious effort to control nuclear power, reluctant to expose its own internal disorders to foreign inspection. In 1947 satellite regimes dominated Eastern Europe, strong Communist parties reached for power in France and Italy, a revolution threatened to sweep through Greece to the Mediterranean, and Mao's Red Army forced Chiang Kai-shek to flee from the Chinese mainland.

Two bold measures saved the West. The United States undertook to support free people who resisted subjugation by armed minorities or by outside countries. And the Marshall Plan offered Europe some $20 billion over five years to reconstruct its economy, expecting rising production and improved living standards to form an effective barrier to Communism. Two years later the North Atlantic Treaty Organization created an alliance that reached from Norway to Turkey to further containment.

The Russians did not participate in the Marshall Plan and refused to allow Czechoslovakia to do so. Secrecy kept the world ignorant; but the people behind the Iron Curtain paid in terror and deprivation for the mistakes of the Western leaders. The Soviet Union did not want war, but it exploited weak spots by subversion, a tactic that revived old fears within the United States and created serious problems of internal security. Despite ever-present isolationist sentiments, most Americans approved of the Marshall Plan and NATO. As Albania, Bulgaria, and Romania fell into the Soviet orbit, followed by Czechoslovakia and Hungary, Congress passed a new draft law.

The policies that worked for Western Europe and the Mediterranean failed in Asia and Eastern Europe, however. The Truman Doctrine, which asserted that the United States was interested in the fight for freedom and would oppose Communism everywhere in the world, saddled the country with an agenda too broad for its political will, expressed in sharply reduced defense budgets and demobilization in a shrinking military establishment.[36]

* * *

Sensitivity to the issues of freedom antedated the war. Fearful of repressive measures, the American Library Association adopted a Bill of Rights in 1939, in the hope of turning the library into a public forum "to educate for democratic living." Noting the "growing intolerance, suppression of free speech and censorship affecting the rights of minorities and individuals in other countries," it hoped to forestall similar developments at home. In 1939 the Attorney General created the Civil Liberties Unit, forerunner of the Civil Rights Division, an affirmative effort on the part of the Justice Department to protect individuals. Judge Learned Hand summed up the attitudes of most Americans when he declared on "I am an American" Day, "Liberty dies in the hearts of men and women; when it dies no constitution, no law, no court can save it . . . While it lives there it needs no constitution, no law, no court to save it."

But the United States after 1945 found itself in an unprecedented situation. Knowledge that the Soviet Union possessed atomic weapons and an expansive ideology shattered the old sense of invulnerability. Having emerged from the war militarily strong, Americans confronted intellectual and psychological adjustments that left them feeling vulnerable, exposed, and weak. The sense of fear and occasional paranoia cast shadows over the future of liberty.

Civil liberties had not, however, particularly concerned Roosevelt. In the press of wartime, with Nazi saboteurs caught and executed, he acted cavalierly, assuming that he himself would ultimately correct any infringement on liberty. In the 1930s the prosecution of dissenters and mob violence had created a bad time for freedom; the "brown scare," fear of Nazi and fascist infiltration, then provoked legislative inquiries. Under F.D.R.'s prodding, the FBI turned away from pursuit of colorful criminals to tracking down subversives. The President did tighten controls on information, Hitler's secret weapon that operated a potentially dangerous fifth column. No time for finicky concerns with freedom when disunity threatened. Better suppress some vile publications, silence Father Coughlin's *Social Justice,* jail Pelley for disseminating false rumors that impaired military morale, register aliens, deny gasoline to Gerald L. K. Smith's electoral campaign in 1944. A mass sedition case (1942) charged twenty-six defendants with conspiring to cause insubordination in the armed forces, a tactic later used against Communists.[37]

Roosevelt also acquiesced in incarceration of Japanese-Americans, including American citizens, in concentration camps, a brutal violation of their elemental human rights. "A Jap's a Jap, citizen or not," said

General J. L. De Witt. In *Hirabayashi* v. *United States* (1943), the Supreme Court callously approved the relocation of native-born American citizens of Japanese ancestry as a matter that substantially affected the conduct of the war. Such a strictly scientific way made freedom compulsory, the poet concluded, and only man was god (1944).[38]

Questions of loyalty concerned the President even less. In 1933 he had extended formal diplomatic relations to the Soviet Union in return for worthless verbal assurance that it would refrain from undermining American institutions. By the same token, at the time of the Hitler-Stalin pact he jailed Earl Browder, leader of the American Communist Party, for a passport violation long recognized as a joke, and then pardoned him when the Germans invaded the Soviet Union. Browder's liberty mattered little.[39]

Surrounded by people of diverse opinions, Roosevelt remained sure that he could use them all regardless of their affiliations. Furthermore, Eleanor Roosevelt and some intellectuals and social workers in his administration, horrified by the excesses of the 1918–22 Red Scare, did not want a renewed witch hunt. Directed by Moscow to make himself useful in Washington, Michael Straight, a Communist since his days as an Apostle at Cambridge University, applied to Cousin Eleanor, who slipped him into a place in the State Department—after all, his mother was a Whitney. Sympathizers appeared everywhere—Martha Dodd, Laughlin Currie, nice people all. From Eugene V. Debs on, many non-Communist liberals refused to believe the worst of the Soviet Union, casually slandered ex-Reds, despite the Moscow trials and the pact with Hitler. Stalin and, later, Khrushchev charmed even doughty conservatives like Robert Frost. Above all, United Front! Frederick L. Schuman's *Soviet Politics* (1946) traced the Soviet convergence with the American System. In 1941 the Department of Justice therefore failed to act on the list of subversive federal employees produced by a congressional committee. Roosevelt, who often heard himself attacked by conservatives as a Red, tended to make common cause with others so accused. After all, Communists like Eugene Dennis labored to mobilize workers in F.D.R.'s support (although he would later become a defendant in a conspiracy trial); and the best-selling exposé *Under Cover* revealed the true danger—on the right. A few years later, the same author's *The Plotters* revealed the true danger—on the left. In the fall of 1944 the President began to worry about security in atomic projects, but did nothing about it. That year, a nasty congressional race mobilized media celebrities against a candidate falsely accused of fascist sympathies. Liberty and truth suffered as opinions polarized. Passions heated up; a boycott suppressed the movie *Oliver*

Twist, presumed Red and anti-Semitic; its producer, Louis B. Mayer, sought to outlaw the Communist Party and bar its members from employment.[40]

President Truman confronted the issue more earnestly than Roosevelt had. True, the few party cells enlisted but small membership and suffered a high turnover rate. Many, like Vivian Gornick, joined out of loneliness, searching for connectedness and comradeship. Others like Steven Nelson, tougher, went underground and acted as Soviet couriers. However, the loyalty problem concerned not them but government employees who turned secret documents over to spies. Scientists agonized by involvement in the war effort became susceptible to Soviet pleas for help in the interests of peace. Not until years later did the complexities of espionage emerge, and ignorance of the activities of Soviet agents in the British embassy in Washington long concealed the true gravity of the situation. But the exposure of Drs. Alan Nunn and Klaus Fuchs (1950) created serious doubts. Questions raised by congressional investigating committees now called for answers, despite fashionable jokes pooh-poohing it all as a matter of eager female spies lunching together at Schrafft's (1948).[41]

Truman's Executive Order instituted a loyalty-security program exposing all government employees to FBI probes of their "Americanism." Investigations ultimately led to 1,200 dismissals and 6,000 resignations. The Justice Department in the Dennis case successfully prosecuted the Communist Party leaders and also the spy Judith Coplon, and then William Remington, and then Julius and Ethel Rosenberg, not for their opinions but for illegal activities that verged on or included treason. The Supreme Court that upheld these actions did not lean to conservatism; it included only one Republican—Harold Burton, a Truman appointee. The loyalty program aimed at government employees charged with violating their trust. But the zealotry evoked by exposure of devious Communist behavior spread beyond the civil service. Within the CIO, unionists purged their organizations of covert Communists, and in 1947 the House Un-American Activities Committee summoned screenwriters soon known as the Hollywood Ten, ultimately convicted of contempt of Congress, jailed, and blacklisted. Like other panicky party members and sympathizers, they did not defend their opinions but refused to answer questions, on the plea of self-incrimination, then persisted in silence when offered immunity, exposing themselves to charges of contempt. Agitated patriots urged more rigorous action, but occasional instances of repression and deportation remained far less severe than in 1918.[42]

* * *

In the confrontation between Alger Hiss and Whittaker Chambers, the decisive issue for their generation, the tangled threads of melodrama unraveled in farce.

The central character at first clear—all-American boy, clean-shaven product of good schools, a Harvard Law graduate and Frankfurter protégé, who did well in responsible State Department posts and accompanied F.D.R. in Soviet negotiations, instantly recognizable, polished good guy.

Enter right, the reluctant accuser, called to confirm a woman's tale of prewar espionage—a shifty-seeming, somewhat disheveled intellectual journalist. The ring of New Deal officials who funneled secret documents to the Russians, he charged, included Alger Hiss, by then (1950) president of the Carnegie Endowment for International Peace.

Oh, no! Impossible, a most respectable ivy-clad chorus echoed the denial—Dean Acheson et al. Gentlemen don't lie and but a glance reveals which is the gentleman. Hiss charmed them all; he could brazen out any lie. Red herring, pronounced the President. No matter what the jury's judgment, the faithful remained unconvinced for decades to come.

(all good kumrads you can tell
by their altruistic smell
moscow pipes good kumrads dance) (1935)

Alas, not the stage but the political arena provided the play's setting and jumbled all the roles. Hiss gained the immediate support of Francis Sayre, U.S. Representative at the United Nations, of Clarence Pickett of the American Friends Service Committee, of Robert P. Patterson, of Herbert H. Lehman, of Acting Secretary of State Will Clayton, of John W. Davis, of Ralph Bunche, and of Mrs. Eleanor Roosevelt—of all respectable liberals. He also had the instinctive sympathy of such journalists as Alistair Cooke and Fred Cook, of Lord Jowett, and also of Dr. Meyer Zeligs, who put together a scandalous and fictitious psychobiography of the accuser. The *New York Times* and Elmer Davis on ABC counterattacked, charging that Chambers's testimony amounted to a Republican plot directed against the New Deal.[43]

Long after the case had played itself out in a dreary perjury trial, Alger Hiss continued to seek vindication—vainly. He never understood that the weight of all the respectable opinion summoned to his aid could not offset the truth made manifest in the evidence. And shortly the junior senator from Wisconsin, a naïve, simple-hearted, and uninformed man, rose to speak in West Virginia and announced that he had a list (never revealed) of card-carrying Communists employed in the State Department. His demagogic tactics papered over genuine problems and often allowed the truly guilty to escape.[44]

The silly statement bore credibility among the mass of citizens because their leaders, lacking candor, had not explained the relationship of Communism to the war aims for which Americans had battled for a decade, from Pearl Harbor to Korea. As for the intellectuals and journalists who should have provided light, they themselves blundered blindly either out of ignorance or in an excess of pessimism, anticipating a plunge into darkness by a generation of vipers doomed to decay.

Misunderstanding their parts, the characters churned about in confusion. Senator Joseph R. McCarthy pushed to the head of the anti-Communist crusade, determined to root the Reds out of the State Department. Alas, he understood neither Communism nor the Communist threat, which functioned not through a Jersey dentist subverting the U.S. Army, but through espionage. The senator thus lent himself to mockery on television as a buffoon, by big commentators like Edward R. Murrow.

The motley opposition gathered devoted friends of civil liberties sincerely convinced that a renewed Red Scare threatened freedom of speech, deluded fellow-travelers who had backed Foster and Ford in 1932, had accepted the legitimacy of the Moscow trials in 1937, and had never questioned whose lead they followed in the Popular Front, along with a handful of manipulative Marxists pursuing a private agenda who blamed international tension on the United States. The tactics of controversy hopelessly confused the issue, so that loyalty for some became simply a Cold War tactic, a device to win support against a Soviet threat they considered nonexistent.[45]

With the glaring exception of the Japanese internments, overt restraints upon personal liberty proved less oppressive in the 1940s than during earlier American wars. Indeed the courts took notable steps toward expanding freedom, as for instance in striking down the California law that closed that state's borders to the entry of migrants who might become welfare burdens (1941). The administration of the Selective Service Act also permitted more generous interpretations than earlier of the right of conscientious objectors to escape the draft. So, too, the Supreme Court expanded the scope of religious freedom and of the separation of Church and State. In *West Virginia Board of Education* v. *Barnette* (1943), it upheld the right to disobey the law requiring a flag salute in public schools. The Court considered the salute a form of utterance—"a primitive but effective way of communicating ideas," and therefore covered by the First

Amendment. The offensive law required affirmation of a belief and an attitude of mind, and therefore deprived objectors of their liberty.

Accusations of conspiracy on behalf of a foreign power created more difficult issues because they involved not opinions or speech but overt actions. The federal government on those grounds had proceeded against the Christian Front (1939) and the Irish Republican Army, had suppressed Father Coughlin's *Social Justice* (1942), and had prosecuted the Communist Party leaders in the *Dennis* case. After 1945, it also moved against the agents of Soviet aggression and their dupes.[46]

Citizens unwilling to defend themselves proved most vulnerable, particularly employees in higher education who commanded scant popular respect. H. L. Mencken's quip about the three sexes—male, female, and professors—expressed a general view manifest in cavalier faculty dismissals. The American Association of University Professors from time to time raised feeble objections against weak institutions, but to no avail, and administrations regularly barred objectionable speakers who expressed unpopular ideas. The expectation of conformity to the dominant views of trustees and legislators narrowed the scope of free speech among students and teachers; it left some aggrieved but helpless, and readied a few for adventures in subversion.[47]

However distorted in specific applications, the principle remained clear. "The right to free speech," explained Mencken, "involves inevitably the right to talk nonsense," even by fascists and Communists. There was no dissent about the general proposition. The Carnegie Corporation provided funds for a *Bill of Rights Review,* the American Library Association adopted its own Bill of Rights, and the Justice Department created a civil liberties unit (1939). The courts displayed particular sensitivity to press freedom, invalidating a tax on newspapers and limitations on the distribution of pamphlets.[48]

Recognition also dawned that restraints upon liberty emanated not only from government, from the law, the police, and the courts, but also more subtly from the "appalling uniformity" produced by people everywhere seeing the same pictures and reading the same stories. Concern about the limits on free expression and about pornography persisted, but Americans gingerly approached a wider comprehension of the meaning of liberty, at risk not only from the state but from their own neighbors.[49]

Simpler folk conceded that the United States, not yet really a land of fulfilled promise, confronted problems it might not solve, but insisted that only in that place would solutions ever be found. There the only soil, there the only nation capable of achieving fulfillment—whether or not in actuality it would.[50]

In 1950 it faced the challenge of global leadership quite unprepared. "The American Century," "One World," "the Century of the Common Man"—tired slogans inherited from an innocent past—did not accord with the despair of people who had suffered in battle and depression, and still teetered at the edge of the abyss.

Social disorder since the First World War created the means for examining and understanding its own consequences. It brushed away the facile optimism of the preceding half century and laid bare the question of man's destiny in the New World, as no generation had raised it since the Revolution. Their Enlightenment faith had assured Jefferson's contemporaries that man's will could transform the world. The proper organization of free government could create order in society so that a vital productive system could draw from a beneficent nature all human needs in accordance with the natural laws of progress. Americans after 1920 could take no such comfort in their political and economic systems, not even after a costly victory paradoxically forced upon them the rational order that had eluded them in a decade of depression. In 1950, still far from understanding fully the new society about them, they could not shed the despair of the hard times they had experienced as they appraised their personal life's chances.

CHAPTER 4

LIFE'S CHANCES

ONLY THE SUCKERS swallowed stories whole, whether printed in the papers or heard on the radio or at the bar, or even whispered on the street corner or over the general store cracker barrel. In a world full of fakes, with everyone out to put one over on the gullible, skepticism charted the safest course. All those stories about the Belgian atrocities—lies concocted by bankers and munitions-makers, as the Nye Committee had revealed, their hidden aim to drag the country into a war that did no one any good. Tales out of Washington deserved no more credence than those out of Moscow and Berlin. Distrust of every control set up by the past turned goodness into sham morality, and marriage, religion, and law into outgrown survivals.[1]

Trust no one's credentials. Look beneath appearance. Take nothing for granted. The reporter worth his salt peeped beneath the judge's robe, beyond the sheriff's badge. Beware! Buyer, voter, investor, suitor, beware lest the fair appearance conceal a putrid reality. *Your Money's Worth,* by Stuart Chase and Frederick J. Schlink (1927), instructed consumers to seek out the best buy. Remember, the wool and worsted, the silk and crepeline, could drape but not transform the vile bodies they concealed. Balso Snell! In his journey through a world of imposture and fraud, the initials of his name told the whole story (1931).

> . . . a tawdry cheapness
> Shall outlast our days.
> All men, in law, are equals. . . .
> We choose a knave or a eunuch
> To rule over us. (1920)

A dramatic fall in the death rate and a consequent rise in life expectancy reflected medical advances; and the sharp reduction in deaths from typhoid, diarrhea, pneumonia, and tuberculosis sprang from improvements in living and working conditions, in the Depression as well as in the prosperity decade. One after another the dread diseases of the past vanished. Still, when it came to health, the good old snake oil—soothing syrup—persisted, despite federal laws and regulatory agencies. Radio amplified advertising's influence—Listerine for what might ail you or the healing power of Dr. John R. Brinkley of Kansas. Harry Hoxsey prospered from the cancer cure administered in his Dallas clinic (1936); no interstate business accepted. On his desk a reminder: the world consisted of two kinds of people, "dem that takes, and dem that gets took."[2]

Erskine Caldwell, William Faulkner, Daniel Fuchs, Nelson Algren, and other perceptive writers described the breathing heaps of filth along the road in Yoknapatawpha or on the street in Williamsburg. Sharp though the novelists' vision, they did not fully understand. They wrote not about dirt but about humans, steeped in misery there—wherever they were—because however absurd the aspiration, they looked for something, dissatisfied with a purposeless existence. They wanted bread but also some meaning to life and they insisted furiously that no one take them for granted or file them away in impersonal accounts. Hence they made heroes of the confidence men—Samuel Insull or Charles Ponzi—and they flocked to *Little Caesar,* not because they considered Al Capone a Robin Hood, but because they enjoyed watching a hood who robbed get away with it.[3]

The fault lay not in their striving but in the lack of means to achieve or even to articulate their desires. That they received no assistance and little understanding compounded the tragedy.

After 1920, universal education delivered through public schools shaped the aspirations of American youth. The cause for which progressives had long fought triumphed: compulsory attendance and the abolition of child labor drew ever larger percentages of each age group into the classrooms, whether they or their parents willed it or not. By 1920 the almost fifty million registered included everyone aged seven to thirteen, about ninety percent of those aged fourteen to seventeen, and almost forty percent of those eighteen to nineteen. Annual expenditures for education reached well over $10 billion.

The expanded instructional corps included many women, both behind the desks as teachers and, to a lesser extent, as administrators, a sharp contrast to other authority figures in the youngsters' lives. And the "eunuch moms" who operated the little red schoolhouses for the politicians conveyed a soft, smiling, happy-ending message out of accord with the violence and death of the yard and of home and of the street. The developing system's ultimate intention—to give every American an equal chance—required that all pass through the same set of filters. Children everywhere and of whatever background were to receive identical treatment, study from the same books, test themselves by the same examinations. The universal system that processed them therefore had to disregard all particular differences, not only perform nationwide but also transcend class and cultural distinctions.

Immediately, educators confronted the unexpected—the law could force kids to attend; it could not make them learn. In 1922, 83,000 of the 716,000 pupils in New York City failed of promotion to the next grade and a distressing percentage dropped out altogether. Intelligence tests blamed "defective children," especially those from ethnic groups deemed unfortunate. The favored solution—tracking—destined some pupils for lowly manual or secretarial labor, winnowed out the best for further education and the professions, especially after Arnold Gesell and other early childhood educators explained the importance of good preschool training (1924). Toddlers in the primary grades quickly learned the seriousness of the race to get ahead. Expanding high school enrollments widened the field in the competition that led some to factory jobs and others to white-collar desks or to a four-year loaf at college, and usually although not always to higher status. Hence the tendency to differentiate between youth and adolescence in the battle for survival and advancement. In a sardonic story the familiar poor but honest farm boy sought his fortune for the sake of his widowed mother. But pluck led only to persistence in stupidity. His luck, all bad, produced jail, poverty, and violence as rewards.[4]

Faith in success nevertheless endured. Liberty, the ability to act, depended upon what each individual made of life's chances. The message remained the same: opportunity always existed in a society that rewarded merit. Those who did not make it in the first try, could thumb through Dale Carnegie's popular manual as adults and try, try again. The seven hundred thousand copies sold in the year of publication helped readers conquer their fears and develop initiative. Ultimately, eager buyers snapped up fifteen million of the volumes. Numbered aphorisms attributed failure not to faults in the product but to deficient salesmanship; effective speaking and a smile won friends and influenced people. Or they could imitate Dale Carnegie himself—attend acting school and take correspondence courses. A popular preacher praised Moses as a real estate promoter, and Bruce Barton's *The Man Nobody Knows* (1925) identified Jesus as the founder of modern business, justifying every American's struggle to get what he or she could.[5]

* * *

The pace quickened. Dissenters and wanderers from William Blackstone to Willard Gibbs, every one a Railroad Willy or Steamboat Bill, struck forth—away.

> I'll stay no more on my mother's breast,
> my sister can study the golden rule,
> my little brothers can traipse to school,
> my pa he can curse, my ma she can cry,
> they'll all forgive me in the sweet by-and-by,
> I came from heaven and to heaven I'll go,
> but what's in between I'm a-wantin' to know!

Ever restless, Americans accelerated in the getaway, by train or rail, by excursion steamers, and above all by automobile, although not yet by plane. The number of motor vehicles registered grew steadily until it mounted to almost one for every four persons. They all loved to take the wheel and be off for a long, fast ride away to the other side. Of what? No matter. From the patch to town, and from town to country and to the mushrooming sites transformed into tourist destinations; out of the cities reaching toward space; and along the highways dependable stations—clean—in uniform cracker-box style provided facilities for rest and relief. More valued than the bathtub, outfitted with balloon tires, safety glass, and self-starter, the car offered people a means of self-assertion.[6]

They hastened because they had lost faith in heaven as their destination. True, churches that embarked on uncompromising crusades against immorality among the marginal or insecure gained membership. And immigrants, their worship anchored in an Old World culture, formed fellowships as shields against urban anonymity. So, too, the followers of Aimee Semple McPherson and of Father Divine, fundamentalists, Jehovah's Witnesses, and other millennialist sects offered immediate supernatural direction in a confusing world alien to inherited standards. Experience had taught the poor whites and blacks who joined these groups that individuals standing alone enjoyed but slight chances of making it. Bessie Jones of the Sea Island singers visited a strange church where the members talked only about themselves, about the nature of the earth, about the cows, and rocks, and mountains. To her that teaching was not worth a dime. "The preacher said that if he went to telling them how they ought to live, he wouldn't have a church." She knew from her own faith in God, confirmed by signs and spirits, that the Lord fixes it in answer to prayer. So, too, did the believers at Sister Aimee's healing ministry and the million Catholic pilgrims hobbling along on their crutches in 1929 to a shrine in Malden, Massachusetts, lured by hopes of miraculous cures, and so, too, the anxious thousands who turned to spiritualists like Margery for messages from the beyond, to astrology for horoscopes, and to phrenology.[7]

By contrast, the mainstream denominations failed to protect their members against the drift toward atheism, agnosticism, and apathy. Ministers dedicated to the social gospel agenda lost the ability to distinguish between progressive and permissive. No help to confused communicants who simply swallowed Mencken's up-to-date mockery. Some clergymen drifted into a Christian Marxism under the influence of Reinhold Niebuhr or Henry F. Ward. Their utopianism denied the immediate problems of human existence and expected dreams to turn cheaply into reality. Others served psychiatric functions, as when the Emmanuel Movement among Episcopalians found a therapeutic value in religion. Norman Vincent Peale's clinic purveyed the message "Our lives are what our thoughts make them." The healing cults completed the identification of health with worship. In California, Katherine Tingley, the Purple Mother, led theosophists in the quest for physical beauty, intelligence, and spiritual wealth lodged within the self. In her community, former bankers and industrialists listened to lectures in an atmosphere like poppy-scented champagne, while her constant companion, a dog named Spot, reincarnated the favorite among her three former husbands. An American Legion post in Chicago, which heard Annie Besant's Hindu World Master (1926), ended its meeting by singing "For He's a Jolly Good Fellow." In 1923, Émile Coué arrived from Dijon to teach Americans to help themselves by saying, "Day by day, in every way, I am getting better and better." Sister Aimee Semple McPherson used popular music, chorus girls, and stage settings to preach that Christ saved and cured. Physical culture reflected the same identification of body and spirit, as when Bernarr McFadden defined the torso beautiful as the means to health and salvation, and proved it by parachuting from an airplane at the age of eighty-three. After all, the popular musical asked, "And what does worrying net you?" and answered, "Nothing! The thing is to have fun!"[8]

Few church members responded to the European theologians concerned with the nature of man, with his relationship to God, and with the presence of good and evil in the universe. Americans paid no attention to the intellectual anguish stemming from Kierkegaard by way of Karl Barth and Martin Buber. Nor did they feel attracted to the Existentialist philosophy involved in the postwar moral crisis about the use of violence to resist violence. Nor did the apprehension that the world might destroy itself draw the population in fear and trembling to a demanding faith that accepted and thus accounted for the absurdity of the universe. Rather the popular guides included Fulton J. Sheen, Norman Vincent Peale, and Joshua Loth Liebman—Catholic, Protestant, Jew. The reassuring texts—*Peace of Mind, Peace of Soul, A Guide to Confident Living,* and *Faith Is the Answer*—presented religion not as a source of, but as a cure for, anxiety: faith a superior form of psychoanalysis; prayer a method of gaining energy and success; and conversion a means of achieving certitude. Thus soothed, the mind, the search for a place to live over, could settle down "to the making of a home." Relief of personal stress made further self-examination unnecessary. Twelve psychiatrists served on the staff of the Marble Collegiate Church, on New York's Fifth Avenue (1955). Focusing concern upon the problems of the participants rather than upon established rites or prescribed creeds, these movements and churches served individuals impatient with restraint and eager to cast off all external ties, defining liberty as the ability not to act—but to relax. Worshipers could account for the differences among their particular faiths on the grounds of habit and ethnic affiliation. "Go to the church of your choice," said the advertisement; with all equal, only the obligation to belong counted.[9]

Anxiety did not altogether subside, however: did people really believe, who believed because belief was good for them? Or knowing that they would not know again "the infirm glory of the positive hour," did they just "Thank Thee that darkness reminds us of light"?[10]

Important questions remained unasked. The black rain that fell from the mushrooming cloud over Hiroshima never washed away. The rent in the heavens as a Viking rocket passed 244 miles through them (1949) never closed. Americans averted their eyes from matters about which they could have no certitude.

People who thus struggled loose found themselves free—alone—and regarded themselves in an unfamiliar perspective. The hero of a novel in woodcuts, having abandoned his ancestors' religion, failed disastrously to find meaning or happiness in philosophy, astronomy, marriage, fatherhood, or social action, then solved his problem by embracing madness. Or like Hart Crane and Weldon Kees, such people took refuge in suicide—poets unable to integrate their consciousness with the world about them.[11]

Once the Depression pulled down the tottering social order, the rich provided fair targets for mockery, as when the *Daily Mirror* and the *Daily Graphic* raked over the love affairs of Kip Rhinelander and his Alice or of Daddy Browning and his Peaches. But the disrepute of high society extended as well to all social levels. Even in Booth Tarkington's saccharine stories, Penrod and Sam mischievously subverted the good behavior of the dancing school. More acute writers revealed how Spoon River and Main Street stifled the personality, crushed rebellion, and turned their victims into religious and social hypocrites.

Muckrakers and debunkers excoriated contemporary culprits but also national and religious heroes from the past. E. Haldeman-Julius sold by mail millions of little blue books that gave Americans the inside story; others demonstrated that the real George Washington had feet of clay and that the biblical King David, a double-dealing opportunist, could always get someone to kill his giants for him. Louis Boudin's *Government by Judiciary* (1932), Matthew Josephson's *The Politicos* (1938) and *The President Makers* (1940), and Louis Hacker's *The Triumph of American Capitalism* (1940) revealed the sordid self-interest inseparable from American institutions. In a best-seller, Helen of Troy exposed abstract standards of good and evil as delusions; personal satisfaction alone counted. *Strange Interlude* justified adultery—the right thing to do; happiness brought men and women the nearest they could come to knowing good. Thin and vapid talk of freedom meant little in a country in which thirteen million citizens possessed liberty—and nothing else. The smart set snickered when H. L. Mencken debunked democracy, a fraud mob men foisted upon their talented neighbors. Unwittingly he thus joined the masses struggling to pull the elite down to their own level.[12]

Individuals broke away, followed inner inclinations, because they could not trust communal standards. Little Orphan Annie (1924), by herself, recognized the good life; and the analyst Karen Horney recommended self-realization as the ultimate human goal. Rapid social change called all external information into question. The media had become so ponderous—in sheer size and in the numbers reached—that the speakers could not tell who listened, nor the hearers whence the word came. Those who wished to understand the serious problems of their times groped through thickets dense with irrelevancies. Book clubs, paperbacks, the radio, and records distributed literature and music to the multitudes; but the avalanche of sights, sounds, and words effaced consistent standards of selection, made room for the good, bad, and indifferent, but not for calibration or judgment; and static enfeebled all signals. Each person floundered in sorting out the extraneous matter before finding the desired nuggets in the bombardment of information. Even the rebels lacked the positive standards of their predecessors. They knew what they opposed—

the sham of the world around them. But they could not say what they favored.[13]

The uncertainty particularly troubled young people unable to square the pious verities they learned at home with the rows upon rows of Bugsy Siegel's slot machines and Nevada's steepled offices that offered equally easy marriage or divorce. On their way to becoming adults, boys and girls—at the drive-in movie (1933) or in the parked car's intimacy—could neither extricate themselves from the confines of the family, nor evade the obligation to create their own lives through their own decisions in a distressed world. They got little aid in learning to do so, despite the solicitude of fathers and mothers. The media blared forth a vast array of sounds and images—confused, distorted, disordered. Violence peppered sentimental platitudes; with equal coolness viewers or readers believed none of it or all of it, but had to make their own way—even those who read Salinger (1951) and *Lord of the Flies* (1954)—or found the same answer in *Mad,* which mocked the inanities of their elders. All futile, all phony, all crap, moaned Holden Caulfield.[14]

A world organized for power neglected human considerations. Slum clearance wiped out thousands of decrepit homes, replaced them with rows of apartments, unlivable almost at once. On superhighways, vehicles moved with unrivaled speed, but a missed exit carried the voyager forty miles out of the way. The individual became a statistic; for however slight the value of the lone integer, all had worth as components of the measurements that certified achievements—for flagpole-sitting (1924), for marathon-dancing (1928), or for goldfish-swallowing (1939), for instance. Wary readers who trusted the news column no more than the advertisement beside it alternated between fits of weary skepticism and periods of utter naïveté. Deep down, even as they paid the price, they laughed at their own gullibility. It was all ballyhoo, a fraud, bunk—history, society, everything outside themselves.[15]

Motherhood, too? Of course not! Every man said he wanted a girl just like the girl who married dear old dad—even a toughie like H. L. Mencken, even the revolutionary dedicated to a cause: Momma! I must remain faithful to the poor because I cannot be faithless to you! But sung out by Sophie Tucker, the red-hot Mamma, the connotation became ambiguous, just as Al Jolson's blackfaced Mammy did, as if the relationship were less clear than convention made it. The serious plays and movies brimmed over with bitterness. Yes, mother, said Sidney Howard's Robert (engulfed forever), hopelessly tied by the silver cord. Mother love suffereth long and is kind, beareth all things, believeth all things, hopeth all things, endureth all things. Stifleth all things. It became safer, on every account, to reduce the emotion to the formal commercial terms of Mother's Day.[16]

The whole family, in fact, threatened the personality. Grandfather said, "Thee must now and hereafter do my thinking for me, thee must be the continuance of me, thee will forever even if intermittently, or if only every so often consciously, stand in the ghost of a pulpit, in the ghost of a church." Such absolute requirements dragged down those who yielded to the constraints. Clyde Griffiths refused to allow his parents' claims to impede his struggle for success; but his softness in dealing with Roberta's demand for marriage led to *An American Tragedy* (1925). Happiness, in fiction as in life, depended on cutting loose from burdensome relationships, on seeking fulfillment freely wherever possible—even in the thrill of child murder as it did for Leopold and Loeb.

President Hoover (1934) and many social workers still hailed the family as the "hope of the future," the foundation sustaining the country's buoyant spirit—there where a loving father and mother looked down into the cradle in which their firstborn cooed. But the members strained against its restrictive bonds, particularly during the Depression when unemployment prevented the father from playing breadwinner-legislator. The highest obligation for self-fulfillment often demanded defiance of social convention. Marriage, no longer simply the first step in forming a household, became the climax of romantic love, surmounting barriers of class, race, religion, or group, as plays by Eugene O'Neill and Rose Nichols and scores of sentimental movies demonstrated. Sectarian lines ceased to define the permissible. In vain a radio preacher argued that the chances for marital felicity improved when the couple shared the same faith: "The family that prays together, stays together." The Reverend John Haynes Holmes (1931) more persuasively declared that love, the supreme factor in human experience, "must be followed even when it leads across the barriers of race and the thresholds of synagogue and church." A phenomenally popular play delivered the same message. The individual could achieve liberation by casting off inherited ties. Able got his Irish Rose when boy and girl disregarded ancestral differences. At the happy ending, the priest and the rabbi grinned on in approval. The old ways proved not only wrong but ridiculous.[17]

Alas, opportunity did not always materialize; Beatrice Fairfax's column in the *New York Journal* sometimes elicited 1,400 lovelorn letters a day.[18]

Widespread marriage counseling programs did not offset relaxed laws that made divorce easier, by accepting mental suffering as grounds, for instance. A tolerant code of sexual conduct also occasionally recognized extramarital affairs almost as a matter of course, as in the alley-catting around of Hollywood and Broadway. The passionate yet staid relationship of Eugene V. Debs with Mabel Dunlap Curry, a Terre Haute neighbor, stretched over a decade, punctuated with effusions about women's refined, emotionally sensitive, and sympathetic nature. Marital infidelity evoked some disapproval but not surprise. Gaudy magazine illustrations urged men on to adventures of fantasy or reality; and Dr. Kinsey's deceptive statistics informed them that everybody did it. Prostitution no longer seemed evil or a sin, but—as in "Hatrack"—exploitation of working girls, or at best, a device to keep good women pure by diverting male passion elsewhere. Meanwhile the decline in the number of lodgers and boarders increased the privacy and liberty of conjugal couples.

Birth control ceased to depend upon restraint alone; widespread public discussion made contraception familiar. Yet despite its availability in the corner drugstore, carelessness, hedonism, accident, or impatience at the nuisance of the trip still subjected women to "illegal surgery," the usual term for abortion. With marriage a convenience rather than a permanent union of souls, Judge Ben Lindsey recognized the logic of the situation and recommended a period of companionate trial before young people permanently committed themselves. The dating practices of the 1920s and 1930s went a long way toward meeting his suggestion. For the moment no one considered the possibility that only a relationship embedded in domesticity insured children's natural right to continuous parental care. Willingness to experiment reinforced by insistent messages from advertising and popular stories obscured future threats to social stability.[19]

In 1950 the ideal of diminished family size persisted, reinforced by dire scientific warnings that existing population exceeded "all reason, all possibility of support," with no end yet in sight. A shift in attitudes during the Second World War reflected the experience of a generation that had passed through adolescence during the Depression. As adults, its members felt torn between the need for security and the desire to act as free personalities. Pitifully few roots or even illusions sustained them. Enlistment in 1941, they knew, brought not only separation but perhaps obliteration. A burst of battle might finish everything, including their own precious individualities. Neither rebellious nor innocently enthusiastic, they stoically accepted an obligation, having seen *All Quiet on the Western Front* and knowing they were off to no big parade. Homer Macauley might deliver a War Department telegram to any address.

They did not wish the best years of their lives—for some, the last years—to slip away while they reached for the elusive butterfly of romantic love. They thanked heaven that they fought for a free country where a man could still do as his wife pleased. But also hometown restraints dissolved when young men confronted pliant, remote Asian and Australian women. Yet the veterans wished more; before they went off, and after they came back, they wanted to know that some part of them would remain alive, seed immortal, kicking in the belly, running in the sun, surrogate triumphant in the father's empty space. And the girls they left behind, having waited (or not), felt also the wish for fulfillment.[20]

After the Great War came Korea and the permanent draft, and in every newspaper some reminder of the world's dreadful vulnerability that increased the longing for an anchor in posterity. At the same time, returned prosperity put security within reach. The youngsters who chose parenthood believed that they thereby guaranteed their individuality. The birth rate climbed as babies boomed.

Early marriage became the norm. The swain no longer called but took the lady out. Boys and girls went steady in high school, using the family car as a detached, portable bedroom. Many soon after slipped into domesticity. The returning veterans brought baby carriages to college; indulgently supported student couples kept them there—about eight million with the aid of the GI Bill, which also provided housing loans. Later came jobs—of a sort. Those who never finished high school or did not continue beyond it considered themselves as ready for unskilled labor and for household responsibility as they ever would be. Some hastily arranged unions ended in separations and raised the divorce rate, but did not alter the norm of a marital relationship that had become a means of gratifying personal needs rather than a permanent social organization.[21]

Individual fulfillment remained this generation's goal, but its attention shifted to the child, raised by relaxed standards—fed on demand, delayed in weaning and toilet training. Having experienced loneliness, postwar youths cherished security; togetherness best satisfied their needs, along with material possessions that testified to their identity. The intimacy of shared relationships compensated for the inability to manage the great affairs of society and provided continuity in an otherwise uncertain world. The young couples wheeling the cart through the shopping center while the future toddled along ignored insoluble questions and concentrated on those Dr. Spock answered.[22]

The growing autonomy of American women did not alter the trend. The number of female voters, college graduates, and wage earners mounted while earlier inhibitions dropped away. Their habits and clothing revealed that they considered themselves the equal of males. No longer the silly flappers of Ring Lardner stories, they controlled a large part of the nation's disposable income, and profoundly influenced domestic tastes—parasites, Mother Jones called them, "out playing parlor politics instead of raising the nation's children"—prodigal in the waste of opportunity, according to Charlotte Perkins Gilman. The new woman, in actuality and in popular fiction, became a recognized type—free of ladylike delicacies, subject to the same passions as men, able like them to dance and drink and drive within limits she herself set, capable also of achievements in spheres not traditionally theirs—like Aimee Semple McPherson, Amelia Earhart, and Helen Wills.

Choices, however, seemed no more clear to one sex than to the other. Once feminists had argued that women's access to the ballot would purify government; their formal access to power came at an unfortunate time. Ironically, politics after 1920 sank to new lows in scurviness, degeneration, corruption, and chaos. The ability to act in government still depended on informal involvements and organizations, through which some women wielded considerable influence, but most often behind the scene or focused on single causes.

An earlier popular culture reflected the multifaceted adaptation to postwar life. Side by side with celebrations of female achievements, appreciation for their public roles, and even some devaluation of the ideals of domesticity, the Doris Day type and the Jean Harlow caricature sustained more traditional versions of roles and functions. Disaffection and alienation, as well as unhappiness with social expectations and limitations on the capacity to act, affected well-to-do women more than others; lives, shaped by Depression, improved during postwar prosperity that became more liberating than suffrage.[23]

Readjustments in family life bore particularly harshly on the elderly, weakened emotionally and financially when their own powers failed, and particularly when they lived at a distance from their children. During the Depression, a majority of the aged became dependent and wartime unsettlement altered but did not solve their problems. Social Security payments as yet provided but meager relief.

Times had changed since William Osler had suggested that people could expect no great achievements after the age of forty and that anyone over sixty should no longer hold a job. Technical experts would continue to argue that a surfeit of old people in young men's jobs strangled American business and that middle-aged workers became less adaptable and more inflexible—old dogs unable to learn new tricks. In the 1920s, attention to youthful heroes like Amelia Earhart and Charles Lindbergh further undermined the role of the elderly.

These ideas touched off a huge debate and much negative comment. By the middle of the twentieth century, notions of the insidiousness of the aging process had yielded to substantially more positive views that later empowered the Gray Panthers. Earlier battles revolved around efficiency and needs, and the identification of aging and retirement with death. But the Social Security Act shifted retirement decisions from the private process of collective bargaining to national politics. Retirees no longer saw themselves as ex-producers but as consumers whose incomes defined their capacity to act.

Discriminatory treatment therefore called for a remedy. The Social Security Act recognized that the aged had social rights, which to Senator Wagner meant lengthening the period of leisure and contentment, recognizing the value and nobility of life. But such fine sentiments and unfolding programs of aid further distanced the aged from the rest of the society. A secure financial future did not always follow. And since the family had long abandoned its protective functions, its decreasing size and geographic mobility isolated the aged even more.

Between 1940 and 1950, retirement as a way to deal with the aged nevertheless spread, as pension plans multiplied, as Social Security benefits broadened, and as the eligibility age sank. Disengagement provided the rationale for government regulations, leading to the definition of yet another step in the life process—in which the elderly sustained their capacity to act while separating themselves from the workplace and other institutions. Many found themselves isolated in new ghettos defined by the needs of the elderly, in the worst cases but warehouses on the road to eternity.[24]

The lack of agreed-upon criteria for proper behavior forced people to make their own decisions. Delinquencies soared, or at least became more visible. In some states, "sexual psychopath" laws confined to hospitals for the insane persons a probate court deemed dangerous. Other lawbreakers, however, roamed the streets freely. The old numbers game and after 1932 the new slot machines ate sadly into limited resources and accompanied a disturbing rise in crime. True, Dick Tracy, Nick Carter, and other pulp private eyes enjoyed a popular following, but so did various real-life racketeers and hoodlums. The gangs that controlled vice and gambling in the tenderloins of large cities increased their power. Some of them, like Lepke Buchalter's Murder Incorporated, served labor unions—a useful base for racketeering. During Prohibition, the illegal traffic in liquor proved profitable—"My God! How the money rolls in." Sharpies also did well in gambling, whether legalized at the race tracks or outside the law in ubiquitous numbers games. Access to guns and cars often permitted criminals to outdistance corrupt or primitive police, all too often hampered by venal politicians like Chicago's mayor "Big Bill" Thompson, a "low down hound" who degraded himself and his city. Gangs, however, organized the youth respectable society neglected, turning the dominant standards of acquisitive success against the established order. Life under these conditions acquired novel connotations.[25]

The Depression made lawbreakers desperate. Old-fashioned robbers like John Dillinger sporadically shot up banks for needed loot and drifted violently from crisis to crisis until they met a lethal bullet. Kidnappers and thieves enlivened the daily press—detached men, who followed no coherent purpose or calculated plan, but vented their fury on the society that failed to reward them. More forceful types who did know what they wanted organized violence systematically. When Prohibition ended, gangs moved on in other directions—sometimes to legitimate business, but more often to the illicit sale of drugs, and to prostitution, labor racketeering, and gambling. At Al Capone's death, control of his Chicago mob passed to a directorate led by Frank Nitti and Jack Guzik. Frank Costello and Charles "Lucky" Luciano operated out of New York, and the Binaggio crowd tied up Kansas City. Scores of lesser outfits worked other communities, the criminal versions of liberty as numerous as the practitioners.[26]

In the public image, the FBI relentlessly pursued the gangsters. In fact, although the G-men occasionally cornered notorious public enemies like Dillinger, law enforcement depended mainly on the ineffective or corrupt local flatfoot. Ambitious prosecutors like Thomas E. Dewey of New York hunted out the evidence to secure convictions; more often the authorities did nothing unless scandal broke out. Another set of crooks would only replace those jailed. The mayor appointed a committee, said Will Rogers, to stop small graft, which had spread so that it interfered with large graft. Public apathy occasionally gave way to indignation, but citizens had no qualms about patronizing the gangsters. Prohibition, traffic violations, and gambling habituated Americans to minor legal infractions. They less often gave criminals jail terms than publicity.[27]

The socially delinquent usually faced no formal criminal charges. Rape—under-reported and difficult to prove—rarely resulted in convictions. And other infractions also escaped exposure. Al Capone considered stock market speculators and politicians "greater crooks than hustlers in the underworld." Crime, he knew, involved more than hoodlums' violence. From Teapot Dome onward, a succession of scandals revealed the dishonesty of business and politics, as individuals pursued their own ends.

The Depression blocked off careers considered normal by accepted values—to grow up, get a job, marry, have a home. Boys on street corners often would not settle for the relief checks that kept their unemployed fathers going. By 1932, hundreds of thousands of youths wandered the country, hopping rides in the company of the hoboes who also had nowhere to go. But those who stayed behind, immobilized by resignation or despair until the war, also failed in the first duty of earning a livelihood. The continuing discrepancy between what they could and what they should kept the young conscious of defeat. Theirs was the bleakest form of liberty, their capacity to act totally circumscribed.[28]

A taste for violence and widespread hedonism reflected the disillusion with, or disregard for, old standards. Reformers despaired of saving from eternal damnation individuals who loved sinning. Although Prohibition did not put alcohol totally out of reach, the difference between liquor and alternative drugs narrowed; cocaine, heroin, and marijuana spread from the drawing rooms to the street corners and sustained a profitable though illegal organized trade as bewildered users sought the artificial paradise of hashish intoxication.

Such drugs provided relief, although less accessible after the Pure Food and Drug Act eliminated them as ingredients in the old-time syrups, elixirs, and painkillers. Bureaucratic complications impeded the enforcement of federal regulations and contemporary reformers and physicians failed to agree upon the effects of marijuana smoking or its relation to criminality, or the appearance of liberty it offered addicts. But the growing involvement of organized crime in narcotics traffic gave evidence of widespread dependence for release from confining inhibitions and for relaxation from painful tensions. Such stimulants enabled some Americans to attain hazy intervals of freedom.

Other addictions persisted, however. Easy money encouraged speculation by hordes of gamblers, in securities, in real estate, and in business as well as on the numbers, in the slots, and at the race track and other sporting events. Religion rarely imposed restraints, for it no longer wielded credible sanctions to sustain the uncertain guidelines to ordinary behavior. The movies and tabloids more often shaped attitudes and actions.[29]

Elmer Rice, resolute optimist, still described *Street Scene* (1929) as the setting for a symphony. But the smog that darkened the skies over many American cities obscured their social deterioration. Even when factories idled, the stagnant air cast a pall over streets and buildings in want of repair, over men and women out of work, over communities no longer providing their members security. Everything seemed to have happened by accident, without planning, as in a haze of marijuana, out of the chaos of individualism run riot, a sense that penetrated even occasional movies—*Wild Boys* (1933), *Black Fury* (1935), and *Black Legion* (1936). In *Skyline Near Washington Square* (1925), Edward Hopper's isolated building revealed the blank detachment of the integer in the heart of the great city. And in the bleak spaces beyond—where 110 miners died in an explosion of coal dust at Centralia, Illinois (1948), where silent mills crumbled, while new mechanized plants downgraded the skills of labor, and where the soil no longer sustained family farmers—a general feeling of helplessness prevailed. No one had much capacity to act, although many felt it imperative to

> say yes, spoken because under every no
> lay a passion for yes that had never been broken.[30]

What did liberty then mean?

The gap between ideal and reality dismayed acute observers. The disillusioned writers of the 1920s had reacted not only to the war of 1917 and to the peace of 1918, but also to the nation's apparent abandonment of values. The lost generation would not make do with second-hand dreams. Whatever was worth doing, they knew, was worth doing well. And what they could not do well, they would not do at all. F. Scott Fitzgerald believed in the New World that had once flowered for Dutch sailors' eyes and had once pandered in whispers to the last and greatest of all human dreams—space for freedom. In the great treacherous city Gatsby (1925) still had faith in the green light, the orgiastic future that receded before him. That future eluded him now. No matter; tomorrow he would run faster, stretch out his arms farther. In 1950, time had expired; the reaction more complex, no less dismayed. Of liberty only a residue remained—to hope and to die.[31]

In the headlong race, neither participants nor observers accurately appraised the results. Success, the alluring prize, lay within easier reach during prosperity and war, much less so during depression. But how many would win remained unclear. As did the relationship to worth. Will Rogers identified failure with "the fellow that don't want to do manual labor" but "wants to figure out where he and his friends can get something for nothing." The quip became ever less persuasive after 1929 when the ranks of the losers widened.[32]

Shoving ahead, Americans often forgot the contradictory imperatives of competition and cooperation. Nor could they discover convincing explanations for the nightmares of joblessness, divorce, or the failures in personal obligations. They would stumble out of depression as they had stumbled into prosperity. Whose the fault and where the remedy? Awkward questions set citizens asquirm.[33]

Commonly, they escaped to daydreams. In the arenas, on the diamonds or the gridirons, the best men and women won. A contest with winners and losers excited people who regarded life as a striving for success. Bruno "Lefty" Bicek stumbled along imagining his prowess on the diamond—homer! But attention also focused on the stars: Babe Ruth, Red Grange, Jack Dempsey, Bobby Jones, Bill Tilden, and Helen Wills satisfied the craving for heroic individuals who asserted their personalities within the rules of the game, never mind their private lives. Asked to justify his salary, higher than that of President Hoover, Babe Ruth shrugged, "Why not? I had a better year." Even gossip about the stars, purveyed by Walter Winchell or Louella Parsons or Hedda Hopper, found voracious consumers.

In the Rosebud Movie Palace, a happy ending concluded every story. They offended Carol Kennicott's refined tastes, but supplied ten-cent soothing reveries for lonely patrons. On Broadway, the well-to-do sought fun in nightclubs and musicals where gangsters and newly rich butter-and-egg men rubbed elbows with scions of the Four Hundred. Entertainers from the slums supplied diversions under the oversight of Texas Guinan, Flo Ziegfeld, and other promoters. Columnists like Winchell who dished out the dirt on the playboys and playgirls became celebrities in their own right. In the little towns, as in the big cities, romantics swayed in the fox trot to the beat of swing from the bands of Benny Goodman or Glenn Miller. Across the afternoon air waves came the aimless, no bananas, "Mairzy Doats" music, undemanding background for the housewife's chores or the adolescent's studies. Or else, pulsing realistic soap operas described never-ending problems that, even more than in actuality, followed one another in ceaseless complication. Painful situations lost their sting while they granted sighing listeners emotional release in the awareness that others suffered, too.[34]

Daydreams conjured up heroic images—the Lone Ranger or Superman for the young, the private eye for their elders—and gave ordinary people a command of tough argot. A special integrity or virtue imparted the power that enabled the single individual to triumph over seemingly superior hostile forces.[35]

In 1930 vaudeville still struggled to survive, offering performers a close rapport with audiences, winking sensually but not explicitly at the margin of obscenity—"Who paid the rent for Mrs. Rip Van Winkle?"[36] Vaudeville, however, vanished in the next decade, replaced by new mechanical media that decisively separated actors from viewers and listeners. The performer at the microphone had no way of knowing who heard, nor of responding to the distinctive qualities of a vast undifferentiated mass; only the message all would understand came across. Motion pictures had long seemed to some a mechanical menace in their capacity for facile entertainment. Sound increased the threat. In the talking movies, detailed scripts, dialogue timed precisely to action, deprived directors of the old freedom to improvise. Spontaneity disappeared. Expensive productions required heavy financing and depended upon an elaborate star system and upon international distribution; formidable risks therefore impeded departures from tried-and-true formulae.[37]

Radio broadcasting flourished after 1930. The willingness of advertisers to buy segments of time in return for freedom to peddle their wares then created an unexpected and abundant source of income. Furthermore, long-distance transmission lines permitted many different stations to broadcast a single program simultaneously. The networks, money losers before 1929, thereafter increased their sales and their profits. National advertisers able to command the attention of millions paid handsomely for time, and its enormous power drew talented people to radio.

The requirement of a license for access to the air made broadcasting a limited monopoly and challenged familiar conceptions of freedom of speech. Yet no national policy distributed the wave lengths. Nor did the government try to influence the character of programs. It simply handed the air waves to a few entrepreneurs, free to use them as they wished. No federal or state agency regulated program content, though self-censorship by timid corporate officials avoided controversy. They made trouble over a skit entitled "Skiing on the Sabbath or, Are Our Young Women Backsliding on Their Week Ends"; they shuddered when Mae West played the serpent in "Adam and Eve." Restraints on liberty thus resulted not from action but from lack of action by the state. Radio, unrivaled as a speedy transmitter of news, made the informative voices of Lowell Thomas, Gabriel Heatter, and Walter Winchell familiar, more often evoking excitement than understanding. Immediacy also created interest in blow-by-blow reports of sporting events. But most other broadcasts depended on familiar routine and repetition, widening rather than narrowing the distance between isolated people and their real world.[38]

* * *

Tame offerings did not dull the craving for sensation. The girlie pictures from *Esquire* that ornamented dormitory rooms and barber shops offered only hints of the forbidden; and the shared bedroom scene in *It Happened One Night* (1934) remained resolutely decent—Claudette Colbert, the leading lady, having refused to undress even partially, although Clark Gable then revealed that he wore no undershirt, to the distress of the underwear industry. Nevertheless vague images of violence and erotic fantasies, over the air or on the screen or printed page, offered escape from the boredom as much as from the misery of daily life. Stories of tortured nuns, RAPE, out of the Spanish Civil War and Nanking, as earlier out of Belgium, stirred unrecognized feelings. Down in Savannah at the weekly rat hunt, all the neighborhood dogs chased the dozens of rodents released simultaneously on the green. Horror films exploited the taste for the macabre. Elsewhere stronger stuff generated excitement. Brutal shootings and assaults punctuated the stories of Dashiell Hammett and James M. Cain and of the tough movies of James Cagney and Edward G. Robinson, counterparts of the actuality in Chicago's Valentine's Day massacre. Excited crowds witnessed the lynching of white men in San Jose, California; thousands followed accounts of the pursuit of John Dillinger. Liberal interpretations of the law tolerated open discussion of once-taboo sexual themes far beyond the restraints of Puritan morality that excited Mencken's indignation. All-but-nude figures peeped at their audiences from slick magazine pages and from the bare boards of the burlesque stage, and Sally Rand's fan dance proved the hit of the Chicago World's Fair. No restraints inhibited the *Graphic*'s illustrators or Walter Winchell's gossip column. Suggestive movies evaded censorship, while *Woman in the Window* (1944) and *Double Indemnity* hinted at the depth of female sexuality. In the novels of John O'Hara and in the plays of Erskine Caldwell and Tennessee Williams, erotic encounters temporarily diverted attention from real life's other difficulties.[39]

Comedy offered an alternative means not only to forget terrible problems, but also subtly to strike back at those held responsible for them. Blondie, Gracie, Portland—emblematic females, pretty, unthreatening, operated by a silly logic that nevertheless left them in command of every situation. The ambiguous message had it both ways—pleasing men by exposing the dumb blonde beneath the romantic appearance, pleasing women by control over the all-powerful male. The theme extended on into the war when Lucille Ball in a boiler suit appeared in a defense plant; but striving too hard for success destroyed *Mildred Pierce.* Among ethnic comics, dialect sheathed the underlying bitterness. Others exposed all.

W. C. Fields, a total nihilist, boozy, belligerent and lazy, hated all the sacred institutions—bank presidents, motherhood, children, and order. The Marx Brothers turned logic on its head as they careened destructively through race track, college, or store. In *My Man Godfrey,* the idle upper class floundered helplessly until the butler took care of himself and of them. Often the movies converted the tycoon and the politician into figures of fun—pompous, bumbling windbags useless in an emergency. Managers of all sorts, in industry as in government, seemed irrelevant if not hostile to liberty. The Three Stooges represented the type, their gratuitous violence a tactic for survival.[40]

Radio, a less tolerant medium, insulated the most popular comedians; Jack Benny, Eddie Cantor, and Edgar Bergen's Charlie McCarthy stayed away from satire; and Kate Smith conveyed an impression of honesty and integrity with no hint of identity. The wry commentaries of Fred Allen and of the Easy Aces mixed little barbs among the quips in sympathy with the hapless citizens, their liberty under incessant assault. The immense and prolonged vogue of Amos 'n' Andy and the Goldbergs rested on little more than familiar Yiddish or darky stereotyping (1929 ff.). But Amos 'n' Andy also presented a complex picture of day-to-day black life in Northern urban communities. The protagonists, wholesome and clean, scrupulously moral, averse to alcohol and gambling, rarely swore and upheld all the verities attacked in the outside world. Their appeal crossed racial and ethnic barriers, attracting varied audiences, becoming household visitors with whose plight listeners identified.[41]

Serious writers and readers, determined to confront the crisis about them, endowed their work with significance by articulating the anguish of society. Injustice, poverty, and war they treated as causes not for laughter but for change or perhaps revolution. Their merciless internecine warfare about style and about modes of experimentation heightened awareness of the need for action by laying bare the world's ills.[42]

Painters proved the most effective—not the exaggerated blasts from the Grosz or Gropper cartoons, but the bleak buildings and desolate, transient hotel and motel rooms—empty urban scenes of lonely striving in Edward Hopper—and the rigid lines of Grant Wood's country people, with no hint of a curve in *American Gothic.* These canvases, without preaching, conveyed a sense of modern isolation in their subject matter, tight draftsmanship, and manipulation of light and color.[43]

Often the suburbs, too, lost their communal character. The bungalow that originated in California spread after 1915 to other parts of the country. The little detached houses offered low-cost accommodations to people escaping the crowded urban center hoping to find a child-centered, garden-loving community less at war with human nature than the city street, as in Frank Capra's *It's a Wonderful Life.* To assure such places stability and permanence, Los Angeles rejected a mass transit system. Without striking deep roots anywhere, defying social claims, each resident there—a little superman or Dagwood Bumstead within his own walls—behaved precisely like his neighbors yet maintained distance from them.[44]

The tragic futility of small-town life in the 1920s provided an easy target for a facile writer who mocked the dull similarity of Gopher Prairie. A decade later, when the same novelist wondered about *It Can't Happen Here* (1935), he discovered unexpected virtues in the links between the college man and the barber that enabled such communities to resist fascism.[45]

Some authors ascribed to the poor emotionally full lives in sharp contrast to the hollowness of those of the well-to-do. Men and women unencumbered by material possessions attained ultimate freedom. In *The Grapes of Wrath* (1939) or on *Cannery Row* (1945), the toiling farmers, the fisher folk, and the canners, even in failure, coped with authentic problems of survival, as did the Spanish peasants in *For Whom the Bell Tolls* (1940). They would redeem the liberty their oppressors abused. In proletarian novels the heroic workingman appeared, although a less common figure than the tiller of the soil. Vivid photographs by Margaret Bourke-White and Dorothea Lange added dramatic emphasis.[46]

The tendency to exaggerate the virtues of the poor owed something to older romantic notions of the pure and natural redeemed by suffering. But it also expressed the desire to locate the potential for social reform among the least powerful and thus least to blame for existing difficulties. Their strength, properly mobilized, might improve the lot of all. The reformers who came down to raise living standards in the Southern highlands therefore refused to develop an employment agency that would help some but would diminish the community's collective strength. Instead they threw the students into conflict situations to advance an understanding of the class-divided society.[47]

The wish to believe in the redemptive power of the poor extended to the least favored group in American society. In 1917 blacks joined the war effort, assuming that they, too, would profit; the struggle to liberate Czechs and Poles in Europe would also bring equality and self-determination to the underprivileged at home.

Deep disappointment followed. Nothing changed in the segregated

South; riots and lynchings persisted, though fewer in number. Even at the height of the New Deal, efforts to enact the Costigan-Wagner antilynching bill (1935) failed. F.D.R. would not press for it, and the Brain Trust hoped to correct inequities indirectly. Believing prejudice rooted in exploitation, they feared a race war and expected that the abatement of poverty and the elimination of social injustice would cure all other maladjustments. Meanwhile, West Indian immigrants added to the population in Northern cities, giving political power to a few leaders without improving the life chances of most. Urged to "March ever forward, breaking down bars, look ever upward," blacks who lost faith in white willingness or ability to help, abandoned America in search of another promised land. Marcus Garvey's "Back to Africa" movement, rejecting cooperation, briefly kindled hopes that as quickly fizzled out. Everywhere the Depression narrowed choices among those unfamiliar with metropolitan ways. New York City's blacks, 60,000 in 1900, numbered 327,000 in 1930 and 458,000 a decade later. Mothers and their babies died in Harlem at a rate more than double that in the city as a whole. There as in other cities, a color line divided light-skinned from dark-skinned blacks.

The gloom thickened as the conviction spread of the permanence of poverty and of the indelible effects of race ineradicable even in "passing." The urban environment closed in on Richard Wright's *Native Son* (1940) and his *Black Boy* (1945), deserted by the father—religion ineffectual. The Second World War accelerated economic and social change but deepened impatience at the slow pace of reform and at the inequitable distribution of the capacity to act.[48]

Impenetrable economic barriers, fortified by prejudice, made adjustment more difficult during prosperity as well as during depression. Unions rarely admitted blacks to membership or made common cause with those reputed to act as scabs. From 1932 onward, the U.S. Public Health Service callously experimented on black males as guinea pigs in a study of syphilis. Increasingly trapped in segregated slums, discriminated against by social welfare agencies, colored people vainly sought glimmers of hope. The law did not help, for the judiciary continued to tolerate segregation within the confines of *Plessy* v. *Ferguson. Nixon* v. *Herndon* (1927) held the white primary unconstitutional without effect on government power. In 1941 Chief Justice Hughes, delivering the judgment of the Court, held that the *equal protection of the laws* clause of the Fourteenth Amendment meant *equal,* but accommodated separateness. Since Jim Crow patterns in practice made equality nonexistent, the Court's *equal* really meant unequal.[49]

Downtown swells attracted to the easygoing style of Harlem nightlife rarely noted the simmering discontent in the streets whites had abandoned for the suburbs. Violent crime increased. Then riots, weapons formerly used against blacks, turned against whites, as in the Harlem of 1935 and 1943. What happens to a dream deferred? the poet asked.

Does it dry up
like a raisin in the sun?
Or fester like a sore—
and then run?
Does it stink like rotten meat?
Or crust and sugar over—
like a syrupy sweet?

Maybe it just sags
Like a heavy load.

Or does it explode?

Frustration, aimlessness, and the temptation of looting sometimes drew young people out of the tenements and into the streets in a destructive orgy. Their elders more often reflected, "Well, after all, it ain't no worse than it is."[50]

Eleanor Roosevelt, Harold L. Ickes, and a few other New Dealers openly demanded black equality and flouted Jim Crow regulations. Aimee Semple McPherson rejected every form of prejudice and preached the Klansmen out of their gowns. But the unusual individual did not alter patterns of discrimination. The more skeptical and more conservative like H. L. Mencken and George S. Schuyler remained dubious. And even respectable professional colored people could not overcome residential segregation, despite the ruling in *Shelley* v. *Kraemer* that held restrictive covenants unenforceable. Dynamite bombings and riots followed the intrusion of blacks into white neighborhoods, so that only marginal gains resulted from such efforts.

The situation in the South, where law and custom enforced segregation, deepened black poverty and influenced the North, as when deference to University of Georgia sensibilities induced New York University to bench a black football player. In the depressed region below the Mason-Dixon Line, blacks remained the poorest of the poor. And everywhere the harshest burden fell on women, condemned to act as wage earners as well as homemakers, churches their only consolation, ministers the most effective voices of protest.

Radicals who cast their lines in these troubled waters netted a few prominent fish. W. E. B. Du Bois, continuing the quest for a defined identity, had once hoped that education would train the talented tenth to lead others to equality, just as Alain Locke's *New Negro* (1925) wished a common culture to transcend race. Those hopes faded in the 1930s, although Communists did what they could to exploit the Scottsboro case. The need for self-knowledge and self-respect then brought Du Bois to Pan-Africanism and Marxism. Meanwhile, Paul Robeson also sought shelter in a Soviet allegiance. But Karl Marx generally attracted as few blacks as whites; both groups put their faith "in that other Jew, Jesus."

More influential efforts to work within the system kept hope alive, although down to 1950 they brought only meager improvements in black liberty. A. Philip Randolph, for instance, used the labor and socialist movements to bridge the distance between the races, expecting realistic gains, however modest. In 1941 the march on Washington he led persuaded President Roosevelt to create the Fair Employment Practices Commission to secure equal treatment in defense plants. Permanent state laws extended the principle to all jobs and to education, in principle, at least.[51]

Father Divine boldly suggested that individuals might cross lines etched by color as easily as those created by other ethnic divisions, as he himself did in marriage to Sweet Angel. Although his heavens provided low-cost rooms and meals, his optimism proved excessive; even the labor movement failed to help in the face of other needs that seemed more urgent. In the 1930s a few sheltered unions such as those of the railroads and printing trades maintained their pure and simple white character. Others, pressed between recalcitrant employers and radicals who wished to make them instruments of revolution, dragged their feet and held their membership by giving affiliation a social and cultural meaning deeper than that of the pay packet. Their relatively strong position in the 1930s left blacks out, less excluded than disregarded, except for occasional support in abstract protests against racial prejudice.

Perversely, faith endured, despite deep inhibitions against miscegenation; an optimistic civics text (1940) advocated tolerance; and Gunnar Myrdal's monumental study stressed the importance of the creed of equality. On the other hand, America never was America to those who encountered only the same old stupid plan of dog-eat-dog, of mighty-crush-the-weak. And yet some persisted in the oath:

> America will be!
> Out of the rack and ruin of our gangster death,
> The rape and rot of graft and stealth and lies,

We the people must redeem
The land, the mines, the plants, the river,
The mountains and the endless plain—
All, all the stretch of these great green states—
And make America again! (1938)

The darker brother sent to eat in the kitchen when company came would then sit at the table. Nobody would dare say "Eat in the kitchen" then.

Besides,
They'll see
How beautiful I am
And be ashamed.[52]

Poetry moved few people, black or white. But blacks responded to the exhortations of their own religious leaders, whose churches, respected by powerful whites, provided sanctuary against a hostile society. From the Sea Islands Bessie Jones brought traditional spirituals capable of moving listeners' feelings. Messages about the issues of a good life and the promise of a compensatory hereafter stirred the emotions. Some ministers like Adam Clayton Powell, Jr., of New York's Abyssinian Baptist Church also dabbled in politics and gained power by mobilizing votes. Father Divine, who attracted the greatest number of followers, provided practical cooperative programs and advice on urban survival, different from the snooping social investigators whose questions made "the case" ashamed of her life. Promises of millennial redemption attracted lonely white as well as black disciples. By contrast, intrusive Communists made no headway.

Down on the streets, the cool cats, appraising their own meager life's chances, despised the uppity residents on the Hill, "West Indians," they called them, or "Black Jews." On the other hand, the preacher, like the bad man, the trickster, and the signifying monkey, played the folk hero. For the time being, liberty for blacks meant the space numerous other subcultures created for themselves away from the whites. Liberty more often involved resistance than a capacity to act, defined more often by what it opposed than by what it advocated.[53]

A long perspective revealed gains not immediately perceived.

Lynchings declined. The *Gaines* case (1936) began the serious questioning of the doctrine of "separate but equal" education, the number of Negro voters and officeholders increased, and in 1944 the Supreme Court held the white primary unconstitutional. The shift into the Democratic Party after 1928 widened the chances of advance through politics, and opportunities in employment inched open. A 1938 Supreme Court ruling held that sufferers from discrimination in employment could demand not only equal but also preferential treatment. Social segregation did not yet yield to the pressure for equality; in 1945 blacks and whites did not yet serve in the same fighting units. Nevertheless the war had created an impulse that bigots could delay, but not halt. Veterans returning to college demanded a voice in social and academic policy. Those who risked their lives in a common cause would not willingly come home to a society that denied them equal treatment, and the New Deal had armed government with renewed though unused power to advance social welfare.[54]

Hunger for faith stirred people of all backgrounds. Nicholas K. Roerich, an artist who had created sets for Diaghilev's ballets and had stocked his New York museum with his own paintings, had studied in St. Petersburg and had participated in archeological expeditions to Kashmir, Turkistan, and Tibet. In Central Asia he claimed to have discovered an ancient Buddhist chronicle revealing Christ's visit to India as a young man. Secretary of Agriculture Henry A. Wallace, persuaded that evidence of a Second Coming existed there, dispatched Roerich to Mongolia supposedly to search for drought-resistant grasses, but actually to find signs of the approaching millennium. As Vice President, Wallace still sought ways to achieve the kingdom of God on earth. At a Roman Catholic mass he felt an instinctive desire to cross himself and after the conclusion remained kneeling in silent adoration. He studied Darwin and also Presbyterian sermons, Aristotelian logic, Judaism, Buddhism, Zoroastrianism, Islam, and Christian Science. His vision encompassed a land free of bitterness, prejudice, hatred, greed, and fear, where social inventions set hearts aflame with the extraordinary beauty of the country's scientific, artistic, and spiritual wealth. Free-floating faith exposed people seeking certainty to recurrent gusts of novelty, although they usually reverted, as in a Frank Capra film, to a rediscovery of neighborliness, charity, and industry—all three emblematic of traditional capacities to act.[55]

The exciting challenge deepened with awareness that everything familiar changed. New Deal slum clearance altered the urban landscape; and during and after the Great War, strangers filtered into the old ethnic neighborhoods—the East Side and Williamsburg, the North and West Ends, the South Side—as Jews, Italians, Irish, and Germans drifted away to the suburbs. Even in small towns like Haverhill and Lawrence, Massachusetts, the Syrians and Armenians, the French Canadians and Poles, as well as larger groups of Yankees and Irish, abandoned familiar streets when no overseas replacements arrived to rejuvenate aging communities, from which the restless young fled as did Mary Antin, Anna Yezierska, and Laura Ridley, but also John Fante.

The recurrent dream of a return to grandfather's home—the high-columned house under tall elms that looked like a brown Greek temple, for many a shrine of goodness, humanitarianism, and religious freedom—revealed not only that grandfather no longer lived there, but that the house had become a brothel and the neighborhood a red-light district. And two blocks away to the north, in the real world, the most living and lived-in and loving and loved of all houses had been transmogrified and embellished to emerge as the most modern and blatant of funeral homes. Progress—progress![56]

Progress bore a more benign aspect for labor unions that enhanced their members' life chances and thus their liberty. The Great Depression remained fixed in memories, with unemployment a tragic calamity and the union the only bulwark against a repetition. In addition to its role in collective bargaining, it often supplemented or replaced the ethnic communities severely strained by depression and the end of immigration. For the Irish teamsters, Jewish garment workers, Italian plasterers, and other ethnics, balls, picnics, loans, and educational and insurance services counted as heavily as collective bargaining. The International Ladies' Garment Workers Union of the 1930s enrolled people of many ancestries, about half Italian, about thirty percent Jewish, the rest scattered among numerous stocks, but it persistently went beyond negotiating on their behalf to supply cultural and personal needs. A bi-monthly published in English, Yiddish, Italian, French, and Spanish editions, courses and lectures, an athletic program, and instruction in music and dancing served members. The union produced plays, arranged picnics, and operated a health service and vacation resort. Depression guaranteed membership loyalty and the Wagner Act provided legal recognition and security.[57]

The rank and file sought larger paychecks, of course, but also comradeship and a cause that would mediate between the individual employee and the world, in political, cultural, and social, as well as in economic matters. Unable to act on their own behalf, the members willingly surrendered some of their liberty to have the group act for them. The Depression had stifled hopes for social mobility and many expected to remain forever fixed in their jobs, around which they organized their lives. Sporadic sit-ins revealed smoldering militancy and the determination to assert their stakes in the plants. Similar expressions of shared misery appeared in some agricultural regions in organized farm holidays and in rent and mortgage strikes.

Something more now drew together those cut off from abandoned or withered communities when even the simplest duty, like laying out the dead, fell into neglect unless one acted for the other. A helping hand!—life's ultimate necessity. Long before, a sensitive observer had considered it very touching to notice coarse and shabby and beaten people so united, "to see how they felt for one another, how the heart of each to each was softened by the hard trials of their lives." What the poor were to the poor was little known except to themselves and to God. Mid-century needed an equivalent of village neighborliness.[58]

Solidarity forever!—a slogan fleshed out by experience. "We will be our own welfare workers," said Mother Jones, claiming the right to happy homes, a noble mankind, and a great womanhood (1921). During the New Deal and the war, Americans, more than ever before, had assumed responsibility for one another, through the state that could order people to do its will with a profound impact on liberty. But after the peace, honest, decent, hardworking citizens, rich or poor, mistrustful of inept or corrupt politicians, fumbled about in the effort to regain control of their own lives through voluntary action.[59]

Persistent racial prejudice intruded upon unifying tendencies, directed not only against blacks but against other identifiable groups as well, with Asians the most dramatic victims. Since the gentlemen's agreement of 1911, fewer than eight thousand Japanese had annually entered the United States, many for only temporary stays. Yet in California hostility toward them persisted, and the 1924 immigration law barred them entirely, thus unilaterally abrogating the gentlemen's agreement. Then, after Pearl Harbor, with no justification whatever, the United States confined all Japanese-Americans, native-born citizens as well as aliens, in concentration camps—an action the Supreme Court pusillanimously upheld. China's participation in the war as an American ally did not soften anti-Oriental feelings.[60]

Bias also complicated relations with Indian tribes, whose condition had not visibly improved after more than a century's effort at integration. In the East, the Iroquois, Algonquins, and others had worked out stable ways of life; but Western tribes lagged behind. Reform groups vacillated between efforts to assimilate the red men and women into American life as the Dawes Act (1887) had anticipated, or to preserve their identities as John Collier and the Wheeler-Howard Act (1934) sought. Neither policy took adequate account of the Indians' own view of liberty. Both failed.

These policies left the Indians among the most impoverished Americans; fewer than two percent had annual incomes of more than five hundred dollars, and more than half had incomes well below two hundred dollars, derived mainly from leasing or selling land to neighboring whites. Assimilation along with corruption and mismanagement of the Bureau of Indian Affairs undermined family and communal life. Changed attitudes under the New Deal responded to pressures from the Indian Rights Association, a Philadelphia-based group of white reformers backed by anthropologists and artists interested in safeguarding tribal heritage. Government efforts to suppress such native ceremonies as the Sun Dance among the Pueblo raised the issue of religious freedom. John Collier's hatred for Western industrialization with its emphasis on technological change and individual self-interest drove him to enlist in the cause of the Indians, who also rejected assimilation into white culture. In 1933 Roosevelt appointed him commissioner of Indian affairs. With the help of Harold Ickes, himself a founding member of the Indian Defense Association, he attempted to apply some New Deal experiences to improve the lot of the tribes, some of which had their own and different agendas. A few complained that the New Deal reforms only strengthened bureaucratic control. The Wheeler-Howard Act exacerbated existing discontent, and Collier's efforts ultimately foundered on the shoals of traditional rivalries and ancient suspicions that made Native Americans distrustful of their unrepresentative and often ineffective tribal governments.

Shrinking property provided one measure of the tribes' limited capacity to act. The practice of allotting land did not make Indians "competent," it merely "transferred" their land to non-Indian ownership. The policy of "setting the Indians free" merely set them free from their possessions, continuing a paternalistic attitude that had stifled initiative and independence and subjected them to the benevolent despotism of various bureaucrats. By 1948 the Hoover Commission admitted that the efforts to assimilate the Indians by destroying their cultural identity had been a mistake. Efforts to promote pride in Indianhood paralleled attempts to recast the self-governing tribal societies along lines more suitable to the modern age. By 1952 both political parties promised "to remove restrictions on the rights of Indians individually and through their tribal councils to handle their own affairs."[61]

In California, Washington State, and Hawaii, the presence of diverse groups in a fluid society complicated matters. The Anglo (or Haole) elite,

Chicanos, Filipinos, Punjabi, Japanese, Indians, and Portuguese, in agricultural settings, fell into conflicts over employment, intermarriage, and schooling—none resolved in 1950. Proximity to the border put Mexican Americans in a different category. Their numbers had grown steadily since 1920. Some refugees, driven across by the chaos of civil unrest, were recruited by the trainload to work as far away as the Chicago iron mills and the West Virginia coal mines. Repatriation efforts aimed to lessen the problems in the Southwest while acculturation measures in New Mexico considerably improved the lot of the Mexican Americans. But in Texas the widespread violation of civil rights, the wretched conditions of illegal aliens, the poor educational and health facilities, combined to make their lot similar to that of Southern blacks. Political powerlessness and variants of Jim Crow discrimination revealed their lack of liberty. The situation changed only after 1940 when a political awakening paralleled the entry of Mexican Americans into the middle classes, by virtue of wartime employment opportunities and the impact of the GI Bill.[62]

Residues of prejudice affected the life chances of many groups. Persistent patterns of discrimination circumscribed the ability to act of people culturally or socially set apart as outsiders. With places difficult to secure, open and systematic quotas limited the entry of Jews and Italians into medical schools, as the *Dodson Report* amply proved. Although such measures could not close off access to the legal profession, informal practices excluded undesirables from the most prestigious firms, and university faculties also proved unwelcoming. Restrictive covenants barred sales or rental in fashionable residential neighborhoods; clubs, restaurants, hotels, and resorts engaged in similar exclusionary tactics. However, postwar anti-Semitism only rarely matched in intensity the animus of the 1920s and 1930s, and Catholics escaped the hatred the Klan had once directed against them. Indeed, popular novels and movies ascribed prejudice to mistaken identity that goodwill and understanding could resolve.[63]

Discrimination reminded victims of the need for meaningful forms of group identification and expression, alerting them to the gap between their own experience and the promises of American liberty. Men and women who claimed the same rights as other citizens became conscious of the need to assert those rights when they confronted obstacles on the way to higher positions. The organizations structured by their parents bore the stigma of poverty and foreignness, reminders of inequality. However, the emotional drive to unite with others drew many into the hundreds of fraternal societies that flourished throughout the country.

But fearful of rebuff, they also sought the security of renewed identification with their groups of origin, like the hero of T. S. Stribling's *Birthright* (1933), foiled in the effort at improvement. Without quite knowing it, they longed to hear the speech that clung to the ears, tingled in the blood—words about long ago and far away. As in other societies, these impulses strengthened ethnic identification.

Efforts to preserve distinctive group life had a long history. White Southerners and New Englanders in the past had consciously drawn boundaries to assert their own identities. In the 1930s other ethnic groups, including American Indians, embarked on similar efforts, with far-reaching consequences. They thereby affected some aspects of New Deal policy. All persons could remain what birth and heritage made them, yet all deserved equal treatment. Therein lay the intellectual antecedents of class-action litigation, legitimated by the assumption that limits on one person's liberty posed corresponding limits on other members of the same group. An action on behalf of one served the others also.

The "True Democrat" recognized the ultimate value of each person; otherwise all, no longer individuals, would sink into a mass, their freedom lost along with the power to choose between good and evil. Democracy could not survive without the essential belief in the dignity of all God's creatures. Prejudice that diminished life's chances for some enhanced the timeliness of that faith. Preserved cultural heritages provided valuable buffers against degrading imputations of inferiority. Minorities espousing these principles found support in Franklin Roosevelt's vague faith in the common man. And the prominence of children of immigrants in his entourage imparted political momentum to that faith.[64]

The beginnings of ethnic revival during the New Deal gave new meanings to liberty, as each group attempted to square its cultural heritage with the requirements of the larger society. That redefinition proceeded within familiar legal contours, asserted along with rights of citizenship, equality before the law, and other concepts evolved from America's past. Socially and culturally, the United States slowly began to acquire a more open and pluralistic cast. No group could totally salvage a tradition embedded in a remote, irrecoverable place, alien in many of its ghetto survivals, and stigmatized by signs of cultural inferiority. Religious and linguistic bonds could nevertheless tie them all together without the appearance of foreignness.[65]

A growing number of mobile urban blacks shared the dilemma of ethnicity and sought a cultural identity of their own. Some took pride in Harlem's Black Renaissance, or sympathized with Marcus Garvey's "Back to Africa" movement, knowing it a hopeless delusion but welcome as defiance of the white world. A vestige lingered in the Communist insistence that blacks as an oppressed nation deserved the right to self-determination, which some Indians also claimed for their tribes. Others, like Zora Neale Hurston, a Barnard graduate, described the multiple burdens of black women, confronting a hostile world and weak males, and subtly explored the impact of race and sex in black communities and the way in which external constraints shaped private visions of liberty.

Whether Jews formed an ethnic, religious, or national group remained a subject of dispute, furthered by changing demographic makeup, the decline of orthodoxy, growing secularization, and intermarriage. In practice, however, theological compromise and involvement in social and philanthropic activities blurred ideology as ever more Jews discovered their sense of worth and capacity to act outside their faith. The process by which European religious customs adjusted to the American environment further loosened the bonds that elsewhere created tight and often confining communities. The hardships of assimilation, generational struggles, and estrangements from ancestral faith increased the second generation's liberty.

Some Jews joined efforts to create a national homeland in Palestine, in the belief that persistent anti-Semitism required a safe haven under the umbrella of a sovereign state. Zionism had attracted only a tiny minority in the 1920s, for American Jews did not expect to migrate to Palestine, doubting that their own situation warranted a mass exodus. After 1940, the shocks of Nazi anti-Semitism, war atrocities and displaced persons, and the need to find places for European refugees swelled Zionist ranks, as did the wish for emotional satisfaction in group pride.[66]

Other minorities in comparable situations shared the felt need to belong, as did Victor Herbert, eminently successful yet president of the Friendly Sons of St. Patrick and a distinguished member of the Sons of Irish Freedom. Extreme nationalism in that group subsided with the establishment of the Free State, although diehards fought on against the Ulster partition. Some of them became prominent in Father Charles Coughlin's crusade to keep America safe from international Communists or plutocrats. A few extremists, members of the Fascist Christian Front, joined hands with former Klansmen and other isolationists on the "America First" platform.[67]

Their problems and those of other ethnic groups found ultimate resolution within the United States, regardless of the pull emotional ties to old home countries exercised. But in the process, minority attempts to expand their own capacity to act challenged antiquated definitions of freedom and widened the liberty of all Americans after 1940. But when the vast acculturation process repeated itself toward the end of the century, the results proved quite different. In the 1920s the ethnics wanted not to shed their old identity but to make it part and parcel of the rainbow society of the United States. They succeeded because they did not wish to set themselves apart, only to gain acceptance.

Hard-pressed groups struggled to find resources to create institutions they could transmit to their children, a task unprecedented for all but a few. It took time to create alternative educational institutions, and all-day parochial schools proved far too expensive to serve all second-generation children. More useful supplementary instruction and a wide array of business and other vocational courses had at least practical utility. But most often the response took negative, defensive forms—against compulsory attendance laws, against Bible reading, and against secular schools' monopoly of public funds. As for children, the objects of the conflict, neither the parents nor the teachers but rather an emerging autonomous culture of neighborhood and peers provided boys and girls what dismayed reformers called a street education. More than one generation would pass before the advantages of moving apart rather than remaining huddled together outweighed the loss of severed ties.

All voluntary associations suffered during the Depression when lack of funds weakened even well-established fraternal societies. The "spontaneous cooperation," the tolerance for variety and civility in intercourse, once the product of a common journey, faded. Above all, the radical extension of government services preempted tasks formerly performed by voluntary groups. The unintended consequences revealed that even doing good carried a price. The relief measures enacted after 1933 outdistanced private aid, and Social Security overshadowed the insurance and benefit plans of lodges. Even the old cultural and social activities receded in importance as federal agencies underwrote some of them. The age-old methods by which communal activities enhanced people's abilities to act disintegrated once state bureaucracies took over. Much of the provincialism, clannishness, localism, and ethnocentrism thereby went out of American life, considerably widening the horizons of even the most remote and isolated groups.

All along, Americanism exercised a countervailing pull. A rabbi recalled his emotions when he gained American citizenship, when he first voted for an American President, when he watched his eldest child register in a public school: "It was the breaking of a dawn after a long night." America represented a closer fulfillment of the biblical doctrine of human equality and the commandment to love one's neighbor as oneself than he had expected to see on earth, short of the coming of the Messiah. "God fashioned a nation in love, blessed it with a purpose sublime—and called it America," enthused the president of the Zionist Organization. However devoted Jews felt toward the new state of Israel, loyalty to the United States remained primary.[68]

Citizens who sought to compensate for the lost traditional cultures of their parents by forging an ethnic identity all along drifted toward a general American nationalism as an alternative. Advocates of one-hundred-percent Americanization sought to reduce all to a common type by dissolving the distinctive features of origins, class, or section, in place of which only a blank, out of accord with realities, would remain. The survival of liberty amidst the pressures of the hour demanded, they believed, the total obliteration of self-identifying cultures.

However, most people evaded a clear-cut choice; they could have unity and separateness. In racial pageants on the Boston Common, Chinese, Italian, Irish, Jewish, African-American, Russian and Syrian singers performed, and movies like *Guadalcanal Diary* (1943) revealed the multiracial composition of a marine company. The mass of people remained neither fragmented into multiple entities nor totally homogeneous. Waning intellectual support for racism, the New Deal's emphasis on equality and experimentation, the spread of education, and after 1940 the revival of social mobility sustained faith that civilization and liberty would coexist with democracy, that people would learn to live together while retaining their differences, find unity in diversity, if they could but imbue their political relationships with social justice.[69]

In those days, in the decades that tested life's chances, the uniforms no longer marked off the teams, and the players could not tell which side was which, or even what the game and what the rules were. They scurried about, victims "of corroding uneasiness, doubt and fear." Detached integers, some resolved to play it out—no matter why or how, and most in despair—going on for want of anything else to do. Art, the poets hoped, although without conviction, would order or at least resist the chaos.[70]

In the absence of defined common standards, people sought the guidance of diverse social, sectional and ethnic groups or went it alone—defiant individuals at war with ludicrous communal conventions. At the New York World's Fair (1939) they sought a glimpse of the rationally ordered "world of tomorrow," standardized, outfitted in new synthetic fibers, in which even Chanel aimed at the mass market. And the weekly movie tried to form their judgments—sinister men were recognized by the mustaches. But though an "overproduction of organizations" tried to shape their views, they made up their own minds and sought fulfillment through doing what they considered right, just like the cowboys on the silver screen. Whatever the odds against them, they flew their own course. They might lose in the end. But they considered the flight worth making, for the process not the reward mattered. Appeals to individualism therefore resonated on into the 1930s and 1940s, not as political programs but as expressions of deep personal needs for autonomy. In *Casablanca* (1943), Humphrey Bogart emerges from his cynical isolation only through his love affair with Ingrid Bergman, which evokes the desire to sacrifice for a greater cause.[71]

The greatest hero in the history of the human race: fifty-five thousand telegrams agreed with the *New York World.* The feat moved even President Coolidge—silent Cal—to eloquence. Thirty-five hours in the air, nonstop New York to Paris, alone in space above the endless ocean. Between two worlds. Master of the machine. Lone eagle who by will and daring soared in the culminating American adventure. Others had flown the Atlantic before he did in 1927, but solitude made him the absolute individual his country people wished to be. Pre-eminent among celebrities—among those who stood out from the mass on stage, screen, or playing field—because he flew all alone and became what they only dreamed of being, as did Amelia Earhart later and less successfully. Nothing held them down; self-propelled, they moved in response to inner impulses, obeyed codes of their own making, and came through because they wanted to. Or so they wished to believe. Therefore they lost interest in such issues as health and unemployment insurance and old-age pensions, out of fear lest the individual become dependent upon society for security. Like Zane Grey's lone cowboy, hopelessly in love, they preferred to ride off alone, undefeated. Those who sought to escape the bondage to addiction did so most effectively in a setting that protected their autonomy, as in Alcoholics Anonymous.[72]

Not much later, a famous kidnapping introduced Lucky Lindy to tragedy.

Loneliness remained the price of individualism. Having lost the way in the dark, with nothing to escape from and nothing to escape to, always alone, they asked where to go in a world of insanity, anywhere on the other side of despair. What a need for love and communal solidarity the printed pages and flickering images expressed! Never far beneath the surface of the lines in Frost, Cummings, and Eliot resounded the cry of the man or woman incomplete for want of love. And the nostalgic reminiscences of childhood summoned up memories of the kindness of life sustained by family affections. By contrast, old age knew the ache of ungrateful children. The hero who rejected Main Street, home and family, church and clan, all the associations that pinned a person down, also lost their support.[73]

America liberated individuals by offering them hope of self-fulfillment. But the striving also destroyed the sheltering community and disordered the imprisoning family.

> Two people who know they do not understand each other,
> Breeding children whom they do not understand
> And who will never understand them.

With freedom came solitude and uncertainty, which drove people to seek group solidarity beneath the Klan sheets or military uniform or in the suburban bungalow. Was it the meaning of progress thus to set people adrift alone? For the hollow men, that seemed

> . . . the way the world ends
> Not with a bang but a whimper (1925).[74]

Some writers in desperation yielded to hopelessness. Others, lost, nevertheless hoped they would be found. "The life we have fashioned in America and which has fashioned us was self-destructive in its nature and must be destroyed. The enemy was simple selfishness and compulsive greed, old as time and evil as hell. These forms are dying and must die." The country and its people, deathless, undiscovered, remained immortal.[75]

That one who took shelter under the bridge in the shadows, pondering the meaning of social justice, resolved to proceed with no illusions. This was the glory of earth-born men and women, never to yield, but standing, to take defeat implacable and defiant. In this hard star-adventure, knowing not what the fires meant, nor whether any meaning was intended or presumed, people could stand up and look out blind, and say: *all those turning lights offer no clue, only a masterless night, and no certain answers.* Yet their hearts cried out toward something dim in distance, higher than they. And they became emperors of the endless dark even in seeking (1935).

Or the other who left Montana to hug the Spanish earth and fought on in the hopeless battle, with at the end only the dying at which he was no good at all. But as long as Robert Jordan knew what he had to do, he could wait. Let them come! He could fulfill himself (1940). In a world only slightly responsive to his wishes, the individual could do no more than struggle to fulfill his personality as best he could. A novel that began by asserting that no man was an island unto himself concluded that in the end each had to light his own way in the darkness.[76]

Such affirmations, in their echoes of the Emersonian divine spirit, in the 1930s deeply moved some Americans. With less certainty than their ancestors, but with determination, they wished only to be left alone to explore the meaning and to discover themselves.

But the great mass of men and women, like Joe Christmas, could not face up to man's doomed rebellion against himself; they either embraced violence or just drifted as they half-listened to the radio's blared crooning. For a long time they took pride in describing themselves as yea-sayers—to use Nietszche's phrase—but found nothing to say yea to.[77]

The war gave them an affirmation. In the bonding of battle the Jewish boy discovered the faith that he would not have to go home to face anti-Semitism alone.

> trust begets power and faith is
> an affectionate thing. We
> vow, we make this promise
>
> to the fighting—it's a promise—
> "We'll
> never hate black, white, red, yellow, Jew
> Gentile, Untouchable."
>
> The world's an orphan's home
>
> If these great patient dyings
>
> can teach us how to live, these
> dyings were not wasted.

The writings of a few Existentialists, notably Sartre and Camus, that trickled across the Atlantic after 1945 therefore evoked echoes among some intellectuals not so much for the philosophical speculations about being and nothingness as for the bleak vision of no exit from the human dilemma. But most Americans drifted toward a more accommodating stance. Optimistic social scientists outlined reforms needed for a better world. Every social limitation, whether of race, class, or sex, would go, along with "every social institution which teaches human beings to cringe to those above and step on those below." People needed to learn "to look each other in the face." More realistically, *The Caine Mutiny,* a popular best-seller, play, and movie, would soon (1954) set off the mad Captain Queeg, who almost brought his vessel to disaster, against the introspective intellectual, Lieutenant Keefer, who found a loophole in the regulations in order to save the ship. Not Queeg but Keefer proved the villain. "The idea is, once you get an incompetent ass as a skipper there's nothing to do but serve him as though he were the wisest and the best, cover his mistakes, keep the ship going, and bear up. Only discipline and obedience to authority could bring them through trying times."[78]

In the pursuit of life's chances, of course, the losers paid the price of defeat. But the winners got little joy from victory.

In 1919 the solitary people of Winesburg—grotesque emotional cripples, their lives distorted by the inability to express themselves or communicate with others—longed to get away, felt themselves tossed about by the wind like the winged maple seeds of April or the dry autumn leaves. Back then, the prospect of escape persisted—to a lost past or to a promised future.[79]

A generation later in Los Angeles (1939), no further west remained, only the blank despair of a promised land, a world of sunshine and oranges, a well of sickness and despondency, where nothing happened. All their lives they had slaved at some dull, heavy labor, behind desks and counters, in the fields, and at tedious machines, saving their pennies and dreaming of leisure when they finally had enough. At last that day came. . . . Once in California, they discovered that sunshine was not enough and they lacked the mental equipment to enjoy leisure. Did they slave so long just to go to an occasional picnic, return to the Mexican ranch houses, Samoan huts, Mediterranean villas, Egyptian and Japanese temples, Swiss chalets and Tudor cottages that lined the Hollywood hills? (Hard to laugh at the need for beauty and romance, no matter how tasteless, even horrible, the results; but easy to sigh at the sadness of the truly monstrous!) The dull yearning of their lives, under a steady diet of lynchings, murders, sex crimes, focused upon phantoms of excitement. If only a plane would crash once in a while so they could watch the passengers being consumed in a holocaust of flame.

But the planes never crashed.

Therein, the nadir in the slope to despair.

Disappointed people warped by desires with no satisfaction and by miseries with no cure discovered that the false promise was worse than the real pain. Swindled, suckers as well as sufferers, with life a miserable joke, they itched for apocalypse, for a great united front of screwballs and screwboxes to purify the land with a final act in which victims sought only to revenge themselves on other victims. Even that release they never got.[80]

PART II

LEVELING OUT:

1950–1970

CHAPTER 5

THE GREAT SOCIETY

TRACES OF THE DESPAIR that had permeated American society after the First World War persisted in the 1950s. But every decade suffered its own form of malaise. Worries after 1950 often turned upon specific social problems—crime, poverty, health, or family disorders—but also meshed with more general unease about the apparent lack of a national purpose. People who had experienced the trials and disappointment of the great crusade of 1917, who had suffered the frustrations of the Depression decade, and then had slipped into a second, greater war culminating in the trauma of Hiroshima, with good cause wondered where all their striving led. They remembered that the problem of economic order had remained unsolved at the time of Pearl Harbor and feared that its difficulties would recur. As the Stalinist peril loomed over Eastern Europe, Americans confronted unfamiliar questions about the meaning of the national experience, about issues taken for granted since the seventeenth century.[1]

Yet despair and hope proved closest kin.

Despite the Depression of the 1930s and a Second World War, the economy had acquired a new structure, scarcely noticed at the time. As a result, the realignment of productive forces in the 1950s and 1960s brought not a return to depression but affluence. An unprecedented abundance of goods poured into the society, no longer sloping downward, but at least leveling out. Scarcities approached an end, giving birth to the vision of a Great Society providing enough to all.

The unexpected outcome, however, created its own dilemmas. The change touched off an unprecedented and confusing expansion of liberty, challenging inherited notions of freedoms and rights. The millions affected reacted awkwardly to the consequences. A sense of uneasiness therefore persisted, as did social turbulence that erupted into disorder toward the end of the 1960s.

Growing numbers of Americans then confronted the contradictions inherent in their political egalitarianism and private enterprise system, each realm operating according to its own values. The one asserted that all citizens participated in a political process in which the "one man, one vote" formula assured all equality of results. The other promised only equality of opportunity, rewarding individuals according to their prudence, abilities, luck, and skills—with equality of results improbable.

The discrepancy troubled few. Polls revealed a sizable decrease in support for socialism and government ownership of industry in response to war experience and to developments in Europe. In the economic upsurge of the 1950s more Americans experienced social mobility, felt better off financially than ever before, developments that strengthened the core values credited with fostering growth, as did changing orientations in the labor force. The decline of unionism reflected the stronger position of the individual worker. Samuel Gompers's old quip that what the state could give, the state could also take away reflected a distrust of reliance on outside forces, while the new affluent society reaffirmed the values that emphasized success, as a measure of the capacity of all to act.

Old limits to growth dissolved. Although fears about scarcity actually grew, the economy began to use ever fewer natural resources to provide an ever-higher standard of living. Declining prices revealed how independent industry had become and how much processes other than the reworking of basic raw materials fueled the economy.

Nor did the market mechanism function altogether autonomously. Ever-greater investments in defense and the military budget, as well as increased welfare spending, supplemented the allocation of goods and services by private supply and demand. Postwar government expenditures had a built-in growth factor and continued to expand.

Meanwhile tax revenues also increased, although not as fast. The proportion of net national income paid in taxes rose from one-fifth in 1940 to one-third in the 1960s, so that nonmarket decisions governed a larger share of national income. Furthermore, since a major portion of the federal budget comprised relatively fixed costs, such as interest and Social Security benefits, expenditures persistently ran ahead of revenues and enlarged the national debt. Tax policy therefore became an increasingly effective mechanism for regulating private spending, affecting as it did the elasticity of disposable private income.

Postwar expansion also increased the burdens on state and local governments, which had curtailed spending during the war and now rapidly expanded schools and public services responding to urban sprawl, the population explosion, and ever-greater longevity, which meant that people lived longer and thus needed more care.

Government regulation also affected the marketplace. Wage and hour laws, labor and civil rights legislation, and eventually energy and environmental programs increasingly directed the use and distribution of property and income. Nevertheless, the overriding justification remained private property, a free market, and personal liberty—the basic elements of the American free enterprise system. Government intervention broadened the base and increased the growth and security of the private sector, so that the conflict between expanding central authority and personal liberty remained unobtrusive—war, welfare, and big government seemed to diminish as issues in public consciousness as the economy expanded toward abundance.

Slowly the manifestations of growth penetrated public consciousness. The perception gradually dawned that vast economic changes had transformed the world, and not in the anticipated downward fashion. Fearfully people contemplated an uncontrollable future. Yet the hazy shape of things to come also sparked talk of a new frontier and beyond it a great society. The citizens only guessed the nature of the transformation, but hoped that it would bring them closer to a general condition not only of freedom but also of equality—that is, of the universal ability to act.

Since the sixteenth century, some Europeans and many Americans had considered the New World a land of plenty. "O Beautiful, for spacious skies, / for amber waves of grain, / for purple mountains' majesty / above the fruited plain." Ample space and fertile soil then seemed the keys to abundance. In the twentieth century, industrialization and know-how replaced the older imagined sources of wealth.

What the rational planning of the New Deal and of the technocrats failed to achieve, the forced mobilization of combat succeeded in doing. The emphasis upon order born of necessity extended into peacetime; and reorganization of the whole economy followed. During the war, the navy had to build swiftly 750 housing units in Norfolk, Virginia. It asked William J. Levitt to do the job. Experience then persuaded him (in 1946) to construct 17,000 single-family homes for returning G.I.s that sold for $7,990 each. To keep prices low he used precise projections that took account of raw material costs and profit margins, but also of the demographics and the nature of the sites, as well as of more efficient construction methods. Similar mass-production techniques along with standardized kitchen appliances and heating, plumbing, and electrical fixtures multiplied such homes elsewere. And analogous technical planning transformed other branches of the productive system.[2]

Soaring population fueled expansion. The number of residents in the United States had grown by only seven percent in the 1930s, the lowest increase in history, confirming the demographers' dire prediction of declining birth rates and level and perhaps even falling population in the near future. That forecast proved wrong. The census of 1950 counted 151 million persons, an increase of fourteen percent over 1940; in 1960 the numbers rose to 179 million, an increase of eighteen percent; in 1970 they reached 203 million, up thirteen percent, and the trend showed every sign of continuing.

Immigration contributed only slightly to the increase. The tiny opening in the country's closed gates at first admitted but few European refugees. Cuban exiles who fled from the Castro regime after 1958 and migrants from Mexico and Canada added more. But the total between 1940 and 1960 never rose above three million a year. After 1965, more liberal policies and tolerance of undocumented entries added to the numbers, but not enough to affect the population explosion.

Growth stemmed not from events abroad but from a change in the native birth rate, which moved continuously higher until 1970. Despite the availability of contraceptive methods, the number of children in the household mounted. Young people married at an earlier age than before 1950 and they planned to bear offspring sooner and more frequently. The unexpected rise in the birth rate at first seemed a result of the war and of the pent-up demand for family life after 1930. But the baby boom did not subside; it generated an expanding population eager and able to consume shoes, toys, and rompers. The problem of the 1930s—insufficient demand—faded away.

Population expansion in the United States did not operate as a drag on the society as it had in nineteenth-century Ireland or twentieth-century India. Americans used the new numbers to create wealth. A growing percentage found productive employment on terms that enabled them to purchase the output of the farms and factories. The total labor force grew from sixty-three million in 1950 to seventy-two million in 1960 and to eighty-five million in 1970. Furthermore, those people worked more productively and for higher remuneration than formerly. The number occupied in agriculture declined drastically, while that in manufacturing went up moderately, and that in services, professions, finance, and government jumped sharply. The count of white-collar jobs therefore increased while blue-collar jobs did not; and everyone gained in efficiency by the shift from low- to high-yield work.

The rise in per-capita income, although unequally distributed, expanded purchasing power. Some twenty percent of the population in the 1960s lacked enough for necessities without assistance; another twenty percent, somewhat better off, used their income for rent and food, with little left over. But fully sixty percent enjoyed enough to make discretionary purchases. Together, rich and poor mobilized enormous buying capacity.

The complex relationship between low income and the economy emerged in Tunica County, Mississippi, which ranked lowest in level of well-being in the United States. In 1960, fully eighty percent of its households fell below the poverty level; yet more than fifty percent possessed television sets, more than forty-five percent automobiles, and more than thirty-five percent washing machines. Even the very poorest thus joined the army of consumers expanding the internal market for American goods. In 1970, in per-capita number of cars, television sets, and telephones, the United States far outdistanced all other countries.

Abundance diminished further the importance of income disparities. Always more egalitarian in politics than in economics, Americans had affirmed radical equality in government while tolerating inequality in fortunes. The democratic device of universal suffrage did not destroy but ignored economic classes.

The outpouring of goods after the war left untouched the tension between political and economic equality and their relationship to the capacity to act. As of 1960 Americans willingly accepted that tension. As a result, a system utterly committed to fostering political equality left the question of economic equality in abeyance. In expenditures for Social Security and income maintenance, and in the progressiveness of the income tax, the United States usually ranked low among the nations. Having decided that government intervention failed to reduce inequalities meaningfully, most Americans seemed content to leave it at that.[3]

The appearance of a global economy within which capital and commodities circulated with some freedom promptly affected the American productive system. In the 1940s, only the United States could meet urgent military requirements and then provide for postwar reconstruction, relief, and rehabilitation. Markets once opened for those purposes remained available after the peace, while reform of the monetary system facilitated trade and investment. The imperatives of postwar recovery thrust leadership upon Washington. Former allies like Britain and France and former foes like Germany and Japan lay in ruins. All expected aid from the one modern productive system that had survived intact. Americans also understood the desirability of overseas help. With poverty the breeding ground of Communism, countries that failed swiftly to regain their strength might collapse and yield to the Soviets. The replacement of one totalitarianism by another would then prove the ironic outcome of victory. President Truman considered recovery essential to democracy and therefore an impediment to aggression. These views culminated in the Marshall Plan, which provided the means for West European reconstruction.[4]

After 1950, the newly independent nations of Asia and Africa, unprepared to stand alone, also called for help. The United States, having pressed its allies to liberate their colonies, felt obliged to aid, in the naïvely optimistic expectation that all would shortly follow the Western course of modernization. Political expediency also made Latin American countries beneficiaries of assistance, although they had gained independence a century or more earlier. In an assumption of breathtaking boldness, product of pure American faith, policymakers crowded into a single category the Indian Brahmins, the Arabian Sheiks, Congolese tribesmen, and Argentine cattlemen. The category "underdeveloped" implied that any society, any culture, any political order, if nudged in the right direction, could evolve a self-sustaining industrial system. The substantial sums provided rarely achieved the permanent reforms the rhetoric enunciated. But they had at least a palliative effect in suffering regions. A galaxy of private voluntary organizations, heirs of the old missionary tradition, supplemented the work of government agencies.[5]

Military considerations after the outbreak of war in Korea affected some aid programs, but the basic purpose, of easing the free flow of capital and commodities, endured. Between 1945 and 1951 the United States delivered to other countries some $118 billion in goods and services and received in return some $69 billion. About 60 percent of the deficit went as a gift, the remainder on long-term credit. And Europe and Japan, having cleared away the wreckage of war, rebuilt their factories and restored their fields; commercial links forged by aid thereafter gained strength. At the suggestion of the United States, twenty-three nations in 1947 joined in a General Agreement on Tariffs and Trade (GATT) to lower international barriers. The number of participating countries grew, and successive rounds of bargaining produced perceptible relaxation of the restraints upon the global flow of goods.

With aid came American ideas and practices—of political democracy, of personal rights, and of human dignity. The ultimate objective, not always articulated, amounted to the diffusion of liberty by fending off totalitarian threats and by restraints on popular folly and immorality. The attractiveness of certain American ideals prevailed despite objections from intellectuals offended by Coca-Colazation and fearful that democratic notions merely covered up capitalist rapacity, and also from social scientists who followed Max Weber in the insistence that each culture could only pursue its own distinctive social vision. Though the Third World occasionally resisted the spread of America's political versions of liberty, the popularity of cultural exports such as movies, music, lifestyles, and fashions assured the potentially subversive impact of freedom even in countries hostile to its very premises.[6]

Increasingly, as a matter of necessity, the world depended on farm products from the United States. The European and Asian markets opened in the immediate postwar years at first offered only temporary relief, as in 1918 and 1919. Braced for a recurrence of old problems, the government continued to guarantee incomes at parity, to export or store excess commodities, and to distribute some to the needy. But population increases everywhere created would-be buyers of food to stave off hunger and of cotton and wool for clothing. The period of international surpluses had ended; that of shortages had opened.

All producers of primary materials gained, but especially the American growers of grains and fibers, flexible and efficient enough to profit from the dramatic expansion of markets. The primitive Oregon chicken farm lightheartedly described in Betty MacDonald's *The Egg and I* quickly became a nostalgic memory like Jefferson's yeoman or the populists' tiller of the soil, replaced by machines and chemical fertilizers, pesticides and synthetic feeds, and Frank Perdue. Decades of government subsidies had provided small producers with the means either to sell out or to expand and modernize. In 1970 agriculture occupied only four percent of the labor force. The farm population declined from almost twenty-five million in 1950 to about nine million in 1970, while the number of holdings went down from about six million to fewer than three million. Meanwhile the average size rose, as did productivity—yields of corn and wheat per acre soared.[7]

Agriculture adjusted successfully to changing domestic food habits and to the appearance of synthetic fibers; mechanization transformed cotton cultivation in the Southwest; the semen-producing business and new patterns of stock breeding based on genetics met increased demands for milk and meat; frozen foods and advanced processing methods brought fruits, vegetables, dairy products, and poultry to consumers swiftly and efficiently. Technology became central, not only for the contract growers of tomatoes and chickens, geared to the factory, but also for those who raised corn and even cherries for sale in big-city markets. The rising output and improved strains of sorghum for forage demonstrated the adaptability of Great Plains farming. The soybean became a source of oil and meal. In the late 1960s, Illinois, Iowa, and Indiana annually raised on forty million acres about a billion bushels (two-thirds of the world's total), worth $2.6 billion.[8]

Vastly improved distribution strengthened the economy. The national highway network and air-freight systems sent goods swiftly and cheaply to computerized warehouses; even the ailing railroads effectively modernized nonpassenger services. Chains of supermarkets, department stores, and discount houses transmitted cans and packaged goods to consumers efficiently enough to keep living costs from rising despite persistent inflation and intrusive government regulation. The number of intermediaries between consumers and producers shrank, further streamlining the economy, despite hostile federal legislation and five hundred antichain bills introduced in statehouses across the country.[9]

Experience taught Americans not to clutch at the proven past in order to preserve their liberty but to expand their ability to act by adapting to totally new conditions. They did so.

After the war, novel forms of manufacturing and new services augmented efficiency and convenience and provided an ever-increasing share of the nation's productivity, in terms of value added and employees supported. Expectations that artificial intelligence would replace human labor failed as yet to materialize, but computers dramatically speeded up information processing. Moreover, their fabrication itself became an important element in American output. So, too, Haloid, a small, family-owned photographic paper manufacturer in 1946 acquired the rights to the process developed at the Battelle Memorial Institute, spent millions on development, and in 1959 marketed the first Xerox automatic copying machine with sales that rose steadily in the next decade, as it pioneered new marketing techniques such as lease-rental arrangements. Civilian aircraft, space, avionics, defense, chemicals, and pharmaceuticals also created new sources of value and spurred industrialization on the Pacific Coast and along the Gulf of Mexico. The total number of employed workers swelled from sixty-three million in 1950 to eighty-four million in 1970. Meanwhile, fast-food chains, Laundromats, and household appliances eased the burden of domestic labor, and freed all family members but particularly women for entry into the paid labor market.[10]

Since the 1930s, American calculations had turned upon the expectation of stability, discounting entirely the possibility of growth. After

1945, fears persisted that the rate of increase of output might not keep up with that of Japan and Germany or that unemployment would rise. Yet the gross national product zoomed from $7.9 billion in 1950 to $11.7 billion in 1970 (in constant 1982 dollars), a rise that helped offset the effects of persistent inflation. By tinkering with fiscal policy, the government could moderate changes in output and in the rate of unemployment.[11]

Expansion gained force from persistent entrepreneurship encouraged by a steady rise in corporate profits—from less than $50 billion in 1960 to more than $82 billion in 1966. Wildcatters—people who believed that the human will could overcome any obstacles—drifted about in search of a lucky strike, animated by the faith that they would get the most from life by doing whatever they did enthusiastically. Edwin Land, who never graduated from college, proceeded from a simple invention using polarized light to elaborate a large enterprise. Menachem Riklis explored the potentialities of arranging conglomerates that shifted capital and management resources from one area to another. People who retired searched for new ventures, as did Armand Hammer, who thought his business career had ended when he moved to California in 1956 only to wander off into a new life in Occidental Petroleum. Or Harland Sanders, who launched a nationwide food chain (Kentucky Fried Chicken) at the age of sixty-five.

New arrangements encouraged the venturesome. Franchises grouped independent managers in plans that involved local capital and only limited central control, and were therefore more flexible and more responsive to neighborhood conditions than the chain stores. Supermarkets of once-unimaginable size replaced old retailing arrangements, particularly when malls attracted customers away from the Main Street shops. Discounters who handled an ever-larger percentage of trade had the same effect. The "knowledge revolution" that transformed the nation's occupational structure, doubling the number engaged in professional and technical jobs between 1940 and 1964, further altered the economic landscape as did automation, the effort to produce as much as possible with as little human input as possible.[12]

Mammoth scale raised disconcerting questions about the freedom of people enveloped in vast impersonal shops and plants, much the same everywhere. The goods poured out, but sometimes swamped little enterprises unable to compete. The neighborhood grocer and the butcher known to their customers disappeared, replaced by large impersonal bureaucratic firms in which faceless employees dealt with anonymous purchasers. The family unit, the only haven of genuine intimacy, alone still recognized the human being. Elsewhere, whether working at the bench or buying at the counter, the individual discovered that the necessities of mass production qualified the ability to choose. Neither cries of "chain-store menace" nor the Merchants' Minute Men and congressional investigations succeeded in stemming the tide. As in the past, the chain stores generated mixed feelings, since they undermined the foundation of local prosperity by destroying home markets and merchants, "leaving behind about as much as a traveling band of gypsies." But the economies of scale prevailed, and the ability to acquire a wider variety of goods cheaply and efficiently compensated for the drawbacks.

But did the liberty to act widen or contract as jobs and goods came within reach—in forms, colors, tastes, and prices dictated from elsewhere? Did older definitions of liberty apply in the postindustrial era when white-collar workers for the first time outnumbered their blue-collar counterparts? Were people freed from the need to scrounge around to satisfy basic needs really more liberated when offered a vast new array of goods, services, and products designed to enhance the quality of life? No one yearned for a return to the hunger of the 1930s, but abundance after 1950 encouraged more than one-half of American adults to count calories, embarking on one diet after another and exercising to keep fit, be happy.[13]

Overseas involvement after 1950 spread beyond the realms of politics and diplomacy, infusing the whole economy, profoundly affecting the well-being and therefore the liberty of all residents of the United States.

American businessmen had at first shied away from foreign adventures, even in Canada and Latin America. Abundant openings at home and unhappy memories of prewar expropriations discouraged distant adventures. With conditions unstable everywhere, no one could predict what regimes would take power or when recovery would come. Oil, mining, and airline companies had to take the risk; and subsidiaries and affiliates already established reinvested their earnings. But no one else rushed to plant additional good money in alien soil.

The return of stability to Europe and Japan after 1950 eased anxieties about property rights. New consumer markets broadened out, and manufacturers, ready to take advantage of low wages elsewhere, or unwilling by expanding at home to tangle with the antitrust laws, or eager to defend their markets against the effects of tariffs or exchange controls, acquired overseas subsidiaries and set up offshore plants. People who had served in the armed forces overseas or had become familiar with foreign cultures through academic fellowships provided the personnel. In 1970 the book value of direct investments outside the country had risen to $78.1 billion, about thirty percent in Canada, about thirty percent in Europe, about seventeen percent in Latin America, and the balance in Asia, Africa, and Australia. Increasingly European, Canadian, and Japanese firms established or acquired offshoots in the United States; the value of such direct investments amounted, in 1970, to $13 billion. In addition, foreign individuals then held $18 billion in shares in American corporations.[14]

The movement of capital into the country and out of it invigorated the multinational corporation, operating through subsidiaries in many parts of the world, recruiting management, labor, and funds everywhere, its attention focused on global rather than parochial concerns. Such enterprises did not displace the authority of governments, but instead created incentives to international political collaboration and spread American values.

The example of a single large firm revealed the complexity of such operations. In 1972 its annual report showed that Union Carbide—large, but by no means the largest company of its kind—produced over eight hundred different chemicals and numerous plastics, gases, and batteries in addition to managing some nuclear establishments for the United States government. It held majority shares of subsidiaries in the United Kingdom, Canada, Belgium, Germany, Greece, France, Italy, Spain, Sweden, Australia, Hong Kong, India, Indonesia, Japan, Malaysia, New Zealand, Pakistan, the Philippines, Iran, South Africa, the Ivory Coast, Kenya, Rhodesia, Norway, Brazil, Ghana, Sri Lanka, Singapore, Argentina, Colombia, Costa Rica, Ecuador, Mexico, and Venezuela. In addition, it owned minority shares of five companies in Japan, of two each in France, the United Kingdom, and Thailand, and of one each in Belgium, Spain, South Africa, and Sweden. In the United States it employed fifty-one thousand persons directly and fifteen thousand more on behalf of the government; abroad, its payrolls bore more than fifty-nine thousand names. It took special skill and personality to deal with buyers, sellers, the advertising media, bankers, and state and local governments worldwide.

Such operations grew in complexity. The overseas subsidiary managed by local personnel acquired its own identity, reached out for raw materials, and fought for sales where it could find them, sometimes establishing autonomous offshoots. The foreign branches of a single parent company might well battle one another for customers in third countries—the English Ford-Dagenham against the German Ford-Köln in Switzerland, for instance. Only control over basic capital decisions from United States headquarters held the widely scattered branches together.

The ability to act no longer adhered to a single imperial entrepreneur, a Rockefeller, Carnegie, or Ford. Instead hundreds of persons, within defined spheres, enjoyed fragments of liberty.

The central place of the dollar in these far-flung transactions spurred the international activity of American banks. In 1970 more than fifty major firms financed trade and investment; and even those of medium size far from the principal centers joined in consortia for operations outside the country. In all, in 1970 the 536 overseas branches of U.S. banks controlled assets of $52.6 billion, much of that sum free of effective regulation by any authority.[15]

Along with the flow of dollars went advanced technology, management techniques, and marketing methods, so that United States manufacturers occasionally found it advantageous to import from abroad goods made by their own subsidiaries; and sales from foreign affiliates to third countries occasionally diminished the market for American-made exports. Some trade unions resented the trend, which, they believed, deprived their members of jobs. General Motors Opels sold in New York or Mexico City seemed to take wages away from workers in Michigan. But the Opel competed not with the Cadillac or even the Chevrolet but with the Volkswagen or Fiat; and the corporation only covered its flanks against rivalry it could not avoid. Two important sources of gain offset any losses to the national economy—the reverse movement to the United States of branches of advanced German, Japanese, and British firms, and the income Americans derived from foreign investments, which climbed in 1968 to $8 billion. On through the 1960s, the voyagers among the continents carried, along with their bulging attaché cases and their worries about jet lag, the vision of a single global economy inherited from an earlier business generation.[16]

Structural transformations made American industry competitive. The great corporations of 1970 differed in size, form, and spirit from their predecessors. Capitalization of more than a billion dollars no longer seemed exceptional, as it had at the foundation of United States Steel in 1900. The annual sales of many companies amounted to more than that sum. New patterns of behavior developed. The tendency toward concentration, after declining during the Depression, regained force after 1950, but no longer through the simple spread of a single enterprise either vertically or horizontally. In 1952 Royal Little, head of Textron, which had thrived through the war manufacturing yarns, worried about the limited opportunities for expansion in textiles. He picked up small firms in electronics, cement, aluminum, paint, plywood, leather, and aerospace, many stagnant but, he hoped, subject to rejuvenation under new management. Other entrepreneurs followed. The corporation had long since lost its identification with an individual; now it also lost its identification with a static product. Instead it became a device for manipulating investment capital, combining disparate activities in vast conglomerates.

These complex aggregations sometimes encouraged their components to greater efficiency, sometimes concealed costly waste. In the one case, outside influence cut through ingrown bureaucracies and habits to improve performance. In the other, rules imposed from above inhibited initiative, delayed decisions, and covered up failures. Change then ultimately required a violent purge. Either course altered the risks of enterprise. The book publishing and car rental firms acquired by RCA reduced its dependence on the sales of television and radio receivers and on broadcasting revenues and enabled it to absorb losses from a daring and disastrous venture into computers until General Electric ultimately swallowed it up. The promise of stability and long-term growth attracted investors not primarily interested in quick profits and particularly the mutual and pension funds, which in 1970 held about forty percent (in value) of the shares listed on the New York Stock Exchange. Some great enterprises generated their own capital on the security markets; others used banks and insurance companies; but none could afford to sink into pachydermatous lethargy, lest a ravenous outsider overtake and devour it. Growth—the only means of survival—demanded sensitivity to opportunity and responsiveness to change.

The technological side effects of war gave mechanization a new form. In the past, machines replaced skilled with unskilled labor. Ever more often now automatically triggered controls responded to instructions received electronically from stored data and functioned without human intercession. Modern petrochemical plants, for instance, used few workers, skilled or unskilled, other than technicians who monitored the machines. Automation turned laborers into replaceable or dispensable parts. More sophisticated electronic, computer, and nuclear instruments generated intricate adjustments. Knowledge and information became pivotal to economic development; wisdom lagged, with ambiguous consequences for liberty.

The labor force changed drastically. The number of places for the unskilled shrank, even in construction. By contrast, areas in which jobs expanded required technically competent employees—in health care, computer programming, research, office work, and mechanics—all dependent on some formal education distinct from the old patterns of apprenticeship. The dramatic increase in the number of municipal, state, and federal employees after 1950 also came in the white-, not blue-collar ranks. As a result, unionization grew in the public rather than in the private industrial sector. Prudent young people therefore stayed in school, delaying entry into the ranks of wage earners. Those who dropped out rarely got a second chance. Furthermore, the decline of hazardous employment diminished the risk of crippling and disabling accidents, thus extending the expectation of full-time work into old age, usually defined arbitrarily at sixty-five following a convention inherited from Bismarckian Germany. Expectations changed of the point at which people attained the peak of their power—therefore of their liberty—from their twenties and thirties to their forties and fifties. The Social Security system expanded to include in old-age insurance programs groups formerly left out; after 1960 such income transfers began to constitute the fastest growing share of the national budget.

Each decade seemed to replicate its predecessor's experience, as economic restructuring that eliminated some industries while evolving others took its toll on the labor force. Jobs lost would never come back when idled plants shut down for good. Downsizing taught workers who had come to identify their jobs with middle-class prosperity the hazards of private enterprise in a global economy. Labor unions lost some of their power while a new managerial class acquired a new personality—dehumanized, antiindividualistic, less aggressive, and less self-assertive. Yet the critical indices remained favorable: rising life expectancy, declining infant mortality, and a lessening of income inequalities.[17]

Heavy expenditures for research and development sustained change. Government grants and contracts supplemented the resources from private corporate sources. The Bell System, Eastman Kodak, and other large enterprises had early perceived the advantage of moving beyond narrow product improvement to the sponsorship of broad, open-ended scientific investigations. During the war, administrators learned that scientific advances increased profits and that liberally defined research enhanced the chance of success. Texas Instruments (1951), an outgrowth of seismographic oil exploration, arranged with Bell to manufacture transistors and then broadened its line to semiconductors, calculators, integrated circuits, and aircraft control and guidance systems. Managers in such firms less often reckoned efficiency by the mechanical criteria of the stopwatch and more often took account of human factors, as Elton Mayo in the 1920s had recommended. Liberty accorded employees paid off in enhanced productivity.[18]

The new environment required profound industrial reorganization.

The megaplants of earlier decades proved cumbersome. Great postwar corporations divided production processes among numerous branches supplying several assembly plants, or relied upon subcontractors, gaining in flexibility by encouraging small feeder firms that experimented with new techniques. Young men and women with bright ideas attracted venture capital to develop profitable peripheral products. The initial dominance of the computer field by a single large corporation did not curtail the ease of launching new hardware and software devices. The upwardly mobile thus came into their own, using growth to enhance their liberty.

Small companies sought the ability to act by imitating the management style of larger ones. The tough entrepreneur, frugal saver, daring risk-taker, who ran at the fringes of the pack hoping to tear off a prize as proof of personal prowess, belonged to a vanishing species. Wildcatters still roamed the industrial scene. But the great rewards now lay in a subcontract or in takeover by a big outfit, earned in the same way as advancement within the firm—by efficient and unassertive work within a group. The quintessential organization man gained in freedom through a personal contribution within the larger scheme of things. Prepared to deal with colleagues, customers, suppliers, bankers, and regulatory officials in a variety of languages, he also thrived on conformity, eschewed subversive proposals or ideas, opted for security over adventurism and for steady profits over spectacular windfalls. His capacity to act became in fact vastly greater than that of his predecessors but to academic observers he seemed the most constrained of all, because the objective of orderly, predictable expansion had replaced that of the dramatic, spectacular haul.

Enlarged scale, enlarged risk. The wonderful plant churning out vast quantities depended on buyers to carry off its products. Sophisticated market research tested consumer preferences and elaborate advertising prepared the field. Without sensitive feedback to alert managers to unforeseen shifts in taste that halted the flow, unwanted products could drown the firm in red ink, as Ford discovered in a $350 million Edsel mistake. Corporations also had to learn to target their most likely customers and change product lines to meet shifting needs. In an earlier era when the aged ranked among the poor, it made sense to go after younger consumers more likely to spend on upscale products. Advertising strategies then ignored those over fifty on the assumption that luxury items did not interest the elderly, set in their ways, physically infirm, and less consumer-oriented than their younger counterparts. But alterations in consumption patterns after 1950 revealed the instability of the national wealth structure, complicating all economic forecasts.[19]

Changing attitudes also entailed acceptance of unprecedented social responsibility. Corporations set up educational and philanthropic foundations, supported community funds, the Red Cross, and neighborhood projects not only as good public relations—tax deductible, at that—but also as expressions of a redefined understanding of the enterprise as an institution that enlisted employees, stockholders, and subcontractors in a common effort using full-page advertisements not only to sell products but also to establish an identity and to offset antibusiness bias in the nation's leading newspapers. Planted articles also served the same end.

Novel environmental requirements and growing consciousness about scarce resources broadened corporate horizons. As consumers of raw materials, often extracted at destructive costs, their managers felt compelled to generate greater understanding and to overcome the endemically hostile attitude of conservationists. Corporations subsidized symphony orchestras, sponsored park concerts, and financed television series in an effort to stake out a place in the mainstream for their contribution to the general capacity to act, and to counter the prejudices of elite culture.

Rational organization opened up the business environment. Racial and religious prejudice persisted, yet slowly but steadily old patterns of discrimination eroded. The pool of talent from which managers sprang broadened. Some individuals still gained prominence through inherited wealth, windfalls, or speculative gain. But increasingly the top corporate executives moved up by competition through a graded hierarchy. In 1899 sixty percent had started as independent proprietors, in 1960 only fifteen percent. Family and group ties influential for Andrew Carnegie's generation lost importance in the business bureaucracy after 1950.

Objectives shifted subtly. Since impersonal enterprises did not identify their welfare with that of an individual owner, personality clashes intruded upon decisions less often than formerly. The quest for autonomy, stability, and long-term growth favored managers most adept at accommodating the prevailing political and social forces without costly conflicts, regarding government less as an enemy than as a potential collaborator. The new types stressed the public character and responsibilities of the corporation and recognized the legitimate interests of other social groups, conceding labor's right to organize and to bargain collectively. Warfare between employers and employees subsided after the wave of strikes in 1945. Stoppages became tactical instruments in a collaborative bargaining ritual rather than bitter-end weapons wielded by enemies out for mutual destruction—apart from such jurisdictional disputes as over which union should install false bosoms in actresses' gowns. The once belligerent United Mine Workers after 1950 cooperated with employers to mechanize the coal fields in the face of competition from rival fuels. Some companies paternalistically offered their employees stock-ownership and profit-sharing plans, cafeterias, group insurance, medical services, and vacations. Unionization drives enlisted more women, but the changing composition of the work force drained away the power of organized labor. Between 1945 and 1960 the organized portion of the country's nonagricultural workers fell by fourteen percent while the union leadership came to resemble its erstwhile antagonists in middle-class orientation and search for security and stability.[20]

Productivity mounted steadily, although rapid social change complicated statistical comparisons with the past because goods once free became scarce, and services once performed in the household more often involved cash transactions. Internal tourism and travel abroad testified to a changing lifestyle, as did the boats parked in backyards and the private swimming pools dotting the suburbs. National parks and amusement areas like Disneyland met the demand for affordable leisure. The additional paycheck brought home by the working wife provided money for dining out, better clothing, newer cars, and occasionally a second home for vacations.

The shifting boundaries between public and private domains altered the contours of liberty. Many functions once performed in the seclusion of one's castle acquired an open character, subject to novel regulations, requirements, and limitations. The Laundromat replaced the washtub and the fast-food counter the old tin lunchbox. Farmers became city dwellers, proprietors salaried employees, and consumers wanted leisure and goods that satisfied symbolic as well as physical needs. Although pockets of unemployment persisted, the economy's ability to provide a rising output of commodities generated a general impression of abundance.

Almost every year after the Second World War, the Gallup survey asked respondents, "What is the smallest amount of money a family of four needs each week to get along in this community?" After adjusting for inflation, the mean response had risen fifty percent between 1947 and 1979. Mean per-capita disposable income had also risen fifty percent. The conclusion was that popular definitions of "need" rose in tandem with what the average American already had. Moreover, the country put more money into education than into defense. From 1947 to 1957, 12.3 million young people acquired high school diplomas and 3.2 million received college degrees, while enrollment in graduate studies also increased. Education became one of the affordable necessities of life. Meanwhile the market for technologically trained youth seemed insatiable—over eight million new jobs existed at the end of the decade, more than had existed at its start, many of them in electronics, plastics, and computers—fields that had scarcely developed before. Airplanes broke the sound barrier and the United States stepped to the threshold of the space and atomic age, while observers predicted revolutionary transformations in the near future because of new materials, new products, new devices, and new methods.[21]

Few among the contented throng perceived, at once, the subtle intellectual and social adjustments that followed. Like those who clutched their tickets on the Disneyland people-movers, they knew that an unexpected treat awaited them but could only guess the surprise that sprang from economic changes few understood—neither leaders nor followers. People who ceased to regard scarcity as man's inescapable lot came to regard abundance as the dominant conditioning factor in the American environment.

That frame of mind encouraged high—and ever-expanding—mass consumption, stoked by incessant advertising and ever more elaborate ways of satisfying diverse tastes. Constantly reminded that the higher their expenditures, the faster the economy grew, people learned that the more they bought, the more everyone gained. Liberty became a double-edged sword; as indebtedness mounted, the capacity to act diminished, yet the variety and number of available choices created the impression of ever-wider and greater freedom. Fluidity and mobility in society proved congenial to habits of reckless spending. Morose critics then traced the failure of Western democracy to lack of clarity of purpose and resolution of mind along with the usurpation of power by popular assemblies.[22]

Changes in tastes and in art after 1950 followed the shift in values away from the virtue of prudent frugality and toward easy openhandedness. Once people got over the panic that induced them to invest in pre-fab air-raid shelters, they prepared to enjoy—but what? The television mirror offered distorted reflections; and discontinuity, fragmentation, and introversion characterized high culture, whether in the drama of Samuel Beckett or the paintings of Jackson Pollock and Mark Rothko.

As television became the dominant medium, critics judged it harshly, arguing that it reinforced the dominant ideology, fostered conformity, and foisted onto the hapless masses the domestic family orientation of the sitcoms, the patriarchal thrust of the cop shows, the imperialist ethos of the news programs, and the materialist mania of commercials, socializing the younger generation into the capitalist mind-set. It became a tool to engineer consent, not otherwise forthcoming, to the established order, with viewers deemed prisoners of captains of consciousness who fostered the myth of the happy middle-class family in order to swamp potential subversion and discontent. Such critics regarded television as a major shackle on the American psyche, none so deadly in keeping freedom under wraps.

Other social critics like Max Lerner claimed that television had become the poor man's luxury, a psychological necessity, its impact hard to measure. As the numbers of hours the set tuned in steadily climbed, worries mounted about passive couch potatoes absorbing mountains of intellectual trash—the cotton candy of the mind. Advertisers eager to reach large audiences shied away from controversial issues, and producers accommodated to the network needs. Frozen TV dinners introduced in 1954 signaled changing family patterns, determined not by the needs of camaraderie and togetherness but by viewing schedules.

But if television disappointed those who hailed its educational potential, it also for the first time brought the rest of the world into American living rooms. Working-class life formed the substance of "The Honeymooners." People who had never viewed a major league game before could see the World Series, while shows about American ethnic groups and serious drama like "Requiem for a Heavyweight," "The Days of Wine and Roses," "Marty," and "The Rainmaker" treated serious subjects and brought home to many problems they had not known even existed. "Now that the masses—that is, everybody—are getting into the act and making the scene, the problem of vulgarization has become acute." But such disdain for television, guilty of debasing taste, threatening serious art, and celebrating the kitsch of the mass cult, failed to assess its positive impact. Critics feared that its programming merely reconciled consumers to the status quo, serving the interests of capitalism with junk food for the mind, chewing gum for the eyes. But they failed to notice its liberating aspects, which helped eliminate the provincialism, the localism, and the ignorance of the wider world that once characterized the American public. It also turned outside political events into dramas acted out in the living room, in news broadcasts: the Army-McCarthy hearings thus helped attenuate the separation of the public and the private spheres.[23]

Politics adjusted slowly. Harry Truman, old school, moved gingerly until his dramatic election in 1948. He then called on Congress to provide Americans a fair deal by halting rising prices, ending the housing crisis, aiding education, establishing a national health program, enacting civil rights legislation, increasing the minimum wage, extending Social Security, and generating public power projects—all made possible by abundance. He described poverty as wasteful and unnecessary, like a preventable disease. And he believed that no prejudice or artificial distinction should bar any citizen of the United States of America from an education or from good health or from a job that he or she could perform. These pleas met with little response in the face of intransigent opposition in Congress and hostile campaigns by entrenched interests like the American Medical Association. The Kennedy and Johnson programs would revive these proposals.[24]

Dwight D. Eisenhower's avuncular administration after 1953 promised Americans a soothing interlude, despite rising mistrust of politicians and occasional eruptions of scandal. The system of government appeared unchanged—president/governor, Congress/legislature, courts—all neatly in their constitutional places, and parties, conventions, campaigns as well. But anxieties persisted.

Redistricting made necessary by the Supreme Court's insistence on "one man, one vote" made little immediate difference. Elections adjusted also to the requirements of the new communications media and especially of television, which brought candidates into voters' living rooms. Staged performances, as in Richard Nixon's Checkers speech and as in the evolving slick management of the nominating conventions, revealed the power of the medium. The 1960 debates demonstrated the importance of the image and inflated the role of manipulative advisers and handlers who manufactured a favorable impression. Population growth expanded the pool of potential voters, called for complex methods of sampling opinion, and increased the importance of intermediaries able to broker among diverse groups. The reflective citizen able rationally to decide on the basis of the issues faded away.[25]

The novel social context created subsurface turbulence. Increasingly legislators and administrative officials based decisions not only on their own appraisals but also on pressures from a burgeoning array of lobbyists, and a growing White House secretariat filtered out matters requiring the Chief Executive's attention. Military experience induced Eisenhower to rely on the judgment of an experienced chief-of-staff, reserving only the most important problems for the President. His successor surrounded himself with an assembly of the best and brightest minds, dazzling the nation with intellectual brilliance, a hard-nosed approach to problem-solving, and a sense of urgent activism. But their premises were not far removed from those of their less illustrious predecessors, many of whose programs they simply extended, prisoners of a set of government policies, economic agendas, and social and political preconceptions from which they could not shake themselves loose.[26]

Despite the reluctance of government to direct or control the productive system, federal and state action profoundly influenced the way in which people got and expended their incomes, whether during the Truman or later administrations. The war had situated the politicians on the commanding heights of the economy; and the demobilization euphoria left them responsible for full employment. Few challenged the faith that credit manipulation moderated the effects of business cycles. Decisions about the money supply and interest rates would ease the seemingly intractable forces that had formerly produced prosperity or depression, inflation or deflation, rising or falling prices. The level and type of taxes and the volume of public expenditures would also influence the pace of business activity.

The relationship of the federal government to the localities changed. During the entire Depression the New Deal administration had financed a total of 200,000 low-income apartments, mostly through existing state and municipal entities. Within the first four years after the war, Congress authorized the financing of 810,000 such flats. In 1949 Title I of the Federal Housing Act codified the new concept of urban renewal, which made Washington as important as city hall in urban reconstruction. High-rise projects then sprouted, monuments to the folly and thoughtlessness of good intentions, constructed without regard to the character of their future inhabitants. Shortly, Columbia Point in Boston and Pruitt-Igoe in St. Louis (demolished in 1972) proved totally uninhabitable.

The same transformation affected other large projects. Formerly, federal roads had run mostly through open countryside. But the Highway Act of 1944 authorized arterial routes within city limits as well as outside them, and the amount annually built soared until the Interstate Highway Act of 1956 added 6,700 miles to the networks. The role of the national bureaucracy broadened at the expense of municipal authorities, a characteristic trend. The number of federal, state, and local employees climbed from 8.3 million in 1960 to 15.4 million in 1970. Each weekday the *Federal Register* distributed sixty thousand substantial copies of agency regulations. In the United States, at all levels, government became one of the nation's largest employers, with the salary check a form of welfare that augmented the recipients' liberty through payments earned in gigantic bureaucracies which themselves operated to limit everybody else's ability to act.[27]

Having assumed responsibility for providing work to all who wished it, the officeholders modified free-market operations. The New Deal compromise over control survived; banks, fearful of inflation, and government, fearful of unemployment, checked each other. A running feud between the Federal Reserve Board and the Treasury produced an unspoken understanding. However much politicians wanted expansion, the board could check inflation by raising interest rates. Conversely, budgetary deficits and the Treasury's open market operations could offset restrictive credit policies when the admnistration desired. Down through the 1960s, moderation kept joblessness at about four percent of the growing labor force; inflation slowed when industrial output climbed, supplies caught up with demand, and shortages ended. Rising prices in time diminished the value of fixed incomes and of safe bonds and savings accounts, shifting capital into more productive, although more risky, channels.

Government action, however, did not lock Americans into rigid centralized planning or concentrate power at any single point of control. True, the President's annual economic report set forth the administration's agenda. But in fact, the Treasury, Commerce, Defense, Labor, and Agriculture departments operated with their own economic models, as did the Federal Reserve and the regulatory agencies. In addition, the Joint Economic Committee of the Congress had its own staff and views, as did particular House and Senate committees. Those groups also influenced legislation and appropriations. Then, too, banks, universities, the Brookings Institution, the National Bureau of Economic Research, and various think tanks generated a mass of intelligence that supplemented, ran parallel to, or challenged that emanating from bureaucratic sources. Economists peddled information and ideas as they shuttled among public and private agencies, compounding the difficulty of adopting and executing any policy. The data to support or oppose any line of action always lay readily at hand, exploited by specialized or general pressure groups. To compensate, looseness and tentativeness made the planning apparatus sensitive to change.[28]

After 1950, fear failed to elicit direct controls over prices, wages, profits, and commodities such as had served during the war. Eisenhower certainly preferred private action, as when he chose the Dixon-Yates combine rather than the TVA to supply power to Memphis or when he transferred offshore oil lands to the states. The government only rarely invoked the Taft-Hartley Act (1947) to intervene in labor negotiations, but preferred to act as broker between national unions and employers to arrive at bargains acceptable to consumers. Efforts to enact right-to-work laws that would protect nonunion workers floundered.

The regulatory agencies also defined their responsibilities narrowly, although the Interstate Commerce Commission, the Federal Trade Commission, the Food and Drug Administration, and the Environmental Protection Agency assembled vast bureaucracies remote from popular control or responsibility. Constant activity in Washington conveyed a sense of government's omnipresent role in the economy. But administrative officials rarely expanded their activities beyond the resolution of conflicts among contending parties.

Immense obstacles frustrated the occasional efforts of zealous officials to formulate positive policies. Every union, every company of any size, and every trade association maintained representatives in Washington to negotiate with administrators, to provide data to congressional committees, and to foil assaults from rival labor, industry, consumer, and self-styled public interest groups. The judiciary remained apart, growing slowly and generally asserting itself prudently.

The old barriers between public and private activities had collapsed during the war, and industrial concentration and the interrelations between business and government prevented their restoration. Political influences and the altered character of enterprise limited free competitive markets and modified the distinction between them and the public sectors of the productive system.

Subsidies for research and development to enterprises of military value continued, rising from one to ten billion dollars a year in the decade after 1950. Space exploration claimed additional support after 1957 when *Sputnik* left the impression that the United States had fallen behind the U.S.S.R. in science. The electronics, aircraft, and computer industries benefited. The failing railroads also got aid, not by rate increases but by out-of-pocket payments from tax revenues. Washington maintained commodity stockpiles to guard against interruptions of supplies and also to help farmers and miners. These transactions and purchases for foreign aid affected large sectors of the economy, so that it became increasingly futile to pretend that government activity occurred only within a circumscribed sector called *public.*

The description *private* therefore applied to the enterprise only in a limited sense. Political judgments about capital, prices, and profits affected all businesses. Furthermore, serious questions about the corporation's liberty remained unanswered. Did it enjoy constitutional rights that inhered in individuals, like privacy? Did it have standing to represent the aggregate of rights entrusted to it by shareholders? Where did the line fall between the interests of shareholders and those of the corporation as a whole? The courts preferred not to disentangle these relationships, relegating them to the legislative and executive branches. Corporations professed to serve the general welfare; their performances affected everyone; they represented vast investments; and they employed hundreds of thousands of wage earners. They therefore possessed a public character subject to scrutiny and control. However, they remained private, because their investors deserved a return upon their capital. Other than the annual privilege of ratifying management decisions by proxy, the holders of common stock differed from holders of bonds in the same companies or in public authorities in one respect only: shareholders expected risk-rewarding appreciation of values, rather than fixed dollar gains.

Ambiguities in the continuing redefinition of public and private confused policymakers. What benefited General Motors benefited the nation—in a way, but not quite or altogether, with the mere assertion either a truism or a challenge. Recognition of corporate social responsibility did not in itself advance decisions. The conflict between those who justified concentration on the grounds of planning efficiency and those for whom it masked monopoly thus continued. Mergers and acquisitions expanded the scale of enterprise. But hostile critics could summon aid from Kefauver's Senate Antitrust and Monopoly Subcommittee (1957), or from the Justice Department's Antitrust Division under Richard McLaren (1969). And occasionally a giant crashed, as when the courts (1967) prevented Procter and Gamble from acquiring the Clorox Company, on the ground of lessening not immediate but future competition by forestalling potential rivals.

Market power, whether exercised by business or by labor, affected people's right to enjoy the ordinary attributes of life. Quite small unions could affect the liberty of millions. The New York City transit or garbage collection strikes (1966) deprived the whole community of liberty. Yet neither the courts nor the legislature showed a disposition to intervene.

Through the 1960s the monopoly issue—like that of fiscal policy—smoldered unresolved as continued expansion, with gains that benefited many, took the edge off disputes. Although individuals and groups pulled in different directions, few challenged the logic and desirability of growth that widened the liberty to act of all.[29]

Two related difficulties threatened the economy. Inflation and energy shortages questioned the ultimate worth of increasing bigness and revealed dramatic shifts in social values as the political system adjusted to abundance.

At first, monetary difficulty affected mostly business people concerned with foreign exchange and tourists worried about traveler's check rates. But more general domestic consequences soon appeared. Since the war, the dollar had stabilized most of the world's currency and also had financed international trade and investment. The burden on the United States grew heavier in the 1960s when Western and Japanese prosperity increased the volume of commerce and of money in circulation. The fund of dollars overseas grew larger, much of it presentable at the U.S. Treasury for conversion into gold at thirty-five dollars an ounce. Foreign holders who cashed in their American paper for the metal diminished the stocks of gold in the United States, and Charles de Gaulle's perverse hostility made matters worse.

The dollar's weakness threatened consumers at home and all trading partners. But none helped, for resurgent nationalism had accustomed the Europeans and Japanese to shifting the burdens of international order to the United States. Yet without cooperation, unilateral efforts to check the flight from the dollar would have caused inflation within the United States.

Drastic measures showing the government's power to act gained a respite. The United States devalued the dollar slightly and halted its convertibility. Agreement to separate the gold traded in the free market from that used to settle international accounts and the Special Drawing Rights of the International Monetary Fund further protected the dollar against speculative assaults. On the domestic front also, action temporarily braked inflation. Restrictive fiscal policy in 1958 locked the valves on credit, the money supply, and federal spending, and held prices down at the expense of a slight rise in unemployment until the release of controls enabled the economy to lurch forward once more.

Even when the means for action existed, however, uncertainty remained; and competing ideologies offered no clear basis for choice, for government reacted only slowly to the conditions of abundance.

Although some scholars hailed the approach of an imminent science of mankind with "sufficient predictive value" to solve "social problems of global scope," citizens received no easy answers to practical questions. Russell Kirk's *Conservative* (1953) urged government restraint, while J. K. Galbraith's *Affluent Society* argued vigorously for public spending. Economists, deeply concerned, clung to the conviction that ever-improved techniques would infallibly generate solutions. Critics expressed surprise that America—a world empire—clung to small-town standards and values despite the managerial revolution through which it had passed. Yet awkward questions troubled even the confident economists. Could they make their science value-free? Could they speak about the increase of national income without prior assumptions about its distribution? Could they assert general principles about the allocation of resources without a commitment to political and ethical premises?[30]

Beyond the reflex anti-Americanism of such journalists and intellectuals as I. F. Stone and Arthur Miller lay a serious ideological division. The poor had been there all along; but suddenly rediscovered by Michael Harrington, they formed a glaring exception to society's affluence, an outcome of the elite domination of which C. Wright Mills wrote, of the malfeasance of great corporations exposed by Ralph Nader. J. K. Galbraith's *American Capitalism* more moderately described the countervailing power by which interest groups checked one another, but still advocated greater government intervention to protect the liberty of the poor. By contrast, opponents of increased state action drew upon the ideas of Friedrich von Hayek (1944) and of Talcott Parsons and Robert Dahl, who described society as a system uniting people in infinite relationships that advanced each person's ability to act when not interfered with. Indeed, David Potter's *People of Plenty* emphasized the importance of affluence in the formation of national character.[31]

Social scientists, however, devoted little thought to popular liberty. Their central concern focused on abstract theoretical models, although after 1945 development problems shifted attention away from the condition of static equilibrium—how a system worked in the absence of change—to a concern with the dynamics of growth, for which history offered attractive material. (The experience of the United States, Britain, and Germany could test theoretical propositions relevant to modernization in India, Nigeria, or Brazil.) But the economists' basic commitment to abstract models detached from the time dimension remained an inconvenient obstacle to translating theory into action. Agreement in principle that adjustments in fiscal policy could regulate the pace of the productive system did not therefore win support for specific proposals to fine-tune the economy for the general welfare by raising or lowering taxes. In 1962–63, a cut seemed desirable; President Johnson finally got it in 1964—late. After two years an increase seemed equally desirable, but the President, having lost his arm-twisting capability, could not get it from Congress, controlled by his own party, an ironic commentary on the use of state power to expand people's ability to act.[32]

Inflation complicated policy-making. Soaring output in Europe and Japan gave millions the discretionary purchasing power that made them competitors with Americans for increasingly expensive articles. The ability to satisfy many of its own requirements for food, fibers, and minerals shielded the United States from the full consequences. However, in one respect it remained vulnerable—increasing dependence upon foreign sources of energy.

A bountiful providence had in the past always provided Americans with plenty of everything. As a result, they watched undismayed as energy consumption doubled between 1950 and 1960 and then continued to rise, despite the mournful predictions of conservationists. However swiftly industry and individuals drew upon the stores of power, more remained available at reasonable cost, permitting the freedom people enjoyed, to drive their cars, to heat with oil and natural gas, and to escape the summer heat by air-conditioning. New discoveries and improved techniques repeatedly mocked the pessimists who predicted depletion. When wood and coal ran short, water power, petroleum, natural gas, and nuclear plants supplied the deficiencies, despite haphazard government policies, excessively responsive to fads and to consumer pressure. Efforts at control proved futile. The Supreme Court (June 7, 1954) obliged the Federal Power Commission to take jurisdiction over natural gas rates—that is, to fix prices for some 2,300 producers, an impossible task that only led to spot shortages.

Until 1970, such interference mattered little. At any given time, the proven oil reserves covered the needs of only twenty years; and a presidential commission predicted in 1952 that consumption would double by 1975. Yet providentially, fresh fields continued to come in, while the level of demand and price determined supply. When the cost of oil rose, the drillers returned to dry holes with more expensive equipment and also launched offshore platforms. Nor did the forests give out, for the lumber companies replenished the stands depleted. And after 1950, strip- and deep-mining machines—mammoth augers, supergiant shovels, conveyor belts, and bucket-wheel excavators—dug coal out of sites once abandoned.[33]

The familiar structure of politics only slowly adjusted to abundance. Government, having hardly adapted to the New Deal and the war, faced as difficult a task when the conditions of plenty replaced those of scarcity. The most important social and economic changes remained hidden, so drastic a reversal of human experience did they represent. No such radical reform proposals agitated voters after 1950 as had fifty years earlier; the connection to liberty seemed less important than issues of free speech and loyalty.

Officials in Washington, the state capitals, the counties, and the municipalities pursued their business as in the past, despite growing bureaucracies, once unthinkable budgetary deficits, and vaguely understood fiscal decisions with effects that rippled through the whole country. Planning for highway construction, for instance, involved the President and his executive departments, committees of the House and Senate, the state and local authorities, construction companies, labor unions, rival engineers, and competing users—farm, trucking, and automobile organizations, and railroads. The stakes included costs—whether to pay by allocations from general revenues, by taxes on fuel, by bond issues, or by tolls—and also alternative routes—whether expressways or farm access roads—and also the relations to urban renewal, all affecting employment and business. Immense effort went into enacting the Federal Highway Act of 1956, although it enjoyed bipartisan support in Congress. Housing and transportation policy depended on equally complex arrays of federal, state, local, and private forces.[34]

Decisions ceased to depend on head counts in which a majority plus one prevailed. Instead, numerous interested economic, class, gender, and ethnic groups negotiated in maneuvers aimed at influencing public opinion, and then bargained to a compromise, rarely to a clear-cut outcome. Such practices heightened the general sense that the times had changed and that unprecedented threats to liberty called for drastic protection. Some contemporaries believed that economic growth stifled individual freedom, as ever-larger concentrations of powers—government, big business, powerful labor unions—threatened individuals by inducements to conformity and acquiescence, stimulated by the vast expansion of uniform education and of mass journalism, which smothered the sense of independence and turned mediocrity into an accepted standard. The threats generated by the craving for security at any price undermined American liberty.

Cautious observers did not foresee a revolution that would overturn the existing political and social system, nor did they think that the Soviet Union could attain its goals. But they worried about the chipping away of freedoms by forces on both the extreme right and the extreme left. One judge believed that traditional liberty faced less danger from any sudden overthrow than from being gradually bartered away by people willing to exchange it for security. Some foreigners thought that Americans who passionately overvalued promises of social welfare and economic stability failed to consider the price they paid in loss of freedom with its individualistic overtones.[35]

Two ticklish issues of the early 1950s aroused short-term concern but left few long-term effects on the Great Society concepts of the next decade. President Truman's dismissal of General Douglas MacArthur, a popular military commander, in the midst of a burdensome war caused no political damage, affirmed the principle of civilian supremacy, and demonstrated the voters' commitment to democratic values.

But the troubling loyalty issues proved far more difficult, complicated by failure to achieve a satisfactory solution to the Korean conflict. Although the Communist Party in the United States remained small, it still provided a cover for agents engaged in espionage, and it perverted liberal organizations and publications in defense of the Soviet Union. The prolonged agitation of the Hiss Case and the final perjury verdict left a widespread though false impression of some vague FBI conspiracy against liberty. Insistent support after 1950 for Stalinism and for the Maoists by widely read columnists and reporters, despite increasingly clear evidence of Soviet and Chinese tyranny, clouded the issue of freedom of opinion in the United States. Contemporaries realized that the Cold War's special character posed its own challenges, that new methods of warfare demanded appropriate countermeasures. But opponents of restrictive measures warned against turning the nation into a "garrison state" and in the name of constitutional freedoms and human decency urged limits on internal security measures. Loyalty, like love, had no value unless earned and freely given; the definition of such intangibles in legal terms left little room for their inherently personal and moral essence. A government could best preserve the loyalty of its citizens and sustain their liberty by deserving it. For optimistic political scientists like David Spitz, Communism was but a symptom of social injustice, economic insecurity, and political inequality. The United States could do nothing to prevent its success short of eradicating such forces. But as James Burnham pointed out, Turkey and other less advanced nations did not succumb, while the more advanced like Hungary and Czechoslovakia did.

Some radicals after 1950 still identified the Communist cause with world peace and sincerely believed the loyalty issue simply a Cold War tactic. Meanwhile, new revelations in Britain involving the transfer to the Reds of atomic secrets and equipment cast light on the treachery for which the Rosenbergs went to the electric chair. Expectation that the Russians would acquire atomic weapons equivalent to those of the West heightened the sense of anticipation and fear, as did further revelations of sinister fifth-column activity by the British diplomats Burgess and Maclean, and by others in high places, that may well have prolonged the Korean War.[36]

Concern with the betrayal of national ideals earned support for charges that secular humanism purveyed by a hypocritical professoriate undermined education, generating hostile sentiments that would flower in the next decade. The unsettled temper of the times drove many to a new conservatism and also expanded the followings of fundamentalists like Charles Fuller and Donald Swearer. A vigorous revival of Christian academies and Jewish day schools aimed to resist the trend to godlessness regarded as one of a complex of threats to citizens' capacity to act. A nation that had paired liberty and Providence for generations, treated an alien militant atheism as a threat to the Republic's very foundations.

In these emotion-laden times, Justice Earl Warren thought fear, latent suspicion, and prejudice would flourish, threatening the basic rights of all. Everyone agreed that the country had to protect itself, but opinions differed on the extent of the danger and on the countermeasures needed. Since the Soviet Union proclaimed far and wide its readiness to employ all necessary means to hasten the progress of history through the obliteration of capitalism, fears of "secret policies aimed at the destruction of our institutions" flourished. Americans could not grasp how a government could operate without "a belief in the dignity of the individual accompanied by a pervasive sense of intelligent toleration and respect for the rights of others." Those who still professed allegiance to the Soviet regime in the 1950s, in spite of evidence of its true character, had to be victims of brainwashing, "some new psychological technique . . . for which, as yet, no antidote has been found other than our reassertion of faith in the older moralities." Americans in effect confronted beings who had become puppets, and thus lacked any capacity to act.[37]

To deal with the security problem, President Roosevelt had earlier authorized loyalty checks of government employees. By 1951, investigations had cleared three million officials; two thousand had resigned, and 212 had been dismissed. Ample legislative authority to deal with these crimes existed, not only in the laws against espionage but also in the Smith Act of 1940, upheld by the Supreme Court (1949), which prohibited conspiracies to teach the violent overthrow of government by force. Confused citizens seemed willing to circumscribe their own and other people's capacity to act to meet invisible menaces. In 1955 the majority of Americans favored police wiretapping of private telephones and approved of informing to state authorities about neighbors' unorthodox political beliefs; fifty percent of lawyers believed that invocation of the historic privilege against self-incrimination clearly indicated guilt.

The inability to differentiate among various types of radicals and dissenters, as well as passion and ignorance, complicated the persistent concern. The ill-informed Senator Joseph McCarthy of Wisconsin, presiding over an investigation committee, never understood the problem, but jumbled together in blanket accusations earnest Communist Party members moved by a sincere concern about specific issues, actual agents who served the Soviet Union's spy apparatus, well-meaning fellow travelers naïvely drawn into front activities, and old-time dissidents objecting to some feature of American life who simply blundered unwittingly into the Red network and tolerated no criticism of the Soviets.[38]

Meanwhile thunder on the right assailed public opinion. Citizens worried about the loss of China and about the frustrating turn of events in Eastern Europe perceived evidence of a sinister conspiracy that had penetrated the corridors of Washington. They sought explanations from George Lincoln Rockwell, Gordon D. Hall, and Dr. Fred Schwartz, or they followed Robert H. W. Welch into the John Birch Society (1958). Frightened observers on the left saw the Birchites as the mirror image of Communists, their propaganda, tactics, and recruitment apparatus comparable to those of the Reds, the main difference being headquarters in Belmont, Massachusetts, rather than in Moscow.

The Circuit Riders (1951) and various radio evangelists also took up arms against radical preachers. The clamor for action mounted. As the age of anxiety darkened into an age of fear, Francis Biddle, fearful of a surrender of the power that once served the people into the "anonymous womb of the mechanical state," wondered whether personal freedom could any longer exist in America. The laymen who worried about the extent to which Communist influences had infiltrated the Methodist Federation for Social Action, which the public regarded as an official part of the church program, disbanded when their demands were met. But Myers Lowman, who gave up his job as a distributor of air-conditioning equipment to become executive secretary of the Circuit Riders, determined to prove churches and schools unsafe from the Red Menace. Billy James Hargis's Christian Crusade, "a force for God and against Communism," at first tried to balloon Bibles into Iron Curtain countries, then used the same techniques that had made radio faith healer Oral Roberts a multimillionaire with spectacular results. Fueled by anti-Communist evangelism, all brought to their tasks the zeal of true believers.[39]

The political implications of the hunt for subversives became clear when Congress, in response to pressure from patriotic organizations, passed the McCarran Internal Security Act over Truman's veto (1951). The law compelled Communist and Communist-front organizations to register, forbade the employment of their members in defense plants, and excluded anyone ever affiliated with a totalitarian movement from admission to the United States.

These and other measures alarmed observers fearful lest in combating subversion the United States subvert itself. The body of law evolved in response to federal and local security measures departed from traditional procedures that in the past had safeguarded the citizens' capacity to act. Americans had formerly dealt with antisocial activities by warning the citizenry of the consequences of wrongful acts. The state would punish the perpetrator only after the act had occurred. Neither conjecture nor suspicion nor threats sanctioned criminal prosecutions or government interference with basic freedoms. The new measures legitimated actions against communication of ideas by groups such as those on the Attorney General's list of subversive organizations, which formed a sort of bill of attainder and a form of thought control.

The alarming procedures for enforcement of the antisubversive statutes lacked uniformity in definition or procedure and created a great variety of approaches, all quite arbitrary. Administrative rather than judicial bodies inquired into and passed judgment on personal beliefs, associations, and opinions of private citizens seeking government employment. Commissions staffed by experts, often knowledgeable in business and economic problems, but not necessarily able to apply their knowledge to such nebulous matters as ideas and beliefs, conducted the hearings, which the courts ruled merely inquiries and not trials in the constitutional sense. Though an adverse hearing did not deprive the individual of either property or liberty, it often did incalculable damage without trapping the truly sinister, any more than a clumsily wielded fly swatter could catch a microbe.

The Communists, infiltrating other groups, capitalized on civil liberties sentiments. Well-intentioned liberals compounded the confusion by converting the problem from one of security to one of free speech, as when John Huston and other Hollywood figures established a Committee for the First Amendment to block the investigations. Witnesses unwilling to snitch did not speak up in defense of their beliefs but took refuge in the Fifth Amendment and refused to testify on the grounds that they wished to avoid self-incrimination. They thereby created the impression that they hid some crime, while a chorus of sympathetic journalists, entertainers, and commentators stridently proclaimed that the government needlessly pursued phantoms in a witch hunt. Lillian Hellman and Dorothy Parker, among others, served as fronts, unaware that they thereby lent themselves to sinister manipulation. *The Crucible,* Arthur Miller's popular play (1953), thus conveyed the impression that just as the Salem judges persecuted nonexistent witches, so the Committee hunted nonexistent conspiratorial Communists. A little later, Miller, consistently anti-American, wrote a laudatory account of Mao and the Red Guards.

Less myopic observers worried that national shortcomings were a prelude to national suicide, that unjust treatments of minorities, Jim Crow laws in the South, racism in the North, and an inadequate safety net would provide fertile soil to those in whose interest it was to extinguish American liberty. Nations rarely collapsed under external pressure without being ripe for overthrow already. The more the country violated its cherished ideals and deprived its citizens of basic rights, the more unworthy it seemed of its historic mission. In the end, American liberty was more threatened from within than from without.

The universities provided fertile soil for confusion and intrigue. The war had opened up opportunities for academics, enlisted in vast bureaucratic projects related to the military—the atom bomb, radar, sonar, for scientists; the OSS for social scientists; and propaganda and psychological warfare for humanists, all offering tastes of power to no-longer-cloistered scholars. After the peace, the size of faculties increased without a corresponding rise in status. Seething discontent with a society that failed to reward the possessors of knowledge merged with an arrogant certainty that the academic elite knew better than politicians and businessmen, to create in some sympathy for an alternative system and to draw a few into acts of betrayal. Anti-Communism they regarded as either a delusion of warped minds overreacting to Soviet progress or a calculated screen for massive, needless defense spending.

Even academics aware of the Soviet threat feared that the damage done by government measures to combat subversion posed a greater menace. Widespread regulations to prevent sabotage injected a totalitarian principle into American morality, sanctioning any means necessary, whether by an anonymous official in the post office who refused to deliver mail from Russia or by anonymous military officers who decided to deny a security risk work in a privately owned defense plant. The New Deal had proved how impossible it was to limit governmental authority once it asserted itself. Concern grew lest the experience in the 1950s be no different.

McCarthy, as chairman of the Senate investigating committee, blurred ideological lines, for some conservatives regarded him as a neo-populist rabble-rouser, who contributed to the split between traditionalists and libertarians, between those who stressed positive action to affirm moral values and those who objected to all state interference. The damage created by the resulting confusion cast a shadow across American politics for decades, obscuring both the issue of free speech and of Communism.

From the outpouring of words, at the time and later, it would be hard to guess either that almost no one suffered for opinions but for actions, or that Communism presented a genuine, not a fanciful, global threat to free institutions and to human rights.[40]

Although President Eisenhower refused to become involved, McCarthy fell afoul of the U.S. Army and the Department of Defense when he poked about in the miserable case of Major Peress, a dentist, promoted and honorably discharged despite his refuge behind the Fifth Amendment. Televised hearings discredited McCarthy and led to a Senate vote of censure in December 1954. The fact that for the first time the majority of American households had television sets made those hearings especially important. Viewers fascinated by the Kefauver investigation into organized crime, with its thrilling exposés of contacts between the underworld and big-city Democratic political machines, now shared newer sensations. The Wisconsin senator came across poorly, the destruction of his image a sign of television's growing influence on the political process. The hearings also showed that, contrary to contemporary opinion, McCarthy enjoyed no nationwide following. The more people watched him in action, the less credible he seemed, the more boring his repetitiveness, the weaker his cases. Most viewers came away persuaded that the senator was a sadistic bully.

But they continued watching because the hearings acquired the patina of a genuine soap opera, its thrills augmented by the uncertainty of its outcome—drama at its best, unrehearsed, unscripted, unfolding before the very eyes of the nation. When NBC decided to withdraw from the live broadcasts, a deluge of telegrams descended upon the Senate, held responsible for the blackout. Television was particularly cruel in highlighting McCarthy's lack of self-control. Its negative impact on his fortunes was enhanced in the hands of skillful manipulators like Edward R. Murrow, whose editing techniques spliced film clips to show the senator in the worst possible light, while yet seeming to speak for himself. The camera focused on his haggard features, poor diction, squinty eyes and shifty lips, all suitable background material for McCarthy's sloppy logic. McCarthy's opponents, like Murrow, relied on pictures rather than text to bury him, and they succeeded.

Murrow himself had become a symbol of the power of the broadcast journalist, which made his savaging of McCarthy that much more effective—a war hero, symbol of the nation's achievement in 1945, reminder of that happy time when unity reigned along with clear distinctions between good and evil. Everyone remembered how his nightly radio news broadcasts from London became part of everyone's life. His trustworthiness beyond reproach, he satisfied the need in the 1950s of the nation forever in search of father figures. Later Walter Cronkite would play the same role. Murrow presented his case against McCarthy in cosmic and highly moralistic tones that the audience loved. "This is no time for men who oppose Senator McCarthy's methods to keep silent. We can deny our heritage and our history, but we cannot escape responsibility for the result." Murrow called on each and every citizen to make a stand. "We proclaim ourselves, as a nation, the defenders of freedom, what's left of it, but we cannot defend freedom abroad by deserting it at home." Unless those who valued liberty made their views known, McCarthy would win, and freedom would suffer. The senator merely exploited a national mood that the people had to dispel, since "the fault, dear Brutus, is not in our stars but in ourselves." Demagoguery may have benefited by the new means of communication, as Hitler proved; but the visual medium that exposed buffoonery could also destroy it.

By this time McCarthy's influence had waned; significantly, Columbia University took as the theme of its bicentennial celebration that year "The Right to Knowledge and the Free Use Thereof."[41]

The rapid rise and fall of Joseph McCarthy demonstrated the integrity of the nation's democratic and libertarian values in spite of occasional breakdowns. The Senate voted to censure in accordance with established procedures, without recourse to extralegal means. Though later scholars viewed the phenomenon as an extension of Democratic-Republican battles, clashes between elites and masses, or as a logical extension of policies that legitimized the idea of a Communist threat, the importance of the phenomenon to intellectuals and academics far outweighed its impact on the nation's life. The fact that the country managed to survive both McCarthy and some of the menaces he exploited, as well as sustain its liberties, testified to its resiliency in the face of the challenges a genuine Soviet threat presented.

Amidst what some considered a reign of terror, Merle Miller's widely read *The Judges and the Judged* (1952) showed the readiness of many Americans to exercise their capacity to prevent the nation from defaulting on its moral standards. Even the American Civil Liberties Union agreed that in a free society the government had the right and duty to keep potentially subversive individuals away from sensitive positions. But this organization, like many others, rejected methods "morally indefensible in a democratic society" that deprived people of the freedom to think what they wished without having to prove their loyalty. Amidst the difficulties of the Korean War, the strange and unprecedented nature of the Communist threat, the political commotions caused by the dismissal of General

MacArthur, and widespread frustration on the home front over unresolved political and social issues, the most important facet of the McCarthy era was its limited deleterious effects.

The most intense scrutiny focused on aliens still vulnerable even after the McCarthyite furor subsided. The case of Ephram Nestor revealed the petty meanness of prosecutors. Nestor, a native of Bulgaria who arrived in the United States in 1913, became a Communist Party member in 1933 and remained one until 1939. Employed, he regularly paid Social Security taxes and in 1955 drew benefits from that coverage. But in 1956 the government, with no other cause, ordered him deported and terminated his benefits, with the approval of the Supreme Court.[42]

By 1960, anxieties evoked by the Cold War and subversion drowned in the rising tide of abundance. A new generation acquired political power—younger than its predecessor, urban rather than rural in outlook, better educated, or at least more schooled, and less scarred by the Great Depression. The war against fascism had restored a sense of purpose and confidence to millions of men and women, who considered a future worth fighting for a future worth living for. Heirs of the New Deal voter coalition, their outlook influenced by professional teachers and professional social workers, they wished, like Holden Caulfield, to do good, save little kids; a perceptive observer saw them dying nobly for some highly unworthy cause.[43]

The wish to do good permeated the decade after 1960, as affluence permitted ample indulgence in benevolence, administered through government agencies. It remained only to agree on goals and methods. New people assumed political leadership. Old problems lost relevance. The New Dealers and their opponents of the 1930s, the interventionists and the isolationists of the 1940s, no longer dominated the scene, and loyalty and security receded in importance. Those familiar instruments of political liberty—the two major political parties—experienced a steady decline in influence, as ticket splitting and slogans such as "I am voting for the man, not the party" (1952) gained popularity. Allegiances declined as voters seemed satisfied with Eisenhower in the White House and the Democratic Congress. Although congressional committees still emphasized seniority, fresh legislative voices and youthful governors took command. The issues that had shaped the fate of liberty down to 1960 seemed dead. Symptomatically, the eligibility of a Catholic for the Presidency created no difficulty in the election of 1960 as it had thirty years earlier. The sense of a new beginning and of an unprecedented range of choices hinted at expanding freedom in all aspects of life.

The three Presidents of the decade differed among themselves in background, character, and experience. But they differed even more from their predecessors. Younger than Truman and Eisenhower, they had survived depression, world war, and Korea, and regarded the United States as the free world's leader. Although foreign policy absorbed much of their attention, they also had domestic agendas to strengthen the country internally. All three also presided over a nation with a booming economy, which nonetheless made increasing demands for difficult changes in basic life patterns. In the early 1950s youngsters typically graduated from high school, spent time in the military, then got home, took a blue-collar job, and married, a pattern increasingly difficult to replicate after 1960. It depended on an economy with plenty of entry-level jobs that required no higher education and paid what labor leaders called a family wage. Changes became evident in population patterns after 1960, when none of the heavy-manufacturing states gained population at a rate higher than the national average, while the United Auto Workers conducted highly publicized campaigns to guarantee workers' jobs—a sign that growth in these industries had ended. Kennedy, Johnson, and Nixon would preside over a nation whose abundance masked a period of great social readjustment.

John F. Kennedy had grown up a rich kid—private schools, summers in Hyannis Port, travel, Harvard, six months in London where his father served as ambassador. During the war he behaved heroically after the sinking of a torpedo boat he commanded. The wound he brought away left him frequently in pain. Driven by insecurity and the need to assert himself, sustained by his grandfather's reputation, by his father's wealth, and by ambition, from 1956 onward, under parental pressure, he reached for the greatest political prize. Glamour and money, but also the sense of freshness his campaign conveyed, proved decisive. His slogan, the New Frontier, recalled past Democratic achievements but also looked forward. "I think it's time to get America moving again," he declared in one of the crucial television debates against his opponent, and a closely divided electorate agreed.

His thoughts then turned to a place in history, spurred by a sense that the torch had been passed to a new generation. He had to confront the hard issues he had evaded as a senator. Serious. F.D.R. had become a remote memory, but the Truman legacy remained vivid and particularly the social programs of the Fair Deal (1949) frustrated by congressional opposition. Those aspirations became the basis of Kennedy's domestic policy. From his congressional staff he brought an able speechwriter and tough political operators; he added to them his brother Robert and his brother-in-law Sargent Shriver. But John Kennedy wanted more, and quality, the best money and fame could acquire in the academic marketplace—Walt Rostow and McGeorge Bundy from Yale, Dean Rusk from the Rockefeller Foundation, Robert McNamara from the Harvard Business School by way of Ford Motors, and Jerome B. Wiesner of MIT—a youthful contrast to Ike's old-timers. Coming to power at the end of a painful though short recession, these men hoped to stimulate economic growth by raising wages, not by redistributing income; by creating growth that would make everyone richer. Most voters agreed, especially since the President and his entourage formed objects of curiosity and fascination unprecedented in the nation's history.[44]

Strengthened by the economic advances since the war, Kennedy hailed the onset of a new Augustan age, of a power forever leading from its strength and pride to a golden age beyond a new frontier. Americans, "born in this century, tempered by war, disciplined by a hard and bitter peace," would "pay any price, bear any burden, meet any hardship, support any friend, oppose any foe to assure the survival and the success of liberty." He offered his fellow citizens a set of challenges and the promise of sacrifice instead of security: "Ask not what your country can do for you—ask what you can do for your country." Yet the net effect of the decade's changes widened the scope of what the country did for its citizens.

The Peace Corps, designed to channel youthful idealism into foreign affairs, spread technology rather than Christianity in this twentieth-century version of the missionary impulse. Earlier disseminators of American liberty had aimed to save souls for the hereafter. Their young twentieth-century counterparts hoped to spread freedom by improving the lot of people everywhere through teaching English and practical skills.[45]

Television now possessed the technology to compete with newspapers, in providing information on a day-to-day basis; its coverage of the emotion-laden desegregation struggles in the South and of the war in South Vietnam reduced them to concrete problems brought into the nation's living rooms. In response to the segregationists' intransigent denial of basic liberty to Southern blacks, Kennedy unsuccessfully proposed a sweeping civil rights bill, including a ban on racial discrimination in public accommodations and in employment, federal enforcement of school desegregation and stronger protections of voting rights.

Kennedy also took an imaginative view of the federal role in education and science and significantly expanded the space program. The illiteracy rate nevertheless did not fall. He managed to get through Congress some improvements in Social Security and in the minimum wage, and also a Housing Act that authorized loans for middle-income buildings and for park and transit development. Persuaded that economic growth would provide the means to dissolve residual inequalities and end poverty, the President sought moderate changes to aid the less fortunate, relying on his Whiz Kids to apply modern management controls, statistically based, as in industry. An approving observer described his Secretary of Defense as "an IBM machine with legs." Yet the administration left the impression of a golden interlude, a product partly of youth, partly of skill with words, and partly of self-confidence.

When an assassin's bullet cut Jack Kennedy's effort short, power passed to quite different hands. Few could manipulate the government mechanism better than Lyndon B. Johnson, or match his political intuition, charm, and self-assurance. Few had proven more adept in handling the opportunities the media granted or maneuvered better among the labyrinthine bureaucracy that the New Deal bequeathed to Great Society Washington. Kennedy's death and the hopes his short term in office aroused, together with the country's economic well-being, provided the perfect setting for a bold effort to eradicate the nation's glaring problems. Furthermore, LBJ never erased from his memory his personal hardships during the Depression and the encompassing poverty of the hard-hit county in which he grew up.

As a President by accident he wished to put forward his own agenda and yet to maintain continuity with his predecessor's efforts. Johnson's mastery of congressional tactics got measures enacted that had languished in committees since 1961. Moreover, the dignity of office brought him a clearer sense of purpose than before, which his talent converted into legislation. Remembering his poverty-stricken youth and his labors on a road gang, and moved by heartbreaking descriptions of America's poor, trapped in misery without any capacity to act, Johnson grasped at theories that located the source of the problems not in the individual victims but in the surrounding society. A comprehensive attack could end the conditions that caused deprivation and create the Great Society, free of want, affording liberty to all. In March 1964, he expressed the aspiration to use the country's wealth to enrich and elevate national life—to eliminate poverty and racial injustice, improve the quality of urban existence, beautify the countryside, control pollution, and advance education, all without sharp internal divisions through consensus for the common good. Johnson's State of the Union address in January 1965 assumed that America was in the "midst of abundance." Men, freed from the "wants of the body," could seek fulfillment of the "needs of the spirit." He thereupon boldly declared war on poverty. In a flush of optimism, he and his supporters assumed that all problems had solutions. He also assumed that every grievance in need of redress had a social origin, which the statesman could discover by asking "Where have we gone wrong?" Every form of protest by definition became legitimate and expressed a righteous cause. That vision left no room for freedom, with each and every being merely the puppet of forces beyond personal control, with results that became clear before the end of the decade.[46]

The problems of poor farmers early received attention. The Food and Agriculture Act laid out a fresh omnibus program for modified price supports and accelerated cropland retirement. New laws provided for the development of Appalachia and other depressed regions and created a Department of Housing and Urban Development, with the injunction to devote special attention to the needs of low-income groups. A mass transportation act aimed to ease the life of urban residents. Federal contributions to welfare programs increased, although the law remained silent on experiments on human subjects and lax on the use of new medications, as the Thalidomide scandal (1962) revealed. The desire to expand opportunities for the children of the poor shaped measures for support of education, vocational training, the Job Corps, and Upward Bound programs. Public and private elementary schools received aid in proportion to the number of their pupils from low-income families, and college scholarships and work programs provided for the needy. The federal government financed libraries, the construction of college facilities, and the purchase of equipment. A National Teachers Corps set about recruiting instructors for depressed areas. Social Security benefits rose, as did provisions for wilderness conservation and for space exploration. Although Johnson lacked the smoothness of style and failed to evoke the instinctive affection of Kennedy or F.D.R., his resounding electoral victory in 1964 showed the country's approval of his program.

The campaign that year involved a rare clash of ideologies, a referendum of sorts on the kind of liberty Americans envisioned for themselves and the rest of the world. Barry Goldwater, the Republican candidate, represented a conservative agenda that harked back to an earlier era; his refusal to repudiate associations with the John Birch Society needlessly allied him with right-wing elements irrelevant to the times. Despite the clear outcome, however, important changes detached the once solidly Democratic South from its traditional moorings. Republican gains in many states, despite the landslide Electoral College defeat, revealed a realignment with effects on liberty that became clear later.

For the moment, Johnson, heir to the Truman-Kennedy legacy, represented the future and with it the liberty appropriate to late-twentieth-century life. The fluidity and mobility of American society and its abundance frame of reference proved congenial to the vision of a Great Society that would provide for the poor and spread the ability to consume to everyone, without sacrifice by anyone.

Reelection in 1964 gave Johnson definite control of Congress. In February 1965 he assembled the assistant secretaries in charge of legislation for each agency—about thirty in all—and asked them to push through the greatest expansion of social legislation since the early New Deal days—Medicare for nineteen million, widened Social Security, aid to education, air and water pollution control, help for Appalachia, and highway beautification—life, liberty, and the pursuit of happiness, guaranteed by state action for all.

This expansion of social legislation occurred while economic security seemed within everyone's reach. To restore the nation's moral legitimacy, the President targeted problems theretofore left unsolved. But while attaining his legislative objectives, he did not mobilize the political strength to sustain his vision once he passed from the scene. The capacity to act, which the Great Society aimed to expand, later shrank when programs proved unworkable or controversial, leaving behind a bitter residue detrimental to liberty.[47]

Medicare (1965) extended the Social Security system in a totally new direction. The burden on the aged of proper health services had long called for remedial action, but Truman's efforts on their behalf had failed, blocked by the quaint image of the traditional family doctor with his black bag who kept his accounts in his head and treated the poor without charge. The inadequate Kerr-Mills Act of 1960 had depended upon a means test, yet Kennedy's suggestions for reform (1962) had met no response from Congress. Johnson succeeded where his predecessors had failed. The new law provided health insurance for people over the age of sixty-five, with supplementary benefits to cover hospital and nursing home costs. Without much forethought a parallel program, Medicaid, extended service to welfare recipients, until then treated only through local philanthropic and legal aid organizations.[48]

For the first time, tighter control of the environment to make life safe and pleasant seemed a proper concern of government. The President also called for and got laws to restrict advertising along highways, to screen junkyards, and to control pollution, remove urban blight, and plan the proper use of water resources. National foundations provided support for the arts and the humanities of the same sort the government already gave to science; and a Corporation for Public Broadcasting aimed to encourage educational radio and television.[49]

The Great Society tried finally to bring all Americans the liberty that many already enjoyed, but of which significant portions of the population remained deprived—liberty in tune with needs evoked by a vastly greater involvement of state power in the management of everyday life, reflected in a federal bureaucracy that swelled from 1,960,000 in 1950 to 2,981,000 in 1970. State power also limited citizens' capacity to act by narrowing the scope beyond which their freedoms might harm others. The poor, having become beneficiaries of government, suffered particularly from official paternalism, as when welfare and youth bureaucrats imposed their own standards of proper conduct on the recipients of aid, and particularly when ethnic or racial differences complicated even well-intentioned benevolence—"welfare colonialism," the HARYOU people called it. The two-faced concept of liberty that emerged in those years resisted analysis along liberal or conservative lines, terms irrelevant to the issues at stake.

Significantly, influential segments of the public concluded that protests outside of politics could accomplish more than within it. Harnessing the system to make it work for an objective proved laborious in a country where the average citizen did not share goals that met the approval of social reformers. That awareness helped undermine government by consent, on which traditional definitions of liberty depended. Consent acquired a different meaning when it involved responses to blackmailing attempts, and that affected everyone's capacity to act.

Deep social changes in two decades after 1950 lent plausibility to the expectation of the Great Society that everyone would share the abundance the economy produced. Perennial restlessness and mobility increased the outlook for an ever wider diffusion of the goods Americans created. Complex movements of peoples reshuffled the population geographically and socially—from East to West and from countryside to cities, and also from the South to the Northern industrial belt, and from the Northeast to the Southwest.

Improved status accompanied moves voluntarily taken in expectation of a better life. And even young people who remained in the places of their birth gained confidence that effort could improve life chances, provide access to desirable occupations, and earn incomes above those of their parents.

Education more than ever became the avenue of social mobility. In an economy that required ever less unskilled labor and ever more advanced training and technical proficiency, schools served as gatekeepers. Presumably they sorted out the entering cohorts according to character and ability, determining who would advance and to what destinations. Institutions of every sort, public and private, multiplied, and local expenditures for education soared, boosted by federal grants that rose from $281 million in 1959 to more than $2 billion in 1967. Unavoidably, politics and issues of racial equality intruded, but without impeding rapid expansion before 1970. Only the unskilled lagged behind or dropped out entirely.

Complaints multiplied. Back in 1953, Rudolf Flesch, in *Why Johnny Can't Read,* blamed poor teaching. Nevertheless, literate or not, the number of college students reached 7,900,000 in 1970—more than thirty-two percent of Americans aged eighteen to twenty-one.[50]

Not much good it did them. Youth devoted a large part of its life to formal education. In 1970 more than sixty million Americans attended school, almost the whole of the eligible age group. Elementary school, high school, college, and career followed one another in automatic sequence. Even marginal students went through the motions because the labor market had no use for them.

Yet however much the learning experience helped some become doctors, engineers, lawyers, or businessmen, it threw little light on their own problems as persons. Overwhelmed by numbers and by the competition for places, education served as a filtering device, testing as much as teaching. Changes in the traditional curriculum made little difference; the new subjects, like the old, remained unresponsive to the serious questions of the student; often study only stifled the impulse to ask.

Upward social mobility rewarded survivors. Inherited wealth no longer assured the fortunate places at the peak of the social pyramid. New money, talent, and technical skills earned admission to the most prestigious circles, as did political and military achievements. The vast expansion in the number of white-collar positions made room for the sons and daughters of laborers and farmers. Racial discrimination or lack of skill dimmed the prospects of some. But a steady lowering of barriers justified the expectation that the United States stood on the verge of an advance across new frontiers of human relations.

As in the past, so too often after 1950, the family environment influenced life's chances—whether home offered a space congenial to study, whether parents and siblings encouraged youths to persevere, to conform to the code William H. Whyte described in *The Organization*

Man, to work in smoothly functioning units, ruled by togetherness of the whole. Neurotic career women, "the lost sex" described by Marynia Marnham and Helene Deutsch, suffered tensions intensified by the need to abandon children to the indifferent care of others. Although mobility weakened old ties, kinship paradoxically remained important in determining individual success by shaping readiness to adapt.

The strain of making good put pressure upon young people—whether they succeeded or not. For millions of viewers, Lucille Ball of "I Love Lucy" remained the ideal wife, even beyond her heyday in the 1950s. But frequent travel by spouses and long hours took a toll of home life, cutting into the time spent with children. Successful men left wives behind stuck in the suburban starting point, creating responsive readers for Betty Friedan. But failure also poisoned marital relations so that the rising rate of divorce reflected the grievances, sometimes of those who got ahead, sometimes of those who lagged behind.[51]

Mobility also transformed communities ever less likely to encase men, women, and children permanently in mediating institutions, ever more likely to serve as arrangements of convenience, incapable of cushioning the shocks of unfamiliar social forces that subjected people to unprecedented pressures. Men and women spurted off in unanticipated moves and halts, challenging the planned controls, darting away from programs mapped out, whether by federal or local governments, by the Ford Foundation, or by well-intentioned organizations inspired to help by Saul Alinsky's theories.

Theretofore unacknowledged anxieties crowded in on Americans, no matter how prosperous. In 1963 Rachel Carson's *Silent Spring* created needless hysteria about the use of pesticides; consumers, no longer concerned about hunger, worried about the safety of the food they ingested, as had their grandparents who had read Upton Sinclair's *The Jungle.* Concern about the destination to which the Great Society led mounted, reflecting in part raised expectations and wildly unrealistic anticipations. At the same time shortcomings in every arena of life became evidence of societal failings, undermining the legitimacy of institutions traditionally deputed to handle such difficulties. And advocates of improvements failed to see how unhappy voters became with the situation around them. Though citizens paid higher taxes and voted commendable programs into being, problems only got worse.

In 1965 New York's Landmarks Preservation Law created doubts about accepted criteria of progress and about the claims to space of each new generation. Confusion increased when what many considered wanton destruction of property and unbridled violence was portrayed as a form of political protest—legitimate, given the grievances of participants against constituted authorities. And as some rioted and others marched, the slogans still sounded good but not the price paid, for increasingly, within the Great Society, reality pulverized individuals and caught people like shovelfuls of corn in a hammermill.[52]

In 1969 Richard M. Nixon, a moderate Republican, moved into the White House, no longer the shaggy dog type who bitterly taunted reporters a few years earlier that they would not have Dick Nixon to kick around anymore. His successful presidential campaign reflected the skills of handlers who understood the power of television and how candidates appealed to the electorate—one idea at a time, articulated in simple words and short, sound-bite sentences. He also understood that the Great Society programs had moved out of the Democratic platform to become part of what ordinary Americans expected from their government and would not tolerate their repeal. Foreign affairs occupied most of his attention and the Democrats still held power in Congress. But in addition, the Great Society changes revealed unexpected shortcomings in the assumption that people would live happily ever after once abundance quieted Depression-era fears. That expectation proved not at all sound, especially when higher crime rates and riots showed that some of the programs had failed.

Unexpectedly the controls ceased to function. Early on, the brightest politicians had noticed warning signals, had tinkered with the programs, had made alterations as needed. Unavailing. Some malignant virus had crept into the system. No method of getting it out seemed apparent without destroying the whole configuration. The tone of politics in Washington grew increasingly bitter as Richard Nixon, an essentially liberal president, confronted an exceedingly hostile establishment for which he had nothing but contempt. The bread-and-butter issues over which the nation had split in the 1930s had become largely irrelevant. Instead, the focus of the heat and fury shifted to more elusive but equally divisive matters like values and mores, whose impact on the capacity to act was as great if not greater than that of the income redistribution questions of an earlier period.

The Great Society dream of benevolent total control with equality its object never worked out—even in prisons or mental institutions operated by absolute authority, much less in pluralistic open communities. Not every story led to a happy ending—no more often in a time of abundance than in a time of scarcity. In business and in politics, not every whiz kid imbued with a ruthless will to win succeeded and early retirement or (like F. C. Reith) suicide were the losers' lots.[53]

In 1960 the United States, a society in the process of change, prepared to advance beyond the new frontiers of an economy transformed by technology. John F. Kennedy and Lyndon B. Johnson peered across the edges of the territory ahead, hoping to map out patterns of government action that would expand the liberties of all in the manner appropriate to a Great Society. Richard Nixon carried that vision forward, proposing to remedy the Great Society's shortcomings by a guaranteed annual income, the first President in American history to do so. With the help of mavericks like Daniel Patrick Moynihan, he would have expanded the scope of liberty not by having government try to change people, which it had already failed to do, but by handing out money more generously, thus granting the handicapped a capacity to act and allowing them to lift themselves out of their misery. The Family Assistance Program met with bitter opposition from the National Welfare Rights Organization, whose clients stood to lose, especially in states that provided generous benefits, like New York and California. And the more liberal Nixon's domestic proposals, the more opposition he met. For the Great Society had also contributed to deepening polarization between what journalists called Middle America and trend-setters sympathetic to the fringe. Yet the loftier the aspiration, the deeper the disillusion with the results, the more ominous the complaint: what was so great about the Great Society?

Poverty did not vanish despite the vast sums lavished on its eradication. New construction did not keep up with spreading slums; instead, abandoned buildings blighted whole urban areas, which became focal points for drug dealing and crime.

These pathologies appeared most visibly in a deepening underclass that threatened to become permanent, and observers who lacked other means of accounting for the development linked it with the deprivation of an underprivileged minority defined by race. Ominously the Kerner Commission appointed to seek the causes of riot (1967) concluded that divisions split the country in two. Yet the Great Society had made dramatic efforts to redress the legitimate grievance of the minorities, achieving more in the decade of the 1960s than in the whole century since the Emancipation Proclamation. Scarcely noticed by the political engineers at the controls was an ominous shift in objectives from the goal of equality of opportunity to the novel goal of equality measured by results.

And none of the numbers could probe a profound change in the human integers and in the values by which they governed their lives, which therefore escaped inclusion in the formulae and found no place in the most elaborate programs for doing good. After 1960 more than ever before, Americans revealed that creatures of will and passion did not fit into the statistical series the knowledge people compiled.

In this game, the same prize rewarded all the winners—an early death. J.F.K. and Bobby, M. L. King and Hoffa, Mary Jo Kopechne, chosen to ride along, and also LBJ and Oswald's Ruby. Even Marilyn, who knew almost all of them (as well as the stars of stage and diamond), but couldn't take any more. And later Andy Warhol, who put her face on canvas.

Survival in a great society became a hard, tense thing where no rules bound lonely persons except the imperatives to gain equality and to gratify each impulse.

CHAPTER 6

WHERE EQUALITY LED

BETWEEN 1950 AND 1970 a striking diminution in discrimination dramatically improved relationships among most American ethnic groups. Prejudices persisted, in some respects deeper than earlier, but the form and context changed. Efforts to revive the Klan came to nothing, and the anti-Catholic and anti-Semitic movements of the 1930s and 1940s faded away. Relics of an earlier era—G. L. K. Smith and Gerald Winrod—got nowhere in attacks on the Kike-Ike (1952). The rate of intermarriage across religious and color lines mounted, and political expressions of hostility all but vanished.

Even the Communist issue did not evoke old hostilities; the agitation generated by the Rosenbergs' conviction and execution ignored their Jewish identity. Nor was creed a factor in the McCarthy controversies; indeed, two of the senator's aides, recognizably Jewish, drew bitter criticism, but not because of their faith. Increasingly, Americans viewed their society as organized into three religious communions—Catholic, Protestant, and Jewish—a misleading formulation, but one that demonstrated the decline in prejudice, especially when memorialized in the commemorative stamp of the chaplains who drowned together when their troop ship sank (1943).[1]

The war dissolved formerly divisive hatreds. Labor shortages made discrimination unpatriotic when it impeded the flow of planes and munitions. In 1960 a Roman Catholic became President, and a majority of his countrymen in public opinion polls said they would accept a Jew in the highest office in the land. Americans no longer considered people with Italian or Polish surnames inferiors unworthy of admission to the best schools, and Japanese Americans overcame the traumatic effects of internment to which a stupid blunder had confined them. Even later when balance-of-trade problems touched off a wave of Japan-bashing, hostility did not extend to residents of the United States. The anti-Oriental prejudices of an earlier postwar era revived only rarely. Instead, barriers against Chinese, Indians, and Filipinos in education, housing, employment, and social accommodations collapsed—not all at once but in a steady process. Abundance after 1950 expanded the supply of goods, made enough available for all, so that a majority perceived themselves as middle class, effectively minimizing economic issues in politics. The perception, ever more often, that each profited through the increase in others' well-being, generated tolerance of conflicting opinions and ways of life, adjusted in a "therapeutic mode" by compromise.[2]

Racism as a consistent philosophy with respectable scientific support disappeared. Social scientists in the 1930s and 1940s concluded that genetic differences did not divide humans into distinct and separate species. The war hastened acceptance of the idea that most defining traits stemmed from cultural and social sources and changed with time. People of all sorts, having learned in fighting together that they shared strengths and weaknesses, fears and emotions, recoiled from the revelations of the Nazi extermination camps—the logical corollary of the doctrine of Aryan supremacy.[3]

Ever more often, those treated unequally came to consider themselves underprivileged minorities, denied the full measure of liberty to which the Constitution entitled them. Those who considered their capacity to act circumscribed by external factors sought what they regarded as justifiable redress. They expected government intervention on their behalf, and in time acquired enough political power to secure it. Twenty states and many municipalities by law forbade discrimination in employment, in housing, and in education. After long evading the issue, the Supreme Court in April 1952 upheld the constitutionality of statutes against group libel, a decision that further inhibited racist propaganda. The mere enactment of such measures did not secure compliance, but even without stringent enforcement they established standards of proper action that gained gradual acceptance. And in the 1950s, growing understanding of the complex sources of American national character induced most citizens to value their society's plurality.[4]

Slowly, the long-agitated immigration controversy reached a resolution undistorted by prejudice. In the early 1950s serious concern persisted about the reception of displaced persons and undocumented aliens from Mexico and the West Indies. But increasingly, experience demonstrated the emptiness of restrictionist fears and generated support for return to the more open nineteenth-century policy. A Catholic's election to the Presidency revealed the subsidence of ancient fears about the danger to the Republic from the pope's legions.

The immigration and nationality act of 1965 abolished racial quotas and increased total admissions to 176,000 annually from the Eastern hemisphere and 120,000 from the Western. By then, cheap and simple air travel brought once-remote areas within reach of America, and relaxed border controls eased entry for newcomers without documents. In an unanticipated effect, the numbers arriving from Asia and Latin America soared, with the largest share from Cuba, Mexico, the Philippines, Vietnam, India, and South Korea.[5]

Many newcomers belonged to racial, national, and religious groups once mistrusted, but no resurgence of prejudice followed. Nor did demands for one-hundred-percent Americanism revive, as after the First World War. The melting pot image faded, replaced ever more frequently by acceptance of diversity as the characteristic national experience.

Although group hatreds subsided, the hazards of modern life demanded some comforting form of solidarity. Yet for many Americans the cohesive family and its network of related associations no longer provided the emotional safety of a secure framework for daily life. Churches, particularly in the suburbs, made few credal demands on communicants other than a vague commitment to goodness. People had to "learn to live without those consolations called religious," which belonged to the childhood of the race—so ran the popular consensus. Nor did contemporary philosophy provide a helpful guide to better living—too rich in answers, each canceling out the rest, and often disdainful of popular needs, as well as of liberty. With the quest for meaning thus foredoomed, human life signified nothing. Men and women had only their own human trinity to see them through: reason, courage, and grace. And the first plus the second equaled the third.[6]

Fundamentalism survived, its regional strength reflecting sectional differences. Among the Protestants, Billy Graham carried on the revivalist tradition; in 1952 his great revival in Washington, D.C., attracted national attention. Radio and television evangelists commanded sizable audiences, particularly when they joined healing to the Gospel or attacked the modernism of the World Council of Churches. In 1957 in response to a census inquiry fully ninety-six percent of the population gave a specific affiliation. As a matter of course, a law (1954) inserted the words "under God" into the Pledge of Allegiance. Nevertheless periodic efforts to reinstate school prayers and the predictable judicial rulings that struck down such local ordinances testified to the survival of more secular impulses. All along the Supreme Court struggled to draw the line between opinion, with which government could not interfere, and practice, which it could regulate. The kosher butcher therefore won exemption from the Sunday closing law (1961), but not the Seventh-Day Adventists (1963). Meanwhile, fearful that subsidized education might strengthen parochial schools, Protestants and other Americans United mobilized to defend the separation of Church and State. But liberals did not have it all their own way. Father Leonard Feeney exhorted Catholics to resist tendencies to change in the Church; and immigration added to the number of the Hasidim and other Orthodox among Jews.[7]

Whether religious or secular, associations reflected the patchwork character of American society. As in the past, ethnicity provided a comfortable basis for social action, yet far from the confining or unmeltable affiliation some intellectuals argued it should be, particularly since government and trade unions supplied the social security and fraternity once provided by lodges and orders. Group identity ever more often sprang from gregariousness, from the desire to fill cultural needs, and from the effort to create activities to extend young people's loyalties through to the next generation. Members sought to satisfy immediate, present needs rather than to adhere to familiar, inherited old patterns. But the habits of association could also turn into potent political tools to expand the members' capacity to act.[8]

Blacks remained a category apart, twenty-two million of them in 1970—some ten percent of the total population, roughly the same percentage as in the previous century. Overt racists like Theodore Bilbo had passed from the scene, and the Supreme Court in 1950 declared the white primary unconstitutional. The goal of equality ceased to be an idle dream. The NAACP began a direct and open fight against segregation, on the grounds that there could be no such thing as "separate but equal," since segregation meant inequality. In Virginia and other border states black voters and officeholders began to assert themselves.[9]

But Jim Crow lines persisted, North and South, although in different fashions. Migration from below the Mason-Dixon Line and from the Caribbean increased the size of the colored population in New York, Chicago, Los Angeles, and Philadelphia, which re-created some old patterns of Southern segregation. The newcomers arrived ill-prepared for urban life. Destitute and lacking resources or training, they fell into ill-paid unskilled jobs and moved into cheap available housing that other people deserted. For want of alternatives they clustered in their own districts, where they found the familiarity of their own kind, with ready access to soul food—yams, greens—known from back home. Here, their own argot provided means of communication. Here, defensively, they rebuffed the advances of even well-intentioned outsiders. "That's how it is," commented a sympathizer. "I give my heart and they kick me in my teeth."[10]

The family adjusted to the father's absences and wanderings, hustling out from under responsibility while the mother and granny took care of the kids and welfare provided the support of last resort. With school an alien place, the street served as classroom as well as playground. Blacks, like everyone else, needed others to hang around with; Holden Caulfield, far from poor, missed even the phony classmates he despised. At the corners, on the blocks, in the ghettoes—as in other groups, black gangs took form, with their own leaders, codes, languages, and habits, marked by loose standards of sexual conduct and by obscene talk and games. Monkey-chasers from the Caribbean, different, nevertheless fitted in, somewhat—color made them kin. Dealing drugs, running numbers, muggings, and car theft brought spurts of cash, but nothing like a living. Bragging, scoffing, teasing black youths, like "signifying monkeys," matured worlds apart from that outside their own districts. Denied respect by others or the prospect of improvement, able like other gangs to act only on their own turf, they found freedom in self-segregation.[11]

Whatever separation existed in New York, Chicago, and Los Angeles resulted from residential patterns, partly though not entirely the products of people's voluntary preferences to live among those of their own kind, free of the embarrassment or humiliation of contact with others. Lending agencies, including those of the government, and real estate brokers reinforced black and other ethnic boundaries in order to stabilize values. The narrowed range of choices that resulted from red-lining and other discriminatory practices blurred individual qualities, set limits to personal liberty, and amounted to *de facto* segregation that influenced access to jobs and education.[12]

The consequences affected all those who bore the marks of color. The ambitious who made it in business or the professions could move away but could not escape identification with race, a source of frustration for many, expressed sometimes in self-hatred, sometimes in delusions of high society, sometimes in indulgence in liquor and sex. The long-term results also included a developing division between the more prosperous—middle class in outlook, status, and expectations—and an inert underclass, inadequately schooled and unprepared in skills and work habits for desirable places in a modern industrial society.[13]

* * *

Already before the New Deal, Northern blacks had developed political leadership, allied with their churches, that sought redress in alliance with one party or the other. After 1950 the influentials in each community reached out for a more permanent identification with the heirs of Truman's Fair Deal.

Furthermore, the independence of the new African nations in the 1950s imbued colored people in the United States with pride. Disillusion with brutal dictatorships, political oppression, economic exploitation, impoverishment, and famine would not come until later. Meanwhile, in international councils, Nigerians in the 1960s sat as equals with white Europeans; colored people in the United States could do the same. Racism at home deserved the same opprobrium as imperialism abroad. Many recalled Wendell Willkie's warning, in *One World,* that peace depended upon extending freedom to everyone, whatever their color. Unless the United States distinguished itself from the Boers of South Africa and cast out the residues of prejudice, it would irreparably damage its standing in important parts of the world; millions in development aid would not repair the loss. The more extreme advocates of change even referred to "American apartheid" despite differences between disabilities in South Africa and in the United States. White colonialism, everywhere the same, ultimately abrogated liberty and called for resistance by the same means in Africa and in North America.

Above all, blacks in the United States appealed to a historic creed to which almost all their fellow citizens adhered—the faith in equality of opportunity, individual dignity, and personal responsibility. Responding to the challenges of that faith, millions of white men and women learned to cast aside inherited attitudes, to break through old customs, and to make room for the formerly disadvantaged. Dissenting Southerners, lagging behind the times, resisted bitterly. Inadequate social and political structures for a time tragically sustained those whose sense of superiority demanded the oppression of others. But the changes proceeded inexorably. When under court order the University of Oklahoma admitted George W. McLaurin, the administration assigned him a seat in an otherwise empty row, separated from his classmates by a railing. White students, shocked by his treatment, ripped the sign proclaiming "Reserved for Coloreds" from the railing that set apart the area assigned to McLaurin (1949).

By 1950, blacks had begun to utilize the law effectively to improve their situation. Executive orders against discrimination in federal employment and for equal treatment of contractors by government, as well as against segregation in the armed forces (1948), bore some results during the Korean War. Truman was the first President in American history elected on a platform calling for civil rights, and he made the first appointment of an African American to a seat on the U.S. Circuit Court of Appeals. Meanwhile, state fair employment practices acts helped blacks particularly when supported by the labor movement, by Jews, and by other aggrieved white ethnics. These measures appealed generally for justice for everyone discriminated against in hiring, education, and housing. State commissions could combat unfair practices much more effectively than could judicial prosecutions in isolated individual civil or criminal suits. In response to a verified complaint, the government financed the investigation. Action therefore speeded up, and the burden of proof shifted away from the complainant to the party suspected of prejudice. Instead of a jury, an administrative board determined the extent of discrimination; although the right of appeal to the courts remained, defendants rarely exercised it—compliance generally proved less costly.

Southern legislatures, still protected by restricted voting patterns, enacted no such laws. In that region, blacks had therefore turned to the judiciary and had, at first, accepted the decision in *Plessy* v. *Ferguson* (1890), which had sanctioned segregation as long as it seemed to provide equality. The doctrine of "separate but equal," however, enabled Southern states after 1920 to set blacks apart as inferiors, unfit to share with whites a seat on the bus or train, a table in the restaurant, or a desk in the school, despite the implications of the Fourteenth Amendment. Case after case laboriously brought by blacks insisted on genuinely equal facilities in schools, in trains, and in buses. In response, a succession of decisions dealing particularly with higher education tested that formula and ruled against segregation that simply cloaked inequality.

The Supreme Court confronted the issue more squarely in 1954. A unanimous ruling in *Brown* v. *Board of Education* then held that the Jim Crow pattern, established by law, did in fact produce inequality and therefore deprived blacks of their rights. In declaring racial separation inherently unequal and therefore unconstitutional, the Court turned its back upon precedent and reversed Plessy, clutching instead flimsy social science postulates and disregarding abundant evidence to the contrary. In establishing the principle that only integration led to equality, it saddled communities with a rigid and unworkable formula. Holding that any form of separation, even that not established by law, created a condition of inequality, it directed the offending states, with all deliberate speed, to integrate their schools.[14]

The well-intentioned decision rested upon a faulty basis and therefore established inadequate guidelines for future policies. One critic explained,

"If the Fourteenth Amendment did not enact Spencer's social statistics, it just as surely did not enact Myrdal's American Dilemma." The Court traced black inequality to state action. An end to Jim Crow laws would allow the disadvantaged to rise to equality. But the ruling also implied that any form of separation, whether mandated by the government or the product, *de facto,* of settlement patterns, created unacceptable conditions that the schools had to rectify. No one foresaw the implications of the ruling, some of the consequences of which became clear soon enough. A black reporter summed up the reaction of his community at the time. "We won . . . we took the white man's law and won our case before an all-white Supreme Court with a Negro lawyer. And we were proud."

Erroneous assumptions thrust the nation into decades of controversy. A few cities in large border states complied at once and admitted colored and white children to the same schools. Elsewhere, progress lagged. Year by year, the issue arose, and the number of integrated places increased only slowly. When segregation by law vanished, separation persisted when it reflected residential patterns, cherished even by those who moved away to the suburbs yet retained nostalgic ties to the old neighborhood they hated to see decline. Families that could afford to do so sent their children to parochial or private schools.

Lethargy and pusillanimous leaders prolonged the implementation of the Court's decision, which would have been difficult under the best of circumstances. Most citizens remained oblivious until some spectacular outbreak attracted attention to the latest trouble spot. And politicians courting votes skirted the problem until a crisis erupted. In the campaign of 1956, both presidential candidates studiously evaded the issue; President Eisenhower later expressed no opinion beyond the vague wish for observance of the law, although his television address from the Oval Office stated that "mob rule cannot be allowed to override the decisions of our courts. . . . The foundation of the American way of life is our national respect for law." Virginia, South Carolina, Georgia, and Alabama set about circumventing the Court's ruling. Racists reasserted themselves and talked of reviving the Klan. White Citizens' Councils appeared in many parts of the South, bent on maintaining segregation.[15]

However, responsible men and women, aware of the costs, wished to conform to the ruling in *Brown* v. *Board of Education.* They understood that progress depended on industrialization and a rising standard of living—unattainable with part of the population permanently depressed in a society forever divided against itself. Desegregation, however painful, offered the best means to discard the heritage of slavery in favor of the hope of freedom. Others, tired of the gradualism represented by an older generation, determined to assert their own ability to act by changing the focus of the struggle from the courtroom to the streets. Legal briefs gave way to direct action and civil disobedience.

Segregation depended not on laws alone but also on residential patterns of separation, many of them old, well-established, and sustaining their own ethnic or cultural traditions and values to some extent mirrored in their schools. Householders in such areas regarded any strangers, black or white, with suspicion. Then, too, in some places the well-to-do lived apart from workers, whatever their colors; such uptown districts often accommodated prosperous black as well as Asian residents, few in number and ready to accept prevailing customs. Their children entered without incident into the general institutions. By contrast, insecure whites who had only recently attained skilled or managerial positions and had fled inner-city dangers to nearby suburbs sought overwhelmingly homogeneous safe schools. Little more than token desegregation could develop there for years, even without Jim Crow laws. In New Orleans, for example, in 1969, black children outnumbered whites in public schools two to one. And in nearby Jefferson Parish, where whites and blacks had earlier often lived in adjacent streets, more than half the public school students were black. On the other hand, in suburban Whitehaven, south of Memphis, the population multiplied in three years while the number of black voters remained fixed at only three percent. Self-segregation effectively defined such communities.[16]

In 1957 the Eisenhower administration collaborated with moderates in Congress to secure passage of the first civil rights law since Reconstruction. Its details, much watered down in the course of enactment, mattered less than the demonstration that a determined majority could overcome resistance. But the same year the President vacillated when Governor Orval Faubus of Arkansas defied the desegregation order of a federal judge. Eisenhower finally called out troops to enforce limited compliance in Little Rock, but did so hesitantly and without expressing any commitment to equality. Only after repeated turnings of the cheek, in the face of Orval Faubus's obstinate disobedience, had the Chief Executive acted at all; and several more years passed before the Arkansas schools began general desegregation. A foreign correspondent likened the attitude to those of the Roman general Fabian: "Mr Faubus may one day be commemorated by a reference in a military lexicon: Faubian tactics, or the technique of fighting a losing battle in such a way as to cause the greatest loss to all concerned."[17]

The delay gave convinced racists and other demagogues an opportunity to make themselves heard. John Kasper descended upon Clinton, Tennessee, in search of trouble, and White Citizens' Councils organized defiance. Unease spread in the region after President Kennedy used federal marshals to secure admission of a black student to the University of Mississippi. Politicians did not create the stubborn resistance but lent it authority. Orval Faubus of Arkansas, Ross Barnett of Mississippi, George Wallace of Alabama, and Lester Maddox of Georgia built upon the old Dixiecrat movement once led by Senator Strom Thurmond, who had created a third party with its own presidential candidate in 1948.

Time ran short for moderation. Increasingly blacks wondered whether white Americans had the will to enforce the law. Set against the hope that the intransigent racist minority would change its mind was the immediate reality: while others moved ahead, colored people fell behind by standing still. Without education, without access to opportunity, they sank hopelessly into the pool of excess, unskilled labor the economy no longer required. Each recession in the 1950s left larger numbers unemployed in Chicago, Detroit, Cleveland, New York, and Los Angeles, and narrowed the hopes of escape from Georgia, Alabama, and Mississippi. To wait indefinitely meant forfeiting a share in the promises of life in the United States, because it assumed that some would long lack the capacity to act.

A small but significant number gave up, turned against Christian deceit, and rejected the false god of whiteness. Early in the 1950s, Ralph Ellison had still wished to be visible, to have others look beyond color to see him as an individual (1952). Interracial marriage in the postwar decades became fashionable among blacks, as it did for LeRoi Jones. At last, in 1950, the *New York Times* began to capitalize "Negro"—a sign of progress. Then some lost hope. A few left the country. James Baldwin, a decade younger than Ellison and burdened with homosexuality, felt trapped; consumed by hatred, he dreamed of the fire next time. Younger still, Imamu Amiri Baraka (LeRoi Jones) proclaimed *It's Nation Time,* and sought to shake off all vestiges of American identity (1968). He moved into a Marxist phase, then became an ideologue and provocateur attracting attention by senselessly shrill, shocking attacks on the white devils.[18]

Passionate books found more readers in guilt-ridden white suburbs, where they conveyed the thrill of impending doom, than in housing projects or in urban or rural shanties less given to literature. But some blacks, perceiving nothing but cruelty and betrayal in the record of Africa's contact with Europe and America, wished to end an association they thought brought them only hardship and degradation; Islam provided an alternative. "Say it loud, I'm black and I'm proud," sang James Brown. "We're tired of beating our heads against the wall and working for someone else. Now we're people, we like the birds and the bees but we rather die on our feet than keep living on our knees." Robert F. Williams, head of a North Carolina NAACP chapter, thus formed a rifle club that drove Klansmen off with gunfire. But that capacity to act depended on temporary force that left others as badly off as before.

Every defeat in the struggle for equality added to Black Muslim membership and encouraged separatism. The followers of Elijah Muhammad perceived an ineradicable, inevitable conflict between the races and supported the idea of a distinct black nation. Taking up Marcus Garvey's old standard, they rejected integration but also the Back to Africa movement; independent African states proved unwelcoming for Americans of every pigmentation. A sharp distinction thereafter divided people who foresaw total separatism from those who foresaw total integration. At one extreme, until he turned to the more universal aspects of Islam shortly before his assassination, was Malcolm X. In 1960, as a Black Muslim, tired of nonviolent begging, of sitting-in, sliding-in, eating-in, he called for "the creation of a black state for the black man" somewhere on earth. "When our people are being bitten by dogs, they are within their rights to kill those dogs." Blacks might as well run the ghettoes since white oppressors would allow no escape. His was the most extreme form of empowerment, of securing liberty in America through black capitalism as harbinger of black independence, with violence unavoidable. "Liberty or death was what brought about the freedom of whites in this country from the English." Blacks could do no less. "When you are begging for rights, you are putting it in Uncle Sam's lap. You are . . . asking the criminal to solve the crime." At the other extreme, Bayard Rustin, a follower of A. Philip Randolph, spoke for "Negroes" who "organized themselves to demand to become an integral part of all the institutions of the United States."[19]

Few Americans, white or black, defined the issue so starkly. Most uneasily explored the implications of disappointing immediate results of desegregation. Schools in New York and Chicago, like those in Richmond and Atlanta, remained inadequate without legal Jim Crow as they had been earlier with it. Nevertheless, hope for improvement through integration endured, although not among embittered intellectuals.

Time, however, would not wait for gradualism. The comic exchange between President Eisenhower and Governor Faubus persuaded many Americans of the inadequacy of old-time flabby goodwill. The advocates of black civil rights occupied a commanding position not only by the moral force of their arguments, but also by virtue of growing political power and out of fear of ever-threatening violence. To clear the guilt of an ancient wrong, whites began to acknowledge the debt that only equality could dissolve. But neither the cautious approach of moderates nor the apocalyptic visions of intellectuals revealed a convincing prospect for progress toward that goal. Instead, a movement from below, peacefully but uncompromisingly, successfully challenged the Jim Crow system.[20]

Young black leaders came forward, some of them ministers like Martin Luther King, Jr., others dentists, lawyers, students. Unwilling to settle for anything less than absolute equality of rights and opportunities, North and South, they made nonviolent protest their preferred weapon. Ordinances enacted by local governments in violation of the Constitution, they argued, did not deserve obedience. Recourse to the federal courts meant years of costly litigation and further evasion by officials contemptuous of the judicial process. The militants therefore appealed directly to the country's moral sense. Support from the Ford, Taconic, Field, and Stern foundations encouraged voter education and civic disobedience projects launched by the Southern Christian Leadership Conference (SCLC), by the Student Nonviolent Coordinating Committee (SNCC), and by the Congress of Racial Equality (CORE). A boycott of segregated buses in Montgomery, Alabama, showed the way; and lunch counter sit-ins, pray-ins, and freedom rides followed. Youngsters like John Lewis of SNCC (born 1940) let themselves dream things that never were, asked "Why not?"—then acted. Such tactics required the courage not to strike back and the willingness to suffer the brutality of depraved jailers. In Birmingham, Alabama, the police used dogs and fire hoses to break up a protest led by King (April 1963) and made more than a thousand arrests before a federal emissary arranged a truce. Although sporadic bombings and shootings continued, as when four little girls died in the Sixteenth Street Baptist Church, the sight of brutality on millions of television screens aroused the country.[21]

Nonviolence and the simultaneous pursuit of legal remedies sounded a call to conscience. Journalists, better educated and more liberal than formerly, witnessed repression at first hand, became patrons of the oppressed, and confirmed the television images. Clergymen—Catholic, Protestant, and Jewish—responded and summoned their congregants to support the cause of human brotherhood. The surge of protest culminated in a massive peaceful march on Washington that persuaded the Kennedy administration to adopt the civil rights cause as its own.[22]

Recalcitrant Southern tactics forced the President to act, despite his previous aloofness from the tissue. He had responded vigorously to the jailing of Martin Luther King in 1960, and his Justice Department proceeded against state officials who defied federal court orders. But the mass outpouring at the march on Washington convinced him of the urgency of rectifying the wrongs of segregation. By giving official recognition to the demonstration, he affirmed the federal government's commitment to equal rights. Refusing to consider the problem sectional, he envisioned a great change at hand—the country's task, its obligation, to make the "revolution peaceful and constructive for all." Neither repressive police action nor increased agitation in the streets could resolve the crisis. The time to act had come—in Congress, in state and local legislative bodies, and above all in daily lives. Since failure to secure the liberty of each citizen threatened the liberty of all, concern with civil rights had to take precedence over concern with states' rights.[23]

President Johnson, for whom principle and necessity blended, inherited Kennedy's civil rights initiative. Recognizing the need to earn black voter support, he also considered equality a key component of his emerging concept of the Great Society. "I moved the Negro from D+ to C−," Johnson said. But "he's still nowhere. He knows it. And that's why he's out in the streets. Hell, I'd be there, too."

Hard-core Southern resistance remained intransigent, however. By the end of 1964, neither Alabama nor Georgia nor Mississippi had altered its attitudes toward race, and ominous indications showed that this defiance might take more overt, forceful forms. The eighty-seven percent of the vote that Barry Goldwater gained in Mississippi (1964) measured the distance separating that state from the rest of the nation; and four years later, George Wallace mounted a significant third-party segregationist campaign for the Presidency.

In Louisiana a hysterical woman brandished a Bible at the archbishop responsible for her excommunication; in Georgia night riders burned down a church where blacks had heard a summons to vote; in Alabama the Freedom Riders' bus went up in flames; and in Mississippi a tight-lipped governor said no, no, to every hint of change in God's own plan of segregation. These areas had long stood lowest in the Union in income, wealth, education, and literacy. Theirs were the smallest proportions of persons eligible to vote. They had subjected the growing cities to a decaying countryside. Their stubborn leaders rejected change that would uncover their guilt, and though they destroyed themselves and their world in doing so, they resisted what they could not prevent from coming.

Not even the rural Deep South could hold out indefinitely, however. In the end, prejudice could not withhold from part of the population a share in the abundance the American economy yielded, and the liberty it ensured. Blacks, too, had a valid claim to security, without which they would remain forever alien, a source of irritation from which no suburb could isolate itself. President Johnson's civil rights bill (June 1964) included provisions he had earlier stricken out as Senate leader. Moreover, he helped surmount the longest filibuster in history. The new law forbade discrimination in any public facilities, in places of accommodation and amusement, in any program receiving federal aid, in education, in employment, and in union membership. The literacy test could no longer cloak exclusion of colored voters. The Attorney General and the Civil Rights Commissioner received added enforcement powers along with a new Equal Employment Opportunities Commission. A Community Relations Service helped in the voluntary settlement of racial disputes.[24]

In 1964 the ballot had become central. Despite the intent of the Twenty-third (1961) and Twenty-fourth (1964) Amendments, and despite Supreme Court rulings against unequal electoral districts, blacks still suffered from discrimination; they formed about twenty percent of the Southern voting-age population, but they constituted only about seven and one-half percent of the region's registered voters. Disenfranchisement aided demagogues and left control of the rural counties to local courthouse groups, callous toward minorities and willing to tolerate violence, even murder, directed against dissidents, such as Medgar W. Evers, field secretary of the NAACP, killed in 1963. The refusal of juries to convict whites guilty of crimes against colored people outraged Americans everywhere, but to little effect before 1964.

National judicial and legislative action gave the formerly disenfranchised access to political power. In *Baker* v. *Carr* (1964), the Supreme Court struck down devices by which the states manipulated the boundaries of legislative and congressional districts to nullify the influence of minorities. Chief Justice Warren there expounded the doctrine of "one person, one vote" to assure equal representation.

Lyndon B. Johnson determined to go further. A Southerner who had always played within the system, he understood the necessity of breaking through informal and formal barriers to participation. But fair electoral districts did not go far enough. Johnson understood that the formerly disenfranchised also needed protection in learning to use the ballot effectively. Unlike Kennedy's glittery Ivy League types, he remembered from his own youth what poverty and hatred could do and how democracy functioned at the local level. After a bitter congressional battle, he had pushed through the new Civil Rights law, defining discrimination in terms of intentional behavior treating an individual differently on account of race, color, religion, sex, or national origin, and the Twenty-fourth Amendment to the Constitution (1964) banning the poll tax as a requirement for participation in national elections. Then the Voting Rights Act (1965) provided blacks the assurance of full rights that enabled them to act as citizens.

Federal intervention had roots in the Fifteenth Amendment. The concept had remained quiescent for almost a century, but its reaffirmation led to a gradual transfer of political power to the formerly underprivileged. Active enforcement of civil rights legislation and the assignment of federal registrars to secure equal voting rights in the South led to substantial advances.[25]

By 1966, blacks held state and local office not only in the North but also in Alabama and Georgia. James Meredith's march against fear that year symbolized the distance traversed, while the murder of Andrew Goodman and Michael Schwerner, two Northern civil rights volunteers in Mississippi (1964), had shown the way yet to go. The vision of the Great Society had not yet become a reality. Indeed, the Department of Labor concluded that the situation in the ghettoes was dismal, their high unemployment rates "primarily the story of inferior education, no skills, police and garnishment records, discrimination, fatherless children, dope addiction, hopelessness." But Americans had inched forward toward the objective of a society as blind to color as to religion and place of birth.

In politics, success rewarded obstructionist tactics only until party leaders perceived the self-defeating results of stubborn resistance. The Dixiecrats and their successors could not prevail. The formal rhetoric of equality became commonplace. Less clear, however, were the varied meanings given the word "equality" by the diverse groups that fought for it.[26]

Since the Second World War, reformers had shifted emphasis away from the leaders expected to define goals and toward the grass roots, where followers could best judge their own interests and tactics. Community organization became the preeminent task for radicals, informed of how-to-do-it by popular handbooks and manuals of rights. Sensitive observers of the urban scene felt the crying need for a force to hold people together, keep them from going adrift, anonymous, isolated, as family cohesion slipped away. The cry of the vigilant neighbor, seated at the window, no longer warned the street kids, "I'll tell your mother on you." The kids more likely ran about around the corner or in the playground. The no-longer-vigilant neighbor now sat, a couch potato, in front of the TV set. And with strangers moving in and out, families no longer really knew one another.

Saul Alinsky, who had worked with the unions in Chicago, perceived the need, though he pushed no particular social agenda. His simple idea: let people help themselves by assisting them to form equivalents of the lost communities. With funds from Marshall Field III and the support of the Catholic Church, he established the Industrial Areas Foundation to help in such efforts.

The Southern Christian Leadership Conference (SCLC), the Student Nonviolent Coordinating Committee (SNCC), and CORE (Congress on Racial Equality) took to the field below the Mason-Dixon Line beside older organizations. The strain of repaying hate with love, or reacting to brutality with nonviolence, informed some of the new groups, which repudiated the white man's law with scorn and self-satisfaction and also shrugged off the commitment to nonviolence. "We believe in a fair exchange. An eye for an eye. A tooth for a tooth. A head for a head and a life for a life. If this is the price of freedom, we won't hesitate to pay the price." Others retained an interracial orientation, while still others split into Northern and Southern cliques.[27]

Years of inaction after the school desegregation decision of 1954 had touched off a revolution, tending toward direct action rather than debate. Sit-ins, boycotts, and demonstrations challenged the legitimacy of government. The protests, gaining momentum, appealed eloquently to the conscience of Americans committed to the ideal of equality, even if only in the abstract. Others came to regard the very emphasis on civil rights as a pacifier, an effort to dull the pain of inequality through false promises and cant. Since life for blacks in a white society was but a modern form of slavery, they would never enjoy liberty no matter how hard others tried.

But all along, a touching faith survived—in the capacity of government to do good and expand citizens' freedom. "I know that government cannot resolve all these problems," President Johnson declared. "It cannot make men happy or bring them spiritual fulfillment. But it can attempt to remedy the public failures which are at the root of so many of these human ills." The end result, he hoped, would provide all with "a living place which liberates rather than constricts the human spirit . . . to give each of us the opportunity to stretch his talents; and . . . permit all to share the enterprise of our society." "The measure of our own success will be the extent to which we free our people to realize what their imagination and energy can achieve."

As the decade drew to a close the United States approached fulfillment of the dream Martin Luther King, Jr., had described in August 1963, that one day the nation would rise up and live out the true meaning of its creed: that all persons were created equal—thus transforming jangling discords into a beautiful symphony of brotherhood. "With this faith we will be able to work together, to pray together, to struggle together, to go to jail together, to stand up for freedom together, knowing that we will be free one day. . . . when all of God's children, black men and white men, Jews and Gentiles, Protestants and Catholics, will be able to join hands and sing in the words of the old Negro spiritual, 'Free at last! Free at last! Thank God Almighty, we are free at last!' " Fannie Lou Hamer, who led the Mississippi Freedom delegation to the Democratic Convention in 1968, stated the case more bluntly as she sat barefoot in a loose white housedress, rocking on her porch: "I don't want no *equal* rights any more. I'm fightin' for *human* rights. I don't want to become equal to men like them that beat us."[28]

The larger problem of liberty therefore persisted. "I believe in the brotherhood of man," Malcolm X declared shortly before his death, but "here in America we are in a society that does not practice brotherhood." Improvement, however genuine, remained gradual. "They taught you to sing 'sweet land of liberty' and the rest of that stuff," "they came up . . . with a civil rights bill that . . . would lead us to the promised land of integration," all a "foul trick . . . another foul trick." Mere wishes for change could not alter the habits and attitudes of centuries, and equality left a sour taste when everyone shared the same miserable degradation. Leveling governmental barriers did not remove the handicaps under which colored people labored. The vicious cycle of slum housing, poor schools, lack of skills, and low income widened rather than closed the gap between many of them and others in the society. Deprivation hopelessly handicapped them in the competition for desirable places. The simple neutrality of government would not remove these shackles; only positive action to compensate could do so. State intervention could assure the disadvantaged a due proportion of well-paying jobs and balance the population of neighborhoods and schools in a thoroughly integrated pattern.

Of course, abundance began to make a difference; the gains of some did not have to come at the expense of others. As President Johnson noted, "the community, the place where each individual knows his neighbors and has a sense of his own belonging, is being eroded. The growing gap between the common experiences of the generations threatens the family. The complexity of machines and the enormity of our society leave the individual frustrated in the presence of forces he feels far too weak to master." But a great society could "preserve old values amid the constant search for the new" beginning with the "ancient ideal that each citizen must have an equal chance to share the abundance man has created." And on a level playing field, all contestants had some chance to win. It remained only to work for true equality of opportunity. Hence Fannie Lou Hamer could not believe in separatism. Common sense informed her that a house divided could not stand and neither could a nation.[29]

For the time being, not everyone, black or white, North or South, shared King's dream or Johnson's or hers. White racists kept the flame of segregation flickering; ordered to desegregate, Albany, Georgia, sold its swimming pool and removed the seats from its library (1962). Let all suffer equally! And black nationalists refused to lower their guards, sustained by an array of separate institutions that served the needs of their communities—not only churches, but also newspapers, radio stations, and cultural organizations. However loyal to the ideal of ultimate integration, such institutions meanwhile thrived on separatism, pandered to the presumed special tastes of their audience. "King Cretin bleatin'. The *King* is here. So let them phones go ding-a-ling, so we know who you want to sing, I mean sing 'n' swing. Man, ain't I cool? A living fool! Gonna get off my stool 'n' kick like a mule. LET'S *GO,* Baby!!!" Crass commercialism laced the messages, as in the religious program in which Brother Bob assured his listeners that he had

> also experienced some of these troubles which I know many of you, my good friends, are also experiencing right now. I know, for example, that some of you are out of work, in debt, and that when you do find a job, there'll be garnishes against your salary. But I also know you need a new car. Well, you know, just this morning I was discussing your problem with my friend, Friendly Phil—a truly fine, sincere, upright, understanding gentleman—over at Friendly Phil's Fordolet. And Friendly Phil assures me that he understands too. So he told me to come on over to the station tonight to tell [about the great deals available].[30]

Self-segregation, a defensive response to the unwelcoming society about them, became a form of suffocation blacks inflicted upon themselves. Confronting entrenched institutional racism, they withdrew. Their bleak outlook premised a liberty tied to color, where one's capacity to act could only be enlarged among one's kind. Separatism also gained strength from the American understanding of social mobility, which linked status and position to the open competition of talents. With the hurdles of prejudice and discrimination lowered, everyone raced toward the same goals—thus ran the common assumption. In the novel, Addie wanted to do more than "work, work, work every day" at the sewing machine, "stand all evening over the hot stove, go to bed, get up, do the same thing all over again." She knew from the movies and television that people did different, exciting things. Yet unlike her, others, ambivalent about integration, sought a distinctive black community with its own values that rejected white dominance.

But preferences counted less than inescapable realities. Isolation offered escape only to a few. In the end blacks formed part of a wider society that imposed its norms on all, regardless of skin color. Preparation to compete depended upon training—that is, upon education, and upon the sharpened incentives and conditioning derived from sound family life. The heritage of slavery and the trauma of migration put blacks at a disadvantage in both respects and evoked calls for group solidarity to gain compensatory treatment. Elijah Muhammad and Malcolm X followed a long line of black radicals who envisioned a vast reparation program to compensate for the years of unrewarded labor as slaves. Later would come calls for a domestic Marshall Plan, on the pattern of aid extended to Europe at the end of the Second World War. Meanwhile, white resistance delayed consideration of long-range goals and narrowly focused attention on tactical issues, so that the civil rights movement became an uncoordinated congeries of disparate efforts. Weak organizational controls and uncertain leadership left confusion about how to define salient objectives; issues cropped up of their own accord, with reactions sporadic, local, discontinuous, and unrelated to any general standard of importance. Some intellectuals influenced by Franz Fanon called for redeeming acts of violence; and explosive activists, ready to precipitate conflict, grasped opportunities to determine the questions over which to fight while the established leaders tagged along to maintain their influence.[31]

Other ethnic groups also faced a choice about integration. Japanese and Mexicans had known the shackles of racial prejudice but made largely voluntary decisions. However, in some places the courts plunged head-on into dubious social science, ruling that "Hispanos and Negroes" had a great deal in common and had suffered identical discriminatory treatment of which municipal officials had to take account. Private and parochial schools offered some Catholic and Jewish parents an alternative to integration, particularly attractive after 1962 when the *Engel* case outlawed school prayer in public institutions. Some black parents, unwilling to expose their children to desegregation experiments, used the METCO program, which bused a few of the very best students to suburban white schools, leaving behind other ghetto families set apart by color, but with far less choice in education. Efforts to explain disparities occupied governments, the legal profession, sociologists, psychologists, economists, and a vast array of specialists for the next decade. In the end each answer, accompanied by a plausible remedial plan, floundered on the shoals of experience. Black liberty remained circumscribed.

The impulse to separateness spread to other groups that also felt deprived, not least to white working people struggling with the harsh conditions of urban life, yet operating within the rules. In the effort to rear their children in decency, they depended upon the solidarity of neighborhood institutions and particularly of local schools and churches. The appearance of strangers with different habits and lifestyles challenged that solidarity. When government snatched their children away to spend time in distant schools, to learn strange ways of dressing, eating, talking, the parents felt a deadly assault on cherished values, particularly since the Civil Rights Act of 1964 (Title 4) had explicitly barred "court orders requiring 'busing' in order to achieve racial balance." The desire of unelected district court judges, who generally resided securely in distant suburbs, to impose an illusory concept of racial balance on society by daily transporting students to remote districts amounted to an assault upon all the neighborhoods held dear. They resisted. Judicial activism ran counter to government by consent.

Arrogant jurists who substituted their values for those of elected state and local officials in administrative matters accomplished nothing good—nothing at all. Social scientists pontificated that "given the unwillingness of elected officials at any level of government to devise their own policies to end segregation in American cities, the Court's solutions were usually the only solutions there were." They conveniently forgot that those elected officials represented their constituencies, after all, and that an effort to rule by judicial fiat went counter to national experience. The resulting costly experiments ultimately fizzled out, having needlessly stirred up group hatreds. Further complications followed when evidence showed that changes in schools had little effect on either achievement levels or students' career patterns. And other reports judged home influence more decisive than academic environment in shaping children's futures, and regarded the middle-class home, despised by intellectuals, as the nation's most effective educational institution.[32]

"Liberty's Chosen Home," as some labeled Boston, became one of the American cities that experienced serious turmoil as a result of multipronged efforts to use the schools to redress racial imbalances. Action-oriented, "don't just stand there, do something" bureaucrats and social scientists, along with a few judges, combined to lead where the people had no wish to follow. Though told that there was no way "to stop court-ordered desegregation short of a constitutional amendment," Bostonians unwilling to abrogate short-run liberty in the name of worthy though ill-defined goals ultimately prevailed. They needed no constitutional amendment to abrogate disastrous policies that burdened those least able to bear them and seemed unlikely to benefit anyone. Learned disquisitions on "resentment politics" could not obliterate the result—"a war nobody won," one which actually left all losers.

The slogan of equal rights as individual and citizen attracted general support, as long as the vague terms remained undefined and unrelated to a program of action. The calls for brotherly love sounded on the platforms did not reduce the intensity of hatreds in Birmingham or Harlem. The California vote on Proposition Fourteen in 1964 provided a better measure of white resentment at black demands than did the national vote against Goldwater. Before long, civil rights leaders with unimpeachable credentials acknowledged that "continued emphasis on racial balance remedies was a suicidal strategy for the civil rights movement."[33]

Inflammable images crackled into violence. In the ghettoes teenage gangs nursed self-destructive highs, visions of sex and good feeling with no head-breakers around. Along the uneasy periphery neighbors tightened up, fearful of an incident that would become a license for looting. Radical babble from the sidelines blamed the "corporate bourgeoisie" for the black problems and urged whites to join the Minutemen. All the while television brought the flames into the living room. In 1964 and 1965, Harlem went, then Los Angeles, then Washington, Newark. "Riots for fun and profit." In Detroit forty-three people lost their lives, and damages amounted to $50 million. Self-defense became imperative on both sides of the color line. The report of the National Advisory (Kerner) Commission on Civil Disorders (1968) mournfully concluded, although on the basis of feeble evidence, that the nation moved inexorably toward becoming two societies, one black, one white—separate and unequal. In response, President Johnson called for an attack on the conditions that bred despair and violence—"ignorance, discrimination, slums, poverty, disease," and unemployment. By shifting the entire blame to white racism, the Commission evoked some sense of guilt, but it obscured the other factors that contributed to the disorder.[34]

White sympathy and guilt helped some blacks move up the corporate or political or educational ladders; many others broke through barriers on their own. James Farmer, who organized the Freedom Rides, became a sub-Cabinet officer, and Floyd McKissick left CORE to promote capitalism with the help of Chase-Manhattan. James Forman moved through SNCC to the Black Economic Development Conference, which aimed to shake down the churches for substantial sums in reparations. Others unwilling any longer to acquiesce in deprivation turned to non-political, extralegal means of attaining liberty. Eldridge Cleaver and the Black Panthers denied the possibility of improvement without a change in the economic system by revolution; in 1968 Cleaver ran for the Presidency on the ticket of the Peace and Freedom Party. White sympathizers condemned the "hopelessly corrupt social order" of the United States, and even Martin Luther King advocated some form of socialism. By then, however, the suffrage could not bottle up disruptive forces; the Panthers turned to terrorism. Stokely Carmichael, Charles Hamilton, and other intellectuals proclaiming black was beautiful condemned "white Negroes" who sought an accommodation (1967) and joined in the demand for a domestic Marshall Plan and preferential treatment. Black Muslims and others campaigned for separateness instead of integration.

In the ghettoes, calls for the redistribution of income and wealth meant nothing. Violence meant something. Self-conscious men cursed their own cowardice and trembled as they wished for a masculine impulse to course through their bodies and send them screaming into the streets, shooting from the hip. John A. Williams wrote with relish of an impending race war. Black women looked at their men as if they were bugs. Violence, like a homing pigeon, floated around seeking a brain in which to roost for a season. For a time, confused young followers of Malcolm X rustled about, like Alan Donaldson, in quest of an alternative god, among those whose liberty remained the most circumscribed.

The general climate of public incivility and lack of respect for authority made everyone a loser. Attacks and mutual recriminations among forces expected to set the standards of proper behavior compounded the tragedy. When disgruntled whites appropriated the charms of guerrilla theater, black advocates of forced egalitarian measures reconsidered some of their premises. Meanwhile, whoever could fled to the suburbs, declared off-limits, however, to those seeking to escape forced desegregation in the inner cities.[35]

Separateness acquired practical advantages from the unfolding implications of Great Society legislation. The congressmen who framed the civil rights laws intended them to operate in a negative fashion, to prevent discrimination on the grounds of color or religion, and indeed inserted clauses explicitly forbidding the use of quotas in hiring or education. Ultimately, pressure upon a flabby but activist judiciary subverted those intentions, converting equality of competition into equality of results. The civil rights movement thereupon ventured upon unsure ground.

Demands for personal security, for the ballot, and for decent schools, comprehensible in Alabama and Mississippi, deserved long overdue redress. Evasion of those obligations cast doubt on the abiding good faith of whites. But the same issues blurred in the newer context of New York, Chicago, Atlanta, or Los Angeles, where the failure to define appropriate goals created future difficulties. Disappointing results generated searches for scapegoats. For some the fault lay with the elite, accused of backing lukewarm, piecemeal desegregation that exempted the upper classes from bearing any of its burdens. Others, out to prove American liberty a sham in a class-ridden society, described all desegregation efforts as feints to ward off serious threats to the social structure. Still others, regarding occasional explosions of racial animosity as forms of ritualized rebellion, pointed to results that seemed to reinforce existing segregation. And the more extreme argued that all reforms generated through civil rights litigation benefited the white majority and in no way expanded blacks' capacity to act.

In the 1960s, the struggle for equal citizenship and equal opportunity nevertheless moved a step forward. Intellectuals and many policymakers ceased to regard equal opportunity as the measure of civil rights and instead used as a test equality of outcome among the discrete minorities thereby permanently fixed in the American population.

The impetus came not only from the failure of existing programs to alter the effects of past discrimination, but also from a clash between perceived needs and political realities. Reformers fixated on the notion of a backlash, which they discerned every time the electorate voted contrary to their recommendations. Talk about traditional values, they assumed, only disguised racism, and any deviation from the line they laid down amounted to ipso facto protofacism, calling for drastic steps as remedy. Magic in words: the law barred "quotas" but mandated "affirmative action." And then in the race to succeed, people who obeyed the rules and tried harder resented the preference in appointments to jobs and in admissions that employers, universities, and professional schools gave black applicants.[36]

Almost at once the irony became apparent. Desegregation required segregation. Integration as a goal yielded to identification by group. With life indeed a zero-sum game, one person's gain meant another's loss. Each expansion of the capacity to act therefore resulted in a lessening of that same ability on the part of others. And in this struggle of all against all, group affiliation improved chances of success.

Counting by color, always difficult by virtue of the long history of miscegenation and passing, became more difficult still by virtue of the shifting advantages of identification. How to classify the children of a Supreme Court justice—father black and wife Hawaiian-born of Filipino ancestry? The marginal candidate—could be in, could be out—settled the issue by checking the black line or the white on the questionnaire. Community control and empowerment that would help kids learn required teachers and principals of their own kind as role models. The demands that seemed outrageous when voiced in South Boston by the white Irish became plausible when voiced by Brownsville blacks. President Johnson supported preferential treatment, arguing in 1965 that in view of the breakdown of ghetto family life, disadvantaged youngsters required special help. They resembled, he said, racers whose legs had been chained, competing with others in training all along. To the argument that discrimination against whites was an unconstitutional as discrimination against blacks, Justice Thurgood Marshall replied, "You guys have been practicing discrimination for years. Now it is our turn."

In 1968 the strike by mostly Jewish teachers against the actions of the local black school board in Ocean Hill inspired one of the pupils to verse read over the radio:

> Hey Jewboy, with that yarmulke on your head,
> You pale-faced Jewboy, I wish you were dead.

Some sectors of the civil rights movement, including the Black Panthers, tragically blurred into a kind of blue-jeaned totalitarianism. Elsewhere confrontational tactics brought out the worst in people of both colors. Hysterical whites foresaw a time when malice would outweigh mischief—dynamiting of bridges and water mains, firing of buildings, and assassinations. Distorted media images routinely presented the deviant and the extreme as representative of the mainstream, and the more outrageous the pronouncements, the more excitement they created, the greater the news value. The remarkable economic progress of blacks in the 1960s did not extinguish but fanned the fears.[37]

Members of other ethnic groups, also covered by civil rights legislation, in time discovered the advantages of minority status as a means of expanding the ability to act.

Puerto Ricans only slowly arrived at that understanding. They remained a small self-contained entity as long as the sea voyage provided their only access to the mainland. The largest concentration had formed at the port of landing in New York City where they lived in tight clusters near Harlem and in Brooklyn's Navy Yard district. But persistent poverty on the island and cheap air fares increased the numbers of arrivals, for as American citizens, the Puerto Ricans faced no immigration barriers. The postwar demand for labor offered them places on the mainland with better conditions than available at home, and the ability to shuttle back and forth eased the shock of migration. As their numbers grew they spilled over to contiguous districts in Brooklyn and in Manhattan, with smaller clusters in other cities. They maintained a distinctive way of life, forming tightly knit neighborhoods set apart from both blacks and whites. In the barrios they communicated in their own language, found familiar food and drugs, and heard music that preserved links to the past. Hardworking and devoted to coherent family life, they helped each other out, guided by the belief that "whatever is going to happen when you grow up is predestined from the day you are born." But destiny was not all. "You yourself have a part in deciding what you are and what you do. Before you can do that you have to know yourself. And it's up to each of us to know himself." The freedom offered by life in America presented both a challenge and an opportunity.[38]

At the edges of the barrios, they ran up against rivals—Jews, blacks, and Italo-Americans—but generally maintained safe distances, each group within its own turf. The gangs young people formed also followed ethnic lines, although Cha Cha Jiminez of Chicago's Young Lords, under the influence of Eldridge Cleaver, called for Brown Power. Rising politicians, however, took an interest in peace and accommodation, for political lines generally crossed ethnic boundaries. Thus Vito Marcantonio, an Italo-American congressman, long successfully represented a multiethnic district. Communal empowerment could at first develop within large enclaves, in which one's own ethnic identity did not need to assert itself at others' expense.[39]

The local press had an interest in maintaining group identity, which provided it with circulation and with an advertising base. New York's *El Diario,* the largest newspaper, had some influence; but partial literacy limited readership. In addition, ethnic newspapers competed with widely read English-language tabloids. In New York City and elsewhere, also, Spanish language radio and TV programs attracted many. In the first decades of its growth, the Puerto Rican community did not measure its capacity to act against a universally valid standard defined by the mores of the white upper-middle class. As most inhabitants of the barrios saw it, their liberty, infinitely wider than it had ever been in Puerto Rico, left them no desire to return permanently to the places of their birth.

Outside the areas of heaviest concentration, the Puerto Ricans encountered other Spanish speakers—in Chicago and Los Angeles, for instance, people with Mexican antecedents, whose numbers grew with continuing immigration. The entry of aliens from across the border increased ethnic diversity, as did the arrival of a steadily growing Cuban contingent along with quite different Spanish speakers from Central America, Colombia, and Venezuela. By contrast, some Southwestern Hispanos descended from families in place long before the conquest by the United States maintained their separate identity. The needs of the census-takers, however, jumbled them all together as Hispanics or Latinos because this defined their potential benefits.

The Great Society welfare programs after 1960 eased the hardships of settlement, and the civil rights movement revealed the strategic utility of cooperation in pursuit of common objectives. By the same logic that had operated among blacks, some Hispanics learned to value their definition as an underprivileged minority. Others remained ambivalent, torn between the impulses to go it alone and to cooperate with others. Among New York City's Puerto Ricans, the influence of the public schools and of organized labor offset the pull toward separateness of the Economic Opportunity Act; and the California grape pickers, led by Cesar Chavez, ultimately depended upon support from the AFL–CIO for their boycott's success.[40]

In effect the law thus operated to create ethnic groups where none had existed before. Signs reading "White Power" or "Polish Power" thus surprised Martin Luther King in the North. Earlier, the aggrieved had asked the government to ignore differences of color, religion, and antecedents, and to treat everyone alike. Blacks and Puerto Ricans considered restrictive barriers products of prejudice. Redress called for the equal treatment guaranteed by the Constitution, with desegregation the appropriate response to segregation. Relief from discrimination therefore attracted widespread support. Americans of all antecedents regarded that struggle as in accord with their own creed of individual dignity and equality of opportunity, basic to human liberty.[41]

In the 1960s the search for a remedy gradually and imperceptibly shifted from desegregation to integration, from a definition of equality as the condition of lowered barriers to a definition of equality as a state of uniform outcomes. The shift, fueled by disappointment and impatience at the seemingly meager results of past efforts, rested on basic misconceptions about American society and revealed profound shortsightedness about the nature of the desirable goals. It occurred without awareness of the consequences.

In 1970 the word "integration" sometimes referred to the openness of society, to a condition allowing individuals the maximum number of choices without regard to ancestry. Used in that sense, the term envisioned a level playing field in the competition for employment, education, and political action, with the outcome governed by rules based on personal ability, tastes, and preferences. But at the same time, integration sometimes also referred to a condition that distributed individual members of each racial or ethnic group randomly through the society so that every activity contained a representative cross-section of the whole. Within the latter view, the objective of social policy became the attainment in every occupational, educational, and residential category of a balance proportionate to numbers among all the constituent elements in the population.

The antithetical consequences of the two positions thereupon governed debates over public policy. One demanded improved opportunities for everyone in jobs, housing, and schooling, even though blacks, Hispanics, and whites remained separate in some experiences; the other stressed balance achieved through commingling. Though buried beneath the passionate rhetoric of the 1968 campaign, civil rights efforts increasingly tilted toward a social organization racially apportioned within every sector.[42]

The emphasis on group identity had deleterious consequences. Equality mandated by the state entailed a loss of liberty. The stress on being part of a self-defined entity demanded rigid codes of behavior and allegiance, at a time when the dominant cultural values stressed individualism, autonomy, and independence. People compelled to classify themselves according to fixed, if artificial, norms lost the ability to interact with others; agendas formulated in response to past injustices, or out of tacit admission that only thus could members get their share of the American pie, clashed. Constant comparisons with others reinforced feelings of inferiority and insecurity, generating repeated efforts to compensate for shortcomings through group pride. A capacity to act dependent upon group identity would thereafter lend itself to measurement only in terms of units, and not of persons—of race norming. If empowerment depended on group strength, one individual standing alone did not have a chance.

* * *

The quest for equality concerned other Americans as well. The long tradition in the United States of sentimental and paternalistic concern about the Indians now seemed inadequate to the needs of those who joined the roster of underprivileged by substituting a presumed ethnic identity for the tribal characteristics and associations of the past. A recasting of history, not altogether accurate, portrayed these people as perennial victims of white rapacity, at one with nature, shielded by the organic coherence and stability of their communities. Using themes borrowed from old captivity narratives, novels juxtaposed the pure English maiden and the noble red warrior against the grasping Yankee. The claim to the designation "Native Americans" arrogated to Indians a privileged status, entitled as the only legitimate segment in the society to civil rights protection as victims of past prejudice.[43]

The definition of group lines depended upon governmental decisions, often of the most arbitrary sorts. Asians—a recognized category—jumbled together people of diverse cultural and social characteristics, associated by birth or ancestry with Japan, China, Korea, Indonesia, and the Indian subcontinent but with no elements of cohesion in the United States, while Italian Americans, Irish Americans, and Jews, Poles, and Arabs in the eyes of the law arbitrarily commingled in the general "white" category.

The number of claimants to ethnic status multiplied, if only to escape the sense of guilt that adhered to membership in the exploitative majority. The harried Bureau of the Census hastened to collect data in support of the Civil Rights Act of 1964, of the Voting Rights Act of 1965, of the Civil Rights Act of 1968, and later of the Equal Employment Opportunity Act of 1972, and of the Older Americans Act of 1965. The bureau's data and the categories embedded in them became critical—affecting political elections and redistricting; the awarding of government contracts, university grants and admissions; access to housing; employment practices; and marketing research and advertising tactics in business. Ever more often, also, access to benefits depended upon one's position within an ethnic group. That status would later become critically important in debates over multiculturalism, but it acquired immediate value as people learned to dip into available entitlements, allocations to which depended on group size. Yet the basic ethnic categories themselves had all the validity of rooms in a house of cards.

By 1970 other groupings newly conscious of their interests further confused expectations in the unabashed pursuit of benefits. The elderly, women, and the disabled increasingly sought to advance not by asserting the right to equality as persons but by claiming entitlements as members of categories damaged by past prejudice. Senior citizens, having won recognition in the Social Security System, which in 1960 carried 10,454,000 on its rolls, perceived the value of organized action through such bodies as the American Association of Retired Persons, then gained by enactment of the Medicare program, and then battled for cost-of-living increases to offset the effects of inflation. Attacks on "ageism" focused on various forms of presumed discrimination and particularly on mandatory retirement.

Women pursued a more complex agenda. They had long since gained political visibility and also admission to the workplace; now their objective became eradication of the image of a separate feminine maternal role in society situated in the home rather than in the office or factory. The federal Equal Pay Act became law in 1963, the year that saw publication of Betty Friedan's militant *Feminine Mystique.* Thereafter, disparity in the number of employees became evidence of discrimination that justified counting by gender.

But preferential treatment for women discriminated against men. If maternal leaves, why not paternal leaves? Flextime adjusted for a mother, but denied a father? And why deprive childless employees of the benefits their co-workers enjoyed? The vast influx of women into the work force, for the paycheck rather than in quest of careers, reflected massive shifts in mores and in the economy. The idea of a living wage no longer held, nor did the once-clear separation between private and public life, between home and office. Facile definitions by groups and efforts to resolve disputes by categorizing ever-larger numbers of people along artificial lines complicated everyone's capacity to act and in the end left everyone with less liberty than before.[44]

In the general haste to discover and compensate victims of past mistreatment, a wave of antiinstitutionalism released patients under treatment for mental disorders. True, the asylums rarely cured, only warehoused inmates. But cut adrift by misguided reforms, these people thereafter wandered the streets unattended. There they joined the "homeless" category, a recognized group also entitled to compensatory treatment.[45]

Change created anxiety. New forms to complete, strange bureaucrats to appease, the unrelenting threats of time- and money-wasting prosecution set people on edge. Jews, long in the forefront of the civil rights struggle, now found themselves on the defensive against black extremists, as at Ocean Hill. By contrast, reformers like Michael Harrington interpreted the same incident as evidence that the Ford Foundation used

"Black Power" to strengthen the status quo. Loony intellectuals did not help—as when the *New York Review of Books* cover (August 24, 1967) carried a diagram showing how to make a Molotov cocktail.[46]

Some Americans considered the pace too fast; others wished more speed. No vote decided the issue one way or another. The critical decisions rested with judges and administrators, some obsessed with the obligation to keep up with the *New York Review of Books.* Most citizens preferred a gradual adjustment to the new conditions underwritten by the economic strength of the nation. The nagging questions remained open: to what use would the beneficiaries put the wealth, and by what criteria would it pass to personal hands?

Hence the lurid fear that public and private power in the reformed state, sustained by the overwhelming force of technology, formed an inhuman structure that would crush individuality.[47]

In the past, Americans had assumed that society consisted of free individuals each equal in rights although occupying diverse situations. The corollary, seldom articulated because taken for granted, endowed all such persons with moral responsibility for their actions; the ability of each to act depended on general acceptance of that condition.

After 1950, the effort to correct the injustices of prejudice had increasingly shifted emphasis away from the merits of individuals to entitlements as group members; and that raised questions about the meaning and purpose of liberty, particularly since other forces at the same time altered views of moral responsibility.

CHAPTER 7

GRATIFICATIONS

IN THE GREAT SOCIETY, blacks often became emblematic of all Americans: each person alone, ancient ethnic bonds broken, all deprived of satisfying affections and avid for gratification, indeed, for any sensation to inform them that life beat within. And then the Hispanics. And the Asians. Anyone who nurtured grievances. The poor and the unmarried mothers. Never mind the realities that showed no change in rates. So many suffered. And not only the underprivileged, but everyone in whom rage welled up at life's shortcomings. The white Negroes envied those able to lay the blame on society for its faults.[1]

Back in 1928 the incomplete poet had described the loneliness he dreaded as but the fear of life. He wished to believe that no death existed, only laughter, accessible through love, "Man's hope flaming toward the stars."[2]

His expressions of longing fell on infertile ground in depression and war, but bloomed in the welcoming soil of the Great Society—although often in the unexpected psychedelic shapes of *Yellow Submarine* (1968). For surely human beings entitled to life, liberty, and the pursuit of happiness could claim also the rights to companionship and love that validated all others. From isolation in the dark, yearning to hold and be held, avid men and women reached out for sensation, hoping that the violent spurt of blood, the needle's jab, or sexual release would at least testify to the capacity to feel—that is, to their own authentic existence. Even self-inflicted cuts provided release from otherwise unbearable pain.

No strangers to violence, the mixed multitudes settled in their portions of the continent had jostled against one another since the seventeenth century; in a wild place, abatement of fears of punishment along with relaxed traditional restraints after 1950 let loose expressions of passion in blows, in thrusts of steel, and in hails of bullets. Along the successive frontiers, in the past, individuals beyond the reach of law had satisfied grievances, genuine or fancied, in their own ways. And in the great cities, the hastening crowds carried along such as often felt the impulse to strike out, moved by passion, greed, or the felt need for self-defense. Formal government rarely restrained individuals' urges to challenge authority and even less frequently tangled with organized gangs or bands in town or country.[3]

After 1950, science and war brought men and women to the verge of a new frontier where the potential for violence evoked a mixture of fear and anticipation. On the plane, returning from that first fateful mission with Hiroshima only a few miles behind him, a crew member wrote to his four-year-old son: "The days of large bombing raids are finished. That means that nations will have to get along together in a friendly fashion. This terrible weapon may bring the countries of the world together and prevent further wars." The letter-writer then paused: Alfred Nobel, he reflected, had thought that his invention of high explosives would also make wars too terrible to contemplate. Unfortunately, the opposite happened. Reluctantly Americans understood that the atomic shadow created by the physicists and engineers would cloud the world indefinitely. The reflection that the same power could take humans to the moon and beyond offered scant consolation.

Why they wished to explore the newer worlds they found as difficult to explain as it had been for Columbus five centuries earlier. Competition with rivals, the desire to prove the venture feasible, discontent with the older world, and the inability to make more immediate use of available energy—the same elements sent off caravels and rockets. Americans had come full circle—back where they had started from when the Atlantic had limited the known universe.

Already in 1939 when the war erupted, the old stable communities had dissolved and had left their members drifting toward despair. Released from previous ties, clutching at confidence in the capacity to transform the world, men and women remained proud of their individuality, though unprepared for the shocking disorder into which affluence would plunge them. In the trauma that followed, retreat to little closed groups tempted many, some to the plenty and self-sufficiency of the suburb, others to enclaves the youth generation created for its own counterculture, which C. Wright Mills identified as the truly radical agency for change. The analysis profoundly impressed young Tom Hayden, convinced that he stood at the dawn of a new age, beyond the industrial era. Now as at the beginning, and through their whole history, these men and women in space headed for great achievement or great disaster, exposed themselves therefore to the violence of the unstable. Lacking confidence in their power of persuasion they embraced violence. "The fucking society won't let you smoke your dope, ball your women, wear your hair the way you want to." That's our way. Action, by way of assassination, terrorism, and self-immolation.[4]

A sign of the times—brutality inflamed athletics. Earlier in the century, the fury that infused intercollegiate football had led to a temporary ban on the sport. After 1920 the game came back and, in addition, professional teams enlisting older, larger, more powerful players, intensified competition, which involved ever larger sums of money generated by television. The twentieth-century gladiatorial contests became regular fixtures in millions of bars and living rooms, "show business with blood," said Budd Schulberg. The thud of crashing bodies on the ice also raised interest in hockey, as did malicious body checks and forbidden blows with the stick. The uniformed teams, disciplined, ready for battle, poured onto the fields or rinks like well-drilled military squads.

So, too, after 1920 the inhibition that once led many states to outlaw prizefighting had dissolved. Instead, under the pretense of regulation, boxing commissions cloaked contests with legitimacy; his position on the New York State board thus made James A. Farley a power in the national Democratic Party and ultimately in the New Deal. Earlier in the century the fight between Jack Dempsey and Gene Tunney attracted to its ringside Charlie Chaplin, Andrew Mellon, and W. Averill Harriman, as well as millions tuned in via radio (1926). Efforts to suppress boxing as unrepublican and a throwback to barbarism fostering criminality failed. Instead, bored consumers demanded sharper fare and entrepreneurs who turned sports into gigantic businesses met their needs. Athletes became heroes, their success a validation of freedom and personal achievement as well as of social mobility, the winner a self-made man. And the more civilized, artificial, and constrained life became, the greater the attraction to the unconstrained, the natural, the elementally violent, whether in the arena or on the gridiron. At a time when the masculine ethic suffered increasing attacks, male brutality governed by intricate rules validated its strengths.

The weekly football combats became antidotes to the counterculture, to the breakdown of law and order. The contest became a metaphor for cherished American values—team spirit, tenacity, and iron discipline. President Nixon suggested that the same impulse that drove coach Vince Lombardi, regarded by many as an insensitive slave-driver, suited the nation as a whole. "Let's always try to be number one. In the spirit of American football at its best, let's be for our team." Spiro Agnew explained that he would not want to live in a society that "did not include winning in its philosophy." Football represented the American competitive ethic Lombardi espoused. Callous brutality proved virtue, only winning counted, and military metaphors, peppering sports language, symbolized the rules by which successful players lived: "Be angry. Be violent. Be mean. Be aggressive. Break his spirit. Bust his butt. Bruise his body."[5]

Then, too, righteous causes justified violence—in defense of the self, the group, the neighborhood, or the nation. Millions of young men learned to kill the hated enemy in Asia, Europe, around the world. They brought home the habits of hitting out, plunging steel, spraying lead. Earnest whites manning racial barriers shot innocent strangers, bombed black churches, and rioted in defense of threatened values. And blacks no longer placidly accepted the role of victims, but struck back where the opportunity appeared.

The new heroes and thus role models became celebrities, celebrating precisely those qualities the rest of society attempted to banish from daily life, albeit unsuccessfully. But the violence all deplored also expressed the qualities ambiguously valued, such as aggressiveness, great physical courage, and the abandonment of constraints. The vicarious thrills derived from watching a football game provided a catharsis from the streamlined features of modern life. Athletes utterly dependent on their own ability seemed the freest of all individuals, though their incessant training and strict regimen, and the constant threat of serious injury, made their freedom a mirage. Their public façade fulfilled daydreams without challenging society's shortcomings.

A science fiction movie of the 1950s, *The Incredible Shrinking Man* (1957), expressed the secret fears of males overwhelmed not by society but by their homes and wives. As the character progressively shrank, his wife became an overprotective giant and the home a collection of threatening booby traps. In contrast, Norman Mailer set up boxing prototypes for whom life consisted of war. Freed from the phony inhibitions of civilization, the boxer practiced the art of the primitive. That attitude required little more to glorify the accompanying criminality, deemed only "the morality of the bottom." At that level, "all situations are equally valid . . . the worst of perversion, promiscuity, pimpery, drug addiction, rape, razor-slash, bottle break." None could achieve more liberation than those free to disobey all codes, not even conscious of rule violation and thus unhampered by pangs of conscience.

Feeding upon itself, criminality escalated and increased the number of rational homicides, those incidental to some particular line of business—burglary, bootlegging, drug dealing, extortion, loan sharking, kidnapping. So Francis Ford Coppola's *The Godfather* (1972) lived by the brutal code of his family in a world where all rules of loyalty, religion, and patriotism had broken down, and only force mattered. Mario Puzo, the author, adopted the gangster theme to compensate for the lack of success of his earlier, much more sensitive account of the Italian-American experience in *The Fortunate Pilgrim* (1964), a realistic portrait of the hardships of ordinary immigrants to the United States. Not violence but hard work and family solidarity enabled these people to survive. But gore, and plenty of it, brought *The Godfather* gold.

More commonly, simple greed sufficed to account for violence, as when Dr. Raymond B. Finch killed his wife after a dispute over the property settlement in a divorce (1959). And ever more frequently, killings sprang from family disputes, jealousy, and petty thievery, callous responses to petty provocations. But in addition, seemingly senseless random slaughter erupted, as when a young man on the University of Texas tower sprayed the crowd below with bullets. No doubt he thereby acted out some personal disturbance, but also revealed a loosening of social restraints that had once kept such impulses in check.[6]

Supernatural sanctions had faded away. Evil and sin had lost their places in the teachings of the churches; the person who pulled the trigger did not believe he or she would roast an eternity in hell for doing so. New-fashioned ways of thinking made right indistinguishable from wrong, truth from fiction, and lies from reality. Morality became "largely a rationalization" of position in the power pattern, sacrifices for social ends needless. When General Dwight D. Eisenhower wrote to Chief of Staff George Marshall, at the end of the war, that he planned to divorce his wife in order to marry his secretary, Marshall responded that if Eisenhower ever again mentioned "a thing like that, he'd see to it that the rest of his life was a living hell." Times changed. The prevailing understanding held that mental illness or emotional disturbance caused marital disorder and criminal behavior, just as the environment made *Bonnie and Clyde* and *Klute* break the law—poor things. Too bad for the victims, but all those enraged killers deserved sympathetic treatment, not punishment. Intellectuals took up the defense. Truman Capote's *In Cold Blood* sympathetically described the brutal Clutter murders in Holcomb, Kansas (1959). And Norman Mailer went all out to secure the release of a convicted murderer who proceeded to repeat the crime. State after state abandoned capital punishment and, to relieve overcrowding in the jails, paroled the convicts who drifted away to endanger others. After all, lawbreakers had an especially broad view of society, a radical scholar argued. "More of them see the need for radical change." Did not the Attica prison uprising, that harbinger of revolution, presage a dawning consciousness, especially among society's most unjustly condemned and greatest outcasts? Meanwhile weapons became ever more readily available.[7]

The blood lust infected good, law-abiding citizens who never themselves harmed anyone. "Bang!" "Pow!" "Sock!"—the little balloons and subtitles that once punctuated comics and silent movies now, on the big screen, gave way to the knockabout slugging of the Three Stooges or spurted gore in glorious Technicolor, as the old inhibitions of the Legion of Decency and the Hays office dissolved. Even men and women who never raised an arm against a stranger got a jag on at the bar or in the parlor from observing the action as well as from the beer. Desperate to hold audiences against television competition, Hollywood tried CinemaScope, Cinerama, 3-D and spectacles, then discarded double features and refocused on younger, more affluent patrons who paid higher ticket prices to view films "suitable for mature audiences" and free of external review. The movies competed not only with over-the-air plays but also with docudramas presented as actuality and above all with the news, which displayed the "attributes of fiction, of drama" live, in short clips. Viewers could see people killed in the Dominican Republic and Vietnam, as it happened. Match that for thrills on the big screen![8]

Subtly the shifting boundaries of permissible behavior made the vicarious thud of fist on flesh gratifying. Those who disapproved stood by helplessly—with no solution to violence in view. Prisons did not reform but only hardened the guilty amidst degrading overcrowding. Parole, release time, and other reforms provided no acceptable alternative. Ever more intense, the sense of forces beyond control alleviated guilt and nurtured a feeling of victimization. No one had any liberty; everyone was locked into a vast, terrifying anticommunity, stripped of personal uniqueness, formed into a productive unit for a mass technological society. So it seemed.

No one therefore bore responsibility—not for being fat, not for criminal activities, not for drug taking, alcoholism, smoking, child molestation, or murder. Readers of Jack Kerouac learned the advantages of being on the road rather than at home where women had to purvey spontaneity, softness, cooperation, and lovingness while men, locked into a tender trap, suffered from an excess of responsibility. Husbands who abused their wives blamed feminism, which made them feel helpless and powerless. Fathers ceased to be authority figures dispensing blows and bribes. Instead they became figures of fun competing for the affection of their offspring. The average household size therefore dropped off after 1950. Murderers claimed that mistreatment in childhood made them strike out once they reached adulthood. The blame fell not on evil or sin but on "cultural psychosis"—on external forces that made individuals do what they did. Not only those raised in ghettoes and thus victims of discrimination, but everyone, to some extent, suffered from the impact of giant forces run wild—first the atomic menace, then pollution, then ozone depletion, and always machines. The American Medical Association heard the accusation (1969) that it had created a vast shortage of health manpower and thereby caused the needless death of countless millions; and Saul Alinsky charged that the war on poverty he had inspired had become a feeding trough for the welfare industry. Having come to regard prizes as entitlements of which others deprived them, everyone felt cheated, and not altogether erroneously. By any comparative standard, the country did well, better than in the 1920s, 1930s, and 1940s. Yet in the light of the enormity of the problems, little incremental improvements seemed pitiful. The culture of whining, fostered by pseudo–social scientists, instant experts, health professionals, soul quacks, and environmental fanatics, therefore left everyone to some degree a victim, insensate but blameless. A professor in the Yale Law School summed it up in 1970: a steady erosion in civil liberties for twenty years—that is, since 1950. The urge to feel a victim obliterated recollection of what mattered in 1950: loyalty oaths, McCarthyism, Hiss, and all that; and of changes since then, of birth control, desegregation, and the end of censorship.[9]

Narcotics, gambling, and sexual stimuli aroused and intensified the craving for extreme feelings.

Unwillingness or inability to delay gratification contributed to diffusion of the drug habit, which spread to all ranks of society, and which in turn affected education and the prospect for social mobility. Better production methods, wider cultivation in the Third World, and more efficient transport routes, as well as the growing market for illegal substances, greatly increased the inflow of forbidden drugs that soon outpaced the abuse generated by overly indulgent physicians alleviating their patients' complaints. In the general revulsion against anything that smacked of self-control, self-abuse became a national pathology in the mistaken notion that it reflected personal liberation.

The general designation "drugs" covered a variety of controlled substances, regulated by law and available only by medical prescriptions or through costly illegal traffic. The needs of consumers varied—relief from pain, urge to alter mood, desire to escape unbearable realities, quest for a high or for exaltation unattainable in mundane existence, or some combination of these impulses. People who had suffered unhappy childhoods, who lacked the support of whole families, who could not find stability in religious, cultural, or traditional values, more frequently than others teetered over the line to addiction, at whatever cost. Like the Tyrones, each alone, they wished not to see life as it was, and therefore hid from the world, hoping thus to hide the world from themselves.[10]

Alcohol, no longer illegal, remained popular, though time-consuming and sometimes messy in getting to a high. The Hollywood-Broadway-literary-film-stage world had a long tradition of boozing. After 1950 stimulating wartime experiences and plenty of money eased recourse to the bottle; whiskey flowed freely in a setting that shrugged off drunkenness. Those worried about their weight, but still determined to feel good, soon enjoyed "light" beers, testimony to industrial resilience, dietary phobias, and a vastly expanded range of choices that seemed to broaden ad infinitum the American consumer's freedom. Defining alcoholism as a disease eased the stigma of secret drinkers but brought sufferers within the purview of a vast array of professionals eager to augment their prestige, power, and income. Bureaucracies ranging from the American Hospital Association to the American Psychiatric Association called for larger funding of existing programs, and alcoholics increasingly charged discrimination by comparison with people suffering from other maladies. Since alcoholism reflected wider problems than merely excessive drinking, social and economic factors had to enter into consideration of the problem. The wail for grants swelled. "Urgently needed are greatly increased public and private monies for research, expanded research institutions and programs, and large numbers of fully-trained personnel. . . ." Only "a major shift in social attitudes and policies" would cope with "the prevalence, the persistency, the complexity and the interrelatedness of the alcohol problem."

Tobacco sales also held up, despite the links to cancer exposed in 1954; mildness in immediate consequences obscured the long-term effects of smoking. The cigar remained a symbol of wealth, power, and masculinity, the long thin white cigarette a symbol of women's liberation. "You've come a long way, baby" reigned unchallenged until feminists discovered its paternalistic overtones. More advanced thinkers made the little pale sticks phallic symbols and soared from there. Meanwhile the tobacco industry, like the alcohol industry, denied that it produced a harmful, habit-inducing drug and argued that in a free society the individual consumer was the best judge. But in a culture where self-mastery and self-control had become contentious values, activists agitated for greater government involvement. The state had the duty to stop weak people unable to restrain their own suicidal impulses from killing themselves.

Widespread social disapproval expressed by some states in hostile legislation did not suppress addictive gambling, particularly since lotteries in other places aimed to solve local fiscal problems. Wagers on the ponies or the fights, on the point spread in basketball or football, bought not only a chance to win but also the thrill of vicarious involvement in the contest. Bingo at church, the punch board at the corner newsstand, and the ubiquitous one-armed bandit swept in small sums from patrons who got by from day to day in heated excitement over the outcome. Ever more gaudy casinos lined the Las Vegas strip in nonstop activity, creating a never-never world given over to dreams, where reality fell by the wayside and feverish anticipation of potential gains counted almost as much as the win itself. A congressional investigation (1950–51) revealed that Americans annually spent more on gambling than on national defense, a situation that did not change thereafter.[11]

But increasingly the thrill-seekers turned to hard narcotics for results fine-tuned to the mood sought. Respectable arguments defended marijuana as harmless. Heroin, easily transported, now replaced morphine; peyote buttons containing mescaline and long sold by mail, and also LSD, heightened sensation. Aldous Huxley and Timothy Leary extolled the mystic states available at the pop of a pill, and very likely aphrodisiac at that. A trip exposed voyagers to intense sensations—interesting, meaningful, fascinating, or terrifying.

"Drugs are the religion of the people—the only hope is dope." The offer of "the new vision of the divine" aimed at "a new internal freedom." Why not? How different was that freedom generated by the use of consciousness-expanding experiences from the conventional sacramental substances—alcohol, nicotine, penicillin, or vitamins? The right to get high was the equivalent of "freedom—letting go," since "man's natural state is ecstatic wonder, ecstatic intuition." Metal people struggled against the flower people, who merely wanted to blow the eight million minds of New York City and ponder the meaning of *Siddhartha.* In those unenlightened days when LSD augured the psychedelic revolution, one of its unenlightened gurus recommended it to cure homosexuality and lesbianism. "Turn on, tune in, drop out." "Current models of social adjustment—mechanized, computerized, socialized, intellectualized, televised, Sanforized"—made no sense when everyone could see American society becoming an air-conditioned anthill. "Sorry, LBJ, it's time to mosey on beyond the Great Society." The ultimate liberty: each person would become his own Buddha, Einstein, and Galileo. With everyone divinely made, history as determined by mendacious white men would come to an end.

Some physicians encouraged the use, prescribing "uppers" or bennies (Benzedrine) and "downers" (barbiturates) to modulate feelings. Later, Prozac served more effectively. The expensive habits, on the margin of illegality, spread among the affluent with cash to spare, and also among the poor with nothing to lose. Whatever the source, the dependency fed off itself, became addictive, especially when it merged with other mind-altering forces—sexual, musical, religious. People of all classes, eager for relief from unbearable burdens, trapped by forces they deemed beyond control, had lost their liberty—that is, their capacity to act. Drugs provided a release; ironically, users felt liberated by subjugating themselves to chemical dependencies that turned them into nomads existing in a grotesque idyll of drifting through a mad, mad world.[12]

For centuries procreation, the ostensible purpose of the licit sexual act, lay embedded in a context of family life. Though not every embrace of husband and wife produced a child, any could have. And deviations in practice—no matter how frequent—did not diminish fidelity to norms, sanctioned by religion and the state, and by the oversight of snooping neighbors, as well as by the dangers of unwanted pregnancies. Respectable people ignored available alternatives—in urban red-light districts or in the more discreet flats on the Back Streets—where illicit passions thrived. Such indulgence became more common after 1920, in the era of closed motor cars, jazzy flappers, reckless girls, and unrestrained men. The addiction of the wealthy like Joe Kennedy and William Randolph Hearst to fast sex with Hollywood playthings became common gossip. Then, too, the knowledgeable used contraceptive devices—condoms, pessaries, and jellies—although awkward, frowned upon by law, and unreliable. And physicians routinely helped their female patients evade restrictions. In *United States* v. *One Package of Japanese Pessaries* a New York federal district court judge declared the importation of diaphragms for legitimate medical use legal. Unable for the time being to influence elected officials to alter their attitudes, birth control advocates chose the judicial route to legalize the practice. What had become an acceptable medical practice would, they hoped, before long apply to the whole population, giving everyone the right to make the decision until then restricted to licensed physicians. But in view of widespread Catholic opposition and fears of a declining population, the movement to liberate women from the fetters of male tyranny and unwanted childbirth stagnated.[13]

After 1950, science effected a dramatic liberation. Behold: Enovid (1960). An eccentric chemist in Mexico, a devout Catholic who sought to remedy the causes of infertility, and a biologist studying steroids created a safe, secure pill that, taken by women, prevented conception with a high degree of certainty. A decade later, the law caught up when the courts invalidated limitations on the dissemination of the medication and of relevant information about its use.

A concerted drive, directed less at public opinion or at legislatures than at the judiciary, ultimately eliminated all restraints on birth control. Its advocates ranged from those wishing to free women from bearing unwanted children to those who hoped to limit the reproduction of undesirable social types. Proponents of family stability and social mobility considered a lower birth rate a guarantee of both, and the vastly expanded middle class after 1950 agreed. "Times have changed," the Reverend A. McCormack noted, "since a Catholic couple was prepared to raise ten or fifteen children in a tenement, a flat or house meant for four or five. A modern couple are not to be blamed if they feel unequal or unwilling to face this task or feel . . . they could not really bring up their children well." The Planned Parenthood League, in the forefront of the campaign, drew support from the American Civil Liberties Union, which interpreted the issue as one of free speech—that is, of liberty—and from the National Council of Churches, which published *Responsible Parenthood* (New York, 1961), a powerful polemic in favor of planning.

The doctrine of *stare decisis* long impeded change in old laws forbidding contraception. Earlier courts had upheld the constitutionality of such state statutes. *Poe* v. *Ullman* (1961) still refused to sanction a change, demonstrating the difficulties in the way of judicial action. But Justice John Marshall Harlan's dissent was a portent. He deemed the law prohibiting dissemination of contraceptives an unjustifiable invasion of privacy, and thereby turned the issue away from the old questions of search and seizure into a matter of civil liberties.

Four years later, in *Griswold* v. *Connecticut* (1965), the Supreme Court abandoned precedent and invalidated a Connecticut statute insofar as it applied to the behavior of married couples. The majority argued speciously for the necessity of bringing the law into line with modern conditions and attitudes. But it made no effort to ascertain or define those conditions and attitudes, other than as stated in the plaintiffs' briefs, and it simply disregarded the facts that the Connecticut legislature, presumably in touch with opinion, had refused to act, and that popular referenda in that state, which certainly expressed public opinion, had also opposed change. In the end, the Court relied on the amorphous right to privacy, a right vaguely recognized in the past, though never defined or expressed in any constitutional document. Justice William O. Douglas found "emanations" and "penumbras" coming from the Bill of Rights to support the decisions, and his activist civil libertarian court majority followed. Only the unenlightened like Robert Bork disagreed, and the enlightened wrote them off as part of a backlash.[14]

By 1965, all effective restraints on obscenity and pornography had vanished as the justices, brandishing the First Amendment, struck down the old statutes. They first applied the nebulous criterion of redeeming social value to counter expressed legislative intent, then lashed out at all inhibitions, denying any power to police expression or to implement community standards. Bold civil libertarians, fresh from numerous victories that struck down all forms of censorship, found themselves defending child pornographers as well. As skillful litigation enabled students, prisoners, women, the poor, gays and lesbians, the handicapped, and the mentally retarded to find their own voices, could pedophiles be left behind? The newsstands and the mail thereafter peddled or disseminated all manner of garbage to people thrilled by peeps at the no-longer-forbidden. Before the decade closed, 500,000 people gathered at Woodstock, New York, for a countercultural anything-goes concert, innocent of sanitary facilities, but as symbolic of attitudes toward community values as the Chicago Seven trial in Chicago a month later.[15]

When the Days of Rage fizzled out and the summers of love came to an end, the quest for new lifestyles rather than political activity generated the decade's final hurrah. Transferred to the countryside, the guerrilla offensive rejected the morally bankrupt society in favor of music, Oriental mysticism, and drugs. The sense of freedom and exhilaration Woodstock represented masked paranoia and anxiety. "I just thought you ought to know where my head was at, Pig Nation." So many people together, "and everyone stoned on something. . . . Flower Power ain't dead at all, brother. All we gotta do is get our shit together and grow some thorns. Power to the People. Power to the Woodstock nation." The obsession with excrement paralleled the mud in which torrential rains mired the new nation. But participants reveled in this sense of "the very primitive—precivilized, pastoral, America before the white man came . . . really loving kind of communal images." Rain, the natural force, actually a good thing, created "such community there that it did not make any difference that everybody's blanket was muddy and wet." In the end "there was a lot of garbage. I mean a lot of garbage," a huge mess, "but the airplane was chartered." "We are stardust, million year old carbon/We are golden, caught in the devil's bargain./And we got to get ourselves back to the garden."

The permissive parents could not take it in. Having felt the after-shocks of depression and war and the displacements of repeated moves, they knew the penalties of failure, but never guessed the greater pains of success; they remained cautious, insecure, disposed to shy away from controversy. As the decade of the 1960s drew to a close, they learned to what goal their efforts brought their offspring. *On demand*—cuddled sleep, feeding, toilet training (easy does it). Now the products squatted heedlessly in the Woodstock grass.

Somehow a gap had opened between the generations that easy tolerance could not bridge. The family had drifted from "Beaver" to Bunker. Abundance had wiped away the economic problems; those determined to find evidence of joblessness and hunger had to look hard in society's obscure corners. Eloquent numbers described the steady rise in life expectancy, in per-capita income, in available housing. They could not easily describe the changes in attitudes of benevolent welfare agencies and public officials, no longer geared to police cheats but to aid the needy—deserving or not. In 1968 the Great Society's program lay well within reach of fulfillment. It could afford a parasitic and subversive counterculture.[16]

But those who looked back could not describe to those who looked forward the nature of the road traversed and its implications for the future. How meet the escalating demands from those who never lacked.

I want mine.
I want mine now.
I want mine right now.
Make the world perfect.
Stop the world; I want to get off.

Loosened inhibitions brought some relief to people once locked into traditional families with burdensome restraints and obligations. But liberation did not lead to relaxation, not for women freed from the burdens of unwanted pregnancies, not for men liberated from unwanted wives through easy divorce, not for others able to follow inclinations, however deviant. All these presumed extensions of the capacity to act proved but new restraints and fresh sources of anxiety because they did not really offer what the people wanted. ". . . All they ever think of is doing It and it doesn't matter much with who half the time but the other half it matters more than anything . . .

"... Around and around they go all hunting love and half the hungry time not even knowing just what is really eating them."[17]

Uninhibited, the media—television, film, and magazine—pursued the exploitation of bodies for sexual titillation; attractiveness no longer turned on *it*—character or personality—but matched the images purveyed on the big or little screens. A family on vacation could take its cues on what having "a good time" meant from Coca-Cola ads. Images on the screen could also govern "gender behavior" when patterning oneself on media productions resolved uncertainties. The more "natural" an action seemed, the more contrived in fact, the ideal conception of the sexes perhaps unmatched by reality but acceptable enough to provide models. In the realistic soap opera world, people lost their memories, jobs, spouses, minds; battered by shady business deals, drugs, and infidelity, they kept afloat with difficulty, brave reminders of enduring hope.[18]

In spite of the nascent feminist movement, the means to lure men remained the key to female behavior. Viewers unfortunate enough not to resemble the stock faces and bodies flashing on the screens could proceed through a variety of self-improvement methods designed to hide or obliterate the true self. The booming sales of deodorants and makeup revealed the almost universal reliance upon chemical aids to self-improvement. The more venturesome path to attractiveness led to breast augmentation and other types of cosmetic surgery, scientifically designed forms of self-mutilation. Intrusive commercials, some directed at men, most at women, urged the insecure to spend and act, thus to liberate themselves.

Publishers flooded markets with manuals for those unable to curb their appetites, touting the latest form of restraint guaranteed to end the battle against bodily craving, setting the self free from its entrapment in fat. Weight could be laughed off, walked off, or danced off. Cheaters learned how not to, lovers learned that love could regulate eating disorders. Fat became a feminist issue, the slim body yet another version of patriarchal oppression, an effort to keep women frail and weak, preoccupied with irrelevancies unthreatening to the male power structure.

Still, however available sex became, some individuals felt deprived or wanted more—the thrill of the unsafe, forbidden. Reported cases of incest and of child abuse soared, perhaps because greater openness encouraged victims to speak up, perhaps because the number of offenses actually increased. The shift to isolated nuclear households created private spaces free from observation by obtrusive aunts and grandparents; relaxed family ties and enfeebled communities removed restraints that had earlier inhibited or concealed such impulses. Newspapers increasingly reported sexual misconduct on the part of psychiatrists, physicians, clergy, and other caretakers whose positions of authority provided numerous opportunities for violations of fundamental ethical and religious codes. Herbert Marcuse, the puckish philosopher, urged the young onwards, in favor of that "polymorphous perversity" that would revolutionize society through an assault on middle-class values by the children of that very class—the new revolutionaries who would use sex, drugs, bizarre appearance, and behavior as their weapon. Everybody's doing it now.

Other compulsive disorders—bulimia, anorexia, obesity—also owed something to the altered social environment and to the loss of universally accepted moral values sustained by custom and religion. No fear of purgatory stayed the urgings of appetite. Nor did Metrecal advertisements that urged diet to protect the American way of life and preserve freedom. In the privacy of the home, more commonplace victims of addiction sat hour after hour waiting for the telephone's ring or watching the TV screen, stuffing themselves with munchies, enslaved by habit and inertia. Controlling one's food intake turned into a political issue, the anorexic an extreme example of difficulties encountered by women entering a masculine world. Specialists provided medicalized diagnoses, compensating for their starving patients' sense of inferiority. Social scientists found these obsessions an extreme rebellion against society's iron grip on its female subjects. Turning inward upon one's body and obliterating the self through starvation became the ultimate liberation.

The obsession with thinness responded to the unprecedented abundance of food and to its ever lower price. Diets became healthier as proper nutrition got credit for prolonging life and improving its quality. Items once exotic and costly now graced supermarket shelves everywhere while gigantic industries churned out ever better and more appetizing products. Choice widened as scientific jargon replaced old-fashioned ways of extolling the virtues of different foods. So well off did Americans become that no presidential contender after the war repeated the promises his predecessors once made—Hoover's "a chicken in every pot" or McKinley's "full dinner pail." The impact of the counterculture expressed itself in ever-greater attention to produce raised "organically," a term few understood but for which many were willing to pay more. Ever accommodating, business fostered the recurrent myth that related disease to diet, providing consumers with foods presumably free of the harmful effects of pesticides, fertilizers, and other chemicals. Products labeled "natural" cost more but seemed worth it, as were countless other items touted as good for one's health and also for the environment. People ate to win, as low-fat, low-sodium, low-cholesterol, and high-fiber products proliferated. A New York socialite who declared in the early 1970s that "you can never be too rich or too thin" articulated an emerging outlook that ironically circumscribed people's choices as never before. Faced with an unprecedented availability of food, they learned that most of it was bad for them. And since the family no longer gathered around the dining table in the evening, new eating patterns centered on fast-food restaurants and grazing.[19]

The rapist joined to ecstasy of penetration the excitement of assault and domination. Potential victims drifted among the crowds of unattached—unprotected young women, alone in rooming houses, traveling from work, seeking friends. Harvey Murray Glatman met his prey through lonely-hearts clubs or by answering personal advertisements (1951–59). Will they, nill they, he had his way with them before killing and photographing them. The Boston Strangler committed at least thirteen murders (1962–64), repetitious in the method of expressing Albert De Salvo's brutal lust.[20]

Plausible disguises cloaked other violations of the body. The scoutmaster, church organist, teacher, priest, relative reached out to touch, caress, possess unsuspecting boys or girls—mute, sometimes lacking words to describe the act, sometimes thrilled at being singled out, "special," sometimes afraid of hostile disbelief. The surreptitious act, undiscovered and without immediate consequences, lent itself to repetition, with the added zest of novelty. Uncontrollable appetites moved the predators, often once themselves victimized.

Not all restraints dissolved, however. The ancient biblical injunction against sodomy left a residue of loathing for homosexual practices. Those in the know remained in the closet or winked at what went on there, but public exposure or even the hint of scandal brought calamitous retribution as Walter Jenkins, President Lyndon B. Johnson's aide, discovered in 1964. Pressure from homosexual liberation activists undermined the earlier view of homosexuality as a pathology. In 1973 the American Psychiatric Association responded to such pressure by removing homosexuality from its list of mental illnesses, though with no more scientific basis for doing so than for the earlier opposite judgment. Not yet widely endorsed as but an alternative lifestyle, homosexuality gradually won tolerance. Decriminalization began in the early 1960s when the Illinois Model Penal Code condoned all private relations between consenting adults. As states revised their codes, sodomy statutes disappeared with the help of the American Law Institute, whose widely copied model facilitated change without public controversy. Elsewhere appeals courts helped out. However, in 1970, forty-nine percent of the respondents to a national survey agreed that homosexuality was "a social corruption which can cause the downfall of a civilization."

The Stonewall Riot in New York's Greenwich Village in 1968 marked a new phase in militancy. Inspired by the tactics of black liberators, the out-of-the-closet movement joined the vanguard of a rainbow of causes in the name of participatory democracy. Lifestyles of "moderate hedonism," already widespread among the young, embraced ever more marginal groups. With consensual sex for sheer fun condoned, the question arose: why not other forms of bodily contact, equally harmless and consensual? Once "normal" became a four-letter word, anything abnormal was in. Science helped with apparently persuasive examples from other, more accepting cultures—the Siwan men in Africa who lent their sons to each other for purposes of sodomy, or the Keraki anal intercourse considered essential to the right development of growing youngsters. Science, however, failed to examine the social and cultural concomitants—disease rates and life expectancy, for instance. Nor did it consider the more usual course of nature. Behold, the albatross! With the blessings of Herbert Marcuse, who had described homosexual rejection of genital tyranny as a social critique of immeasurable significance, "being different," no longer out, became so in that the unfortunate heterosexuals deserved pity as the least liberated of all.[21]

Senses aroused by the needle's plunge, the spurt of blood, the victim's stifled cry brought surcease, relaxed the nerves. In pursuit of that calm, others sought the easy-does-it state that once the beat of music furnished—cool rhythms, familiar lyrics, undemanding. No longer. Blues be gone. Assertive rock and roll blared, more strident in the 1960s than in the 1950s. Excitement rose—defying all constraints, duties, and obligations, so that only me, me, me counted. Even on the dance floor, couples drifted apart in impersonal steps, each an isolated individual. For the concert hall, John Cage offered blank silence or the jangled sounds of twelve radios tuned at random. Culture gone mad—Joseph Heller summed it up in *Catch 22* (1961).

> This is the dawning of the Age of Aquarius . . .
> Sympathy and understanding, harmony and trust abounding.
> No more falsehoods or derisions,
> Golden living dreams of visions,
> Mystic crystal revelation and the mind's true liberation.

Rock and roll appeared as a vital revolutionary force. "It blows people all the way back to their senses and makes them feel good, like they are alive again in the middle of this monstrous funeral parlor of Western civilization. . . . We have to establish a situation on this planet where all people can feel good all the time." Bob Dylan, the Rolling Stones, and Jefferson Airplane thus became harbingers of the new New World. The Stones' "(Can't Get No) Satisfaction" (1965) led into the Rascals' 1968 hit, "People Got to Be Free," and Carole King's 1971 "It's Too Late/I Feel the Earth Move." Don McLean summed up the decade in his "American Pie" (1972):

> Now for ten years we've been on our own,
> The moss grows fat on a rollin' stone
> But that's not how it used to be . . .

An alienated youth complained to the *New York Times* (1967) that "with so much freedom, I am left with no value system and in certain ways I wish I had a value system forced on me so that I could have something to believe in." Meanwhile his peers asked him to submerge himself in the tribe, with rock as a means of communication in the face of general inarticulateness.[22]

At Altamont, which followed Woodstock, violence and aggression burst forth, sugarcoated by words about love and community. The free concert provided by the Rolling Stones in 1969 attracted 300,000 listeners who created a living hell of drug casualties, fires, violence, and brutality. Four people died, one of them knifed by a Hell's Angel just as Mick Jagger sang "Sympathy for the Devil." Bad acid trips proliferated. But unlike Woodstock, which received heavy and largely fawning media coverage, Altamont receded to the back pages. Efforts to turn the event into a political rally (two Black Panthers had been shot by Chicago police days earlier) fizzled out, as one of the singers informed the audience that it needed no politicians here; politics was bullshit. Waiting helicopters whisked musicians away, leaving behind mayhem and bloodshed. Bernardine Dohrn further violated the Woodstock Nation spirit when she waxed lyrical about the beauty of Charles Manson, who had the guts to send his women on a mission to kill the rich. In 1969 Jimi Hendrix died from a barbiturate overdose, and in 1970 Janis Joplin suffered a similar fate.

In 1970 the counterculture had defiantly proclaimed its conscious rebellion against the once-dominant morals, values, and modes of expression. Then the steam went out of the movement, not by opposition but by deflation. The appearance of the Beatles had touched off a hair revolution; in 1968 the Supreme Court refused to act in the case of three boys expelled from Dallas High School for wearing long hair. But judicial opinion did not slow the spread of unisex styles in clothing as in hairdressing and in social roles. The revolution congealed in a society tolerant or apathetic enough to accept both longhairs and shorthairs.[23]

The Movement also stumbled over internal divisions. Advice from the left to talk more about the price of milk than about love, to get away from abstractions like "American imperialism" and into issues about which people genuinely cared, evoked no response. As in choosing up sides in a game, all victims of prejudice expected to line up together. The Movement revealed its grasp of political reality in John Lennon's 1971 conclusion that "Japan is ripe for Communism . . . it's all bullshit about them doing so well," and in Michael P. Lerner's assessment that "the same features of American society that move young people to sing 'I can't get no satisfaction' are the causes of what is wrong in the society." Yet at the Montreal Conference (1969) the Black Panthers shoved through their program with scant regard for white sensibilities.

Feminists had a rough time of it at the hands of the New Left. Stokely Carmichael at the 1964 SNCC conference: the only position for woman was prone. At the 1967 New Politics conference: "Move on, little girl," to a female who sought to make a point. "Good-bye to the Weather-Vane," Robin Morgan defiantly responded, "with the Stanley Kowalski image and theory of free sexuality but practice of sex on demand for males. Good-bye to the dream that being in the leadership collective will get you anything but gonorrhea." After 1970 radical feminists pulled out of the left since none of the males seemed as yet sufficiently enlightened to join the struggle for gender liberation; no longer would women define sexual issues in terms of what pleased men. Confrontational politics, acquired during the apprenticeship on the left, now applied to female issues. A sit-down strike in the office of the male editor of the *Ladies' Home Journal* won the movement more space, and in 1972 Gloria Steinem founded *Ms.* The Revolutionary People's Constitutional Convention declared in 1970 that "the nuclear family is a microcosm of the fascist state, where the women and children are owned by, and their fates determined by, the needs of man, in a man's world." But radicalism did not strip away prejudiced language or attitudes.[24]

Organized bodies of knowledge had lost the ability to hold culture or society together. Science had long before ceased to speak to any but specialists; having become incomprehensible to ordinary citizens, it could do little to stem the retreat from rationality, though conceded vast support. Dominated by mathematical and quantitative methods, therefore dependent upon machine computations, its conclusions expressed in private languages, science commanded immense respect but exerted little influence until applied to life through new technology. Few intermediaries or popularizers succeeded in restating the rapidly changing conclusions in a way the general public could assimilate.[25]

Americans took pride in the number of their Nobel laureates, but rarely understood the achievements that earned the prize. Nor could many respond to the intellectual challenges the discoveries raised. Astronomers, looking beyond galaxies to quasars, revised their conception of what lay out in space. Biochemists investigating the nucleoproteins (DNA) wondered about the concept of life itself. So what? Their information drowned in a massive flow of miscellaneous data, written up in *Time* or *Newsweek,* noted by some readers but rarely speculated about. These potentially exciting theories created little wonder or doubt. No reexamination followed of the accepted view of the universe and of humanity's place in it such as Darwinism had occasioned a century earlier. Apart from the Creationists who stubbornly clung to tradition and a literal reading of the Bible, Americans no longer held a coherent view of the world that science could shake. At most, laboratory results only reduced to dust the already shattered fragments of faith.

The respect for science, raised by links to government, industry, and the military and by the command of huge research funds, suffused the world of learning. The pressure of prestigious fields of knowledge like physics and astronomy weighed heavily upon investigators in such subjects as economics, government, and psychology, who studied what they could measure and describe in statistical terms, thereby also distancing themselves from the uninitiated nonspecialists. Sociology, psychology, and social psychology hastened to adopt scientific methods, veiled in their own arcane languages. Broader issues of meaning and purpose became the province of the humanities, which fought futile rearguard battles to preserve a commitment to rationality. Isolated cases of plagiarism, animated by greed for grants, blemished the reputation of some scientists, while others bore the blame for tarnishing their disciplines through uncritical reflection of patriarchal values and invalid conclusions that the influx of more women into laboratories would remedy.

Science and to some extent all learning therefore seemed devoid of moral purpose, suspect because pliant tools, manipulated by unknown hands. The outsider had no way of knowing whom the experimenters served. They produced antibiotics and the hydrogen bomb; they worked for a hospital or a business corporation or the army; their efforts bore little correlation to perceived human needs. Though on the right side, Mr. Spock of "Star Trek," a clean-cut rationalist, found himself ever at odds with the humans guided by emotion. *Dr. Strangelove* (1964) became emblematic—detached, alien, not quite sane. Since the differences between the United States and Russia would one day appear as meaningless as the theological conflicts of the Middle Ages, the non-sense of two superpowers willing to wipe out all human life by accident seemed to Stanley Kubrick the ultimate absurdity. Strangelove became the archetypal mad scientist with a mechanical arm that assumed a life of its own in its *"Sieg heil!"* salutes, animated by the prospect of death. The War Room became the arena where civilization made its final stand against barbarism, where Strangelove's dedication to the Doomsday Machine resembled man's intercourse with technology, both the ultimate sinister love affairs. As a crooner intoned "We'll Meet Again," the doomsday shroud formed a halo around the film's last image, the cloud of the hydrogen bomb and the extinction of life. Courtesy of science, unreality prevailed.

From within the enclosed environment of the laboratory or the think tank, it made sense to think about the unthinkable, to balance one terror with another. On the outside, Mutual Assured Destruction spelled MAD.

Doubts about the uses of knowledge applied to the social as well as to the physical sciences. Economics by the 1960s had developed precise tools, shaped by sophisticated mathematics embedded in elaborate theoretical frameworks. Its models commanded respect. Businessmen and politicians, as a matter of course, studied economic charts. Yet much of the work in that discipline seemed directed merely at finding techniques to implement the decisions of sponsors, just as development economics arose in response to the problems created by the Marshall Plan, AID, and foreign assistance. Furthermore the actual movement of stock values or commodity prices often mocked its predictive value.

History and anthropology lost authority, once every analyst shaped conclusions to fit preconceptions and biases. The relativism that infested science after 1950 deprived it of popular respect. Knowledge conveyed meaning only within the community that validated it. Without that support, the most elegant formulations faded away. Popular horror movies focused on the experimental scientist who tampered with nature, which thereupon broke loose and wreaked havoc everywhere while the master of creation, *Homo sapiens,* became a panic-stricken bit of provender pursued by creatures whose biological arsenal vastly outclassed his. Defenseless man in those visions reverted to an existence of animal pains, dangers, and needs. The alternative vision emerged from *2001.* In its twenty-first-century universe, HAL, a humanized companionate computer, provided almost cuddly warmth for astronauts while programmed to operate the space ship. Narration and speech remained at a minimum, since the future would render language obsolete. A formal emptiness dominated the atmosphere, appropriate to a space where none of the usual orientational marks made sense, where Newtonian physics no longer applied, and machines took over. The final words spoken within the confines of HAL's defunct brain, actually broadcast rather than delivered live, emanated from a prerecorded briefing. The Technish jargon of Mission Control contained no word for "liberty." To the tune of Strauss's "Thus Spake Zarathustra," the surviving astronaut prepared for the next leap forward in man's evolutionary destiny.[26]

Television deprived scientists of the external props to validate their activities. In the studio, anyone could don a white coat, call himself or herself doctor, and chatter glibly, authoritatively, thirty seconds to three minutes. No credentials required. Doctor of what? Degree? Where awarded? No answers to the unasked questions. Assurance alone counted—as in commercials. The designation "scientist" in the 1960s covered a variety of thinkers, experimenters, engineers, and technicians, the more sensitive of them aware that increased information only revealed the greater areas of their ignorance. The *Bulletin of the Atomic Scientists* expressed the puzzlement of some about the moral consequences of their achievements. Physicians for Social Responsibility attempted to broaden their influence beyond the sickbed. Others separated their activities in the laboratory from their external lives and thoughts.

Alas, they learned that outside their areas of competence they had no more insight than laymen. The pronouncements of Nobel laureates on public issues had no more value than those of other citizens. The more earnest reluctantly discovered that they possessed no means to differentiate themselves in public consciousness from the buffoons and frauds who also clamored for attention. A few scientists pursued political careers or mystical faiths, as the vogue for Arnold J. Toynbee and Pierre Teilhard de Chardin showed. Others felt attracted to Nietzsche's aphorisms, which justified embrace of the most recent, the newest forces—analogous to the procedures of science in which the latest theorem superseded its predecessors. Enjoined to doubt their teachers, warned that no particular way was the "right" way, the kiddies learned each to develop his or her own potential—own individuality, own uniqueness. "A conviction of decadence, the rotting of the West" seemed to Czeslaw Milosz "a permanent part of the equipment of enlightened and sensitive people for dealing with the horrors accompanying technological progress."[27]

Explorations in space.
Star Trek.
Out there, what destination?
What heaven or hell?
No sin; no brownie points.
Strive to what purpose?

The loss of certitude disoriented educators, who had once assumed that the school could ingest all the nation's six-year-olds, pass them through its digestive mechanism, and send them forth ten to twenty years later happily to distribute themselves among the tasks the world wished performed. That vision approached fulfillment in the 1960s, as the average years of schooling climbed, as did the days in the teaching year, and as enrollment and instructional staff dramatically increased. Yet results fell short of expectations.

The inherited concept of a unifying culture had, before 1950, justified the certainty that the schools administered to all a common body of knowledge and values in addition to the specific technical skill each individual acquired for a particular role in life. The blithe reiteration of that assumption in manifesto after manifesto skirted the inconvenient problem presented by the dissolution of established standards. Teachers once had known the correct in art, literature, philosophy, and science and, their confidence buttressed by support from European authority and by communal acceptance, had unhesitatingly conveyed the right answers to their charges. No such certainties survived 1950. In the arts the wall between academics and avant-garde finally collapsed, and a disquieting relativism permeated every organized body of knowledge.[28]

Churches failed to supply quiet certitude. A sophisticated intellectual at age sixty-eight could do no more than express belief in a vague, undefined God (1968). Some religious thinkers in the United States had indeed discovered European crisis theology, expressed by Søren Kierkegaard, Karl Barth, and others who argued that rational means could not comprehend the universe or explain the inescapable reality of evil's existence. The more pessimistic saw the impact of these changes on freedom. "The fire of human liberty is extinguished because there are no inalienable natural rights," a Jesuit said. "There are no inalienable natural rights because there is no natural law. There is no natural law because there is no eternal law, there is no eternal law because there is no God—no God, that is, but Caesar." Individuals could apprehend their own nature only through mystical confrontation with God's will. These convictions involved Protestants through Reinhold Niebuhr and Paul

Tillich, and Jews through Martin Buber and Abraham J. Heschel.

But a more benign theology more often attracted Americans. Harvey Cox's *The Secular City* (1965) announced the death of God—that is, of the God that was, not of the God that he would describe in *The Feast of Fools* (1969), nothing harsh but all hope, ecstasy, immanence.

However attractive the message to people on highs, or hoping to be, most citizens passed their lives insulated from fear, anxiety, or doubt—ninety-eight percent of them told pollsters they believed in hell, and sixty percent in the Devil. Some forty-three percent went to church on Sunday. They responded to the certainties of fundamentalism or to the array of offerings by televangelists or megachurches. Though Sister Aimee had died, her Four Square Gospel churches thrived. In Eureka Springs, Arkansas, Gerald L. K. Smith's Christ figure, seventy feet high, visible from four states and serenaded by the taped voices of Kate Smith and Tennessee Ernie Ford, looked quizzically out on a puzzling land and helped attract audiences of six thousand to a passion play enacted on a set four hundred feet long (1968). Among Jews, ultra-Orthodox and Hasidic groups, rooted in Eastern Europe, grounded their faith in ecstasy rather than in reason. Few Catholics who recognized papal authority and the discipline of a worldwide hierarchy responded to the call to a contemplative life advocated by the Trappist monk Thomas Merton, but Liberation Theology moved many. The wider society tolerated all these pockets of faith, although more skeptical of the animal sacrifice and voodoo rites of other sects.[29]

Some searchers turned to Oriental varieties of mysticism, like Zen Buddhism, which offered them a means of contemplating and reflecting upon the unknowable world rather than inadequate explanations of blank chance. Meanwhile rock singers mined the New Testament for appropriate imagery. Pete Seeger paraphrased Ecclesiastes in "Turn, Turn, Turn"; to Theodore Roszak, the young revolutionaries resembled early Christians undermining a decadent pagan empire. Others sang of the Eve of Destruction, the apocalypse articulated by Phil Ochs's Crucifixion.

> And the night comes again to the circle studded sky,
> The stars settle slowly, in loneliness they lie.
> Till the universe explodes as a falling star is raised;
> The planets are paralyzed, the mountains are amazed.
> But they all glow brighter from the brilliance of the blaze;
> With the speed of insanity, then, he dies.

Still other seekers found their way to unavailing gurus. A new age had dawned, revealing more things in heaven, on earth, than ever known before, more than even *2001* exposed. The universe by now formed too big a job for one deity. No one could guess the limits. Uri Geller's visions convinced a prominent New York publisher: Uri's powers came from outer space—force by way of an interstellar council called the Nine who appeared to him as flying saucers. Sure enough, sightings of UFOs proliferated, as did accounts of molestation by small-bodied, large-headed aliens. On the other hand, chance encounters drew many a young man or woman to the ordered life of the Reverend Sun Myung Moon, who purported to answer all questions. Others turned to Hare Krishna and, saffron-robed, took up stations at city corners.

Still others drifted off in more hazardous encounters. Holly Maddux, class of 1965 at Tyler, Texas, High School, cheerleader, pretty, high honors—voted most likely to succeed; then the shock of Bryn Mawr, where the Bible is literature, not the Word of God. Experiments in sensation led to an abortion in 1969, a year of wandering in Europe and Israel, and ultimately to a return to Philadelphia where a bright lower-middle-class kid would do her in.

Ira Einhorn in 1970 made a good thing of Earth Day, Fairmont Park, Philadelphia. He had dipped into earlier phases of the counterculture—apocalypse now, behold the millennium ushered in by the psychedelic revolution. Timothy Leary, LSD, Marcuse, Wilhelm Reich, McLuhan, pollution, population, guaranteed annual income, cancer—Einhorn knew about, lectured on all the trendy subjects. Inspired by events in California and New York, he brought the hippie scene to Philadelphia and organized Be-Ins, replete with body painting, exchange of daffodils, floppy hats, burning dollar bills: "Down with capitalists." Now smile on your brother, "everybody get together, try to love one another right now." Holly took it all in, took in Ira, too, then later disappeared; he fled to Europe when accused of her murder.[30]

Einhorn—unicorn—remained a small-time retailer of thrills, though he got himself a fellowship at Harvard's Kennedy School. He did not play in the same league as Charles Manson, who ordered his followers to commit bizarre murders in Bel Air, California, in preparation for an apocalyptic Helter-Skelter. Ultimately, the Manson family—the select—believed that they would emerge from their refuge to build a new society. The identities of the victims—well-known Hollywood figures—attracted prominent nuts, among them a psychic, a stylish hairdresser, and Truman Capote, instant murder expert. The assumption that drugs played a part in the killings set toilets flushing all over Beverly Hills and stoned the entire sewer system. But the panic proved unfounded; the family did not depend on narcotics. Sadie, Squeaky, and Sandy, like Manson the products of broken homes, supported by welfare, theft, and hustling, drifted like others through the tolerant counterculture in San Francisco's Haight-Ashbury—feckless, high even when not drugged. Jerry Rubin fell in love with Manson at the mere glimpse of the cherub face on TV.[31]

The nine-month, million-dollar trial, starring expert psychologists on both sides, played to a national audience.[32]

The wish to believe fed off the wish to feel that animated others, besides hippies doing their things, all avid for gratification. Well-to-do women, untroubled by fear of poverty or of childbirth, free to escape inconvenient marriages and to seek pleasure elsewhere, with what male or female companions they chose, exposed their unhappiness on analysts' couches. In vain! These *Ladies in the Dark* lacked Gertrude Lawrence's good fortune. Their restless discontent burbled along like that of their husbands. Neither fathers nor mothers found compensation for their own frustrations, by displacing their own personal—individual—desires into hopes for their children's achievements. Immediate gratification, now, defined all life's goals.[33]

Young women in the "underground" were sure that "the world could be cleansed of all domination and submission, that perception itself could be purified of the division into subject and object, that power playing between . . . sexes, races, ages, between animals and humans . . . could be brought to an end." Feminists began to agitate for their own agenda by protesting in street theater and symbolic gestures of defiance their subservient public and private roles. Dramatic action, as at the Miss America demonstrations (1968), attacked the notion of gender differences even when unrelated to inequality—trashing objects of female torture like girdles, bras, and curlers, and calling for a share of power, as blacks had. Less dramatic but more consequential, the fashion spread for bearing children out of wedlock, in defiance of all conventions. Sex as liberation was more than the "Cheap Thrills" about which Janis Joplin sang, which ended, as another of her songs put it, with "Woman Left Lonely." The disarray that pushed some over the edge drove others into the political arena.[34]

Women who defined themselves as a minority moved beyond the demand for equal rights to the goal of liberation. Encouraged to do so by Betty Friedan's *The Feminine Mystique,* they attacked the Freudian interpretation of a uniquely female role and also the dedication to motherhood espoused by Dr. Spock. Small local consciousness-raising groups formed centers out of which the National Organization for Women (NOW) developed. Mary Daly's feminist theology challenged patriarchal images of God, heightened sensitivity to sexist implications in language, and bitterly criticized accepted norms of family and personal life as threats to the ability to act. Women's participation in the work force rose, less often for personal fulfillment than out of the desire for income to surmount the inadequacies of a one-wage-earner household—no longer to stave off starvation, but to maintain a desirable standard of living. For most, the motives for taking a job in the 1960s were the same as those a hundred years earlier—the urge to add to personal or family income, whether out of necessity, the desire for independence, escape from domestic monotony, or the pull of a career.

No precedent guided the youth rebellion. Earlier generations had left home, struck out on their own, and rejected parental values. They had responded to the need to do something to stay alive, to achieve something to validate their individuality. But they had not clutched credit cards that made a mockery of their rebellion. Sandra Butler in the commune did not worry; she knew "there would always be people to raise the crops," stack the supermarket shelves. The sixties people believed that since they would all live in "a temporary society," it mattered more to develop interpersonal competencies (such as deeply intensive human relations), to learn how to cope with ambiguities, and how to let go. In the face of "chronic churning, mobility and unconnectedness," youth needed to follow John Cage's proverb for the age: "We carry our homes within us, which enables us to fly." Many interpreted the People's Park revolt in Berkeley as a harbinger of future victories, and Columbia's abandonment of its Harlem project as a sign of capitalist weakness.[35]

In the 1950s, civil rights had attracted young people who registered voters in Mississippi and protested segregation, at the risk of assault by hostile rednecks. Others later joined the Peace Corps to bring literacy and sanitation to Third World countries. Still others just empathized with the *Rebel Without a Cause* (1955) and *The Defiant Ones* (1958), or made a cult of Jimmy Dean. And some just quit:

> Goodbye I'm walking out on the whole scene.
> Close down the joint.
> The system is all loused up.

Growing up, leaving home, had always involved a rejection of parental authority. The 1960s experienced breaks deeper than ever before, because the young now turned their backs on the most monstrous Daddy of all—Uncle Sam. For Stokely Carmichael, the United States was "the biggest monster in the world," and Jane Fonda, in her calmer moments, vilified its way of life as "racial superiority, male supremacy, private enterprise, opportunism, military success and the success-oriented 'money is sacred' kind of principles." By 1970 she was sure that "We are right now, at this moment in history, locked in a struggle for survival against a monster which has been created and which we are perpetuating if we allow it to exist; and that monster is the American society." Meanwhile she raked in the cash. The road from Cat Ballou to the Black Panthers, from sex symbol to political revolutionary, led to Hanoi, a workers' paradise despite American warmongers.

Everything about the United States reeked of decay. The American Revolution was "just sons fighting their parents for who's going to take the loot"; the antipoverty programs aimed to split black communities and black families, a shrewd method to obliterate black militancy; education was Western brainwashing, an aspect of "the Thalidomide drug of integration." Anti-Americanism infused the rhetoric of the youth rebellion, fed by European intellectuals, Maoist slogans, and anti-Vietnam propaganda, but most of all by deep disappointment at the discovery that the world's hard edges bruised, unlike the shapes in dreams. Abbie Hoffman's failure to levitate the Pentagon in the course of the March on Washington yielded an insight: the United States would give birth to the most fearsome totalitarianism the world had ever known.[36]

The rebels turned against it all. They had drifted in with the Beats, destination uncertain—but aware of the wish to get away, seeking a belief by crossing accepted boundaries. Well off (more or less), they read Alan Watts and Norman O. Brown and Timothy Leary, or heard about them. They could not doubt that a clearing wind approached, and the Weathermen at least proved their toughness by gratuitous acts of violence. They made Ho Chi Minh and Che Guevara the new icons and deemed disruptions of high school classes and clashes with teen gangs revolutionary acts. The joy of seeing oneself on the evening news tempted many into publicity stunts and street antics—waging guerrilla warfare in front of TV cameras to destroy bourgeois morality.[37]

Many tried drugs—anything that might turn them on, ecstasy their goal, to escape the bondage of conformity. Why did some take drugs? Because they were "tired of comic books," answered one of them, Patrick Gleason. And the Hula-Hoop craze had ended. Somewhat younger, the Hippies in San Francisco's Haight-Ashbury and elsewhere suffered a spiritual hunger that small tribal groups might assuage. "If the thing moves you," said Peter Mackanass (1966), "you got to move with it." Tarot, Kabbalah, astrology, the occult, ESP moved them—to participate, to let go, create and perform without script or forethought. Feeling repressed, they empathized with other victims of society—"the blues singers and John Dillinger, Willie Sutton and Billie Holiday . . . all people who got burned for what they did . . . being repressed beyond recourse" (1967) by the unkindness of a mad universe. When he read *Howl,* Peter Borg knew he had nothing to lose.[38]

No longer children, not quite adults, functionless, they cried out against the elders who had failed to supply them a purpose in life. Slightly older leaders exploited them by appealing to their narcissistic self-importance, their instinctual reasonings and blind sense of self-righteousness, as well as profound ignorance of the encompassing world. I. F. Stone labeled them "the seed corn of a better future," the kind that "in every generation has written the brightest chapters in our American history. They are the spiritual sons of the Jeffersonians and the abolitionists." He wrote of course in blithe ignorance of Jefferson's warnings against involvement with student disputants as from "the infected subjects of yellow fever." Like patients in Bedlam, they needed medical more than moral counsel. No good would ever result from efforts to correct these fiery zealots. Get by them as by an angry bull; "it is not for the man of sense to dispute the road with such an animal" (1808).[39]

Told that their capacity to act would expand tenfold, the rebels sought release from the time schedules and other shackles on their liberty maintained by the society around them. In reality the tribalism that followed deprived them of any ability to act. The anguish of the smart kids in *Portnoy's Complaint* and *Fear of Flying* arose not from lack of money but from lack of goals, from the sterility of the lifestyle to which destiny condemned them. As a result, everything sounded like a meaningless yammer.

> You just put on your coat and hat
> And walk yourself to the laundromat
> And when you finish doin' that
> Bring in the dog and put out the cat.
> Yakety yak!
> "Don't talk back." (1958)

Strangers like Edmund Tyrone, they never felt at home, even at home. Shrugging off advice—share your toys, brush your teeth—they struck back with ridicule, chortling over the Teen-Age Werewolf and the Teen-Age Frankenstein (1957). Do the opposite:

> Well, he never washed his face
> And he never combed his hair
> He had axle grease imbedded underneath his fingernails.

In the muscle of his arm was a red tattoo
A picture of a heart
Sayin', "Mother I love you." (1955)

Clown around like the Beatles or Charlie Brown:

Who walks into the classroom cool and slow?
Who calls the English teacher Daddy-O?
Charlie Brown
Charlie Brown
He's a clown
That Charlie Brown. (1959)[40]

The mournful Elvis songs had expressed the misery of the unattached—transients, as in "Heartbreak Hotel." All alone, all alone. Young men and women, adrift, heard themselves in Sergeant Pepper's Lonely Hearts, a club always crowded that always made room for lonely people to cry in the gloom and tell themselves that love would rout the Blue Meanies. The dismal alternative: "Eleanor Rigby," who "died in the church and was buried along with her name. Nobody came."

Having turned against the parents, youth turned also against the values of the older generation and especially against material success, which sought to draw *The Graduate* into the plastics business—the fake substance of a fake life. Floating in the swimming pool, Benjamin nurses his grievance as he nurses his beer. Doomed like the parents who abuse him with gifts and kindness. Make something happen, or in five years he will be like them. Initiated into sex by a mom—the indignity: he likes it. So he breaks into the church, steals the girl, and rides triumphantly off to nowhere.

Children born after 1945 did not understand the attitudes toward work and wages of parents who had lived through war, depression, and unemployment. Why sweat now, when all came so easily? Anthony Burgess's *A Clockwork Orange* encapsulated the results in its portrayal of Alex, truly liberated only with everyone else in bondage, the Ludovico Technique of mechanical (clockwork) imposition of goodness by aversive therapy a harbinger of an ethically and morally meaningless life, governed as by B. F. Skinner's behavioral psychology, its simplification of human nature a denial of the existence of evil and original sin. No wonder American readers and later viewers of Stanley Kubrick's version of the novel found the message unsettling.

Schools did the youngsters in, having become the training ground for the staffs of the Great Society's new economy, which demanded in successful men and women traits somewhat different from those of past achievers. Fixed ties to a place, a family known in the community, and a personal reputation among neighbors in the 1960s proved not as helpful as readiness to move, adaptability to new circumstances, and sensitivity to the opinions of colleagues, collaborators, and customers. The ability to work in large groups, not as a mechanical cog, but as a responsive participant, became the primary qualification for advancement. Since the individual functioned as part of a team, the aggressive, assertive personality proved effective only when pliable enough to take account of others.

A complex technological productive system met social needs by drawing upon an open pool of talent, which included a large part of the whole population. Every sector of the economy competed for personnel, and the millions of young people who annually sought careers sorted themselves out for one calling or another by an intricate pattern of decisions that reached back to early childhood.

No centralized control directed the flow to jobs. The process of appraisal and selection consisted of myriads of decisions shaped by employer and family preferences, by resources and social values, all weighted in one direction or another by the differences in rewards attached to various occupations. Numerous particular combinations determined who passed into which calling. All were scarcely predictable, shaped by chance as well as by individual preference.

Educators and administrators, however, expressed a heady confidence that the schools could prepare youth for life, sort them out for appropriate careers, and also further equality. These institutions commanded knowledge vital to all and transmitted skills essential to the operations of modern technology, along with information deemed useful to citizens. Education thus molded its products for appropriate places in life. Graduates emerged sound in body, trained to read and drive cars, expected to vote and to marry, and directed toward congenial careers. Such claims gained force with expansion of the corps of teachers and the administrative bureaucracy, which disposed of formidable political power and commanded substantial budgets.

Children moved through the four-tier system, each level locked into its predecessor and essential to the next step. Elementary to secondary school to college to professional school; six, fourteen, eighteen, twenty-two—with the ages also fixed. The product got no immersal in practice until well on to thirty. *And everyone,* the expectation ran, *would follow the same course.*

Reality in the sixties had not quite approached the ideal, as yet. Substantial numbers, by choice or necessity, fell out of the race, and a significant share of the winners ran by paths of their own choosing. Aggressive types, impatient with the prescribed course, broke away, and some of them prospered, especially if they enjoyed the lead of inherited wealth. At the other extreme, the children of blacks and of poor white families started with such heavy handicaps that they rarely caught up. Expectations for women differed from those for men, and that affected the course of careers. And between the very rich and the hopelessly disadvantaged lived blocks upon blocks of solid craftsmen, proud of their skills, protected by unions, situated in comfortable neighborhoods, and satisfied with the gains of the post-Depression years; often their sons aspired only to take up the same trades.

Despite these exceptions, the society affirmed the norm of open competition. Any boy or girl qualified by ability and effort could arrive at any destination. The schools, into which the whole population passed, sedulously nurtured the expectation that everyone would run the same race, and the more open the terms of entry, the more intense the competition.[41]

Aggrieved young people seethed quietly until the disaffected made a target of higher education, which presumed to stand *in local parentis*—and especially the bright kids. Having gotten SATs in the seven hundreds, having been anointed by admission into the elite colleges, they could not tolerate rules, requirements, subordination. And for what? To secure entry to a good graduate or professional school, with the distant reward a gray flannel suit in some other large, impersonal organization. Savio and Rudd rose up in arms long before they heard of Saigon or felt threatened by the draft. As youngsters saw it, the victors in the rat race remained rats.

The rejection of all authority in part animated the upheavals in the universities, where students considered faculty and administration emblematic of wider problems. Only a small minority participated in the rebellion. But the ease with which so many university governing bodies caved in justified the optimistic student belief that they could subdue the rest of society as easily.[42]

The termination of student military deferments kindled the conflagration; until then the Vietnam War had been remote, abstract—one of many protestable evils. Now the draft made it personal, close. Anger flared at the prospect of taking orders from a horny-handed sergeant whose scores may not even have gotten into the six hundreds. A little demonstration, unchallenged, ballooned; building occupations went unpunished; unconditional demands met acquiescent responses. News from Paris, Berkeley fanned the flames. Timid faculties turned the other cheek, encouraging escalation; their ranks had swelled in the expansive years with para-intellectuals, who had some scraps of knowledge, but had never learned to think for themselves or to pursue truth. "Free universities" sprouted, and administrators hastened to buy off the attackers. At Harvard unqualified rowdies thrust a radical course into the curriculum, luring the unwary by easy grading. Fun and games but empty of content—a sad mockery of the *Veritas* emblazoned on the college seal. There as elsewhere, the eclectic left took command—a fashionable brew of Marxism, deconstruction, and radical egalitarian populism. The decade then ended in farcical crisis from which the universities did not recover.[43]

For the time being, Dwight Macdonald found it fun—exhilarating, exciting, pleasant, friendly, joyous, as a revolution should be. But the outcome mocked the goals eloquently stated by Tom Hayden, Students for a Democratic Society, Port Huron platform:

From Free Speech to political correctness;
From cozy relations between teachers and students, family-like, communal, to the impersonal multiversity, a shopping mall dense with administrators, heavily policed to prevent jarring contacts and everyone moving in shock-free grooves;
From the cultural compatibility of people of all origins to separatist multiculturalism;
From participatory democracy and humanism to a stratified chain of command to stimulate competition.

The rigid bars of a bureaucratic cage thus replaced the silken bands of authority.[44]

At the Ivy League commencements of 1969 the valedictorians let the grown-ups have it. At Brown, one orator confessed that society had very few realities for him. "They exist, but they are not real. When I watch the news every night, it's not real to me. These can't be realities to me. I acknowledge that they exist but I can't allow myself to see them in my real world because, if I do that, then I am willing to accept them. The way things should be has got to be the way things are or none of us should be able to sleep well at night." And Wellesley heard a summons to search for a more immediate, ecstatic, and penetrating mode of living.[45]

Whereupon Ira and Hillary shrewdly embarked on careers that would earn them substantial incomes and prepare them to do good—in the long run.

The abundance of the Great Society set the decades apart. In the 1950s, people made such choices as the following: less income or more;

security or risk; child care or career; tomorrow or today; passion or fidelity—each decision the product of individual reflection or impulse, eased by the whiskey's burn or the narcotic high, by media stimulus and commercials' avarice, all of which swamped the calm, reflective, virtuous citizen cherished in the past. The 1960s required no choices; the great equalizer, the lust for immediate gratification, won out, made it possible to have it both ways, or either, or neither.

At a progressive wedding ceremony, the reverend asks the bride, "Will you, Jane, marry Tom and will you try in this marriage to grow together, to be honest, to share the responsibility for your children and to maintain a sense of humor?" Whereupon the happy couple sets out to stage a little guerrilla theater outside President Nixon's Western White House, with a cookout, dubbed "the starve out."

They could not, however, have what some knew they most wanted, a real community where each was known: not just held together at a distance as were all who took the L.L. Bean catalogue, but in some equivalent of the older group life that forced each to be with the others. Failing this, they might unwittingly find themselves among the Blue Meanies. Hence the popularity of encounter and sensitivity training groups. Meanwhile others cashed in. After the Beatles left Kansas City on one of their American tours, the hotel manager sold their bed linens, to be cut into small squares, mounted on cards, and peddled at ten dollars apiece—affidavit attesting to authenticity attached. In New York, cans of Beatle Breath went on sale, while backstage at concerts disabled people, wheeled into dressing rooms, received the healing touch. Amidst the customary swipes at "this decadent American society" and "racist capitalist government," black student unions plaintively demanded "an education for our people that teaches us how to survive in the present-day society. We believe that if the educational system does not teach us how to survive in society and the world, it loses its meaning for existence."[46]

Society, acquiescent, lowered the barriers against hedonistic impulses. Its churches, seeking understanding, tolerantly reaching out for strays, rejected inhibitions. "Wet Dream over You" and "Group Grope," popular songs, did well, and Jimi Hendrix titillated listeners with orgasmic grunts and suggestive moans. Jim Morrison of the Doors declared, "I am interested in anything about revolt, disorder, chaos, especially activity that has no meaning. It seems to me to be the road to freedom." By 1969 he faced six warrants issued for lewd and lascivious behavior in public. Two years later he died of a heart attack. Meanwhile, millions drifted into alternative religious and spiritual movements. Only the fundamentalist rear guard still insisted on the reality of evil. The law no longer policed personal behavior except for old-style felonies and gang-related drug traffic. Youth achieved full liberty, denied nothing, its petulant prayers answered, granted ever more independence, its hands untied, external controls relaxed. And so they stumbled toward a future in which they would once more beg for government.

Harry Nilsson sang the elegy to the flower children in "Driving Along" (1971):

> Look at those people standing on the petals of a flower
> Look at those petals pumping for a little bit of power

What happened in the 1960s? "Nothing happened except we all dressed up," said John Lennon. "The same bastards are in control, doing the same things, people living in fucking poverty with rats crawling all over them." It's just the same, "only I am thirty and a lot of people have got long hair."[47]

The self-defined genius, absorbed in the ego, self-centered and exploitative, rejected the role of brother's keeper, just as Ezra Pound had shrugged off loyalty to country in defense of Fascism, taking refuge in anti-Semitic obscenities broadcast on Rome radio—his private rebellion against the liberty modernity imparted. Robert Brautigan, author of *Trout Fishing in America,* once the bible of the Woodstock generation, later shot himself in a remote cabin; his body lay undiscovered for several weeks. The Beatles broke up, and that icon of political art, Bob Dylan, took a hike. Senator Edward M. Kennedy's presidential ambitions drowned in Chappaquiddick while over four hundred universities experienced strikes or closed in chaos. Four students died at Kent State. The Census Bureau reported that the number of people living with unmarried partners of the opposite sex had risen 70 percent since 1960, and on the fiftieth anniversary of the women's suffrage amendment, eighteen-year-olds got the right to vote. The year's hit songs included "Leaving on a Jet Plane" and "Raindrops Keep Falling on My Head." The 1950s returned to style, and popular demand brought back Chuck Berry, the Everly Brothers, and Little Richard. Attention-grabbers like Elton John had to dress like Donald Duck to generate publicity, while "Yummy, Yummy, Yummy, I've Got Love in My Tummy" also reflected the distinctive taste of 1970.

That year the War on Poverty showed signs of failure, despite the hopes lavished on it. New York City's welfare rolls grew by 50,000 in August 1968, absorbing a quarter of the municipal budget. For social reformers, no alternative in sight. Blank. Disillusionment strengthened some appeals of religion, made *Jesus Christ Superstar* a hit, while Billy Graham's Christian Woodstock drew thousands of clean young people to praise the Lord in a Texas football stadium, in front of a huge backdrop with the word *Jesus* in psychedelic colors. Though demonstrations in Washington continued, a poll showed that two-thirds of the students had tired of marching in the streets, and the campuses became quieter.[48]

By then, Americans identified with the *Easy Rider* who drifted unattached through space, no destination in view, riding where impulse led, gratifying whatever whim popped up. People ranged along the road

> on freeways fifty lanes wide fifty lanes wide
> on a concrete continent spaced with bland billboards
> illustrating imbecile illusions of happiness
> . . . maimed citizens in painted cars
> . . . and engines that devoured America.

"Be delighted!" No other injunction made sense in a world of accidents. By the time the innocent hedonists understood that, "We blew it," they could not turn back on the thruway, except at the price of surrender to the three-piece suit.[49]

Meanwhile, let everyone equally do the same—where, as on hardly passionate Marlborough Street,

> Even the man
> Scavenging filth in back alley trash cans
> Has two children, a beach wagon, a helpmate
> And is a "Young Republican,"

they were all one in the assessment of values.

Or in Africa, for a while the residual hope of indefatigable rebels like folk singer Phil Ochs, who journeyed to meet Idi Amin but instead met three thugs in Tanzania who stole his money and ruptured his vocal cords. Nevertheless, an infatuated anthropologist observing the Mbuti Pygmies, part of the ecosystem, who shared everything and copulated openly without hang-ups, concluded they were like "our own hunting and gathering ancestors." He admired what his ignorance perceived as the commitment to equality, although conceding that the Mbuti indeed helplessly became slaves of the neighboring entrepreneurial cultivator tribes.[50]

The commitment to equality shifted emphasis from life and liberty to the pursuit of happiness, increasingly defined as an entitlement. But since happiness lacked a universal cash equivalent, Americans tended to understand it as the hedonistic gratification of whatever impulse moved them. The absence of restraints deprived men and women dripping with guilt of guides to action, so that, leveling out, their liberty often left them flapping in gusts of uncertainty.[51]

That new definition of liberty, which placed individuals' rights above those of society, would show its deleterious results in the next decades. In that brave new world, the idea of suffering as a consequence of doing right would often fall by the wayside. Assaults on the traditional family would continue unabated, a legacy of the belief that it was an ultimately fascist institution, irrelevant and destructive, oppressive to women and children. In its place, as a legacy of the 1960s, would come calls for greater government paternalism, with social agencies providing what people no longer could. The rights pie would grow enormously, as would varieties of sexual identification, replacing the perverted eroticism of the 1950s. Its deconstruction deliberately blurred antiquated, Western, Eurocentric genital sexuality. The stress on asceticism and voluntary poverty, on doing with less—"small is beautiful"—remained influential, especially among those who had more than enough to begin with. Having banned Dow Chemical and ROTC from their campuses, universities adapted to new consumer demands, as did good purveyors of commodities, by expanding their bureaucracies and offerings. From learning institutions they transformed themselves into instruments for doing good, to further social change.

The more articulate babbled about creating an antiauthoritarian society, comforted by anarchist revivals, lifestyle changes, radical Christianity, and passionate involvement. Experimental politics became all the rage, guided by sex roles, gay liberation, and a variety of environmentalist activities, united by assaults on industrialism and capitalism. The psychiatry of adjustment was out, maladjustment and abnormality took center stage.

Yet in the end revolution proved no solution. Forces other than those assembled at a giant rock concert to raise money for it settled the fate of Bangladesh. And do-it-yourself politics proliferated to such an extent as to cancel out the effectiveness of any specific effort. Sincerity and passion, dripping with love of human kindness, proved no match for the fundamental resilience of a society still governed by consent that survived in spite of the assault.

The once flourishing counterculture meccas reverted to what they had always been, blots on the landscape. Lifestyle revolts subsided into wood-burning stoves and alfalfa diets. Individual self-discovery left few comfortable with what they found. Efforts to define the center by the margins rather than by the core brought greater tolerance and acceptance. Yet radicals who hoped to liberate not only themselves but everyone else found fewer takers than anticipated. Worse, they failed to calculate the cost of the battles involved, or their outcome, which ultimately restricted everyone's liberty. Nor did they foresee the results of efforts to fragment the polity—the response to the Black Panther litany of black power for black people, red power for red people, yellow power for yellow people, brown power for brown people, white power for white people. "All power to the people," enunciated almost as an afterthought, turned out to mean less than its advocates thought.[52]

The 1960s thus left a two-faced legacy to the history of liberty in America, and the battle over whether the positive or the negative would ultimately prevail consumed the next quarter-century. Whichever aspect endured would not efface the 1960s heritage of style expressed in a sensate, psychedelic culture devoted to gratification of the self.

The past recalls precedents—the Alexandria of Ptolemy Philopater (221 B.C.), the Rome of Petronius (54 A.D.), the Carthage of Augustine (354 A.D.), the Fatehpur Sikri of Akbar (1605), and the Restoration London of William Congreve's *Way of the World* (1700).

Whoever peers at the years after 1970 can make out tantalizing perspectives of changes, all potential, none certain, not susceptible to description or analysis; and which an epilogue can only glimpse. The opening of a fresh page may head into a new chapter, or an altogether different volume, or may simply extend the old story. Breaks in the story, no matter how abrupt, rarely completely rupture links with the past.

EPILOGUE:

1970–1994

EQUALITY'S CHALLENGE

THE MEN, WOMEN, YOUTHS, AND CHILDREN who moved into the twentieth century's last decade confronted an alien universe everywhere in the United States. That the tools of observation brought them ever more data sharpened understanding not at all. "It's the information age and no one knows anything," said a pundit.

The United States remained the world's envy. Europe, Asia, and Africa heard incessant cries of those who wished to migrate to what they still called the New World, and thousands crossed the scarcely guarded borders. Then, too, from every corner of the globe pleas for assistance sounded. With all alternative visions of a sound future having faded, with even the Soviet Union in need of aid, this society and its fortunate inhabitants still showed signs of vigorous growth, still enjoyed liberty of a sort, not what their seventeenth-, eighteenth-, nineteenth-century forerunners would have understood, not even what would have seemed familiar in the decade of the 1960s, but still recognizable.[1]

Steadily, remorselessly, after 1970 several forms of authority collapsed—at every level of society, in government as in community life. The very idea became suspect. The erosion came quickly, in no comprehensible sequence—made manifest in a total crumbling of respect for rules, for rank, and for established roles. As a result, familiar relationships became fluid—of parents to children, of teachers to students, of citizens to officials.

The success of the insurrection against the universities had immediate consequences. It effaced control by faculties and also undermined the validity of the disciplines they taught and the rules they administered. Nor did political authority withstand the challenges reared against it after

1968. True, the darlings of youth—Eugene McCarthy and George McGovern—could not win election; but Richard Nixon's victories in 1968 and 1972 proved hollow, incapable of resisting the challenges that drove him from office and that also ate away at the Chief Executive's prerogatives, which his successors could not restore. Congress did not thereby expand its own powers; cumbersome rules still emphasized seniority and maintained the dictatorial grip of committee chairmen on procedures. Since 1930 the national legislature had functioned largely through guidance from the White House, without which it churned about in disarray after 1970. To make matters worse, vastly expanded staffs and rising campaign costs—products of television elections—further shackled congressmen's ability to act.[2]

The venerable political parties endured, but wielded little power and rarely controlled elections. From the 1950s on, political scientists pointed to the growing weakness of those organizations—their diminished institutional relevance and inability to muster voter support for coherent programs. In the absence of ideological cadres, identification shrank in importance as the electorate focused its attention on leaders who happened to enjoy an affiliation but communicated with the public directly, presenting themselves and not the organizations behind them as problem-solvers. Experts in advertising and in manipulating opinion like H. R. Haldeman and Patrick Cadell advised candidates on electoral tactics and on policy. Although each of the fifty states displayed unique characteristics reflecting its distinctive strengths and weaknesses, a general pattern of diminished authority showed up in their capitals as it did in Washington. And nothing that happened after 1970 significantly added support to the crumbling structure of local government, which faced in disarray unprecedented social, economic, and cultural problems. Hope for grassroots reform vanished. A tax revolt in California culminating in the referendum on Proposition 13 revealed deep mistrust of politicians. And New York City abandoned the liberal policies of the 1960s: low transportation fares, excellent free schooling, and well-paid, uncorrupted municipal workers. In the 1970s one million of its eight million residents abandoned it, as the city slipped into bankruptcy and services deteriorated. Ominously, neighborhood life disintegrated when districts turned into quarters for lodging, not for living.

Once authority dissolved, only commands supported by force or threat of force elicited obedience, whether by gang leader, Mafia boss, cop in cruiser, teacher, or even dear old Dad. Power replaced persuasion among people not really free because unattached, adrift.[3]

* * *

The demand for immediate gratification called into question the evolving commitment to equality, but in doing so shifted emphasis from opportunity to results. After 1970, insistence on prizes for all replaced the historic understanding of equality as a product of open competition. The elevation of victim status to an art form by black activists excluded reasoned discussion of the change. Faults in society responsible for all personal deficiencies called for compensation, not for an assessment of blame—not even for self-defense against violence, as Bernhard Goetz discovered.[4]

Americans had always interpreted the inalienable right to the pursuit of happiness referred to in the Declaration of Independence as access to equal opportunity. In life's race, each runner deserved the same chance to win. A free society assured its members neither perfect equality of results nor perfect equality of opportunity; individuals bore responsibility for their own destinies even though they lacked complete control over them.

However, in the closing three decades of the twentieth century the failures and their sympathizers lost confidence in the fairness of the course, and asserted that the fault lay not in any lack of ability but in some tilt in the track or some incapacitating handicap. Competitors who identified themselves as a group—blacks—compared with others—whites—traced their lack of success to external conditions. Equal results then became the true measure of the equal opportunity guaranteed by law. In the 1970s, minority demands for remedies shifted from negative to positive government action, from nondiscrimination to affirmative preference. Flabby, though fashionable, redefinitions of justice encouraged the trend.[5]

One inflexible constraint for a time hampered those who sought the shift. The Constitution treated only of individuals, not of collectivities. Not merely "color blind," as Justice Harlan's dissent had put it in *Plessy* v. *Ferguson,* it also took no cognizance whatever of aggregates. But group-think circumvented the limitations on application of the Equal Protection Clause of the Fourteenth Amendment. Ingenious lawyers argued that a state which did not exercise its general police powers to forbid discriminatory behavior in effect condoned that behavior. And class-action suits could supply the remedy, rather than impractical litigation on behalf of all individuals who considered themselves discriminated against on various grounds. Neither legislation nor fanciful judicial decisions could, however, evade the awkwardness in the effort to allocate desirable results by quotas; the original charter and the Fourteenth Amendment recognized only persons.

Nor did social reality provide a basis for such allocations. Increasingly, categories aimed at compensation for past injustices through slavery and discrimination lost contact with actuality. No evidence whatever confirmed the argument that the heritage of slavery left an indelible stereotype impressed on the descendants of former plantation owners, much less on the great majority of Americans who lacked any contact, actual or inherited, with bondage. Moreover, "black" had ceased to refer to pigmentation and ever less often described people descended from the past victims of bondage, since immigration brought in large numbers from the Caribbean and from Africa unaffacted by that heritage. Past miscegenation and passing also confounded the matter. And the related category "Hispanic," totally fanciful, resisted efforts to make it a basis for quotas.

In 1970 a broad consensus still affirmed faith in equality of opportunity. Americans mingled respect for achievement with insistence upon fundamental human equality. Success, in whatever field, wrote Lord Bryce back in the 1880s, earned popular esteem—in business, politics, the Church, battle, or philosophy. A Vanderbilt, Webster, Beecher, Grant, or Emerson became an object of interest, perhaps of admiration, though deemed "still of the same flesh and blood as other men," because each had grasped the chance to assert personal merit.

Not only defenders of the status quo but also progressive and socialist critics regarded broader opportunity as the remedy for present faults. "Not human equality, but equality of opportunity to prevent the creation of artificial inequalities by privilege"—thus John Spargo proclaimed the essence of socialism, in terms that Jefferson, Jackson, and Wilson would have accepted. So stated, the creed triumphed over conflicting realities.[6]

In managing the passage of decisive civil rights legislation through the Senate, Hubert Humphrey made the distinction unambiguously clear. The law would not become a pretext for quotas or for the allocation of places among groups.

It would soon do so.

President Lyndon B. Johnson's success in prying out of a reluctant Congress a potent civil rights law (1964) and a statute on suffrage (1965) transformed the politics of the South and of the Northern cities. The quest for equality then reached a new stage, based upon the power of black Americans to meet their unsatisfied needs. Although politicians in 1972 rejected the idea that all citizens had a right to government support, the sense of obligation grew in the years that followed—with respect not only to citizens but also to aliens, including those illegally in the country.

And "compassionate politics" imperceptibly raised the acknowledgment of entitlement to include housing and health.

Increasingly, in this context equality referred to results rather than to opportunity. The aggrieved expected government to eliminate the effects of past discrimination, and also to assure each underprivileged group desirable places proportionate to its numbers. To do so, the state had to take positive, not merely negative, steps. Nondiscrimination clauses attached to appropriation bills would bar those who thought otherwise. Though many condemned prejudice in matters of race or ethnicity, no such consensus supported the expanded definition of nondiscrimination. But the Supreme Court ruled in *Workers* v. *Weber* (1979) that the no-racial-discrimination provision of Title VII of the Civil Rights Act did not proscribe preferential treatment based on race, and in *Fullilove* v. *Klutznick* (1980) affirmed as constitutional the congressional use of racial classifications. It thereby legitimized reverse discrimination—indeed, made it a requirement of government and private sectors alike.

The advocates of affirmative action showed no awareness either of the underlying premises or of the consequences of the course they advocated. To assure equality of results, they assumed that within each segment of the population similar numbers of individuals shared similar goals; that as many people of one kind as of another wished to be basketball players or engineers or physicians. Affirmative action also assumed that the distribution of abilities and personality traits necessary for success appeared in each group proportionate to its numbers. Both assumptions proved invalid, as the composition of athletic teams demonstrated. Major league baseball, once lily-white, signed up attractive black players not in response to law but in recognition of superior talent. Quotas in the interest of balance did not work in sports, where ability counted; race norming made no sense on the gridiron or diamond. But flabby college faculties and other educators yielded supinely to the demand; success as a student after all required vastly less demonstrable skill than success as a basketball player.

Only immediate, all-out reform would spare society the imminent conflagration that threatened total destruction in the fire next time. Riot remained an ever-imminent threat. Whatever the encouragement afforded by entry into white-collar and professional positions and admission to Ivy League colleges, the inert inner-city, dependent poor remained a danger that only empowerment through politics could blunt. The 1982 amendment to the Voting Rights Act still rested on the old "one person, one vote" premise, aiming to clear away obstacles to participation. When no improvement followed, since former nonvoters cast their ballots just as former voters had, emphasis shifted to racial redistricting to protect black and Hispanic candidates from white competition. That compromise with principle did assure the election of minority legislators; and white flight from the cities led to the choice of black mayors in Cleveland, Detroit, Los Angeles, and Washington, D.C.—none of which in the least improved the situation of the ghetto underclass.[7]

The intractable problem early attracted the attention of foundation executives. Having spent a quarter of a century curing the maladies of the Third World, often with meager or negative results, Ford and Rockefeller determined to do as well for Harlem and Watts, with community organization the favored instrument. The Tax Reform Act of 1969 cleared the way for them to act. Voter registration drives had long attracted their support; after 1970 they also aided black defense efforts and, in time, also the Mexican American Legal Defense and Educational Foundation (MALDEF). The mixed results revealed the limits of such external aid, which had less effect than underlying social structure. In terms of sound family life and low rates of crime and of gang participation, Mexican Americans did better in San Antonio than in Los Angeles, whatever the amount of external support.[8] In a volatile society where swiftly changing currents concealed all traditional moorings, events blew in unpredictable fashions and people drifted to unanticipated destinations unless guided by an inner sense of direction.[9]

The battleground of the struggle for expanded civil rights shifted after 1970 from the floor of Congress to the courtroom and the bureaucratic office. Radical change thereafter came by judicial and administrative rulings rather than by legislation. Advocates of reform could no longer mobilize popular majorities required for enactment of statutes in this area; increasingly the courts and the executive acted instead. Thus the dilatory tactics of building trade employers and unions induced the Secretary of Labor by executive order to "set aside" a quota of construction jobs for minority contractors in order to secure a fair hiring pattern. The practice became common in employment, as well as in admission to schools and colleges. Acquiescences in goals established by bureaucrats became the price of freedom from prosecution and eligibility for lucrative government contracts. Legal theorists, having cut themselves off from precedent and legislative texts, propounded strange new concepts of compensatory justice by which unequal future treatment would make up for past deprivations of equal opportunity. Quotas, disguised by the designation "affirmative action," aimed to expand freedom by making inroads into it. They resulted in "an increasing consciousness of the significance of group membership, an increasing divisiveness on the basis of race, color, and national origins, and a spreading resentment among disfavored groups."[10]

Judicial and bureaucratic actions differed from legislative remedies, even in cases that correctly diagnosed the malady and prescribed appropriate treatment. The necessity to garner a majority forced legislators to consider the general effects of a statute. Judges did not have to do so; they could and did write their opinions out of their own understanding of right and wrong, with only a casual link to constitutional texts. Let justice be done though the heavens fall. Without hesitation, the jurists proceeded to pronounce the correct in education and schooling, in prisons, in military policy, and in environmental issues, so that ever more controversies dropped into the laps of the judiciary. Holding office for life, free of the need to seek re-election, the occupants of the benches arrogated to themselves power unwarranted by the nation's founding documents. The colossal impudence behind their rulings violated the core theme of American government, that it consisted of a process defined through a limited, procedural covenant, entered into for limited purposes. But in the absence of authority on crucial, frequently moral issues, no one knew where else to turn.

The judiciary, too, had grown in size and complexity. Aside from the familiar divisions between state and federal jurisdictions and the distinction between trial and appellate courts, a complex array of administrative judges dealt with matters ranging from bankruptcy to broadcasting. New issues and new procedures crowded calendars. Highly complicated class-action suits in effect amounted to kinds of legislation; settlements in product-liability cases on the civil side and plea bargaining on the criminal bypassed usual trial procedures, although all remained subject to appeal and review, with the apex in the Supreme Court. Animus toward lawyers, and mistrust of the courts, were the results, which turned vigilantes into folk heroes. The *New York Post* thus hailed Bernhard Goetz (the Death-Wish Gunman): "Here at last stands a man who knows that the courts cannot be trusted, that the police don't care a dime for justice, that the law is a joke."

The civil rights issue inched along within this complex array of attitudes in the vain hope that an authoritative ruling once and for all would settle matters. In April 1971, the Supreme Court, without approving racial balance as a constitutional right, upheld mathematical ratios as a starting point and endorsed busing as a remedy in systems that had previously practiced segregation by law. Since the judges held office by appointment and for life, they gave scarcely a thought to the consent of the governed—once the foundation of the Republic.[11]

The Court could decide; but it lacked the power of enforcement. In 1978 it struck down (5–4) a University of California medical school plan that set aside a fixed number of places for minority applicants. The school had never in the past discriminated and its arrangement violated a white male's rights under Title VI of the Civil Rights Act. The decision did not, however, end affirmative action, justified either on the grounds of previous abuses, or as a means of serving underprivileged communities, or as a way to add diversity to a student body. The view of the dissenters in the case at hand ultimately won out. With no evidence whatsoever, four justices asserted that the academic deficiencies of minority applicants derived from past discrimination, and that opinion prevailed in the future.

Activism in time created mind-racking problems for the judiciary enmired in reinterpreting the Bill of Rights. Judges only later began to explore the complexity of privacy, lightheartedly enunciated in *Roe* v. *Wade,* which protected the mother's right to choice but remained silent on the father's. Did it also extend to Senator Packwood and Senator Kennedy? Protection went to homosexuals, but not to those victimized by "acting out." Forms of expression covered by free speech extended to street musicians but not to bootblacks, to child pornography but not to removal by stripteasers at the Kitty Kat Lounge of their G-strings. The theft and destruction of dissenting newspapers at the University of Pennsylvania got by as a "form of protest" but not offensive fraternity T-shirts.

Nor did the Second Amendment stand in the way of gun control, any more than did well-defined property rights prevent takings by the EPA or other governmental agencies.

Liberty did not depend simply on the absence of interference by government. It required positive fortifications either by law or by associations sanctioned by society; it thus presented insoluble problems for jurists not bound by tradition and precedent.

Administrative acts also lacked the sanction of a voter majority, indeed often aimed to resist popular pressures. Yet the number of government employees—state, local, and federal—grew inexorably, from 13 million in 1970 to 17.5 million in 1988. That vast body of appointed officials, diverse in function, designation, and discipline, made its own rules. Theoretically officeholders occupied places in graded hierarchies leading upward to the agency head or Cabinet secretary and ultimately to the President, governor, or mayor. But in practice other forces intervened laterally, as for instance in pressure from congressional and legislative committees, with their own staffs and agendas, using control over appropriations to shape decisions. In the higher administrative echelons, men and women of similar backgrounds formed tacit alliances with congressional staffers, like them typically well-educated and out of touch with the rest of the nation, able to work well with the vast array of nonbusiness lobbyists who crowded Washington and whose reform values they shared. Such people found the chaos and disorder of the world outside the Beltway disturbing and regarded practical arrangements already in place with loathing. The complex interplay of forces left the citizen-subjects powerless unless also enlisted in some pressure group.

Bureaucratic measures differed from both legislative and judicial ones, for although bounded by statutes and decisions, they expressed the intentions of officeholders maneuvering among competing pressures. The Equal Employment Opportunities Commission staff thus pursued its own agenda, consciously or unconsciously acting in accord with their own assumptions and prejudices, which often turned about statistically measurable definitions of dubious value. So, too, the publications and hearings of the U.S. Commission on Civil Rights expressed not the views of the commission but of its staff. When it came to race, officials took any variance from uniformity as a *prima facie* sign of discrimination; *de facto* and *de jure* segregation thereupon merged into one, an outcome never tested at the ballot box. To yield to the greatest pressure provided the easiest way out. Renewals of the voting rights law in 1970, 1975, and 1982 strengthened the treatment of blacks as a group apart and also extended equivalent guarantees to some linguistic minorities.

Abandonment of the historic conception of equality created inescapable problems. Judicial gropings toward consistent case law and freewheeling administrative rulings on the new concept left Americans uncertain about vital aspects of their lives. In *Griggs* v. *Duke Power* (1971), the Supreme Court condemned "neutral" employment and ability tests that did not offset the presumed effects of previous discriminatory practices. But subsequent rulings withdrew from that position, further confusing the issue. Equality consultants came into their own as various lobbying organizations, determined to "make a difference" and priding themselves on challenging society's most fundamental perceptions, offered to untangle the results.

Uncertainty spread. *Brown* v. *Board of Education* held race an improper ground for school assignment. By tortuous logic various courts, however, subsequently held race a necessary ground for assignment in order to implement *Brown,* which held the opposite. Only head counts of black and white students could measure the presumed effects of *de facto* segregation. Furthermore, only balance in numbers based on race could demonstrate desegregation. Pathetic judicial contortions aimed to create satisfactory district boundaries, thereby damaging the already wounded schools. Busing drained financial resources from education. Not everywhere—not in Detroit, for instance, but in Los Angeles and Boston, depending somehow on how judges read past intent. White flight, however, emptied the process of meaning; while New York City and Los Angeles experimented, pupils became victims. Those blacks who could joined the exodus. Since shuffling inner-city children about rarely improved student performances, the effort to create a semblance of equality of outcome required further compensatory treatment. Reformers resolutely rejected abundant evidence that success in learning had less to do with school assignment or racial balance than with the quality of homes and of family life. The mere suggestion of that link unleashed a torrent of ill-informed abuse on the "Moynihan Report."[12]

Affirmative action acquired an identity of its own, independent of the presumed benefits to its beneficiaries—embodied not only in an ideology, but also in a growing cadre of functionaries who policed its application to specific cases. The concern with victims and underdogs papered over the actual disdain for the wider implications of policies that rested on a simple version of anti-Americanism, one which assumed the existence of a rotten society ripe for subversion. Crusaders by definition could not bother about the costs or about assessment of the actual benefits their actions generated. Few acknowledged that blacks rarely benefited except when employed in enforcement. The most disadvantaged failed to gain at all, for lethargic white society preferred to lower the bars for occasional underqualified individuals rather than struggle to educate a whole minority so that it could compete. The few pushed ahead by racial preference did not offset the stigma of inferiority attached to their favored treatment and rarely avoided a loss in self-esteem.[13]

Change moreover eroded the presumed polarity of the races. The growing number of middle-class and professional blacks formed a stabilizing element. The concessions easily made by comfortable suburbs remote from the urban reality bore a different aspect in working-class neighborhoods where the great majority of poor white men and women regarded the preferences extended to blacks as unfair—discrimination in reverse. The descendants of immigrants and other Northerners did not believe they shared the guilt of slavery; many of them had only recently themselves been victims of prejudice and saw no reason why compensation should come at their expense.

In some districts the issue in practice differed from its legal or theoretical forms. Such areas, white only in the abstract sense of "not black," contained small, compact, homogeneous clusters that shared common places of origin and common social, cultural, and religious institutions. They defined themselves as Italian, Greek, Hasidic, Korean, Arabic, or Cambodian. Some such communities had survived for generations; others had taken form recently. The districts and the groups that occupied them each possessed its own identity, some in constant flux, others quite stable. Each provided informal though important means of adjustment to the great variety of differences dictated by the environment and by the quality and status of the residents. Local public schools accommodated themselves to these diverse situations, as did the Phelan School in Queens, New York, which enrolled children from forty-three different nationalities.[14]

Radical blacks, unwilling to operate within the old rules of the game, directly threatened the survival of these neighborhoods. Although the population changes, coinciding with increased crime and use of drugs, with disrupted families, violence, and loose sexual behavior, caused trouble enough, the new people made matters worse by insensitivity to the existing population. When the intrusive outsiders showed no respect for the identity and institutions of others, they not only asserted a demand for space but also threatened existing cultural and social norms of behavior. The unqualified language in which the new arrivals made their claims for preferential treatment, and the readiness to resort to violence, left the neighborhood borderlands tense. The established populations at first responded defensively. Demands for favored positions seemed inequitable to those who had always regarded discrimination and quotas as unjust.

The revival of immigration, especially after the liberalized law of 1965, increased the size of the groups that competed with blacks, not only in numbers but also in the assertion of ethnic identity. Refugees from Central and Eastern Europe displaced to the New World the patriotism they could not express in the Old. Palestinians added to the swelling ranks of Arab Americans. All such people fell haplessly into the inadequate category "whites." In addition, Pakistanis, Cambodians, Laotians, and Chinese, along with many others, counted as Asians.

In the aggregate the ethnics, thus defined, formed a significant political force. Federal law recognized the legitimacy of the search for heritages and funded its support. Indeed, added diversity and the presumed stimulus to self-esteem had justified affirmative action. School systems therefore provided bilingual teaching and ethnic studies. African-American, Chicano-American, American Jewish, and Italian-American courses, among others, dotted the nation's multicultural offerings. By contrast, classes for the academically gifted, "Eurocentric" curricular materials, and competency testing met fierce opposition because of their presumed disparate impact. Indeed, efforts to establish race-normed gradings even in mathematics and science revealed the persistence of separatist intentions.[15]

Powerful vested interests supported the maintenance of ethnic identity. Numerous intellectuals earnestly worked to discover, describe, and disseminate the cultural values and traits associated with their heritage. The phenomenal popularity of Alex Haley's fraudulent *Roots* (1976), despite its flimsy research and plagiarism, showed the strength of the impulse. Such efforts proved largely worthless, though welcomed by communal functionaries, journalists, and politicians with a stake in solidarity. Separatist professional associations—of black physicians, psychologists, and lawyers—pursued their own agendas under cover of group loyalty.

The Constitution and the statutes had taken cognizance only of individual persons. But administrative and judicial rulings after 1970 treated groups, which the government therefore had to define—an issue by no means clear, even in the case of blacks. Was one grandparent enough? Could families that had once passed, pass back, when advantaged? In the absence of answers, self-identification generally sufficed until challenged. Hence Mark Stebbins, who ran as a black, lost his seat on the Stockton City Council because his birth certificate listed his parents as white. Ralph White, who was black, replaced him.[16]

To complicate matters, many other claimants to privileged underprivileged status joined the blacks after 1970. Indians, Asians, and Spanish-speakers found manifest advantages to minority status, as did Italian Americans and Polish Americans. Women's voices joined the chorus, charging that sex more often than ethnicity had served as a cause or pretext for deprivation; and their claims won significant support, although not enough to secure adoption of the Equal Rights Amendment. The elderly and the disabled also gained some measure of protection. An ordinance against "lookism" in Santa Cruz, California, responded to the grievances of people not physically favored. The Civil Rights Act had explicitly rejected the idea of quotas. But elaborately calculated goals, the euphemistic designation contrived to meet competing claims, made inequality of access a necessary condition of equal results, even when it came to college scholarships.

The law knew how to categorize group membership only by self-identification, and treated each category as fixed and homogeneous—a necessary fiction. The offspring of three generations of well-to-do middle-class college graduates remained black on the university's admission form, as deprived as a youth from the slums, while children of migrants from Appalachia became white, as advantaged as other WASPs (although the Cincinnati City Council in 1992 did forbid discrimination based on "Appalachian regional origin").

Preferences gave beneficiaries a stake in preserving group solidarity. Blacks who lived apart from whites possessed a distinctive voice and displayed high group consciousness because community-based and culturally and psychologically rooted. Although in the 1990s, some thirty percent of metropolitan black households resided in the suburbs and enjoyed annual incomes of more than $25,000, the advantages of affiliation linked them, however tenuously, with inner-city residents. By the same token, marginal people like the Bravas who once emphasized their whiteness now emphasized their color.[17]

Juggled terms masked fictitious terminologies. *Hispanic* applied to several groups totally dissimilar in actuality—Puerto Ricans, Mexicans, Cubans, Peruvians, and Colombians—and incorporated people of Indian antecedents with mother tongues not Spanish. All this apart from the fact that the migrants who came from south of the border to San Antonio differed markedly from those who came to Los Angeles. Native Americans included Sioux, Cheyennes, Iroquois, Navaho, Mohawk, and Algonquin; blacks included Nigerians, Caribbeans, and Alabamans. Hard-pressed Census Bureau officials struggled in vain to escape the problem. Aware that the "situational" concepts of race and ethnicity changed in definition with time and place, they nevertheless felt obliged to come up with precise numbers to fit fuzzy boundaries because their enumerations affected political representation and access to jobs and education.[18]

Perversely, group lines refused to remain fixed. Already *blacks* encompassed people from the British Caribbean; in the 1980s French-speaking refugees from Haiti shared the statistical category. The immigration law of 1965 opened entry to Pakistanis, Koreans, and Arabs among the Asians. But whether the half-million Israelis fell in with the Asians (place of birth) or with the whites (like other Jews) remained unclear.

The pathetic obsession with self-naming displayed the concern with identity, as if the proper word would create group consciousness and cohesion. True, the term *"Indian,"* product of European misapprehension, never bore much meaning even to the members of neighboring tribes. But neither did "Native American," by which activists sought to arrogate a unique legitimacy to themselves. The generation of W. E. B. Du Bois had worried about whether to capitalize "Negro" and "Colored People"; the next generation flaunted black as beautiful; in time, the quest for roots focused on Afro- or African American. As a token of kinship, some American blacks believed that the Kenyan drug Kemrow Kemron alleviated the symptoms of AIDS. Others asserted that their folk religion had demonstrable continuity with the traditional faiths of West Africa, despite scholarly evidence to the contrary. Such usages assumed a cultural and social identity with the people of Africa—an identity utterly meaningless to the Ibo and Yoruba, the Xhosa and the Zulus who actually lived there. But the link term supplied pleasing illusions to self-deceptive teachers and journalists, and to the politicians who pandered to them. Though Kwanza aimed to substitute for a white Christmas, Santa Claus prevailed; and the little child with one white parent could not join the black festivities. Rarely, however, did the choice satisfy the urge to create a group identity. Nor did it ease the pursuit of status.[19]

The search for roots also affected Jews, Italian Americans, and Polish Americans and an immense variety of smaller groups. Armenians, Slovaks, Greeks, and scores of others embarked on the quest for the traditions of their ancestors, with a turn inward the result. Interest shifted from the shared qualities that bound people together to the distinctive features that separated various clusters of them. The result threatened the balance that had long stabilized the country.

Worldwide counterparts to this fragmentation revealed the danger. While the ethnic revival occurred under unique American conditions, bitter struggles elsewhere showed the destructive potential—in Quebec, Cyprus, and Ireland, in British Wales, Cornwall, and Scotland, in Flemish and Walloon Belgium, and in the Breton, Basque, and Corsican regions of France, to say nothing of the former Yugoslavia and Soviet Union. Everywhere men and women no longer sheltered against life's hazards by village, neighborhood, or intimate community drew together in the effort at least to discover the solidarity of a shared heritage.[20]

To make results the measure of equality in the United States required the audacious assumption of a random distribution in society of occupational abilities and preferences so that deviations from the norm became evidence of discrimination that called for corrective government action. Emotion, prejudice, interest, and politics then removed the issue beyond the point of rational consideration. The relationship of intelligence, aptitudes, and criminality to genetic heritage became a subject taboo not only in policy discussion but also in scientific research. But other tangential evidence demonstrated that values—whether genetic or environmental—embedded in family and community shaped young people's aptitudes and choices of careers; and those reflected the immense diversity of American society. Nor did verbal and mathematic skills manifest themselves equally in all groups. The relation of ethnicity to career choices and ability, irrelevant so long as the law treated only individuals who sorted themselves out without regard to group lines, became relevant when government rulings proceeded from the expectation that every population cross-section would contain the same admixture of elements.

Moreover, incontestable evidence—historical, anthropological, and sociological—revealed undissolvable bonds between calling and culture reflected in lifestyle, values, family strength, tradition of mutual aid, and attitudes toward the world, as relevant in Japan as in the United States. Even discounting the effects of any differences in the distribution of abilities, lifestyles helped or hindered in the pursuit of success. In the absence of ever more frequent government intervention, the social and intellectual traits people valued shaped their careers. Ironically, at the very time that results became the measure of equality, blacks, Indians, Chicanos, and others began to stress their cultural particularity, emphasizing especially the unique traits bound to produce heterogeneous outcomes. By contrast, Laotians, Vietnamese, Cambodians, Koreans, Japanese, and others, though set apart by color and victimized by prejudice, drew support from families and communities, proved achievement-oriented, and got ahead.[21]

The incalculable social effects of quotas or goals set by affirmative action included at least the possibility of a significant deterioration of competence in tasks vital to all. Schools, having become the gateways to social advancement, immediately felt the effects, especially since the turmoil of the 1960s had seriously sapped their strength. Charges of Eurocentrism in many places emptied curricula of meaningful content in the interest of diversity and of self-esteem for all. The unifying elements in national culture receded to the background, as did attention to hard subjects of study. The government report *A Nation at Risk* (1983), which warned of the danger of placing self-esteem and multiculturalism before learning and rationality, did not halt the retreat from basic knowledge without which graduates could not find rewarding positions or ascend the scale of high-income employment. Instead many schools mechanically processed students toward an imaginary world that excluded distinctions of intellect and values. If the measurements did not yield the desired results, throw away the yardstick! The universities could not halt the trend, as they had a century earlier. Heedless expansion in the 1960s, capitulation to rowdy students, and then the professional corruption that followed upon inundating government and foundation grants, rendered them helpless. Insidious developments in the humane disciplines like literature and history completed the utter debasement of the academy.[22]

Social theorists long knew an alternative method of achieving equality of results. Uniformity of incomes would dissolve all incentive for any position for which individuals lacked fitness. In Edward Bellamy's *Looking Backward* (1888), benevolent rulers evened out differences and imposed centralized standards on a uniform and homogeneous populace. People performed tasks appropriate to their talents and interests because all enjoyed the same rewards. Such equality resembled that of prison camps and military battalions. Indeed, Bellamy called his labor force "the Industrial Army."

After 1970 such egalitarianism more often attracted manipulators disappointed by the outcome that equality of opportunity produced. Bold philosophers refused to modify their views of justice; if it did not fit reality, they preferred to alter reality. John Rawls, in *A Theory of Justice* (1971), and Ronald Dworkin, in *Taking Rights Seriously* (1977), elevated equality over efficiency as a social goal, even if less for everyone resulted. From that point of view, individual rights mattered not at all, nor did consent of the governed, since the majority would resist the sacrifices entailed. Instead, change would come at the hands of an all-powerful judge (Hercules) who would deduce the correct rules from knowledge of the law, and impose them by force. Other theorists advocated a social order modeled on the monastic barracks or army camp—in which religious orientation and military discipline offered a chance for survival (Red China the model in 1975).

More than two centuries earlier Rousseau had outlined the concomitants of equality of results: enrichment of the state; impoverishment of the people by the removal of surpluses through taxation; and destruction of the arts, sciences, and civilization that he regarded as the cause of inequality. In theory, at least, he considered the price worth paying.[23]

Americans did not. A sociologist foresaw the outcome—"a population made up of deviants, delinquents, alienated, anomic, bored, narcissistic and troubled souls," of collapsed families, and of escape in idle nostalgia and apocalyptic visions of the future. The dire warnings did not provide slogans for action. But the historic concept of equality of opportunity through free competition, which gave people the ability to act—that is, liberty—did not require slogans. Americans had no desire to surrender personal freedom as the price of equality. Hence the uncertain consequences of the vital transformation demanded of them after 1970.[24]

Changes in political idiom revealed the popular unease. President Carter referred to a pervasive malaise since the country had entered upon an "era of limits" with solutions out of reach, with all institutions—government, unions, and corporations—fallible, and with social problems intractable. Though all signs pointed to a substantial decline of absolute poverty in the nation, as a result of the achievements of the 1960s and of economic growth, "the rise of a national pattern of brute social inequality" appalled the National Advisory Council on Economic Opportunity, which demanded a debate on how "to create an ethic of fairness and compassion in America" (1980). A commission headed by John D. Rockefeller concluded that no benefit would result from a further increase in population. The end of the era of growth made small beautiful. However, behavior, expressed in style of life, did not reflect acceptance of the dire nightmare warnings; and expectations, far from shrinking, swelled. And most Americans affirmed the commitment to liberty.[25]

In the last quarter of the century an unfamilar word enriched the American vocabulary: *entitlements*—payments to individuals assumed by government since the New Deal, but magnified by the Great Society programs; not only Social Security for the elderly and unemployment insurance for those out of work, but also Medicare and Medicaid, and aid for the mothers of dependent children and for veterans, as well as access to an elaborate complex of educational programs. Every need deemed authentic had become a full-fledged right. The beneficiaries and their spokesmen evoked slogans of inclusion that would improve everyone's lot by redistributing income through taxation and government action. The totals swelled remorselessly, year after year, with no end in sight. The Food Stamp program, begun in 1965 with 426,000 recipients, in 1980 covered more than 21 million, while the number of people defined as poor also increased and continued to do so whatever the conditions of the economy. Tricky definitions and pliable statistics easily manipulated to make a political point explained part of the trend. But more important, the swelling welfare roles revealed the growth of a permanent underclass, born to poverty, with no prospect of extrication by its own efforts or by public assistance.[26]

The outcome satisfied few, not even the recipients, in the absence of agreed-upon concepts of "enough." No amount of transferred cash sufficed to even out levels of happiness, contain violence, and establish security, and to provide each individual the loving, supportive family that converted shelters into homes and promised offspring a fulfilling life. Nor could the impersonal welfare check replace the supportive neighbors who helped each other out as old-timers did in rural Cape Cod or urban South Bronx. How to deal with dying, a persistent question posed to radio talk-show hosts—ten steps, please. Meanwhile, off on the fringe, John Sinclair of the Ann Arbor hippie community called for "rock 'n' roll, dope and fucking in the streets," while analysts of "full-fledged rights" not served by the marketplace pointed to such "truly human needs" as "meaningful participation in sexual intercourse." Unrequited love for a movie actress he did not know drove John W. Hinckley to attempt to assassinate President Reagan.[27]

Some of the aggrieved concluded that since no policy could raise all to the same level, then at least furious destructive protests could lower all to equality, as in a hurricane or earthquake. Prime-time activism became all the rage, on the assumption that issues represented on the nightly TV newscast thereby acquired social legitimacy. Guidebooks instructed aspirants on the road to instant fame. After all, even true revolutionaries, convinced that the very media were in need of "re-aligning," and fighting for "a democratic restructuring," had to know how to write a press release, or what colors looked good on TV. The result? Justice for sure, in the Rawls-Dworkin style. Perhaps "the death of this hateful world as we know it" would make room for another, different world "in which longing would be realized in glory" (1982)—as by James Jones and David Koresh.[28]

The gloomy forecasts, like the controversies over equal rights, raged after 1970 oblivious to profound economic and social changes that rendered predictions and complaints irrelevant. "Before the blight of Reaganism, we were on our way to an increasingly friendly cultural ambience. . . ." "We have a low-grade disease . . . ultimately it may come down to a question of survival . . . some think it is already too late . . . the damage is irreversible. . . ." Such slogans burbled freely without regard to actuality.

But the basic conditions of 1990 differed from those of 1970 even more profoundly than those of 1970 had from those of 1950. The pace of change accelerated, carrying all people in unpredicted directions. Recurrent waves of poitical rhetoric obscured the significance of transformations that revolved about continuing expansion of the American economy. The numbers that bewitched economists and politicians—GDP, interest rates, prices, unemployment rates—proved useful in debate. But other data, rarely mentioned, conveyed more significant implications. The employed labor force, which had grown from 60 to 84 million between 1950 and 1970, leaped at an even higher rate from 84 million in 1970 to 125 million in 1990, more than forty-five percent female. In four decades it more than doubled. The factors responsible for multiplying the bodies that swelled the labor force included a rising population (from 203 million in 1970 to 250 million in 1990) based on a continued high birth rate; a steady influx of more than 10 million immigrants, particularly after 1980; and the absorption of women into the ranks of workers at an unprecedented rate.

But something else had happened that drew those bodies into the *employed* labor force, a development not visible to commentators who glued their attention to the statistics for *unemployment.* After 1970, a transformed economy vastly expanded output and sustained lengthening payrolls.

The heavy industries of the past—steel, automobiles, chemicals, mining—did not supply the new places; indeed, they lost ground. Even greater job losses marked the light consumer industries—clothing, shoes, and textiles. Rather, the fastest-growing occupations included medical and health aides and technicians, financial services, travel agents, computer analysts and programmers, and various "human service" employees, among them teachers and jailers.

Technological change did not, as earlier, increase the size of firms, but actually favored the small entrepreneur who could tie into a communications network and swiftly make and implement decisions. The elaboration of franchising provided scope for family firms, including those of immigrants who could begin with limited capital and plow profits back into the business. Koreans, Cubans, and Arabs thus prospered. The computing industries, although briefly dominated by a single large firm, promptly spurted in new directions to exploit successive new inventions—transistors, integrated circuits, miniature chips, minicomputers, and many software operating systems. Bell Laboratories, the Defense Department, NASA, and the technical universities helped, as did the availability of venture capital; but the impetus to growth came from dozens of ingenious youths, immigrants from Hungary, Bulgaria, and natives of every part of the United States, able to develop new ideas into substantial enterprises. Biotechnology followed an analogous course. With artificial intelligence domesticated, the sinister HAL of *2001* became the lovable R2D2 of *Star Wars.*

Few Americans perceived the consequences of the momentous alterations in their economy. Politicians and journalists continued to babble about unemployment, unaware that joblessness had quite a new meaning in two-wage-earner families less mobile than formerly. Debates about social policy proceeded in utter disregard of the forces that wiped out low-paying, unskilled jobs, although the trend had a direct effect on affirmative action, welfare costs, and ghetto life. Historical surveys of attitudes toward the poor noted the persistence of ways of thinking labeled antiquated, like emphasis on the work ethic and like the country's refusal to abandon its traditional social philosophy despite the substantial changes experienced in the twentieth century. Scholars drew comfort from the fact that the government welfare agencies mushroomed in spite of popular hostility to "welfare" (substituting the euphemism "public assistance" did not help). Perhaps as a result, the political process lost the capacity to handle fundamental national issues.[29]

Sustained growth provided jobs and incomes even for undocumented aliens and for the increased number of legal immigrants admitted by an act of 1990. For a time, expansion provided the means to meet demands for entitlements, in part at least. The paid work force absorbed ever-larger numbers of women and minorities. The goal of the Great Society—abolition of poverty—nevertheless remained out of reach. Dependence on public aid persisted and, despite the creation of many entry-level jobs, increasingly embraced black youngsters unprepared for work and unemployable.[30]

The incorporation of the American productive system into an integrated world economy raised efficiency and industrial output. At the same time, modernized agriculture eliminated sharecropping and substituted for much of the depressed migrant labor force the large-scale, scientific, mechanized operations that fed much of the world and also adjusted to changing dietary habits within the United States. Most of the old farm problems of the past disappeared.

Meanwhile the transformation that shifted manufacturing away from the old heavy industries to services, information, and biotechnology caused an adjustment of labor requirements. The number of farmers, assembly-line workers, and machine tenders declined; the number of health care and entertainment workers, computer engineers, and programmers and teachers rose. The occupations for which demand increased required some skill and training and called for some exercise of judgment, with a consequent alteration in the nature of the employees. In studios and theaters, at the publishers and the agencies, a very real though not always perceptible line set apart writers, editors, directors, "on air" personalities, and producers from gaffers, cameramen, electricians, and typists, just as physicians and nurses moved along separate paths in the hospitals. Lifestyles and union affiliations recognized the difference. Technical competence counted heavily on both sides of the line; but neither editors nor typists, directors nor electricians made good the claim to professional status as doctors or lawyers did. The skilled craftsmen at least could often flash a license granted by the state. But no college degree, prescribed course of study, or governmental certification qualified reporters and producers for their positions. They therefore fell into a large but amorphous group of para-professionals, possessed of some particular skill but half-educated and insecure in the large organizations that gave them employment.

The developments of the 1970s contributed to the global triumph of democratic forces over worldwide challenges from the right and the left. The cartel of oil-producing countries led by Saudi Arabia (OPEC) thus failed to exploit energy as a political lever. Its 1973 general embargo inconvenienced motorists in the United States, but the resilience of the American productive system surmounted the challenge, albeit at the cost of some inflation and a brief recession. The strength of the United States also blunted the challenge of Communism. The Soviets withdrew from Afghanistan and negotiated arms reduction because they understood (as some lugubrious American "scientists" did not) that they had lost the productivity race and could not compete against the U.S. Strategic Defense Initiative.

The Union of Concerned Scientists fulminated against the "political fantasy," but as events proved, the guilt of fantasizing fell upon the Concerned Scientists. More imaginative critics traced the Strategic Defense Initiative to "a vital element of American politics, the idealistic utopian element that is beyond criticism, out of touch with reality, a response to a utopian vision." Others described the program as "the product of a satirist on human perversity rather than the vision of a statesman," on the basis of evidence from such reliable sources as the *New York Times* editorial page, the Public Agenda Foundation, the *Nation,* and the Committee of Soviet Scientists for Peace Against Nuclear Threat. Opponents labeled the Star Wars project, a "regression to an idealized golden . . . past," to those "blissful years from 1945 to 1950 when the United States had the Bomb and the Other did not," deluding Americans into the belief that they would get a chance to experience "a second childhood." In fact, critics charged, the SDI program combined "material avarice (the arms lobby), military pursuit of advantage (point defense), and . . . ideological self-delusion" that would prove "the terminal dementia of the nuclear age." Sad to tell, events soon exposed the authors' own dementia.

Released from oppression, democratic forces in Eastern Europe asserted themselves in a turbulent and inconclusive effort to develop independent social and political forms. In Nicaragua and El Salvador, genuinely free elections brought shares of power to the very forces that the United States had backed against the Sandinistas and the FNLA. Similar changes began to resolve conflict in South Africa, Angola, and Mozambique. None of these countries approached utopian perfection, but the United States encouraged their attempts at democratic self-government.[31]

Nevertheless, intellectual criticism of the United States persisted, amplified by the growing number of para-professionals and by their influence on the media. Anti-Americanism did not display the random characteristics of individual, personal expressions. Uniform, predictable, ritualistic in nature, the hostile utterances emanated not from free-thinkers, each wandering off in his or her own direction, but rather from those keeping time to the beat of a drummer, albeit a drummer different from the one who set the pace for their countrymen and countrywomen. The critics behaved as a group, although without recognizing their identity since they generally presumed to speak for society at large. Nor did they understand that they pursued their own economic, social, and cultural interests and agenda when they claimed to represent the whole country. Nevertheless, their distinctive lifestyles, atttitudes, and views, disseminated through increasingly influential means of communication, remained important.

The decline philosophers—Paul Kennedy, Edward Luttwack, and Paul Fussell—reiterated a monotonous theme: "As a people we will never be as rich again." Demoralized leadership in the balkanized society and the corrupt legal system of an entrepreneurial decade had brought the country down, said some critics—quite unaware that such fears had resounded through the American past, in the jeremiads of the 1680s, in the breast-beating of the Great Awakening, in the reform ferment after 1830, and in the 1870s fear of the spread of insanity, corruption, and degeneracy. Few contemporary evaluators of the American scene recalled the 1950s fear of mass culture—the anticipated result of television, a soulless mass of consumers smothering creativity and individuality. The critics did not realize that change in an open, dynamic society always undermined the hegemony of elites and of privileged interests.[32]

The hostility of the intellectuals sometimes aimed simply to outrage, often through sophomoric humor. "Go with your worst instincts"—instructions to the staff of the popular *Animal House.* For Robert Coover, the country displayed its true character when the national mask of pious rectitude slipped, as in the case of the Rosenbergs, regarded by the author as hapless victims of judicial injustice. Reaching for sensation, his gross novel *The Public Burning* ended with Uncle Sam, the spirit of brute power, sodomizing President Nixon. Most often, however, other than to set them cackling in the faculty lounges, the justification rested on dislike for American materialism. True, most of the world depended upon food exports from North America—Asia, Africa, Latin America, and Western and Eastern Europe, including the Soviet Union, having become net importers of grain in the 1970s. But the ability to feed a large part of the world less often provided the reference point of criticism than the record of exploitation and environmental damage, revealed in the standing contrast with the Indians. In a flimsy novel (1981) the villainous seventeenth-century Yankee minister lost the hand of the white heroine to a red man who cherished the natural world in which each living thing had a place. (Forget the desert-making role of the Anasazi.) Museums returned to the tribes of presumed origin for reburial bones collected for scientific study. The needs of archeology and history counted for nothing, with the objectivity they espoused only a rationalization for oppression. The Native American gambling casinos provided only tokens of compensation. And ecopsychologists, having traced the world's ills to the invention of agriculture, urged a return to the hunter-gatherer stage.

"Small Is Beautiful" propagandists, in the effort to undo what they regarded as the horrendous damages caused by economic expansion, ignored the vastly more important beneficial results of ways of life that provided economic security at an undreamed-of level to countless individuals. Suburban sprawl and shopping malls became symbols of excessive affluence, but critics remained blind to the potential problems that would follow upon the diminished upward and increased downward mobility that a lack of economic growth would create.

Journalists and social commentators focused on the decline of "the American empire" and mourned the passing of the New World spiritual and temporal dreams—democracy, individualism, progress. Capitalism they considered in retreat—in Guatemala as in Detroit, all part of "the collapse of the moral scaffolding on which [their] . . . forebears erected monuments of freedom."[33]

Of course, the critics rarely had much good to say of those forebears, either; but after 1970 emphasis fell upon "a strategic struggle against contemporary American normalizing bio-powers, which increasingly extend their fields of operation into other countries." Those struggling against the patriarchal family had an obligation to combat its wider extension in the form of American imperialism. The new "aesthetic of liberty" meant "a new politics of truth" that excluded "universalizing" because it eradicated heterogeneity. Nothing less would do because some features of late capitalism subjected individuals to "fragmentation rather than the homogenization produced by normalizing power relations." Most criminal of all, "the institutionalization of a standard language" reinforced "pedagogical normalization and surveillance with mechanisms of self-surveillance," as students learned to write and speak themselves into standardized objectivity. Instead of enforcing a single spoken and written English (a racist concept), the country should recognize "a legitimately American language . . . a language including Nebraska, Harlem, New Mexico, Oregon, Puerto Rico, Alabama, and working-class life and freeways and Pac Man." Black children then would escape the "censorship of their living particular truths, past and present." All could escape bondage to the official language—"exclusive and exclusionary, white, class-privileged, masculinist . . . an act of collaboration with domination." The result, "liberty and self-stylization," would enable people to transform themselves and truth. In the words of an unsympathetic observer, "the cult of otherness" had taken over. Alas the champions of bilingual education never considered actual issues. Would Hispanic kiddies learn Castilian or the language of their Mexican families? Would Chinese learn Mandarin or Cantonese?

Anti-Americanism also called for a reconstructed past, along lines that invariably cast the United States in the worst possible light. Novelists and historians rose to the challenge. Nothing that the United States had done since 1945 deserved commendation or reflected honorable motives. They recast the Cold War along lines partial to the Soviet Union, that largely guiltless victim of American imperialism. The horrendous results included a loss of America's soul and a degeneration beyond repair. Even the presumed battles for worldwide democracy and human rights after 1950 consisted merely of subterfuges to guarantee docile markets for the products of American capitalism throughout an unwilling world. The Soviets and their Western sympathizers had often enough said all this before. The later acknowledgment of radical scholars that perhaps the failures of Communism had something to do with the downfall of the Soviet Empire struck the only new note.

There were other hostile accusations: that the United States victimized those it purported to help, at home as abroad; that it made the poor the major victims of the welfare state. Intellectuals now also voiced a charge once associated with aristocrats, of Coca-Colazation—that is, of a pervasive vulgarization of life. Such assessments usually took place at the nation's elite universities, often at luxurious resort hotels where seminars and conferences, financed by the taxpayer, assembled the pundits to moaning sessions in which they judged their country harshly as the source, or at least the prototype, of a society built upon possession, upon the idolatry of property and material things. A legal director of the American Civil Liberties Union said, "We are not yet a fascist state in general," implying that he manned the last barricade before the end.

A scarcely concealed animus against the ordinary lives of ordinary humans crept into the animal rights and environmental movements that set the snail darter and spotted owl above Joe Six-Pack in the scheme of creation. Their elitism gained strength from a distaste for the culture of ordinary people, for precisely that feature of American life that represented the triumph of democratic ideals. From "Beaver" (1957) to Bunker ("All in the Family," 1971) to "Serial Mom" (1994)—from the neat little lovables to the uncouth brute or psychotic housewife. "Fifty percent of Americans are basically Paleolithic." If given political power they would all act like Idi Amin. "What sense does democracy make if all members of society are robots from different genetic castes?"

Timothy Leary offered hope (1982), ready to jump ship into a better socio-biologic future where he would lead the elite joined by members of the ACLU, NOW, the Children's Defense Fund, and various think tanks, all mercifully free of the need to pander to the morons who made up the vast majority of the population.[34]

The outpouring of material goods coped with, if it did not satisfy, the consumerism that swayed intellectuals as it did other Americans. Just let everyone possess Calvin Klein jeans and $125 pump-up Reebocks to spread contentment.

Not at all! There was no end to the cry for more, joined paradoxically to complaints against the excess, against the rat race, and joined also to the longing for a simpler, less pressured existence. When James Dean and Marlon Brando wore jeans in the 1950s, their outfits made statements of genuine proletarian hardscrabble toil. In the 1960s jeans became the counterculture costume, symbol of a new, humanized American consciousness, assertion of a dream of classlessness. In the next decades older and more affluent folk followed, some to escape the stigmas of their age, others, courtesy of expensive designers, to bridge the gap between their social status and wealth on the one hand and their proclaimed ideologies on the other.[35]

This context made the omnipresent cult of the body comprehensible—nutrition, diet, and exercise workshops, calorie controls, all of which persuaded anti-American intellectuals that phobias about moral, historical, and transcendental ends had become corporal obsessions; that whatever went in one end went out the other. The "messianic aspirations" that "should have ended in the tragedy of Vietnam" revived in "the pitiless askesis of the dieter." The antiwar protesters of the 1960s became the health fanatics of the 1970s, with the passions that had fueled their activism redirected into a preoccupation with their bodies. "In a sense the war had come home," a writer pompously pronounced, for now with our bodies under siege, rather than those of the Vietnamese, "only the most unremitting vigilance could save us from the chemicals bombarding us from every supermarket shelf." Jane Fonda provided the evidence; the rhetoric of the antiwar radical turned apostle of the Keep Fit resonated with disconcerting echoes of the battle in Asia and suggested that the forbidden pleasures of American imperialism had resurfaced in the very discourse of their exorcism. "Even the diet Fonda recommended, high fiber, complex carbohydrate, low animal protein, low fat, corresponded to that of the prewar Vietnamese peasant," as if to atone for the defoliation of that country by stuffing American bodies full of leaves. Fiber suggested that "the falling moral fiber of America might be rescued by heroic mastication of the indigestible integuments of vegetables." Slimming, too, depended upon the same amnesia that sustained utopianism; the next diet would produce the miracle, the next war would be victorious and just, with all past failures merely aberrations in the progress to beatitude. Fonda's injunction "to go for the burn" simultaneously expiated and relived the Vietnam napalm raids and hinted that the sacrificial rites of exercise provided a way of enjoying apocalypse now.[36]

Such feverish effusions illustrated the degraded state of literary criticism in the 1990s and also the passionate anti-Americanism that clouded the understanding of people who agonized about their bodies and their health. But the antiauthoritarian mood of the academy that hailed the death of all "canons" (presumed to be the concoction of white, Eurocentric, and dead males) legitimized excrement deconstruction. Controversial theorists became culture heroes, who enlisted under the banner of the New Historicism in which anything went. Its counterpart in the legal profession was Critical Legal Studies, and other disciplines constructed their own versions. Skills once strictly literary applied to history, justified the discard of notions of causality and influence. Everything became merely a text, no less fictive or figurative than a novel or a poem. Race, class, and gender, the new trinity, invoked in the name of an agenda determined not merely to reinterpret the past but to master it, justified the belief that control of the past meant control of the future as well. Ultimately supporters of the redefined disciplines denied the possibility of freedom. If no one could transcend constraints of race, gender, and class, all were utter prisoners.

The anguished longing for love did not subside after 1970; indeed, it grated the more harshly on those who, possessing all else, nonetheless felt deprived. Hot wants would no longer do. For many Americans, the central institution of the family unraveled. Frequent divorce and serial marriages unsettled husbands, wives, and most of all children left adrift by working mothers. External restraints having dropped away, sexual relations had become as open and uninhibited as the most lurid earlier imaginings, although not exactly free because dictated by peer expectations. Communities, however, no longer intervened, and marital ties and restraints of age and gender no longer counted. Yet the results exposed on TV talk shows less often seemed erotic or stimulating than gross and perverse, less a liberating, joyful force than—as for the Bobbits—a mode of domination, an expression of pain and power. Counterparts of Barnum's freaks entered twentieth-century living rooms daily via tabloid talk shows. Bewildered old-time radicals like Herbert Marcuse denied that the new practices signified sexual liberation, only a flow of instincts. The woman who really valued people's being sexually attracted to her nevertheless hated any traditional display of affection and concluded that "the key to happiness is loving myself."[37]

Eroticism, pushed to an extreme by Madonna, Michael Jackson, and other gender-benders, seemed more perverse than provocative. Laced with sadomasochistic words and images, sex as thus presented focused on hurting the other, on control, and on domination, not eased in the least by easy talk about pluralistic social forms. Although taken seriously only by obsessed academics able to deconstruct any text, the new attitude penetrated popular consciousness by way of cosmetic advertising, X-rated movies, and television. The relaxed understanding of sex also eased tolerance of pornography, no longer punished as criminal, and subtly insinuated into the mass media, despite its degradation of female victims. Indeed, feminists seemed to withdraw from efforts to enter the structure of patriarchy, having, according to Betty Friedan, only succeeded in allowing women to become as bad as men. Their high visibility in prominent positions, whether on the Supreme Court, as university presidents, in the U.S. Senate, or as appointees of administrations embarked on redressing former imbalance, mattered little. To their critics, such women, having been unable or unwilling to infuse society with new values, seemed betrayers of The Cause—in the end less liberated than before since their situations required the assimilation of masculine values.[38]

Numerous scraps of evidence revealed the calamitous effect on family life. Crime: the juvenile justice system floundered, torn between the desire to protect the community and the wish to advance the welfare of the child, between the inclination to take offenders out of circulation and the wish to restore them to their families, between blaming malfeasance on the society or the individual. Attitudes toughened in the 1980s with the rise in the number of homicides and the increase in gang and drug wars.[39]

In the 1990s the count of children born out of wedlock soared; single women gave birth to two-thirds of all black infants. But two-parent households were not enough to sustain sound family life. Mothers and fathers who worked outside the home passed their offspring around like pets for whom busy schedules allowed little time. Shocked citizens who subscribed to the Moral Majority and sought a restoration of traditional values focused on only the lesser part of the problem in preaching the right to life in an antiabortion crusade; the greater part of the problem was the kind of life open to unwanted children in fragile families. In an age of counseling, which interpreted unhappiness as a sign of oppression, parents who stumbled no longer seemed the best judges of their children's welfare. The time had come to pay the price for a choice many wished to avoid—between self-expression and social responsibility. Often the burden fell on women, not liberated but victims of altered attitudes, although men, too, complained of the change. The inchoate longings of individuals who blindly threw their lots in with James Jones and David Koresh revealed the deep and futile desire to belong to a family.[40]

Other forms of sexuality detached from the family also emerged from the closet, no longer hidden by the assumption that heterosexual love alone was licit, since only the union of male and female could serve the end of procreation. After 1970 advocates openly, defiantly defended, described, and practiced sexual relationships earlier only discreetly referred to in novels or hinted at on the stage. "In Your Face." San Francisco and New York allowed bathhouses and singles bars to serve as places of assignation until the virulent spread of the AIDS virus closed them down. And the antics of extremist groups like ACT-UP and Queer Nation antagonized many willing to accept the existence of other forms of human relationships. Self-appointed zealots eager for publicity and bent on furthering their agenda at any cost took to "outing" those who preferred to keep their sexual preferences private, in violation of their liberty. But supporters of nonconforming sex did not feel that the AIDS epidemic should force them to abandon their lifestyles, in favor of "mainstream sexual mores." Quietly the San Francisco bathhouses reopened.

Some communities tried to give spousal status to such unions—or at least to those with a defined, permanent quality. But arguments presented for their tolerance could not deny that their essence ran counter to the values traditionally associated with a family that provided continuity across the generations. Supporters of same-sex alliances proclaimed their right to pursue happiness in their own way, and pointed to high divorce rates among heterosexuals and to the stability of so-called Boston marriages (where sexual relations, apparently, were not a factor). Furthermore, lifetime bondings, often contracted for hypocritical motives, reflected "cultural imperatives" and resulted in "lost affiliation with a larger community, erotic desiccation and the perpetuation of female dependence." As long as anatomy shaped the destinies of men and women, there would be little liberty for any, gay or straight. But this sentiment papered over many questions, and in the days when fear of controversial results hampered scientists' research, answers would be long in coming.

Violence still thrilled as sexual encounters in the flesh or on the page or screen no longer did. Custom and law continued to forbid the injury or pain caused by one person to another, which, however, evoked quivers of excitement even in hardened observers. Norman Mailer thus drooled with anticipation as he watched Ali prepare for THE FIGHT. But the fist soon paled in the capacity for arousal as the gun, the knife, and the bomb asserted their superior power to draw blood, to smash down, to blow up the solid façade of persons or structures, to violate the humanity of others. And more explicit and more dramatic media soon outdid descriptions in print. The inhibitions that had formerly exercised some restraint upon the offerings of movies and television quietly collapsed. Fanciful notions about "oppositional cultures" actually encouraged denigrations of civilized behavior, as ever more nihilistic teenagers turned their communities into free-fire zones. Black-on-black violence became a national concern, as did the romanticization of brutality and the subversion of traditional values. The wave of pointless homicides in the streets paralleled outrageous lyrics and forms of entertainment, with a white-owned record industry cashing in on black alienation and the kicks teenagers derived from listening to, and viewing, glorifications of self-destruction. Such fragmentation reached down to the primary schools amidst heated battles over curricula and textbooks, as outraged parents, unsympathetic to the wider goals of social reformers, fought back. Not all mothers and fathers considered a homosexual lifestyle a legitimate alternative. Nor were many happy when a series of books suggested to students that in the end they might "adopt the views of a feminist, a humanist, a pacifist, an anti-Christian, a vegetarian, or an advocate of a one-world government." After 1990, in all forms of expression, anything went. Neither the law, nor community sentiment, nor organized voluntary efforts effectively stood in the way.[41]

Faith in government declined as people became ever more dependent on it. Revelations about the old Tuskegee syphilis experiments meshed in with fear about AIDS ascribed to conspiracies to wipe out blacks or homosexuals. Loss of faith in science connected with the Thalidomide, *Challenger,* and Chernobyl disasters evoked demands that only black or homosexual physicians treat their own victims. The bewildered, lacking anchors in family or troubled institutions, agonized in confusion. Some tuned out reality with the help of their Walkman and plugged into a private world of music that obliterated surrounding squalor. The more articulate consoled themselves by assuming that they had a monopoly on compassion and goodness, and labeled all their critics simply mean. At the same time, redefinitions of such matters as sexual harassment widened the scope of criminal behavior.[42]

So what? A deep sense of futility spread among men and women who paused, now and then, to consider the purpose of their striving. The popular song no longer asked them to wait for tomorrow; it made no better offer than the day after tomorrow. Even escape to the rural countryside or small town did not help. And those who had a decent job, a satisfying spouse, and good kids woke up to wonder "what for?" and failed to relate their own experience to the vast universe within which they spun about. Civilized to the point of tedium, safe, threatened only by the storm within, they had no one to call, no one to consult. Well might they ponder whether that mad, mad world was too big a trap to afford floundering humans scope for the ability to act—that is, for liberty.[43]

The nineteenth-century thinkers who had envisioned the ultimate choice people would confront as that between bread and liberty could not have foreseen a situation in which an abundance of bread and an absence of all restraints would still leave humans aggrieved and unable to act.

Even doing good did not suffice to earn freedom.

Grievances about the national inadequacies had resounded throughout the American past. Extraordinary expectations invited deep disappointments—a pilgrim people rearing a city on a hill, a land of liberty, light for the world, the last best hope on earth, a world made safe for democracy—such the standards by which the citizens measured themselves. Alas, the men and women, creatures of flesh and blood, of passion and prejudice, frequently blind and ill-informed, all too often fell short of the hopes vested in them. Hence they seemed to many critics, as they did to Holden Caulfield, phonies one and all, who talked a good line but always let you down when needed, driving to desperation whoever wished to do good by saving little kids.

Mark David Chapman could not stand it (1980). He reread the book and came to New York to retrace Holden's steps—the lagoon in Central Park, the Museum of Natural History—then proceeded to shoot John Lennon, one of those rich phonies, who preached poverty and claimed to have greater influence on youth than Christ.[44]

Neither the victim nor the assassin understood where they were, because neither of them knew whence they came, nor of what that liberty they claimed consisted. Spiritual heirs of a four-hundred-year quest for something rarely defined, yet always known as precious, they had arrived at a critical juncture at which they grasped for answers without knowing the questions. Their countrymen and women, diverse in color, culture, and faith, the hundreds of millions of them strewn across a vast area or heaped up in dense towns, reached across the centuries for an identity yet scarcely knew what they sought.

Liberty, the ability to act, once denied to men and women wedged into old societies encrusted with institutions and rules, had drawn on the Europeans who crossed the ocean to the world new to them. They had blundered into a land of great spaces, unsettling because established rules did not apply there. To survive they had improvised, sometimes out of ignorance, sometimes out of necessity.

Only the most articulate could explain why they wished to be free; however, all but the slave, all others including the indentured servants, having exercised some choice in the decision to come to America, understood why they wished to slip away from the restraints of the Old World, with its limited opportunities, its ancient traditions and confinements; why, that is, they wished to make a fresh start across the ocean. Moral individuals, deemed capable of judging right from wrong in the eyes of God and under the scrutiny of their neighbors, all bore at the very least responsibility for their own actions. To that extent, the least of them enjoyed liberty—that is, some ability to act.

Status conditioned the extent of their freedom—whether rich or poor, whether gentle or simple, married or single, mature or childish, man or woman; every degree marked out its scope for action. So, too, did the sphere—within the home and family, the village, the parish, the county, the province. That much was familiar, transferred from the European background whence they came.

In America, as in the Old World, only the proper organization of power could safeguard the liberty of each. People who did not wish to descend to the level of beasts in the field learned to live by laws. But having arrived in a distant land, almost empty, with one settlement remote from another, circumstances forced changes in inherited ways of acting—and two in particular. To survive, in peace if not in amity, these people had to recognize that the liberties of others set limits on the liberty of even the greatest among them. And so, too, the rulers discovered that they could exert authority across the New World's great spaces only through the consent of the governed.

The necessary use of force they therefore encased in respect for the rights of the citizens.

The Fourth of July, independence and all that—those came later; Americans had gained the essential victory before the shot heard round the world. The war only confirmed an existing reality; the inhabitants of the states along the Atlantic, citizens of a Republic, ruled themselves by constitutions of their own devising that recognized popular sovereignty and guaranteed individual rights.

Thereafter they directed their attention to expansion, spurred on by the seeming emptiness of the continent to their west, but also by the global opportunities for trade. The urge to spread out incorporated personal and national elements—personal, in the attractiveness of space within which families could hope for future rewards and compensate for past failures; national in the opportunity to fulfill the manifest destiny that justified the Republic. Expansion amplified the ability to act of yeomen, merchants, artisans, and planters—considered new types of beings in the liberty to transform the world about them. Expansion also sustained the reform impulse that aimed to transform all humanity by eliminating the imperfections that stood in the way of improvement. The certainty that the United States moved in the vanguard of progress endowed these efforts with cosmic significance, so that even a great civil war did not dilute confidence in the ability to perfect a land of liberty—

that is, one that endowed all its people with the ability to act.

Success, however, brought unexpected penalties. Along with the expansion of agriculture came the development of a great industrial economy that moved far beyond the rural textile and shoe manufactories of the early nineteenth century and rested rather on extractive and heavy industries such as coal, iron, oil, and steel. A massive reordering of life followed after 1870 as the immense labor force required to till the soil and man the machines rapidly raised the population. Millions of families drawn from migration out of Europe and from a high birth rate spilled across the continent and piled up in great cities. Neither the high price society paid nor the sheer human suffering entailed dimmed the optimism of Americans, but rather spurred them to more insistent schemes of reform. The less-than-perfect results did not still efforts to perfect society, even though they coincided with an expansionist impulse that extended overseas and that soon involved the United States in a great world war. In a half century of confusion about the relation of power to liberty, the government of the United States ever more often resorted to the tools of repression rather than of persuasion.

As a result the country sloped downward to despair in the twentieth century; the contrast between the high expectations of human perfection in the New World environment and the reality of political corruption, venal business practices, and persistent problems in agriculture and industry eroded the stubborn optimism of an earlier era. Then a prolonged depression that resisted the unavailing political remedies of the New Deal and a greater world war brought the nation to the brink of disaster. The ultimate revelation of nuclear force over Japan seemed to herald the inglorious finish to the New World experiment.

It did not end thus. After 1950 the economy recovered; earnest efforts made a start at solving great social problems; and ever-wider circles of the population enjoyed greater ability to act than ever before—perhaps not enough, but still significantly more than any previous generation.

A sobering thought then intruded: perhaps liberty, a necessary condition of happiness, would prove to be not a sufficient condition of happiness.

December 31, 1993

Fragments:

With the approach of a new millennium comes assessment time.

What fools these mortals be!

Most of all they lack the ability for self-assessment.

But also they lack the knowledge of the past to set the present in context.

Regard the agonizing over the economy, as the doctors monitor its every heartbeat.

One way or another it produces all the nation needs and enough besides for a good part of the rest of the world. Some get more, some less, some too much, others too little. The wiser would do it better. But one infallible index measures it all: year by year in every class, race, gender, at every age level, life expectancy rises.

No more favorite numbers adorn the newspaper pages than the statistics of unemployment—none more rarely appear than the statistics of employment. Yet while the percentages of people out of work fluctuate, the number of people at work rises steadily—surely an index of economic health.

Review next the agonizing about the strains of arriving at some approximation of racial justice and equality—with always the emphasis upon what yet remains to be done to achieve perfection. Recall: less than a half century has elapsed since 1950. Never in modern history has a society carried through a more radical social transformation. A black underclass still presents a massive problem; but one-third of United States blacks fit into the American middle class, and black faces are visible on stage, screen, and television, in city halls and state capitals, in the national cabinet and also in corporate boardrooms. In forty-five years!

We mourned the murder of the university at the hands of the student radicals of the 1960s, the stifling of humane scholarship, and the insidious spread of institutional bureaucracy smothered in foundation and government money that diminishes the prospect of a resurrection. Big bucks brought corruption into the academy; anything-goes permissiveness made it welcome. Plagiarism, faked experiments, networking, peers who made only a pretense of review revealed the insidious temptation of grants, prizes, and patents.

Yet students always learned more outside the classroom than within it. They still do even as they drift through the malls that offer every type of course, every variety of activity. And something different also goes on—detached from the usual undergraduates' pre-one career or another. From the San Diego State University courses of instruction, the bemused visitor learned that the Afro-American Studies Department offered "Fundamentals of Computation," while Mexican-American Studies offered "Review of Mathematics." No doubt addition, subtraction, and long division—a far cry from differential equations—did not vary by ethnicity; but on reflection it made sense to offer remedial instruction in contexts that would enable those who had fallen behind to catch up.

Question: would a way lie open for those good in arithmetic to move on to calculus?

In the 1990s, nontraditional students accounted for forty percent of all those enrolled in American institutions of higher education—older, part-timers, some supporting dependents rather than supported as dependents. Among all those who carry student IDs and among others who drift around the fringes, thinking goes on—in libraries, bookstores, laboratories, and crowded lonely rooms; nothing to do with courses and curricula, only with the tolerance of inefficient administrations. So Bill Gates, bored as a Harvard sophomore, carries away the concept of Microsoft. And thousands sign up for continuing education, after retirement or in intervals of leisure, out of a simple desire to learn, to know, to understand.

And so on. The family in trouble; the cities in trouble; crime, trouble; welfare, trouble; the homeless, trouble. True.

To some extent the fault lies in perspective. Always the family, cities, crime, poverty, and tramps provided subjects for jeremiads. The 1990s, less tolerant of deviance, more insistent upon making the world perfect, insists on doing something about its troubles. Hence the frustration.

What is this speck of dust that we should be mindful of it?

An explorer finding new things—spaced out. The moon? Nothing to it; Hubble intends to reach beyond the edge of the universe.

Back in time, too—before the Hebrews, Egyptians, Greeks, Minoans; before the Nabateans, Hittites, and the nomads of Central Asia and of the farther Orient, scratching, digging into prehistory, finding out ways to find out.

And others who explore the interior of what students once knew as matter or who probe the structure of the gene or who measure the shift of continents, out of the wish to know.

The audacity of it: a speck of dust exercising the will to know in order to exercise the will to act, the unquenchable will to act.

That is to be free.

The New World adventure was one such exploration, an adventure that began with a handful of Europeans audaciously planting a society in what they took to be an empty continent. Their descendants, along with additions from every part of the world, developed institutions that expanded human ability, sometimes unsuccessfully wandering off into error, then recovering and nevertheless after almost four hundred years of trial forming a nation dedicated to liberty.

NOTE ON THE SOURCES

The process of analyzing and describing the recent past created unfamiliar difficulties for historians. The foreshortened chronological perspective drew many of the events here analyzed within our own lifetime, therefore subject to the biases from attitudes formed as they unfolded. We have done our best to offset those distortions.

More important difficulties emanated from the changing nature of the sources. We could glean the data on which the present volume rests from an abundance of manuscripts, newspapers, periodicals, and printed books, as we had for accounts of earlier centuries. Moreover, we could draw on new sources—the statistical accumulations of governmental and private bodies, oral histories, social surveys, and the visual data preserved on films, tapes, and disks.

The changing nature of the materials presented less difficulty than their sheer abundance. True, marvelous electronic devices put at our disposal finding aids, references and entire texts that would have aroused the envy of earlier generations of scholars—when we already knew what we sought. Technology ceased to help when we groped for information we could not define in advance. Then we depended upon older techniques less appropriate for modern data. We could read through a year's file of a respectable Philadelphia or New York newspaper of the 1790s in a few days, but not a month's run of the *New York Times* of the 1930s or 1980s. Even were the time for analysis limitless, sheer volume created a kind of static that drowned out the more important messages with irrelevancies.

To tune out selectively, created difficulties of which we were conscious and with which we may not fully have coped. A vast library of mongraphs, memoirs, and biographies has treated some aspects of our problems and to some extent has offset the complexities of coping with overabundant data. But that secondary literature suffered from its own deficiencies, much of it written by journalists, more often storytellers than analysts, susceptible to juicy gossip and swayed by hearsay evidence, their accounts set in a context shaped by imperfect memories. Yet these volumes contained important evidence that called for judicious evaluation—no simple task in view of our own imperfect recollections and prejudices.

NOTES

CHAPTER 1.

1. H. L. Mencken, *Notes on Democracy* (New York, 1926), p. 49; Robert M. La Follette, *La Follette's Autobiography,* 2 vols. (New York, 1953), 1:667; Andre Siegfried, *America Comes of Age,* tr. H. H. Hemming (New York, 1927), p. 125; Joseph K. Folsom, *Culture and Social Progress* (New York, 1928), p. 452; Walter Lippmann, *Interpretations 1933–1935,* ed. Allan Nevins (New York, 1936), p. 316; Mark Sullivan, *Our Times* (6 vols., New York, 1935), 6:112; Edgar Kemler, *The Deflation of American Ideals* (Seattle, Wash., 1941), pp. 9, 29; Leon Whipple, *The Story of Civil Liberty in the United States* (New York, 1927), p. 327.
2. Andrew Sinclair, *The Available Man* (New York, 1965), pp. 90, 161, 190; William C. Widenor, *Henry Cabot Lodge* (Berkeley, Calif., 1980), pp. 347–48; John A. Garraty, *Henry Cabot Lodge* (New York, 1953); Robert J. Maddox, *William E. Borah and American Foreign Policy* (Baton Rouge, La., 1970); Marian C. McKenna, *Borah* (Ann Arbor, Mich., 1961); Ishbel Ross, *Power with Grace* (New York, 1975), pp. 69, 187, 212, 218; Gene Smith, *When the Cheering Stopped* (New York, 1964), pp. 68–69, 128, 138–39; Michael E. Parrish, *Anxious Decades* (New York, 1992), p. 3.
3. Robert A. Caro, *The Power Broker: Robert Moses and the Fall of New York* (New York, 1974), pp. 104 ff., 615 ff.; James M. Beck, *Our Wonderland of Bureaucracy* (New York, 1932); Robert K. Murray, *The Harding Era* (Minneapolis, Minn., 1969), pp. 415–16; Sullivan, *Our Times,* 6:2 ff.; Henry H. Curran, *John Citizen's Job* (New York, 1924), p. 112; Parrish, *Anxious Decades,* p. 11.
4. Oliver Brett, *A Defence of Liberty* (New York, 1921), p. 31; Siegfried, *America Comes of Age,* p. 245; Arthur N. Holcombe, *The Political Parties of Today* (New York, 1924), p. 384; Kenneth Campbell MacKay, *The Progressive Movement in 1924* (New York, 1947), pp. 164–66.
5. T. Harry Williams, *Huey Long* (New York, 1969).
6. George Walsh, *Gentleman Jimmy Walker* (New York, 1974), pp. 138 ff.; Curran, *John Citizen's Job,* p. 192; Stanley Walker, *The Night Club Era* (New York, 1933), pp. 224, 273, 274; Noal Solomon, *When Leaders Were Bosses* (Hicksville, New York, 1975), pp. 136–39, 141–48; also Joseph F. Dineen, *Ward Eight* (New York, 1936); Edwin O'Connor, *The Last Hurrah* (Boston, 1956).

7. Clarence E. Ridley, *Measuring Municipal Government* (Syracuse, N.Y., 1930); Robert K. Murray, *The Politics of Normalcy* (New York, 1974), pp. 34–35; Curran, *John Citizen's Job,* p. 158; William F. Russell, *Liberty Versus Equality* (New York, 1935), p. 129; Richard T. Ely, *Ground Under Our Feet* (New York, 1938), p. 260.
8. Fred J. Cook, *Maverick* (New York, 1984), pp. 82 ff.; Curran, *John Citizen's Job,* p. 110.
9. Murray, *Harding Era,* pp. 228, 230 ff., 253, 263; Arthur N. Holcombe, *The Foundation of the Modern Commonwealth* (New York, 1923), pp. 284 ff.: Arthur N. Holcombe, *State Government in the United States* (New York, 1926), pp. 453 ff.
10. E. E. Cummings, *A Selection of Poems,* ed. Horace Gregory (New York, 1965), p. 83; Fred Allen, *Treadmill to Oblivion* (Boston, 1954), pp. 203–204; Russell, *Liberty Versus Equality,* pp. 92–114; Mencken, *Notes on Democracy,* pp. 46, 125.
11. Murray, *Harding Era,* pp. 69–70, 514; Stanley Walker, *The Night Club Era* (New York, 1933), pp. 295–96; William H. Harbaugh, *Lawyer's Lawyer* (New York, 1973), pp. 238, 239; Martin J. Wade, *"Down with the Constitution"* (Davenport, Ia., 1924), pp. 17, 31; Clarke A. Chambers, *Seedtime of Reform* (Minneapolis, 1963), pp. ix ff.
12. Maury Maverick, *A Maverick American* (New York, 1935), pp. 142–43; Irving Babbitt, *Democracy and Leadership* (Boston, 1924), pp. 274, 291; Timothy Materer, *Vortex: Pound, Eliot, and Lewis* (Ithaca, N.Y., 1979); George B. Lockwood, *Americanism* (Washington, 1971), p. 38.
13. Manfred Jonas, *Isolationism in America* (Chicago, 1990), p. 3; Lockwood, *Americanism,* pp. 5, 19, 30; Murray, *Harding Era,* p. 517.
14. Edwin A. Robinson, "Demos" (1920), *Collected Poems* (New York, 1937); Paula Fass, *The Damned and the Beautiful* (New York, 1977), p. 345; John H. Schaar, *Loyalty in America* (Berkeley, Calif., 1957), p. 83; Francis Russell, *The Great Interlude* (New York, 1964), pp. 60, 65; Murray, *Harding Era,* p. 518; Parrish, *Anxious Decades,* p. 132; Leon Whipple, *Our Ancient Liberties* (New York, 1927), p. 148; Claudius O. Johnson, *Borah of Idaho* (Seattle, Washington, 1936), pp. 220 ff.
15. Ellis Hawley, ed., *Herbert Hoover as Secretary of Commerce* (Iowa City, 1981), pp. 185 ff.
16. Durant Drake, *America Faces the Future,* pp. 324 ff.
17. Lockwood, *Americanism,* pp. 31–32, 64, 71, 130, 145 ff.; Murray, *Harding Era,* p. 394; Gilbert Chinard, *Thomas Jefferson* (Boston, 1929), pp. 486, 492; Edward M. Easy, *Mankind at the Crossroads* (New York, 1924), pp. 115 ff.; Parrish, *Anxious Decades,* pp. 113 ff.; Drake, *America Faces the Future,* pp. 83, 88, 91; Richard T. Ely and Frank Bohm, *The Great Change* (New York, 1935), pp. 237–40.
18. Oscar Handlin, *Race and Nationality in American Life* (Boston, 1957), pp. 93 ff., 139 ff.; E. Fuller Torrey, *Freudian Fraud* (New York, 1992), p. 50; Richard N. Current, *Secretary Stimson* (New Brunswick, N.J., 1954), p. 39.
19. Henry Pratt Fairchild, *The Melting Pot Mistake* (Boston, 1926), pp. 137, 257; Isaac F. Marcossone, "The Alien in America," and Martin Dies, "The Immigrant Question," *Saturday Evening Post,* 207 (April 6 and 20, 1935): 22, 27; Joseph Gies, *The Colonel of Chicago* (New York, 1979), pp. 112–15; Chalmers H. Roberts, *The Washington Post* (Boston, 1977), pp. 156 ff.; American Legion Committee on Americanism, *Conference* (San Francisco, 1923), p. 31; (San Francisco, 1937),

pp. 12 ff., 44, 285; Daniel C. Brewer, *The Peril of the Republic* (New York, 1922), pp. 56, 210; William F. Russell, *Liberty Versus Equality,* pp. 14–15.

20. Otto Mutz, *What's the Matter with Our Uncle Sam* (Lincoln, Nebr., 1922), p. 176; F. A. Baughna, *Elementary Americanism* (Los Angeles, 1926), pp. 60 ff.; Chester F. Miller, *The March of Democracy* (Boston, 1925), p. 6; John Erskine, *Prohibition and Christianity* (Indianapolis, 1927), p. 173; Lee J. Levinger, *Anti-Semitism in the United States* (New York, 1925), p. 84; Fass, *The Damned and the Beautiful,* pp. 17–19, 76, 358–60; Earl Warren, *A Republic if You Can Keep It* (New York, 1972), pp. 4, 5; Irving Babbitt, *Democracy and Leadership* (New York, 1924), pp. 197, 222, 264; "Battle Flags and Moth Balls," *Independent,* 102 (May 22, 1920); Paul S. Boyer, *Purity in Print* (New York, 1968), pp. 151 ff.; Parrish, *Anxious Decades,* pp. 77 ff.
21. Fass, *The Damned and the Beautiful,* pp. 20–23, 37; Gerald Mast, *Short History of the Movies,* 4th ed. (New York, 1986), pp. 105–106; Upton Sinclair, *Boston* (New York, 1928); Maxwell Anderson, *Winterset* (New York, 1935); John Dos Passos, *Big Money* (New York, 1936); James T. Farrell, *Bernard Clare* (New York, 1946); Henry J. Abraham, *Freedom and the Court* (New York, 1967), pp. 46 ff., 54 ff.; Albert Londres, *The Road to Buenos Ayres* (New York, 1928); Miller, *March of Democracy,* p. 23; Shailer Mathews, *The Validity of American Ideals* (New York, 1922), pp. 28, 56; Thurman Arnold, *The Folklore of Capitalism* (1937; New Haven, 1948), p. 354.
22. Henry S. McKee, *Degenerate Democracy* (New York, 1933), pp. 1–9; Stuart Chase, *The Tyranny of Words* (New York, 1938); Charles A. Beard, *America Faces the Future* (Cambridge, Mass., 1932), pp. 5, 9–10; Vincent Sheean, *Personal History* (Garden City, N.Y., 1937), p. 12.
23. Waldo Frank, *In the American Jungle* (New York, 1937), p. 113; Harry S. Warner, *Prohibition: An Adventure in Freedom* (Westerville, Ohio, 1928), pp. 245 ff.; Boyer, *Purity in Print,* p. 153; Russell, *Great Interlude,* pp. 104 ff.; Ernest Kurtz, *Not God: A History of Alcoholics Anonymous* (Center City, Minn., 1979); Fabian Franklin, *The ABC of Prohibition* (New York, 1927), pp. 48–52; Whipple, *Our Ancient Liberties,* p. 148; Durant Drake, *America Faces the Future,* p. 25; Parrish, *Anxious Decades,* pp. 98 ff.; also Ogden Chisolm, *The Volstead Act* (Ridgefield, Conn., 1929), p. 2; A. Lawrence Lowell, "Reconstruction and Prohibition," *Atlantic Monthly,* 145 (Feb. 1929): 9.
24. Harold L. Ickes, *The Secret Diary,* 3 vols. (New York, 1953), 2:183, 191.
25. Frank, *American Jungle,* p. 25; *New York Times,* August 17, 1937; Frank C. Hanighen, "Foreign Political Movements in the United States," *Foreign Affairs,* 19 (October 1937): 9; Ralph L. Roy, *Apostles of Discord* (Boston, 1953), pp. 26 ff.; Kenneth T. Jackson, *The Ku Klux Klan in the City, 1915–1930* (New York, 1967), pp. 67, 130; Shawn Lay, ed., *The Invisible Empire in the West* (Urbana, Ill., 1992), pp. 127, 205; Harbaugh, *Lawyer's Lawyer,* p. 209 ff.; David L. Lewis, *The Public Image of Henry Ford* (Detroit, Michigan, 1976), pp. 135 ff., 151 ff.; Lee J. Levinger, *Anti-Semitism in the United States* (New York, 1925), pp. 88 ff., 92 ff.
26. *New York Times,* May 31 (IV, 6:1), Oct. 4 (IV, 7:8), 1936; *Life,* July 26, 1937, pp. 19 ff.; George Morris, *The Black Legion Rides* (New York, 1936), p. 5; Morris Janowitz, "Black Legions on the March," Daniel Aaron, ed., *America in Crisis* (New York, 1952), pp. 305 ff.; Leo P. Ribuffo, *The Old Christian Right* (Philadelphia, 1983), *passim;* Morris Schonbach, *Native American Fascism During the 1930s and 1940s* (1958; New York, 1985), *passim.*

27. Alfred Bingham, *Insurgent America* (New York, 1935); William Dudley Pelley, *Nations-in-Law,* 2 vols. (Asheville, N.C., 1938), 1:59, 64, 152 ff., 2:579, 650 ff.; Stanley High, "Star-Spangled Fascists," *Saturday Evening Post,* May 27, 1939, pp. 5 ff.; Ribuffo, *Old Christian Right,* pp. 55 ff., 123 ff.; Lewis Corey, *The Crisis of the Middle Classes* (New York, 1943); William F. Russell, *Liberty versus Equality,* p. 13; Calvin M. Logue and Howard Dorgan, *The Oratory of Southern Demagogues* (Baton Rouge, La., 1981), pp. 157, 214; Shailer Mathews, *The Validity of American Ideals,* pp. 188, 191.
28. Gerald K. Smith, "The Huey Long Movement," Rita J. Simon, ed., *As We Saw the Thirties* (Urbana, Ill., 1967), pp. 46 ff.; Isabel Leighton, ed., *The Aspirin Age* (New York, 1949), pp. 232 ff., 339 ff.; Alan Brinkley, *Voices of Protest* (New York, 1982), pp. 33 ff., 80 ff., 91 ff., 129 ff.; Larry Ceplair, *Under the Shadow of War* (New York, 1987), pp. 190–91; Lippmann, *Interpretations,* pp. 374, 376; Raymond G. Swing, *Forerunners of American Fascism* (New York, 1935), pp. 121 ff.
29. *Congressional Record,* 74 Cong., 1 Sess., Vol. 79, pt. 7, pp. 8040 ff.; Huey P. Long, *Every Man a King* (New Orleans, 1933), and *My First Days in the White House* (Harrisburg, Penn., 1936); Glen Jeansonne, *Gerald L. K. Smith, Minister of Hate* (New Haven, Conn., 1988), pp. 25, 37, 53.
30. Lawrence Dennis, *Is Capitalism Doomed?* (New York, 1932), and *The Coming American Fascism* (New York, 1936); T. S. Eliot, "Tradition and Orthodoxy," *American Review,* 2 (1934): 517; Babbitt, *Democracy and Leadership,* p. 303; Hans Schmidt, *Maverick Marine: General Smedley D. Butler* (Lexington, Ky., 1987), pp. 231 ff.; Ceplair, *Under the Shadow of War,* p. 196.
31. Arthur Mann, *La Guardia: A Fighter Against His Times* (Philadelphia, 1959), p. 222.
32. Ceplair, *Under the Shadow of War,* pp. 183, 184.
33. Susan Canedy, *America's Nazis* (Menlo Park, Calif., 1990), p. 52.
34. Canedy, *America's Nazis,* p. 88.
35. Robert S. and Helen M. Lynd, *Middletown* (New York, 1929), pp. 80 ff.; Raymond C. Mayer, *How to Do Publicity* (New York, 1937), pp. 242, 248; Ernest T. Gundlach, *Facts and Fetishes in Advertising* (Chicago, 1931), pp. 477, 552; Canedy, *America's Nazis,* p. 111; Martin Dies, *Trojan Horse in America* (1940; New York, 1977), p. 175; *Life,* Mar. 29, 1937, p. 20.
36. "The Foreign-Language Press," *Fortune,* 22 (Nov. 1940): 90 ff.; Canedy, *America's Nazis,* pp. 74, 145, 154 ff.
37. *New York Times,* Feb. 18, 19, 1939; Ickes, *The Secret Diary,* 2: pp. 111 ff.; Canedy, *America's Nazis,* pp. 136, 215.
38. Pelley, *Nations in Law,* 2: 452, 456, 459; Erich Fromm, *Escape from Freedom* (New York, 1941); Alva Lee, *America Swings to the Left* (New York, 1933), pp. 105–106; Dennis, *Coming American Fascism,* xii, xiii.
39. T.S. Eliot, "Gerontion" (1920), *Complete Poems* (New York, 1952), pp. 21, 24, 35; Logue and Dorgan, *Oratory of Southern Demagogues,* p. 164; Carl Bode, *Mencken* (Carbondale, Ill., 1969), pp. 81 ff., 228 ff.; Brian Boyd, *Vladimir Nabokov: The American Years* (Princeton, N.J., 1991), pp. 311, 312; Winton U. Solberg, "The Early Years of the Jewish Presence at the University of Illinois," *Religion and American Culture,* 2 (1992): 215 ff.; Irwin Edman, "Reuben Cohen Considers Anti-Semitism," *Menorah Journal,* 15 (Jan. 1929): 124, 303; also below, ch. 3.
40. Lee, *America Swings to the Left,* pp. 166, 305.
41. Elizabeth K. Dilling, *The Red Network* (Kenilworth, Ill., 1936); Steve Nelson *et al.,*

Steve Nelson, American Radical (Pittsburgh, 1981), pp. 44, 57, 102 ff.; Mary Harris Jones, *Correspondence,* ed. Edward M. Steel (Pittsburgh, 1985), p. 227; and *Speeches and Writings,* ed. Edward M. Steel (Pittsburgh, 1988); Sheean, *Personal History,* pp. 253 ff.

42. John Reed, *Red Russia* (London, 1919); Meta Berger, "Seeing Is Believing," *New Masses,* 17 (Nov. 5, 1935): 17 ff.; Theodore Dreiser, *Tragic America* (New York, 1931), p. 417; James W. Crowl, *Angels in Stalin's Paradise* (Washington, D.C., 1982); Harvey Klehr, *The Heyday of American Communism* (New York, 1984), pp. 28 ff., 78, 83 ff., 94, 387, 401 ff., 449; Langston Hughes, *I Wonder as I Wander* (New York, 1956), pp. 65, 66; Max Schachtman, "Radicalism," Rita James Simon, *As We Saw the Thirties* (Urbana, Ill., 1967), pp. 11 ff.; Sally J. Taylor, *Stalin's Apologist: Walter Duranty* (New York, 1990); *Nation,* 149 (Aug. 26, 1939): 228; Norman H. Pearson, "The Nazi-Soviet Pact and the End of a Dream," Aaron, ed., *America in Crisis,* pp. 327 ff.; Rose Wilder Lane, *Give Me Liberty* (1936; Easton, Conn., 1944); Bode, *Mencken,* p. 327; Boyd, *Vladimir Nabokov,* pp. 90 ff., 143, 270; Nelson, *Steve Nelson,* pp. 85 ff.; Irving Bernstein, *The Lean Years* (Boston, 1960), pp. 22 ff., 122; Allen Guttman, *The Wound in the Heart: America and the Spanish Civil War* (New York, 1962), pp. 149 ff.; Sherwood Anderson, *Puzzled America* (New York, 1935), p. xvi; Ralph L. Roy, *Apostles of Discord* (Boston, 1953), pp. 259 ff.; William F. Russell, *Liberty Versus Equality,* p. 13.
43. W. G. Krivitsky, "Stalin's Hand in Spain," *Saturday Evening Post,* 211 (Apr. 15, 1939): 5 ff.; Joseph North, ed., *New Masses: An Anthology of the Rebel Thirties* (New York, 1972), p. 308; Dies, *Trojan Horse in America,* pp. 4, 21, 347, 352, 358; William Gellerman, *Martin Dies* (New York, 1944), pp. 75–79, 199, 201; Ickes, *Secret Diary,* 2:507, 529.
44. "Inner Workings of Congressional Committees," *University of Chicago Law Review,* 18 (1951): 461 ff.
45. "The Revolution That Was Not," *The Independent,* 102 (May 15, 1920), p. 213; Walter Lippmann, *Liberty and the News* (New York, 1920), pp. 22 ff., 35 ff.; Zechariah Chaffee, Jr., *Free Speech in the United States* (Cambridge, Mass., 1948), pp. 285 ff., 306 ff.; Leighton, *Aspirin Age,* p. 330; William J. Ghent, *The Reds Bring Reaction* (Princeton, 1923), pp. ix, 92; Cook, *Maverick,* pp. 69 ff.; Langdon Mitchell, *Understanding America* (New York, 1927), pp. 88 ff.; Otis C. Edwards, *Freedom in Two Centuries* (New York, 1969), p. 48.
46. Babbitt, *Democracy and Leadership,* pp. 195 ff., 221.
47. Chafee, *Free Speech,* pp. 362 ff., 398 ff.; Wayne C. Booth, *Now Don't Try to Reason with Me* (Chicago, 1970), pp. 48 ff.; Abraham, *Freedom and the Court,* pp. 83 ff., 124 ff., 150; Harold Stearns, *Liberalism in America* (New York, 1919); Samuel Walker, *In Defence of American Liberties* (New York, 1990), pp. 53, 60–63; Edwin E. Slosson, "Sheepishness," *Independent,* 102 (May 29, 1920), 285; Jenna W. Joselit, *Our Gang* (Bloomington, Ind., 1983), pp. 85 ff.; Tom Mann, *Americanism: A World Menace* (London, 1922); Boyer, *Purity in Print,* pp. 94, 95, 99 ff., 165 ff.; Edward M. East, *Mankind at the Crossroads* (1924; New York, 1977), pp. vii, 293; Chambers, *Seedtime of Reform,* pp. 3 ff.; Harbaugh, *Lawyer's Lawyer,* pp. 281 ff.; Homer Cummings, *In Memory of Benjamin F. Cardozo* (Washington, 1938), p. 13; Hygrade Provision Co. (1924), 266 U.S. 497; Hannah Sprecher, "Let *Them* Drink," *American Jewish Archives,* 43 (1991): 135 ff.; Ickes, *Secret Diary,* 1:32, 36, 2:417; Ribuffo,

Old Christian Right, pp. 127 ff., 163; Dies, *Trojan Horse,* pp. 359 ff.; Joseph K. Folsom, *Culture and Social Progress* (New York, 1928), pp. 247 ff.

48. Chafee, *Free Speech,* pp. 332 ff.; Nancy F. Cott, *The Grounding of Modern Feminism* (New Haven, 1987), pp. 128 ff.; Francis Russell, *Tragedy in Dedham* (New York, 1962), pp. 452 ff.; Paul Avrich, *Sacco and Vanzetti* (Princeton, N.J., 1991); Cook, *Maverick,* pp. 191 ff.; Walker, *In Defence of American Liberties,* pp. 63–64; William McDougall, *The American Nation* (New York, 1925), pp. 48 ff.; Robert Sklar, *Movie Made America* (New York, 1975), p. 130.
49. *Whitney* v. *California;* and *Fiske* v. *Kansas* (1927), 274 U.S. 357, 380; also *Near* v. *Minnesota* (1931), 283 U.S. 697; Chafee, *Free Speech,* pp. 375 ff.
50. Babbitt, *Democracy and Leadership,* pp. 288, 308, 312; McDougall, *American Nation,* pp. 221 ff.; Durant Drake, *America Faces the Future,* pp. 27, 325, 338.
51. Chafee, *Free Speech,* pp. 318 ff.
52. *Palko* v. *Connecticut,* 302 U.S. 319 (1937); Abraham, *Freedom and the Court,* pp. 26 ff.; Louis Marshall, *Selected Papers,* ed. Charles Reznikoff, 2 vols. (Philadelphia, 1957), 2:957 ff.; Anson P. Stokes, *Church and State in the United States,* 3 vols. (New York, 1950), 1:583 ff.; 3:453; Herbert A. Philbrick, *I Led Three Lives* (Washington, D.C., 1972), p. 3; Shawn Lay, ed., *Invisible Empire in the West* (Urbana, Ill., 1992), pp. 161, 202.
53. Henry H. Curran, *John Citizen's Job,* pp. 13, 29, 252; Nicholas M. Butler, *The Faith of a Liberal* (New York, 1924), pp. 287 ff.
54. Calvin Coolidge, *The Price of Freedom* (New York, 1924), p. 147.
55. Butler, *Faith of a Liberal,* pp. 87, 99, 308 ff.; Homer Cummings, *Liberty Under Law and Administration* (New York, 1934), pp. 122 ff., 136; Louis LeFevre, *Liberty and Restraint* (New York, 1926), pp. 204, 205.
56. Hawley, *Herbert Hoover,* p. 135; Murray, *Harding Era,* p. 387.
57. R. C. Epstein, *The Automobile Industry* (Chicago, 1928), p. 116; William Z. Ripley, *Main Street and Wall Street* (Boston, 1927), pp. 7–15; F. Eugene Melder, "The Tin Lizzie's Anniversary," *American Quarterly,* 12 (1960): 466 ff.; Harold E. Burtt, *Psychology of Advertising* (Boston, 1938), pp. 4, 7, 110; Chambers, *Seedtime of Reform,* pp. 29 ff., 50 ff.; Henry C. Link, *The New Psychology of Selling and Advertising* (New York, 1932); Hawley, *Herbert Hoover,* pp. 91 ff.; LeFevre, *Liberty and Restraint,* p. 280.
58. J. B. Murray, *American Trails* (Melbourne, 1944), pp. 53–54; Oscar and Lilian Handlin, *Liberty in Peril* (New York, 1992), pp. 179 ff.; Link, *The New Psychology of Selling and Advertising;* Hawley, *Herbert Hoover,* pp. 91 ff.; Charles Merz, *The Great American Bandwagon* (New York, 1928), p. 191.
59. Ray Ginger, *Six Days or Forever* (Boston, 1958); Arthur H. Vandenberg, *If Hamilton Were Here Today* (New York, 1923), pp. 50–54; Charles A. Beard, *America Faces the Future* (Cambridge, Mass., 1932), pp. 303 ff.
60. T. S. Eliot, "The Rock" (1930), *Complete Poems,* p. 103; Hart Crane, *The Bridge* (New York, 1930); Booth, *Now Don't Try to Reason with Me,* pp. 133–34; Waldo Frank, *The New America* (London, 1922), pp. 192–93; Robert Littell, *Read America First* (New York, 1926), pp. 73 ff.; H. Mencken, *Notes on Democracy,* p. 209; R. C. Mayer, *How to Do Publicity* (New York, 1930), pp. ix, x; Dreiser, *Tragic America,* pp. 413, 415; Walker, *In Defense of American Liberties,* pp. 73–75.
61. William Faulkner, *Light in August* (New York, 1932), pp. 65, 262; T. S. Eliot, "Murder in the Cathedral," *Complete Poems,* p. 194.

62. James J. Davis, *The Iron Puddler* (Indianapolis, 1922), pp. 269 ff.; Charles E. Coughlin, *A Series of Lectures on Social Justice* (Royal Oak, Mich., 1935), pp. 55, 236; Nancy F. Cott, ed., *A Woman Making History* (New Haven, 1991), p. 15; Edward E. Whiting, *Calvin Coolidge* (Boston, 1924), pp. 48 ff.; Schmidt, *Maverick Marine,* pp. 145–49, 155.
63. Whiting, *Coolidge,* pp. 97, 100; Parrish, *Anxious Decades,* pp. 208, 216; Horace Kallen, *Freedom in the Modern World* (New York, 1928), p. 115; E. Fuller Torrey, *Freudian Fraud* (New York, 1992), pp. 26, 29, 32, 48, 56, 57; Cummings, *Selection of Poems,* p. 64.
64. Charles Beard, "Written History as an Act of Faith," *American Historical Review,* 39 (1934): 219 ff.; Richard Boeckel, "The Man with the Best Story Wins," *The Independent,* 102 (May 22, 1920), 244–46; Walter Lippmann, *Public Opinion* (New York, 1922), p. 18; Boyer, *Purity in Print,* pp. 71, 78; Oscar and Lilian Handlin, *Liberty in Peril,* pp. 268 ff.; Bode, *Mencken,* pp. 44 ff.; Derek Freeman, *Margaret Mead and Samoa* (Cambridge, Mass., 1983); Robert Hutchins, *Higher Learning in America* (New Haven, 1936), p. 66; T. S. Eliot, "The Rock" (1930), *Complete Poems,* p. 132; Victor Rosewater, *The Liberty Bell* (New York, 1926), p. 193.
65. Chalmers, *Washington Post,* pp. 173, 180, 185; Roy Hoopes, *Ralph Ingersoll* (New York, 1985), p. 136; Booth, *Now Don't Try to Reason with Me,* p. 10; Sheean, *Personal History,* pp. 25 ff.
66. Nathanael West, "Soft Soap for the Barber," *New Republic,* 81 (Nov. 14, 1934): 23; Ribuffo, *Old Christian Right,* pp. 64 ff.; Louise P. Henricksen, *Anzia Yezierska* (New Brunswick, N.J., 1988), pp. 166 ff.; Bode, *Mencken,* p. 159; Jack C. Ellis, *A History of Film* (Englewood Cliffs, N.J., 1979), pp. 145 ff., 150, 177 ff.; Sklar, *Movie Made America,* pp. 97 ff.; Chalmers, *Washington Post,* p. 180; Merz, *American Bandwagon,* pp. 177–81; Thomas L. Quinn, *Liberty, Employment and No More Wars* (New York, 1943).
67. James Rorty, *Here Life Is Better* (New York, 1936), p. 13; Floyd W. Parsons, "Golf—A New Industry," *Saturday Evening Post,* 199 (July 3, 1926): 8 ff.; Chalmers, *Washington Post,* p. 184; Geoffrey Perrett, *America in the Twenties* (New York, 1982), pp. 212, 223.
68. Edwin E. Slosson, "The Sheepishness of Americans," *Independent,* 102 (May 29, 1920), 285; Merz, *American Bandwagon,* p. 198; Charles Trout, *Boston, the Great Depression and the New Deal* (New York, 1977), p. 258; David Bradby, *et al., Performance and Politics in Popular Drama* (Cambridge, 1980), pp. 201 ff.; also Stanley High, "Star-Spangled Fascists," *Saturday Evening Post,* 211 (May 27, 1939): 6; Robert Lang, *American Film Melodrama* (Princeton, N.J., 1989), pp. 113 ff., 127; Raymond Durgnet and Scott Simon, *King Vidor* (Berkeley, Calif., 1988), pp. 78 ff.
69. Donald Davidson, "Still Rebels, Still Yankees," *American Review,* 2 (1933): 58 ff.; Allen Tate, "A View of the Whole South," *Ibid.,* 2 (1934): 417; Anthony M. Rud, *The Second Generation* (Garden City, N.Y., 1923); Morris R. Cohen, *A Dreamer's Journey* (New York, 1949); Perrett, *America in the Twenties,* p. 148; Robert L. Dorman, *Revolt of the Provinces* (Chapel Hill, N.C., 1993), p. 32; Le Fevre, *Liberty and Restraint,* pp. 331, 336.
70. Robert L. Burgess, "The Protestant Garrison in America," *American Review,* 2 (1933): 435 ff.; Herbert Hoover, *American Individualism* (Garden City, N.Y., 1922); Arthur Garfield Hayes, *Let Freedom Ring* (New York, 1937), pp. x ff., 7 ff.; Alice

Roosevelt Longworth, *Crowded Hours* (New York, 1935), pp. 313–15; Christopher Hollis, *The American Heresy* (London, 1927), pp. 7 ff.

71. Jane Trahey, ed., *Harper's Bazaar* (New York, 1967), pp. 238 ff.; Zane Grey, *Call of the Canyon* (New York, 1924), p. 247; Carlton Jackson, *Zane Grey* (New York, 1973), pp. 119, 247; Cott, *Grounding of Modern Feminism,* pp. 129, 134; Longworth, *Crowded Hours,* p. 339; Parrish, *Anxious Decades,* pp. 132, 154; Waldo Frank, *The Rediscovery of America* (New York, 1929), p. 185.
72. Mary McCarthy, "Ghostly Father I Confess," *The Company She Keeps* (New York, 1942); C. M. Clay, *The Mainstay of American Individualism* (New York, 1934), pp. 235 ff.; Charles Merz, *The Great American Bandwagon* (New York, 1928), pp. 142 ff., 185 ff., 256 ff.; J. D. Salinger, *The Catcher in the Rye* (Boston, 1951); Marvin Laser and Norman Freeman, *Studies in J. D. Salinger* (New York, 1963); Parrish, *Anxious Decades,* p. 161.
73. Zane Kotker, *A Certain Man* (New York, 1976); Rabindranath Tagore, *Letters from Abroad* (Triplicane, Madras, 1924), p. 43; Faulkner, *Light in August,* pp. 383 ff.; Ralph Borsodi, *Flight from the City* (New York, 1929), pp. xiii, 146; Langdon Mitchell, *Understanding America* (New York, 1926), p. 105.
74. T. S. Eliot, "Dry Salvages," V, *Complete Poems and Plays* (New York, 1952), p. 135; Babbitt, *Democracy and Leadership,* p. 315.
75. T. S. Eliot, "Ash Wednesday," *Complete Poems and Plays,* p. 60; Charles Boer, *Charles Olson in Connecticut* (Chicago, 1975); Mitchell, *Understanding America,* pp. 78, 82 ff., 108; Jim Tully, *Beggars of Life* (New York, 1924), pp. 124, 335.
76. Lewis Mumford, *Herman Melville* (New York, 1929); George Bryan Logan, *Liberty in the Modern World* (Chapel Hill, N.C., 1928), pp. 78, 91, 113, 114.
77. Eugene O'Neill, *Strange Interlude* (1928; New York, 1955), p. 41; Wallace Stevens, "The Man on the Dump" (1942), *Collected Poems* (New York, 1954), p. 202; Eliot, *Complete Poems and Plays,* p. 66; Frank A. Warren, *Liberals and Communism* (Bloomington, Ind., 1966), pp. 227–28.
78. Howard D. Rollofs, "Venite Exultemus," *American Review,* 2 (1934): 529 ff.; Logan, *Liberty in the Modern World,* p. 6; below, ch. 3.
79. Wilfred Parsons, *Which Way Democracy* (New York, 1939), p. 191.

CHAPTER 2.

1. Oscar and Lilian Handlin, *Liberty in Peril* (New York, 1992), pp. 273 ff.; Frank E. Hill, *What Is America?* (New York, 1933), pp. 174–89 ff.; Herbert Hoover, *American Individualism* (New York, 1922), pp. 66 ff., 71; Robert C. Morris, *The Pursuit of Happiness* (New York, 1930), p. 26; Richard Rothchild, *Three Gods Give an Evening to Politics* (New York, 1936), p. 135; Leo Lowenthal, *False Prophets* (1948; New Brunswick, N.J., 1987), p. 13; George Bryan Logan, *Liberty in the Modern World* (Chapel Hill, N.C., 1982), pp. 65 ff.
2. Robert Bowden, *In Defense of Tomorrow* (New York, 1931), p. 202; Harold E. Stearns, *Rediscovering America* (New York, 1934), p. 210; Michael E. Parrish, *Anxious Decades* (New York, 1992).
3. National Bureau of Economic Research, *Recent Economic Changes in the United States* (New York, 1929), pp. 862 ff., 873 ff., 909 ff.; Kendall Beaton, *Enterprise in Oil* (New York, 1957), pp. 177 ff., 374 ff., 511 ff.; Harold L. Ickes, *The Secret Diary,* 3 vols. (New York, 1953, 1954), 1:11, 12.

4. Stearns, *Rediscovering America,* pp. 217 ff., 223; Geoffrey Perrett, *America in the Twenties* (New York, 1982), p. 372; Earl Reeves, *This Man Hoover* (New York, 1928), pp. 7, 233.
5. 251 U.S. 444; Alfred L. Bernheim, *The Security Markets* (New York, 1935); Mira Wilkins, *The Emergence of Multinational Enterprise* (Cambridge, Mass., 1970); Perrett, *America in the Twenties,* p. 324; Homer B. Vanderblue, *The Florida Land Boom* (n.p., 1927), pp. 3–13; Parrish, *Anxious Decades,* p. 93.
6. Parrish, *Anxious Decades,* pp. 55, 80.
7. Ithiel de Sola Pool, *Technologies of Freedom* (Cambridge, Mass., 1983), pp. 101, 113 ff.; Edward E. Purinton, "The Stores with the Right Idea," *Independent,* 102 (June 19, 1920), pp. 388–90; Alfred P. Sloan, *My Years with General Motors* (Garden City, N.Y., 1964); Leo Wolman, *Planning and Control of Public Works* (New York, 1930), pp. xxiii ff.; Howard M. Gitelman, *Legacy of the Ludlow Massacre* (Philadelphia, 1988); Dexter M. Keezer, *The Public Control of Business* (New York, 1930), p. 1; Irving Bernstein, *The Lean Years* (Boston, 1960), p. 169; Alfred D. Chandler, *The Visible Hand* (Cambridge, Mass., 1979); Perrett, *America in the Twenties,* pp. 336 ff., 352 ff.; Judith Sealander, *Grand Plans: Business Progressivism and Social Change* (Lexington, Ky., 1988); Parrish, *Anxious Decades,* pp. 74 ff., 89 ff.; Samuel Walker, *In Defense of American Liberties* (New York, 1990), pp. 51–52.
8. Walter N. Poliakov, *Man and His Affairs from the Engineering Point of View* (Baltimore, 1925), pp. 74 ff., 180; Perrett, *America in the Twenties,* pp. 337, 346; Forrest McDonald, *Insull* (Chicago, 1962), p. 100.
9. Charles C. Carr, *Alcoa, an American Enterprise* (New York, 1952); Perrett, *America in the Twenties,* pp. 337 ff.
10. Logan, *Liberty in the Modern World,* p. 48; Ellis W. Hawley, *The Great War and the Search for a Modern Order* (New York, 1979), pp. 227 ff.; Perrett, *America in the Twenties,* pp. 321, 353 ff., 371, 373.
11. "Child Labor and the Welfare of Children in an Anthracite Coal-Mining District," U.S. Children's Bureau, Publication No. 106 (Washington, 1922), 15–16, 18–20; Jack Conroy, *The Disinherited* (New York, 1933); Thomas Bell, *Out of This Furnace* (1941; Pittsburgh, 1976); E. E. Cummings, *A Selection of Poems,* ed. Horace Gregory (New York, 1965), p. 66; Philip Klein, *The Burden of Unemployment* (New York, 1923), pp. 17, 22, 25, 73 ff.; Nels Anderson, *The Hobo* (Chicago, 1922), pp. 202 ff.; David J. and Sheila M. Rothman, *On Their Own* (Reading, Mass., 1972), p. 145; Abraham Epstein, *The Challenge of the Aged* (New York, 1928), pp. 9, 13; Perrett, *America in the Twenties,* pp. 338 ff.; Mary H. Jones, *The Correspondence of Mother Jones,* ed. Edward M. Steel (Pittsburgh, Pa., 1985), p. 237; Parrish, *Anxious Decades,* p. 84.
12. Bernstein, *The Lean Years,* pp. 5–9; Rothmans, *On Their Own,* pp. 113 ff.
13. Irving Fisher, *The Stock Market Crash and After* (New York, 1930), pp. xii, 257, 260; Earl Sparling, *The Mystery Men of Wall Street* (New York, 1930), p. xvii; Charles Trout, *Boston: The Great Depression and the New Deal* (New York, 1977), p. 8; Poliakov, *Man and His Affairs,* pp. 185 ff.; Lewis Corey, *The Crisis of the Middle Class* (New York, 1935), pp. 230 ff.; Jesse F. Steiner, *The American Community in Action* (New York, 1928), p. 7.
14. Theodore Roethke, *Open House* (New York, 1941), p. 61.
15. Tom Kromer, *Waiting for Nothing* (New York, 1935), pp. 163 ff.; Nelson Algren, *Somebody in Boots* (New York, 1935), pp. 124 ff.; Klein, *Burden of Unemployment,*

pp. 39 ff., 73 ff, 146 ff.; Paul Webbink, "Unemployment in the United States, 1930–40," *American Economic Review,* 30 (Part 2, 1940): 250–51; *New York Times,* Feb. 13, Oct. 22, 1937; "No One Has Starved," *Fortune,* 6 (Sept. 1932), 21, 22–28; Jerome Davis, *Capitalism and Its Culture* (New York, 1935), p. 513; Herbert Hoover, *The Challenge to Liberty* (New York, 1934), p. 204; Bernstein, *The Lean Years,* pp. 55 ff., 263, 440; Harold L. Ickes, *The New Democracy* (New York, 1934), p. 26; J. Joseph Huthmacher, *Senator Robert F. Wagner and the Rise of Urban Liberalism* (New York, 1968), p. 71; Stephen Shadegg, *Clare Boothe Luce* (New York, 1970), p. 51; George Seldes, *The Years of the Locust* (Boston, 1933), p. 251; Albert U. Romasco, *The Poverty of Abundance* (New York, 1965), pp. 33, 63.

16. Frank Freidel, *Franklin D. Roosevelt* (Boston, 1990); Frances Perkins, *The Roosevelt I Knew* (New York, 1946); Ickes, *Secret Diary,* 2:295; Parrish, *Anxious Decades,* pp. 271, 286; Franklin D. Roosevelt, *Government—Not Politics* (New York, 1932), pp. 27–28.
17. E. B. White, *Letters,* ed. Dorothy L. Guth (New York, 1976), p. 171; Bernstein, *The Lean Years,* p. 252; E. Taylor Parks and Lois F. Parks, *Memorable Quotations of FDR* (New York, 1965), p. 6.
18. Russell D. Buhite and David W. Levy, *FDR's Fireside Chats* (Norman, Okla., 1992), pp. 47–49; Ickes, *Secret Diary,* 1:308; Cornelius Vanderbilt, Jr., *Farewell to Fifth Avenue* (New York, 1935), p. 244.
19. Clarence N. Callender, ed., *The Crisis of Democracy* (Philadelphia, 1933), p. 48; Ickes, *Secret Diary,* 2:64 ff.; Maury Maverick, *An American Maverick* (New York, 1937), p. 231.
20. Louis Borgenicht, *The Happiest Man,* ed. Harold Friedman (New York, 1942), pp. 352 ff., 411 ff.; Alfred B. Rollins, Jr., *Roosevelt and Howe* (New York, 1962), pp. 330 ff., 368 ff., 382 ff.; Robert E. Sherwood, *Roosevelt and Hopkins* (New York, 1948); Rexford G. Tugwell, *Industry's Coming of Age* (New York, 1927); Ickes, *Secret Diary,* 1:162; Walter I. Trattner, *Homer Folks, Pioneer in Social Welfare* (New York, 1968), pp. 202 ff.; Clarke A. Chambers, *Seedtime of Reform* (Minneapolis, 1963), pp. 109 ff.; Cleveland Rodgers, *The Roosevelt Program* (New York, 1933), pp. 25–30; Eleanor Roosevelt, *This I Remember* (New York, 1949); Searle F. Charles, *Minister of Relief* (Syracuse, N.Y., 1963); Bernard Sternsher, *Rexford Tugwell* (New Brunswick. N.J., 1964), pp. 39 ff.; James T. Patterson, *Congressional Conservatism and the New Deal* (Westport, Ct., 1967), pp. 139–40; George McJimsey, *Harry Hopkins* (Cambridge, Mass., 1987), pp. 116–17.
21. Ellen Fitzpatrick, *Endless Crusade: Women Social Scientists and Progressive Reform* (New York, 1990), pp. 208 ff.; Parks and Parks, *Memorable Quotations of FDR,* p. 7.
22. Horace M. Kallen, ed., *Freedom in the Modern World* (New York, 1928), pp. 159 ff., 181; Harrison E. Freyberger, *Riches for All* (New York, 1932), p. 20; Henry A. Klein, *America Use Your Head* (New York, 1932), p. 11; Leon Whipple, *Our Ancient Liberties* (New York, 1927), p. 139; Charles A. Beard and George H. E. Smith, *The Future Comes* (New York, 1933), pp. 161 ff.; Buhite, *FDR's Fireside Chats,* p. 55; Parks and Parks, *Memorable Quotations of FDR,* pp. 9, 18.
23. Trout, *Boston,* pp. 81, 85; Meridel LeSueur, "Women on the Breadlines," *New Masses* (January, 1932), 5 ff.; James T. Farrell, *Studs Lonigan: A Trilogy,* 3 vols. (New York, 1938), 3:347 ff.; Ralph Ellison, *Invisible Man* (New York, 1947), pp. 202 ff.; J. B. Murray, *American Trails* (Melbourne, 1944), pp. 36 ff.; Benjamin

Glassberg, *Across the Desk of a Relief Administrator* (Chicago, 1938); Thomas Minehan, *Boy and Girl Tramps of America* (New York, 1934), pp. 245 ff.; "No One Has Starved," *Fortune,* 6 (Sept. 1932): 19 ff.; Nathan Asch, *The Road* (New York, 1937), p. 185; Mauritz Hallgren, *Seeds of Revolt* (New York, 1933), pp. 3 ff.; Sherwood Anderson, *Puzzled Americans* (New York, 1935), pp. 103 ff.; Bernstein, *The Lean Years,* pp. 254 ff., 296 ff.; Romasco, *Poverty of Abundance,* pp. 143 ff.

24. John Dickinson, *Hold Fast to the Middle Way* (Boston, 1935), pp. x ff., 8 ff., 17 ff.; S. Alfred-Jones, *Is Fascism the Answer?* (Hamilton, Ont., 1933), p. 149; Roger W. Babson, *The New Dilemma* (New York, 1934), p. 199; Fitzpatrick, *Endless Crusade,* p. 213; Ickes, *New Democracy,* p. 153; William Rappard, *The Crisis of Democracy* (Chicago, 1938), p. 27; Parks and Parks, *Memorable Quotations of FDR,* p. 21.
25. Richard T. Ely and Frank Bohm, *The Great Change* (New York, 1935), pp. 264, 353; Buhite, *FDR's Fireside Chats,* pp. 61–62.
26. Marvin Olasky, *The Tragedy of American Compassion* (Washington, D.C., 1992), pp. 155, 158, 163; Richard W. Child, "Your Food and Our Farmer," *Saturday Evening Post,* 199 (July 3, 1929): 129; Wolman, *Planning and Control of Public Works,* pp. 169 ff.; Fisher, *Stock Market Crash,* pp. 26 ff.; Buhite, *FDR's Fireside Chats,* pp. 82, 118.
27. Ely and Bohm, *Great Change,* pp. 70 ff.; Parks and Parks, *Memorable Quotations of FDR,* pp. 10, 24; Walter Lippmann, *The Method of Freedom* (New York, 1934), pp. 78, 85, 112; Henry P. Fairchild, *The Foundations of Social Life* (New York, 1927), p. 256; George Soule, *The Coming American Revolution* (New York, 1934), pp. 169, 171; Ellis W. Hawley, *The Great War and the Search for a Modern Order* (New York, 1979), pp. 228, 229.
28. Franklin Roosevelt, *Public Papers,* ed. Samuel Rosenman, 13 vols. (New York, 1938–1950), 3: 288 ff.; Perrett, *America in the Twenties,* pp. 485 ff.; Parks and Parks, *Memorable Quotations of FDR,* p. 69.
29. Carl C. Taylor, Helen W. Wheeler, and E. L. Kirkpatrick, *Disadvantaged Classes in American Agriculture* (Washington, D.C., 1938), pp. 9 ff., 27–38, 39, 48; Soule, *Coming American Revolution,* p. 211; Romasco, *Poverty of Abundance,* pp. 97 ff.
30. John Steinbeck, *The Grapes of Wrath* (New York, 1939), pp. 26 ff.; Harold Barger and Hans H. Landsberg, *American Agriculture, 1899–1939* (New York, 1942); Murray R. Benedict, *Farm Policies of the United States* (New York, 1953); Erskine Caldwell, *Some American People* (New York, 1935); James Agee, *Let Us Now Praise Famous Men* (Boston, 1940), pp. 115 ff., 319 ff.; David E. Conrad, *Forgotten Farmers* (Urbana, Ill., 1965).
31. Soule, *Coming American Revolution,* p. 187; B. D. Zevin, *Nothing to Fear* (Cambridge, Mass., 1946), pp. 8–9, 70–72.
32. Richard C. Overton, *Burlington Route* (New York, 1965).
33. Sternsher, *Tugwell,* pp. 261 ff.; Bernstein, *The Lean Years,* p. 420; Arthur W. Crawford, *Monetary Management Under the New Deal* (New York, 1940 [1972]); Charles O. Hardy, *Warren-Pearson Price Theory* (Washington, D.C., 1935).
34. Winston Norman, *"I Think I Am Slowly Recovering"* (New York, 1934), p. 10; Oliver M. W. Sprague, *Recovery and Common Sense* (Boston, 1934), pp. 4, 75; Soule, *Coming American Revolution,* pp. 238 ff.; Rollins, *Roosevelt and Howe,* pp. 406 ff.; Sternsher, *Tugwell,* pp. 170 ff., 183 ff.; Hiram W. Evans, "The Klan's Fight for Americanism," *North American Review,* 223 (1926): 35 ff., 49; Bernard D. Karpinas, "The Differential True Rates of Growth of the White Population in the United

States," *American Journal of Sociology,* 44 (1938): 269, 273; Bernstein, *The Lean Years,* pp. 323 ff.

35. James D. Mooney, *The New Capitalism* (New York, 1934), pp. 195 ff.; Guys C. Claire, *Administocracy* (New York, 1934), pp. ii, iii; William F. Russell, *Liberty Versus Equality* (New York, 1935), pp. 10, 15, 128; Raoul E. Desvernine, *Democratic Despotism* (New York, 1936), pp. 57, 91; William E. Rappard, *The Crisis of Democracy,* p. 272.
36. William E. Hocking, *The Lasting Elements of Individualism* (New Haven, 1937), pp. 176 ff.; Ross J.S. Hoffman, *The Will to Freedom* (New York, 1935), pp. 79 ff., 101; Floyd A. Harper, *Liberty* (New York, 1949); Ernest S. Griffith, *The Impasse of Democracy* (New York, 1939), p. 340; Arthur N. Holcombe, *The Middle Classes in American Politics* (Cambridge, Mass., 1940), pp. 22, 275; and *The New Party Politics* (New York, 1933), pp. 115 ff.; Parks and Parks, *Memorable Quotations of FDR,* pp. 140, 148, 151; Samuel Everett, *Democracy Faces the Future* (New York, 1935), pp. 161 ff.; Maverick, *A Maverick American,* pp. 181, 187; Alexander Meiklejohn, *What Does American Mean?* (New York, 1935), pp. 125 ff.
37. Frank Adams, *Unearthing Seeds of Fire* (Winston-Salem, N.C., 1975), p. 12; *New York Times,* Aug. 22, 1947, p. 1; Clarke A. Chambers, *Seedtime of Reform,* pp. 87 ff.; Norman, *"I Think I Am Slowly Recovering,"* pp. 49, 58; Soule, *Coming American Revolution,* pp. 190, 281 ff., 300; D. W. Pittman, *A Road to Opportunity* (Los Angeles, 1934), pp. 65 ff.; Herbert Agar and Allen Tate, *Who Owns America?* (Boston, 1936), pp. 297 ff.; Adam Savage, *A Professor's Balderdash* (New York, 1938), p. 39; Bernstein, *The Lean Years,* pp. 417 ff.
38. Frances Perkins, "The Social Security Act," *Vital Speeches,* 1 (1934–35): 792 ff.; Huthmacher, *Wagner,* pp. 80 ff.; Chambers, *Seedtime of Reform,* pp. 61 ff.; Soule, *Coming American Revolution,* p. 304; Agar and Tate, *Who Owns America?,* p. 309, 316 ff.; Ickes, *Secret Diary,* 2:218; Bernstein, *The Lean Years,* pp. 347, 585 ff.; also Glenna Matthews, *The Rise of Public Woman: Woman's Power and Woman's Place in the United States, 1630–1970* (New York, 1992), pp. 182–87; Daniel S. Hirshfield, *The Lost Reform* (Cambridge, Mass., 1970); Mathew Shaler, *The Validity of American Ideals* (New York, 1922), p. 79; Roger W. Babson, *Washington and the Revolutionists* (New York, 1934), pp. ix, 325; Parks and Parks, *Memorable Quotations of FDR,* pp. 65–66.
39. Paul Mazur, *New Roads to Prosperity* (New York, 1931), p. 194; David C. Coyle, *Brass Tacks* (Washington, 1935), pp. 133 ff.; Ralph E. Flanders, *Platform for America* (New York, 1935), pp. 88–89.
40. Handlin and Handlin, *Liberty in Peril,* pp. 359 ff.; Rexford G. Tugwell, "The Responsibilities of Partnership," Address before the Iowa State Bankers Association, at Des Moines, Iowa, June 27 [1934], pp. 1–4, 13, 23–24; Herbert Agar, *Land of the Free* (Boston, 1935), p. 126; Ickes, *New Democracy,* pp. 19 ff.; Soule, *Coming American Revolution,* p. 295; Coyle, *Brass Tacks,* pp. 144 ff.; Willard E. Hawkins, *Castaways* (New York, 1936), pp. 83 ff.; Arthur B. Adams, *Our Economic Revolution* (Norman, Okla., 1934), p. 157; Wilfred J. Funk, *When the Merry Go Round Breaks Down* (New York, 1938), pp. 3, 15; Jules Chametzky, *From the Ghetto* (Amherst, Mass., 1977), pp. 44 ff.
41. Stuart Chase, *Technocracy* (New York, 1933); Howard Scott, *Introduction to Technocracy* (New York, 1940); Thorstein Veblen, *The Engineers and the Price System* (New York, 1921); Thurman W. Arnold, *The Folklore of Capitalism* (1937; New

Haven, Conn., 1948), pp. 378, 388; Arthur N. Holcombe, *Government in a Planned Democracy* (New York, 1935), pp. ix, 141, 155.

42. Warren S. Thompson and P. K. Whelpton, *Population Trends in the United States* (New York, 1933), pp. 48, 57; Franklin D. Roosevelt, *Public Papers,* 1:750 ff.; Freidel, *Roosevelt,* pp. 21, 23; Nathan Silver, *Lost New York* (New York, 1967); David E. Lilienthal, *T.V.A. . . . Democracy on the March* (New York, 1944), pp. 5 ff., 218 ff.; Herbert Hovenkamp, *Enterprise and American Law* (Cambridge, Mass., 1991); Parks and Parks, *Memorable Quotations of FDR,* pp. 15, 115–16.
43. George Seldes, *The Years of the Locust* (Boston, 1933), pp. 274 ff., 335; Nancy Cott, ed., *A Woman Making History* (New Haven, 1991), p. 17.
44. James D. Dingwell, *What Price Economic Adjustment?* (Boston, 1932), p. 70.
45. Henry A. Wallace, *America Must Choose* (New York, 1934); Dwight Macdonald, *Henry Wallace* (New York, 1948), pp. 116–19; Cordell Hull, *Governmental Policies and Their Effect on Economic Conditions* (Washington, D.C., 1932), pp. 3–5; Patricia Clavin, "The World Economic Conference, 1933," *Journal of European Economic History,* 20 (1991): 489 ff.; John N. Schaeht, ed., *Three Progressives from Iowa* (Iowa City, Iowa, 1980), pp. 38–46.
46. Ralph E. Flanders, *Platform for America* (New York, 1935), pp. 89 ff.; Seldes, *Years of the Locust,* pp. 322 ff., 333; Chester M. Morgan, *Redneck Liberal* (Baton Rouge, Louisiana, 1985), p. 214.
47. David L. Lewis, *The Public Image of Henry Ford* (Detroit, 1976), pp. 241 ff.; Soule, *Coming American Revolution,* pp. 213 ff., 259 ff.; John Chamberlain, *The American Stakes* (New York, 1940), pp. 301 ff.; Robert Bowden, *In Defense of Tomorrow* (New York, 1931), pp. 184, 203; David M. Proctor, *Pay Day* (Kansas City, Mo., 1936), pp. 96, 101; Sternsher, *Tugwell,* pp. 154 ff.
48. *United States Statutes at Large,* 49, part 1: 449 ff.; Sherwood Anderson, *Puzzled America* (New York, 1935), pp. 145 ff.; Bernstein, *The Lean Years,* pp. 84 ff., 101 ff., 147 ff., 428 ff., 434; Huthmacher, *Wagner,* pp. 60 ff.; Jones, *Correspondence,* pp. 277, 287; *National Labor Relations Board* v. *Jones and Laughlin Steel Company,* 301 U.S. 229 ff. (1937); Frank Knox, *We Planned It That Way* (New York, 1938), pp. 43 ff.; Samuel Walker, *In Defense of American Liberties,* p. 96.
49. Lewis W. Douglas, *The Liberal Tradition* (New York, 1935), pp. xii, 36 ff., 42; Jerome Davis, *Capitalism and Its Culture* (New York, 1942), p. 519; George Seldes, *You Can't Do That* (New York, 1938), pp. 3, 25, 229; Prestonia Mann Martin, *Prohibiting Poverty* (Winter Park, Fla., 1932), pp. vi, 18, 130 ff.; Guy Stanton Ford, *Dictatorship in the Modern World* (Minneapolis, 1935), p. 179; Thurman W. Arnold, *Democracy and Free Enterprise* (Norman, Okla., 1942), pp. 44 ff., 52; Knox, *We Planned It That Way,* pp. 35, 41, 67; Ralph L. Roy, *Apostles of Discord* (Boston, 1953), pp. 278 ff., 309 ff.; also Sidney and Beatrice Webb, *Soviet Communism* (New York, 1936).
50. Ernest Hemingway, *The Green Hills of Africa* (New York, 1935), p. 191; Booth Tarkington, "Now Ripley Please," *Saturday Evening Post,* 211 (Apr. 1, 1939): 5, 36; John Rustgard, *The Bankruptcy of Liberalism* (Babson Park, Fla., 1942), p. 365; Benjamin Stolberg and Warren Jay Vinton, *The Economic Consequences of the New Deal* (New York, 1935), p. 85; Ogden L. Mills, *What of Tomorrow* (New York, 1935), pp. 30 ff., 41; Bery M. Douglas, *The New Deal Comes to Brown County* (Garden City, N.Y., 1936), pp. 84 ff.; Robert L. Lund, *The Truth About the New Deal* (New York, 1936), pp. 85 ff.; Knox, *We Planned It That Way,* p. 8.

51. E. Pendleton Herring, *Public Administration and the Public Interest* (New York, 1936), pp. 343 ff., 362 ff.; George Michael, *Handout* (New York, 1935), p. 11.
52. John Chamberlain, *The American Stakes* (New York, 1940), pp. 267, 282, 286; Sheridan W. Downey, *Pensions or Penury* (New York, 1939), pp. 12, 113; Richard W. Gilbert, *et al., An Economic Program for American Democracy* (New York, 1938), pp. 22, 56, 65, 91.
53. William H. Harbaugh, *Lawyer's Lawyer* (New York, 1973), pp. 321 ff.; Ickes, *Secret Diary,* 1:529 ff., 466, 499, 2:64 ff.; Maverick, *An American Maverick,* pp. 344, 352; Leo P. Ribuffo, *The Old Christian Right* (Philadelphia, 1983), p. 117.
54. *United States* v. *Darby,* 312 U.S. 100 (1941).
55. Temporary National Economic Committee, *Final Report of the Executive Secretary . . . on the Concentration of Economic Power* (Washington, D.C., 1941), 7–9; Kendall Beaton, *Enterprise in Oil,* pp. 374 ff., 585 ff., 607; Sternsher, *Tugwell,* pp. 109 ff.; also Ellis W. Hawley, *The New Deal and the Problem of Monopoly* (Princeton, N.J., 1966).
56. Robert A. Caro, *The Power Broker: Robert Moses* (New York, 1974), pp. 901 ff.
57. Knox, *We Planned It That Way,* p. 80; also above at note 35.
58. Proctor, *Pay Day,* pp. 107 ff., 130; Stuart Chase, *Idle Men, Idle Money* (New York, 1940), p. 237; Theodore Quinn, *Liberty, Employment and No More Wars* (New York, 1943), pp. 32 ff.; Rustgard, *Bankruptcy of Liberalism,* pp. 367 ff.; Wilfred Parsons, *Which Way Democracy* (New York, 1939), pp. 185 ff.; Edgar Kemler, *The Deflation of American Ideals* (1941; Seattle, Wash., 1967), pp. 69 ff., 107.
59. Leon Whipple, *Our Ancient Liberties,* p. 140.
60. Ernest S. Griffith, *The Impasse of Democracy,* pp. 289, 302, 315; Quinn, *Liberty, Employment and No More Wars,* pp. 66 ff.
61. J. Russell Smith, *The Devil of the Machine Age* (New York, 1941), p. 47; James Harvey Rogers, *Capitalism in Crisis* (New Haven, Conn., 1938), pp. 173–81; Horace M. Kallen, ed., *Freedom in the Modern World* (New York, 1928), pp. 116 ff.; Soren K. Ostergaard, *Into Abundance* (Chicago, 1940), pp. 146 ff.
62. Ickes, *Secret Diary,* 3:394.
63. Page Smith, *Redeeming the Time* (New York, 1987), pp. 666, 688, 689, 845, 850; Parrish, *Anxious Decades,* pp. 383–404; Susan Ware, *Partner and I: Molly Dewson, Feminism and New Deal Politics* (New Haven, 1987); Marion Clawson, *New Deal Planning* (Baltimore, 1981), pp. 253–54.

CHAPTER 3.

1. Max Lerner, *It's Later Than You Think* (New York, 1938), pp. 23, 24, 57.
2. Adolf A. Berle, *New Directions in the New World* (New York, 1940), p. 139; S. H. Hauck, *The Scarlet Fingers* (Scotch Plains, N.J., 1939), p. 103.
3. *Saturday Evening Post,* 211 (Apr. 8, 1939): 24, 25, 211 (Apr. 22, 1939): 22 ff.
4. Leonard Woolf, *The Journey Not the Arrival Matters* (New York, 1969), p. 17; Carl L. Becker, *New Liberties for Old* (New Haven, Conn., 1941), pp. 113, 123; Hamilton Fish Armstrong, *We or They* (New York, 1937), p. 103; Allen Guttmann, *The Wound in the Heart* (New York, 1962), pp. 93, 213; James Marshall, *Swords and Symbols* (New York, 1939), pp. 86, 97.
5. Lawrance Thompson and Ruth Winnick, *Robert Frost,* ed. E. C. Lathem (New York, 1981), p. 68; Frank Freidel, *Franklin D. Roosevelt* (Boston, 1990), pp. 356

ff.; Raymond L. Buell, *Isolated America* (New York, 1940), pp. 327, 455; also Hans Staudinger, *The Inner Nazi,* ed. Peter M. Rutkoff and William B. Scott (Baton Rouge, La., 1981), pp. 31 ff.; Louis H. Pink, *Freedom from Fear* (New York, 1944), pp. 13–14; Edgar Kemler, *The Deflation of American Ideals* (Seattle Wash., 1941, 1967).

6. Alden Stevens, *Arms and the People* (New York, 1942), pp. 3, 4; Rose Wilder Lane, *The Discovery of Freedom* (New York, 1943), p. 262; Freidel, *Roosevelt,* pp. 395 ff., 407 ff.; Francis J. Spellman, *The Road to Victory* (New York, 1942), pp. 5, 49, 112.
7. Hadley Cantril (with Hazel Gandet and Herta Hertzog), *Invasion from Mars* (Princeton, N.J., 1949), pp. 47–54, 162; Isabel Leighton, ed., *The Aspirin Age* (New York, 1949), pp. 431 ff.; Martin Tropp, *Mary Shelley's Monster* (Boston, 1976), pp. 87 ff.; Oscar Handlin, *Truth in History* (Cambridge, Mass., 1979), pp. 316 ff.
8. James P. Warburg, *Peace in Our Time* (New York, 1940), pp. 9, 15; John Mason Brown, *The Ordeal of a Playwright* (New York, 1970).
9. Earl Browder, *The Way Out* (New York, 1941), p. 165; Lillian Hellman, *Watch on the Rhine* (New York, 1941); J. Edward Jones, *My Country 'Tis of Thee* (New York, 1941), p. 61; William D. Whitney, *Who Are the Americans?* (London, 1941), pp. 188, 190; Freidel, *Roosevelt,* pp. 362 ff.; Oswald G. Villard, *Fighting Years* (New York, 1939).
10. Richard N. Current, *Secretary Stimson* (New Brunswick, N.J., 1954), p. 163.
11. Stuart Chase, *Idle Money, Idle Men* (New York, 1940), pp. 243, 249; Nicholas Murray Butler, *Liberty Equals Fraternity* (New York, 1942), pp. 125, 165; Henry M. Wriston, *Challenge to Freedom* (New York, 1943), pp. 167, 169; Page Smith, *Redeeming the Time* (New York, 1987), pp. 1023–24.
12. *New York World Telegram,* Mar. 5, 1942; Archibald MacLeish, *The American Cause* (New York, 1941), pp. 11 ff.; Wriston, *Challenge to Freedom,* pp. 221, 226; Theodore K. Quinn, *Liberty, Employment and No More Wars* (New York, 1943), p. viii.
13. John Erickson, *The Road to Stalingrad* (New York, 1973), *passim,* and *The Road to Berlin* (London, 1983), *passim*; Herbert Agar, *A Time for Greatness* (Boston, 1942), pp. 15–19, 21–25, 288.
14. H. L. Mencken, *Letters,* ed. Guy J. Forgue (New York, 1961), p. 501.
15. Edgar M. Queeny, *The Spirit of Enterprise* (New York, 1943), p. 242; Benjamin A. Javits, *The Commonwealth of Industry* (New York, 1936), pp. 152 ff.; John T. Salter, *The Pattern of Politics* (New York, 1940), p. 241; Albert J. Nock, *Memoirs of a Superfluous Man* (New York, 1943); Jay Franklin, *The Future Is Ours* (New York, 1939), pp. 205 ff.; Albert Y. Romasco, *The Politics of Recovery* (New York, 1983), pp. 244–46.
16. Wriston, *Challenge to Freedom,* p. 209; Nock, *Memoirs,* p. 282; Queeny, *Spirit of Enterprise,* pp. 239, 241; Chamberlain, *American Stakes,* pp. 277, 280; A. J. Muste, *Essays,* ed. Nat Hentoff (Indianapolis, 1967), pp. 10, 25, 153, 253, 261 ff.; Shlomo Shafir, "The View of a Maverick Pacifist and Universalist," *American Jewish Archives,* 42 (1990): 147 ff.
17. Pierre Van Raasen, *The Time Is Now* (New York, 1941), p. 8; Graeme K. Howard, *America and the New World Order* (New York, 1940), pp. 22–23; Mencken, *Letters,* p. 500; Glenna Mathews, *The Rise of Public Woman* (New York, 1993), p. 188; also Peter F. Drucker, *The Concept of the Corporation* (New York, 1946); John B. Whitton, ed., *The Second Chance* (Princeton, 1944), pp. 204–206; Arneson, *America and the New*

World Order, pp. 139–40; Michael Barone, *Our Country* (New York, 1990), p. 156; William H. Chafe, *Unfinished Journey* (New York, 1991), pp. 11–17, 45.

18. Joseph A. Schumpeter, *Capitalism, Socialism and Democracy* (New York, 1942); Vaughn D. Bornet, *Labor Politics in a Democratic Republic* (New York, 1964), pp. 298 ff., 310 ff.; Wriston, *Challenge to Freedom,* pp. 221, 226; William O'Neill, *A Democracy at War* (New York, 1993); Barone, *Our Country,* p. 166.
19. Stuart Cloete, *Yesterday Is Dead* (New York, 1940), pp. 227 ff.
20. Lane, *The Discovery of Freedom,* pp. 211 ff.; Freidel, *Roosevelt,* p. 500.
21. Emil Lengyel, *Millions of Dictators* (New York, 1936), pp. 271 ff.; Mencken, *Letters,* p. 491; Wriston, *Challenge of Freedom,* pp. 211, 213 ff.; Theodore G. Bilbo, *Take Your Choice: Segregation or Mongrelization* (Poplarsville, Miss., 1947); Norman Thomas, *What Is Our Destiny* (Garden City, New York, 1944), pp. 141, 144, 153. See also below, ch. 4.
22. Freidel, *Roosevelt,* p. 567; Melvyn Dubovsky and Warren Van Tine, *Labor Leaders in America* (Urbana, Ill., 1987), p. 229.
23. Joseph Rosenfarb, *Freedom and the Administrative State* (New York, 1948), pp. x, xii, 239; also James Marshall, *The Freedom to Be Free* (New York, 1943), pp. 59, 94; Barone, *Our Country,* pp. 168–69.
24. Stephen K. Bailey, *Congress Makes a Law* (New York, 1950); Max Lerner, *Ideas for the Ice Age* (New York, 1941), pp. 38 ff.; Carl J. Friedrich, *The New Image of the Common Man* (Boston, 1950), pp. 215 ff.
25. "Safeway Stores, Inc.," *Fortune,* 22 (Oct. 1940): 60 ff., 89 ff.; David L. Lewis, *The Public Image of Henry Ford* (Detroit, 1976), pp. 389 ff., 450 ff.; Freidel, *Roosevelt,* p. 519; Barone, *Our Country,* pp. 162–64.
26. Louis Borgenicht, *The Happiest Man,* ed. Harold Friedman (New York, 1942).
27. J. Joseph Huthmacher, *Senator Robert F. Wagner* (New York, 1968), p. 116; Floyd A. Harper, *Liberty* (New York, 1949), pp. 33 ff., 56, 118; Eduard Heimann, *Freedom and Order* (New York, 1947), p. 230; Ernest S. Griffith, *The Impasse of Democracy* (New York, 1939), pp. 337 ff.; Ross J. S. Hoffman, *The Will to Freedom* (New York, 1935), p. 75.
28. Huthmacher, *Wagner,* p. 269; Nathan G. Belth, "The Refugee Problem," *American Jewish Year Book 5700* (Philadelphia, 1939), pp. 374 ff.; Harvey Strum, "Jewish Internees in the American South 1942–1945," *American Jewish Archives,* 42 (1990), 27 ff.; Charles Higham, *American Swastika* (Garden City, N.Y., 1985), pp. 17 ff.
29. Presidential Commission on Immigration and Naturalization, *Whom We Shall Welcome* (Washington D.C., 1953); Charles E. Carpenter, *Private Enterprise and Democracy* (New York, 1940), pp. 211 ff., Lewis H. Carlson *et al.,* eds., *In Their Place* (New York, 1972), pp. 351–52.
30. John Beaty, *The Iron Curtain over America* (Dallas, Tex., 1951), p. 165; Glen Jeansonne, *Gerald L. K. Smith* (New Haven, 1988), p. 89; also Mina Curtiss, ed., *Letters Home* (Boston, 1944), p. 65; Robert Meyer, Jr., ed., *The Stars and Stripes Story of World War II* (New York, 1960), pp. 76–77; Leo P. Ribuffo, *The Old Christian Right* (Philadelphia, 1983), p. 179.
31. William S. Bernard, *American Immigration Policy* (New York, 1950); J. Campbell Bruce, *The Golden Door* (New York, 1954); Salvatore J. LaGumina and Frank J. Cavaioli, *The Ethnic Dimension* (Boston, 1974), p. 317; Carlson, *In Their Place,* pp. 348–49.
32. Robert Conquest, *The Harvest of Sorrow* (New York, 1986).

33. Harold L. Ickes, *The Secret Diary,* 3 vols. (New York, 1953–1954), 1: p. 428; Martin Dies, *Martin Dies' Story* (New York, 1963), pp. 12, 13, 218, 219.
34. Freidel, *Roosevelt,* pp. 581, 587 ff.; Bryton Barron, *Inside the State Department* (New York, 1956), p. 35.
35. Freidel, *Roosevelt,* pp. 600 ff., 604; Max Freeman, ed., *Roosevelt and Frankfurter* (Boston, 1967), p. 742. See also Alfred M. De Zayas, *Die Anglo-Amerikaner und die Vertreibung der Deutschen* (Munich, 1977); Aleksandr M. Nekrich, *The Punished People* (New York, 1978); Miron Dolot, *Execution by Hunger* (New York, 1983).
36. Guy de Carmoy, *The Foreign Policies of France, 1944–1968* (Chicago, 1970); Samuel Walker, *In Defense of American Liberties* (New York, 1990), p. 113.
37. Ribuffo, *Old Christian Right,* p. 193; Beatty, *Iron Curtain over America,* p. 157; Charles F. Croog, "F.B.I. Political Surveillances," *The Historian,* 54 (1992): 441 ff.
38. André Girdner and Anne Loftis, *The Great Betrayal* (New York, 1969), pp. 26 ff., 477; *Fortune,* 22 (1940): 47 ff., 85 ff.; 320 U.S., 83–105 (1943); Current, *Stimson,* pp. 192 ff.; Ribuffo, *Old Christian Right,* pp. 70 ff., 170 ff., 183 ff.; Zechariah Chafee, *Free Speech in the United States* (Cambridge, Mass., 1948), pp. 439; Walker, *In Defense of American Liberties,* pp. 125 ff.; E. E. Cummings, *A Selection of Poems,* ed. Horace Gregory (New York, 1965), p. 122.
39. Will Rogers, "Letters of a Self-Made Diplomat," *Saturday Evening Post,* 199 (July 10, 1926): 3; also "How Can We Best Insure Loyalty," *Town Meeting of the Air* (radio program), Apr. 25, 1950.
40. Freidel, *Roosevelt,* p. 554; Eugene Dennis, *The People Against the Trusts* (New York, 1946), pp. 41 ff., 52; Jay J. M. Scandrett, *What Goes On* (n.p., 1944), *passim;* Eugene V. Debs, *Letters,* 3 vols., ed. J. Robert Constantine (Urbana, Ill., 1990), 3:225 ff.; Thompson and Winnick, *Robert Frost,* pp. 358 ff., 492 ff.; Michael Straight, *After Long Silence* (London, 1983), p. 110; Fred E. Beal, *Foreign Workers in a Soviet Tractor Plant* (Moscow, 1935), p. 7; Ribuffo, *Old Christian Right,* pp. xiii, 191 ff.; Stephen C. Shadegg, *Clare Boothe Luce* (New York, 1970), pp. 196 ff.; Joseph B. Matthews, *Odyssey of a Fellow Traveler* (New York, 1938), pp. 119 ff.; Dies, *Martin Dies' Story,* p. 73; Herbert A. Philbrick, *I Led Three Lives* (Washington, D.C., 1972), pp. 109 ff.; Alan Brinkley, *Voices of Protest* (New York, 1982), p. 272; Mencken, *Letters,* p. 304; Beaty, *Iron Curtain over America,* pp. 83, 94 ff. See also Max Lerner, *Actions and Passions* (New York, 1949), pp. 77 ff.; Raymond Aron, *The Industrial Society* (New York, 1967), pp. 63 ff., 105 ff.
41. 341 U.S. 581; E. B. White, *Letters,* ed. Dorothy L. Guth (New York, 1976), p. 301; John C. Masterman, *The Double Cross System* (New Haven, 1972); Edward Shils, "Science and Scientists in the Public Arena," *American Scholar,* 56 (1987): 185 ff.; Straight, *After Long Silence,* pp. 249 ff.; Vivian Gornick, *The Romance of American Communism* (New York, 1977), pp. 133, 144, 162; Steven Nelson *et al., Steve Nelson, American Radical* (Pittsburgh, 1981), pp. 136 ff.
42. White, *Letters,* pp. 285 ff.; Roy Cohn, *Autobiography,* ed. Sidney Zion (Secaucus, N.J., 1988), pp. 53 ff.; Beaty, *Iron Curtain over America,* pp. 201 ff.; Lerner, *Actions and Passions,* pp. 95 ff., 107; Ribuffo, *Old Christian Right,* p. 227.
43. Whittaker Chambers, *Odyssey of a Friend,* ed. William F. Buckley, Jr. (New York, 1969), pp. 13 ff., 49, 281; Cummings, *Selection of Poems,* p. 101; Allen Weinstein, *Perjury* (New York, 1978); Fred J. Cook, *Maverick* (New York, 1984), pp. 155 ff.; William Harbaugh, *Lawyer's Lawyer* (New York, 1973), pp. 451 ff.
44. *New York Times,* Oct. 29 and Dec. 17, 1992; *Newsweek,* Jan. 11, 1993, p. 66.

45. Mencken, *Letters,* p. 450; Richard M. Freeland, *The Truman Doctrine and the Origins of McCarthyism* (New York, 1972); Michael Sayers and Albert E. Kahn, *The Plot Against the Peace: A Warning to the Nation* (New York, 1945); Michael Sayers and Albert E. Kahn, *The Great Conspiracy Against Russia* (New York, 1946); Albert E. Kahn, *High Treason* (New York, 1950); Ralph B. Perry, *The Citizen Decides* (Bloomington, Ind., 1951), p. 153.
46. 319 U.S. 624 ff.; Cohn, *Autobiography,* pp. 50, 59 ff.; Charles Higham, *American Swastika,* pp. 54 ff.; Chafee, *Free Speech,* pp. 443, 473; Samuel Walker, *In Defense of American Liberties* (New York, 1990), pp. 150 ff. See also below, ch. 5 at note 40.
47. Lerner, *Actions and Passions,* pp. 108, 112, 134. The apologetic attitude hopelessly confuses Ellen W. Schrecker, *No Ivory Tower* (New York, 1986), and Sigmund Diamond, *Compromised Campus* (New York, 1992).
48. Chafee, *Free Speech,* pp. 382 ff.; Philip Kinsley, *Liberty and the Press* (Chicago, 1944), pp. vii, 55, 63 ff.
49. Walker, *In Defense of American Liberties,* p. 125; Horace M. Kallen, ed., *Freedom in the Modern World* (New York, 1928), pp. 24, 182, 294; Lerner, *Actions and Passions,* pp. 207 ff., 116 ff.; Mencken, *Letters,* pp. 454 ff.; Floyd A. Harper, *Liberty* (New York, 1949), pp. 14, 59, 123.
50. Philip Wylie, *A Generation of Vipers* (New York, 1955), p. 6; Carl Sandburg, *The People Yes* (New York, 1936), pp. 72, 84, 179; Borgenicht, *The Happiest Man,* p. 361.

CHAPTER 4.

1. Shailer Mathews, *The Validity of American Ideals* (New York, 1922), p. 26.
2. Nathanael West, *The Dream Life of Balso Snell* (1931), in *Complete Works* (New York, 1957); Ezra Pound, *Hugh Selwyn Mauberly* (1920), *Selected Poems,* ed. T. S. Eliot (London, 1928), p. 174; Daniel Fuchs, *Summer in Williamsburg* (New York, 1934); Stuart Chase and F. J. Schlink, *Your Money's Worth* (New York, 1927); Fred J. Cook, *Maverick* (New York, 1984), pp. 82 ff.; Clyde B. Davis, *"The Great American Novel"* (New York, 1938); James Harvey Young, *The Medical Messiahs* (Princeton, 1992), pp. 152 ff., 258, 349, 363; James H. Young, *The Toadstool Millionaires* (Princeton, N.J., 1961), pp. 247, 260; Harry Hoxsey, *You Don't Have to Die* (New York, 1956); Crete de Francesco, *The Power of the Charlatan,* tr. Miriam Bead (New Haven, 1939); Daniel S. Hirshfield, *The Lost Reform* (Cambridge, Mass., 1970), pp. 28–31.
3. Forrest McDonald, *Insull* (Chicago, 1962), pp. 333 ff.; Geoffrey Perrett, *America in the Twenties* (New York, 1982), p. 400; William E. Lenz, *Fast Talk and Flush Times* (Columbia, Mo., 1985), pp. 200 ff.
4. Philip Wylie, *A Generation of Vipers* (1942; New York, 1955), p. 87; Arnold Gesell, *The Pre-School Child from the Standpoint of Public Hygiene and Education* (New York, 1923), and *The Mental Growth of the Pre-School Child* (New York, 1925); David B. Tyack, *The One Best System* (Cambridge, Mass., 1974), pp. 198 ff., 218, 269, 275; Nathanael West, *A Cool Million* (New York, 1934); W. Lloyd Warner, *Democracy in Jonesville* (New York, 1949); Richard A. Reiman, *The New Deal and American Youth* (Athens, Ga., 1992), pp. 13–14.
5. Dale Carnegie, *How to Win Friends and Influence People* (New York, 1936; 28th

ed., 1937); Giles Kemp and Edward Claflin, *Dale Carnegie* (New York, 1989), pp. 38 ff., 103, 112, 152; Carl Bode, *Mencken* (Carbondale, Ill., 1969), pp. 248 ff.

6. Conrad Aiken, *The Kid* (New York, 1947), p. 11; Kendall Beaton, *Enterprise in Oil* (New York, 1957), pp. 279 ff.; Robert Hobbs, *Edward Hoffer* (New York, 1987), p. 119; Peter J. Ling, *America and the Automobile* (Manchester, Eng., 1990), pp. 5, 10; Raymond Flower and Michael W. Jones, *One Hundred Years on the Road* (San Francisco, Calif., 1981), pp. 109 ff.; also F. Robert Van der Linden, *The Boeing 247* (Seattle, 1991).
7. Robert Weisbrot, *Father Divine* (Urbana, Ill., 1983); Bessie Jones, *For the Ancestors,* ed. John Stewart (Chicago, 1983), pp. 72 ff.; Gayraud S. Wilmore, ed., *African-American Religious Studies* (Durham, N.C., 1989), pp. 85 ff.; Charles Trout, *Boston, the Great Depression and the New Deal* (New York, 1977), p. 49; Manuel Zapata Olivella, *He Visto la Noche* (Havana, Cuba, 1962), pp. 58 ff., 67 ff.; Francis Russell, *The Great Interlude* (New York, 1964), pp. 75 ff.; Reinhold Niebuhr, *Pious and Secular America* (New York, 1958), pp. 4 ff.; No-Yong Park, *An Oriental View of American Civilization* (Boston, 1934), pp. 68, 112; Daniel Mark Epstein, *Sister Aimee* (New York, 1993), pp. 237 ff. See also Henry Glassie, *Irish Folk Tales* (New York, 1985), pp. 76 ff.
8. Kemp and Claflin, *Dale Carnegie;* Isabel Leighton, ed., *The Aspirin Age* (New York, 1949), pp. 50 ff.; Wylie, *Generation of Vipers,* p. 10; Bode, *Mencken,* pp. 264 ff, 276 ff.; Richard Quebedeaux, *By What Authority* (San Francisco, Calif., 1982), pp. 29 ff.; Katherine A. W. Tingley, *The Gods Await* (Point Loma, Calif., 1926), pp. 8, 51, 164, 184; Epstein, *Sister Aimee,* pp. 177 ff., 215 ff., 292 ff.; Ronald M. Deutsch, *The Nuts Among the Berries* (New York, 1961), p. 130; Emmett A. Greenwalt, *California Utopia* (San Diego, Calif., 1978), pp. 116, 169, 183; Moss Hart, *Lady in the Dark* (New York, 1941), p. 17; Perrett, *America in the Twenties,* p. 149.
9. Conrad Aiken, *Ushant* (New York, 1952), p. 220; Norman Vincent Peale, *The Power of Positive Thinking* (New York, 1955), p. 224; Quebedeaux, *By What Authority,* pp. 43 ff., 89 ff., 151.
10. T. S. Eliot, *The Rock* (London, 1934), and *Ash Wednesday* (London, 1930).
11. Henry F. Ward, *Our Economic Morality* (New York, 1929); Lynd Ward, *Madman's Drum* (New York, 1930).
12. Emanuel Haldeman-Julius, *The World of Haldeman-Julius,* comp. Albert Mordell (New York, 1960); Albert Mordell, *Trailing E. Haldeman-Julius* (Girard, Kansas, 1949); Rupert Hughes, *George Washington,* 3 vols. (New York, 1926–1927); John Erskine, *The Private Life of Helen of Troy* (Indianapolis, 1925); Eugene O'Neill, *Strange Interlude, Plays* (New York, 1955), pp. 86 ff., 103; William A. Orton, *America in Search of Culture* (Boston, 1933), p. 73; H. L. Mencken, *Notes on Democracy* (New York, 1926); Everett Dean Martin, *Liberty* (New York, 1930), pp. 8 ff.; Burton W. Folsom, *The Myth of the Robber Barons* (Herndon, Va., 1991); Park, *An Oriental View,* pp. 111 ff.
13. Michael Byrne, *The History and Contemporary Significance of Book Clubs* (Birmingham, Eng., 1978); Clare Brandt, *An American Aristocracy* (New York, 1986), pp. 227 ff.; Karen Horney, *Neurosis and Human Growth: The Struggle Toward Self-Realization* (New York, 1950); Susan Quinn, *A Mind of Her Own* (New York, 1987), pp. 245 ff.; Stephen Becker, *Comic Art in America* (New York, 1959), p. 66.
14. Isaac Rosenfeld, *Passage from Home* (New York, 1946); Eugene P. Moehring, *Resort City in the Sunbelt* (Reno, Nev., 1989), pp. 47 ff.; Flower and Jones, *One Hundred*

Years on the Road (New York, 1981); Harold Bloom, ed., *Holden Caulfield* (New York, 1990), p. 7; James J. Flink, *The Car Culture* (Cambridge, Mass., 1975), pp. 141 ff.

15. Martin, *Liberty,* pp. 267 ff.; Peter L. Skolnik, *Fads* (New York, 1978), pp. 40 ff., 73–74.
16. Bode, *Mencken,* p. 18; Michael Gold, *Jews Without Money* (New York, 1930), p. 158; Sidney Howard, *The Silver Cord* (New York, 1927).
17. Otto Mutz, *What's the Matter with Our Uncle Sam* (Lincoln, Nebr., 1922), p. 220; Herbert Hoover, *The Challenge to Liberty* (New York, 1934), pp. 192–97, 203–14; Walter I. Trattner, *Homer Folks* (New York, 1968), pp. 104 ff., 145; Reiman, *The New Deal and American Youth,* p. 23; Clarence Darrow, *Story of My Life* (New York, 1932), pp. 226 ff.; Hal Higdon, *The Crime of the Century* (New York, 1973), pp. 118 ff.; Anne Nichols, *Abie's Irish Rose* (New York, 1937); Louis Adamic, *My America* (New York, 1938), pp. 283 ff.; Aiken, *Ushant,* p. 112.
18. Paul R. Spickard, *Mixed Blood: Intermarriage and Ethnic Identity in Twentieth-Century America* (Madison, Wis., 1989), pp. 183 ff., 189 ff., 198.
19. Eugene V. Debs, *Letters,* ed. J. Robert Constantine (Urbana, Ill., 1990), 3:97, 238, 243; Nick Salvatore, *Eugene V. Debs* (Urbana, Ill., 1982), pp. 279 ff.; Ring Lardner, "Now and Then," *Ring Lardner Reader* (New York, 1963), pp. 326–38; Armand L. Mauss and Julie C. Wolfe, *This Land of Promise* (New York, 1977), p. 24; Sinclair Lewis, *Main Street* (1920; New York, 1948), pp. 198, 199; Guy Irving Burch, *The Reason for Birth Control* (Washington, D.C., 1940), pp. 12, 14; Alfred Kinsey *et al., American Male* (Philadelphia, 1948); Wylie, *Generation of Vipers,* p. 29; Bode, *Mencken,* pp. 270 ff.; William J. Robinson, *Birth Control* (New York, 1929), pp. 229 ff.; Adolf Meyer, ed., *Birth Control* (Baltimore, 1925), pp. 98 ff.; Steven Mintz and Susan Kellogg, *Domestic Revolutions* (New York, 1988), pp. 107 ff., 117, 129; Park, *An Oriental View,* pp. 54 ff.
20. Francis Cavanah, *Liberty Laughs* (New York, 1932), p. 165; Marston Bates, *The Nature of Natural History* (New York, 1950), p. 251; John Boll, *Dragon Hotel* (New York, 1969); John H. Moore, *Over-Sexed, Over-Paid, and Over Here* (St. Lucia, Queensland, 1981); Mintz and Kellogg, *Domestic Revolutions,* p. 171; William Saroyan, *The Human Comedy* (New York, 1942).
21. Wylie, *Generation of Vipers,* pp. 69, 70; Beth L. Bailey, *From Front Porch to Back Seat* (Baltimore, Md., 1988), pp. 17, 21, 43 ff., 50, 61 ff., 103 ff.; John Modell, *Into One's Own* (Berkeley, Calif., 1989), pp. 12 ff.; Mintz and Kellogg, *Domestic Revolutions,* pp. 153 ff., 162 ff.
22. Mintz and Kellogg, *Domestic Revolutions,* pp. 168 ff.; Modell, *Into One's Own,* pp. 256, 262.
23. Mary Harris Jones, *Speeches and Writings,* ed. Edward M. Steel (Pittsburgh, 1988), p. 260; Mutz, *What's the Matter with Our Uncle Sam,* pp. 218 ff.; Wylie, *Generation of Vipers,* pp. 50 ff., 219 ff.; Epstein, *Sister Aimee,* p. 434; Nancy Cott, ed., *A Woman Making History* (New Haven, 1991), pp. 22, 33; Albert Jay Nock, *Memoirs of a Superfluous Man* (New York, 1943), pp. 204 ff.; Ring Lardner, "Dinner," and "I Can't Breathe," *Ring Lardner Reader,* pp. 214–23, 435–42; Susan Ware, *Still Missing* (New York, 1993), pp. 234–36; Joanne Meyerowitz, "Beyond the Feminine Mystique," *Journal of American History,* 79 (March 1993), pp. 1455 ff.
24. Mintz and Kellogg, *Domestic Revolutions,* pp. 113, 139 ff.; Mauss and Wolfe, *This*

Land of Promise, p. 81; William Graebner, *A History of Retirement* (New Haven, 1980), pp. 6–7, 33, 215.

25. Samuel Lubell, "Ten Billion Nickels," *Saturday Evening Post,* 211 (May 13, 1939): 12 ff., 38; Jenna W. Joselit, *Our Gang* (Bloomington, Ind., 1983), pp. 106, 140 ff., 148; William F. Whyte, *Street Corner Society* (Chicago, 1947); Wylie, *Generation of Vipers,* p. 65; Modell, *Into One's Own,* pp. 223 ff.; Kenneth Allsop, *The Bootleggers* (New Rochelle, N.Y., 1961), pp. 206 ff., 213; Edwin F. Sutherland, "The Diffusion of Sexual Psychopath Laws," *American Journal of Sociology,* 56 (1950): 142, 148 ff.
26. Jay Robert Nash, *The Dillinger Dossier* (Highland Park, Ill., 1983), pp. xxii, 19; Allsop, *Bootleggers,* pp. 275 ff., 282, 309 ff.
27. Philip Slater, *The Pursuit of Loneliness* (Boston, 1970), p. 6; Bryan B. Sterling, *The Best of Will Rogers* (New York, 1979), pp. 90, 92, 93.
28. George Murray, *The Legacy of Al Capone* (New York, 1975), pp. 343, 345; Robert J. Schoenberg, *Mr. Capone* (New York, 1992), pp. 291, 364; Reiman, *The New Deal and American Youth,* pp. 40 ff., 125.
29. David F. Musto, *The American Disease* (New Haven, 1974), pp. 149, 156, 183, 191 ff., 216–20; Sara Graham-Mulhall, *Opium: The Demon Flower* (3rd ed., New York, 1928), pp. 22, 144 ff.
30. Alan Filreis, *Wallace Stevens* (Princeton, 1991), p. 136; Frank E. Beaver, *On Film* (New York, 1983), p. 241; J. Stephen Kroll-Smith and Stephen R. Couch, *The Real Disaster* (Lexington, Ky., 1990), p. 24; Harry A. Overstreet, *The Mature Mind* (New York, 1949), p. 148; Hobbs, *Edward Hopper,* p. 75; Ilya Ilf and Eugene Petrov, *Little Golden America,* tr. Charles Malamuth (New York, 1937), pp. 115–20, 129–30; David DeKok, *Unseen Danger* (Philadelphia, 1986); Renée Jacobs, *Slow Burn* (Philadelphia, 1986); Mauss and Wolfe, *This Land of Promise,* pp. 291–93.
31. Rose Wilder Lane, *Give Me Liberty* (1936; Easton, Conn., 1944), pp. 35, 38, 42; F. Scott Fitzgerald, *The Great Gatsby* (New York, 1925); Sterling, *Best of Will Rogers,* pp. 38, 39.
32. James K. Fitzpatrick, *Builders of the American Dream* (New Rochelle, N.Y., 1977), p. 239.
33. Nathanael West, *Miss Lonelyhearts* (New York, 1933), p. 102; Sterling, *Best of Will Rogers,* p. 96; Nelson Algren, *Never Come Morning* (New York, 1942), pp. 11 ff.; Fitzpatrick, *Builders of the American Dream,* p. 265.
34. Fitzpatrick, *Builders of the American Dream,* pp. 265, 271; Madeleine Edmondson and David Rounds, *From Mary Noble to Mary Hartman* (New York, 1976), pp. 52 ff.; Stuart Cloets, *Yesterday Is Dead* (New York, 1940), p. 245; Skolnick, *Fads,* p. 36; Herman Klurfield, *Winchell* (New York, 1976), pp. 43 ff.
35. Hobbs, *Hopper,* p. 112; Wylie, *Generation of Vipers,* pp. 213, 214; Gerald Mast, *A Short History of the Movies* (4th ed., New York, 1986), p. 228.
36. Robert W. Snyder, *The Voice of the City* (New York, 1989), pp. 150 ff.
37. Snyder, *Voice of the City,* p. 152.
38. Ithiel de Sola Pool, *Technologies of Freedom* (Cambridge, Mass., 1983); Edmondson and Rounds, *From Mary Noble,* p. 40; Alan Havig, *Fred Allen's Radio Comedy* (Philadelphia, 1990), pp. 110, 118, 122, 125; Klurfield, *Winchell,* pp. 58, 64–66; Lloyd Morris, *Not So Long Ago* (New York, 1944), pp. 441, 443 ff., 465.
39. James Hadley Chase, *No Orchids for Miss Blandish* (London, 1939); George Orwell, "Raffles and Miss Blandish," *Collected Essays,* 4 vols. (London, 1968), 3:212 ff.; Bode, *Mencken,* pp. 81 ff.; Wylie, *Generation of Vipers,* p. 201; Aiken, *Ushant,* p.

89; Arnold Gingrich, *The Bedside Esquire* (New York, 1940); William Wolf, *Landmark Films* (New York, 1979), pp. 94 ff.; Beaver, *On Film,* p. 239; Schoenberg, *Mr. Capone,* pp. 214, 221 ff.; Herman Klurfeld, *Winchell* (New York, 1976); Morris, *Not So Long Ago,* pp. 145 ff.; Guttman, *Wound in the Heart,* p. 22.

40. Musto, *The American Disease,* pp. 149, 156, 183, 216–20; Damon Runyon, *Guys and Dolls* (New York, 1931); Leo C. Rosten, *The Education of Hyman Kaplan* (New York, 1937); Arthur Kober, *My Dear Bella* (New York, 1941); Marian A. Dogherty, *'Scusa Me Teacher* (Francestown, N.H., 1943); Havig, *Fred Allen's Radio Comedy,* pp. 155 ff.; Philip Davis and Brian Never, *Cinema, Politics and Society in America* (Manchester, 1981); Lawrence Levine, "American Culture and the Great Depression," *Yale Review,* 74 (1985): 221.

41. Fred Allen, *Treadmill to Oblivion* (Boston, 1954); Fred Allen, *Much Ado About Me* (Boston, 1956); Sam Bass Warner, Jr., *Province of Reason* (Cambridge, Mass., 1984), pp. 44 ff.; Havig, *Fred Allen's Radio Comedy,* pp. 76 ff., 193, 213; Edmondson and Rounds, *From Mary Noble,* pp. 27 ff.; Melvin P. Ely, *The Adventures of Amos 'n' Andy* (New York, 1991), pp. 73 ff., 96, 116–18, 161; Morris, *Not So Long Ago,* p. 460.

42. Aiken, *Ushant,* p. 293.

43. Hobbs, *Hopper,* pp. 97, 98, 103, 124, 125. See also Berenice Abbott, *New York in the Thirties* (1939; New York, 1973).

44. Wylie, *Generation of Vipers,* p. 54; Charles E. White, *The Bungalow Book* (New York, 1923); Harlan P. Douglas, *The Suburban Trend* (New York, 1925), pp. 308, 325 ff.; Robert Fishman, *Bourgeois Utopias* (New York, 1987), pp. 155, 170; C. Page Smith, *Redeeming the Time* (New York, 1987), pp. 951, 955.

45. Lewis, *Main Street,* pp. 264 ff., 268; Sinclair Lewis, *It Can't Happen Here* (New York, 1935); Martin Bucco, ed., *Critical Essays on Sinclair Lewis* (Boston, 1986).

46. David Wyatt, ed., *New Essays on the Grapes of Wrath* (New York, 1990), pp. 76, 79, 83; Louis Owens, *The Grapes of Wrath* (Boston, 1989), pp. 3 ff., 12.

47. Frank Adams, *Unearthing Seeds of Fire* (Winston-Salem, N.C., 1975), pp. 35, 36; Michael B. Katz, *Poverty and Policy in American History* (New York, 1983), pp. 222 ff.; David J. and Sheila M. Rothman, *On Their Own: The Poor in Modern America* (Reading, Mass., 1972), pp. 168 ff.

48. Ely Green, *Too Black, Too White* (Amherst, Mass., 1970); Ely Green, *An Autobiography* (1966; New York, 1990), pp. 239 ff.; Langston Hughes, *The Negro Mother* (Ann Arbor, Mich., 1970); Mbonu Ojike, *I Have Two Countries* (New York, 1947), pp. 17 ff.; Harvard Sitkoff, *A New Deal for Blacks* (New York, 1978), pp. 26 ff., 39, 56 ff.; James Weldon Johnson, *The Autobiography of an Ex-Colored Man* (New York, 1927); Sinclair Lewis, *Kingsblood Royal* (New York, 1947); Mintz and Kellogg, *Domestic Revolutions,* pp. 142 ff.; Michael Banton, *Racial Theories* (Cambridge, Mass., 1987), pp. 159 ff.; Rex Stewart, *Boy Meets Horn* (Ann Arbor, Mich., 1991), pp. 51 ff.; Thomas Hart Benton, *An Artist in America* (3rd ed., Columbia, Mo., 1968), pp. 189, 193–94; George Schuyler, *Black Empire,* ed. Robert A. Hill and R. Kent Rasmussen (Boston, 1991), pp. 274 ff.; Doris G. Anderson, *Nigger Lover* (London, 1938), p. 253.

49. James J. Jones, *The Tuskegee Syphilis Experiment* (New York, 1992); *Mitchell* v. *United States* (1941), 313 U.S., 88–97; David Ward, *Poverty, Ethnicity and the American City* (New York, 1989), pp. 145 ff., 188; Sitkoff, *New Deal for Blacks,* p. 171.

50. Langston Hughes, "Harlem" (1950); Stewart, *Boy Meets Horn,* p. 137; James Weldon Johnson, "The Making of Harlem," *Survey Graphic,* 53 (1925): 635 ff.; Carl Van Vechten, *Nigger Heaven* (New York, 1926); Henry L. Mencken, *Letters,* ed. Guy J. Forgue (New York, 1961), pp. 419, 479; Oscar Handlin, *The Newcomers* (Cambridge, Mass., 1959); Neil Hickey and Edwin Fenton, *Adam Clayton Powell* (New York, 1965), pp. 43 ff.; Benton, *Artist in America,* p. 298; Domenic J. Capeci, *The Harlem Riot of 1943* (Philadelphia, 1977), pp. 79, 138; Cheryl Lynn Greenberg, *"Or Does It Explode"* (New York, 1991), p. 212.
51. Sitkoff, *New Deal for Blacks,* pp. 63 ff., 85, 120, 126, 145; Charles Abrams, *Forbidden Neighbors* (New York, 1955), pp. 86 ff., 93 ff.; Tyack, *One Best System,* p. 229; Martin B. Duberman, *Paul Robeson* (New York, 1988); Sarah Rice, *He Included Me* (Athens, Ga., 1989), pp. 51 ff., 99; Richard Wright, *Twelve Million Black Voices* (New York, 1941), pp. 130 ff.; William H. Exum, *Paradoxes of Protest* (Philadelphia, 1985), p. 12; Anderson, *Nigger Lover,* pp. 249, 252, 254; Davies and Neve, *Cinema, Politics and Society in America,* pp. 181 ff.; Nell Painter, *The Narrative of Hosea Hudson* (Cambridge, 1979); Smith, *Redeeming the Time,* pp. 594, 658; Jervis Anderson, *A. Philip Randolph* (New York, 1973); Greenberg, *"Or Does It Explode,"* 213; Melvyn Dubofsky and Warren Van Tine, *Labor Leaders in America* (Urbana, Ill., 1987), pp. 273 ff.; Darrow, *Story of My Life,* pp. 303 ff.; Samuel Walker, *In Defense of American Liberties* (New York, 1990), *passim;* Epstein, *Sister Aimee,* pp. 267 ff.
52. Langston Hughes, *A New Song* (New York, 1938), and *I Wonder as I Wander* (New York, 1956), p. 60; Gunnar Myrdal, *An American Dilemma* (New York, 1944); Robert Weisbrot, *Father Divine* (Urbana, Ill., 1983); Jill Watts, *God, Harlem U.S.A.* (Berkeley, Calif., 1992); E. L. Angell and G. B. Wilcox, *In a Democracy* (Austin, Tex., 1940), pp. 52–53; Anderson, *Nigger Lover,* pp. 263, 267.
53. Greenberg, *"Or Does It Explode",* pp. 104 ff.; Weisbrot, *Father Divine,* pp. 5 ff., 177, 193 ff.; E. Curtis Alexander, *Adam Clayton Powell, Jr.* (New York, 1983); E. Franklin Frazier, *The Negro Church in America* (New York, 1974), pp. 50 ff.; Roger D. Abrahams, *Deep Down in the Jungle* (Chicago, 1970), p. 63; Alex Haley and Malcolm X, *Autobiography of Malcolm X* (New York, 1964).
54. Greenberg, *"Or Does It Explode",* pp. 132 ff., 210 ff.; Sitkoff, *New Deal for Blacks,* p. 240; Nelson, *Steve Nelson,* p. 288; Andrew Bunie, *The Negro in Virginia Politics* (Charlottesville, Va., 1967), pp. 106 ff., 142 ff., 165 ff.; Ruth Smith, *White Man's Burden* (New York, 1946), pp. 162, 175, 211.
55. Henry Wallace, *Soviet Asia Mission* (New York, 1946); Dwight Macdonald, *Henry Wallace* (New York, 1948).
56. Aiken, *Ushant,* p. 83; John Fante, "The Odyssey of a Wop," *American Mercury,* 30 (1933), 89 ff.; United States W.P.A. Projects (Washington, 1937); Cole, *Lawrence,* pp. 11, 14.
57. Harvey Swados, *On the Line* (Boston, 1957); Dubovsky and Van Tine, *Labor Leaders in America,* p. 271.
58. Jane Trahey, ed., *Harper's Bazaar* (New York, 1967), p. 125; Charles Dickens, *Bleak House* (Harmondsworth, England, 1971), p. 124; Benton, *Artist in America,* pp. 193–94, 196, 298.
59. Mary Harris Jones, *Speeches and Writings,* p. 216; Wylie, *Generation of Vipers,* pp. 326, 327; Sitkoff, *New Deal for Blacks,* pp. 263 ff.; Thomas V. Smith, *The Promise of American Politics* (Chicago, 1936), p. 245.
60. Morton Grodzins, *Americans Betrayed* (Chicago, 1949); Audrie Girdner and Anne

Loftis, *The Great Betrayal* (New York, 1969); Lucie Cheng and Edna Bonacich, *Labor Immigration Under Capitalism* (Berkeley, Calif., 1984), pp. 440 ff., 457; above, ch. 3 at n. 38.

61. Flora W. Seymour, "Thunder over the Southwest," *Saturday Evening Post,* 211 (Apr. 1, 1939): 22 ff.; Angie Debo, *A History of the Indians of the United States* (Norman, Oklahoma, 1970), pp. 282–92, 303; Philip Weeks, ed., *The American Indian Experience* (Arlington Heights, Ill., 1988), pp. 240–59.
62. Cheng and Bonacich, *Labor Immigration,* pp. 572, 585 ff., 599, 602; Cynthia C. Mejia and Hyung-Chan Kim, *The Filipinos in America* (New York, 1976), pp. 7, 15; Angell and Wilcox, *In a Democracy,* p. 53; Carlos E. Cortes, ed., *Aspects of the Mexican-American Experience* (New York, 1976), pp. 96 ff., 1ll; Peter Skerry, *Mexican Americans* (New York, 1992); Julian Samora, ed., *La Raza* (Notre Dame, Ind., 1966), pp. 1–26; Tony Castro, *Chicano Power* (New York, 1974).
63. Max Lerner, *Actions and Passions* (New York, 1949); Marcia G. Synnott, *The Half-Opened Door* (Westport, Conn., 1979); Regna Darnell, *Edward Sapir* (Berkeley, Calif., 1990); Hans Staudinger, *The Inner Nazi,* ed. Peter N. Rutkoff and William B. Scott (Baton Rouge, La., 1981), pp. 70 ff., 80; Charles Higham, *American Swastika* (Garden City, N.Y., 1985), pp. 271 ff.; Arthur Miller, *Focus* (New York, 1945); Laura Z. Hobson, *Gentleman's Agreement* (New York, 1947); also Evelyn Walsh McLean, *Father Struck It Rich* (Boston, 1936), p. 137; Winton U. Solberg, "The Catholic Presence of the University of Illinois," *Catholic Historical Review,* 76 (1990): 765 ff.; *Fortune,* 22 (Dec., 1940): 186; Michael O'Brien, *The Idea of the American South 1920–1941* (Baltimore, 1979), pp. 185 ff., 213 ff.
64. See, e.g., Fredrik Barth, *Sohar* (Baltimore, 1983), pp. 37 ff., 191 ff., 204 ff., 246; also Bonaro W. Overstreet, *Freedom's People* (New York, 1945), pp. 8, 10, 105, 109; *I'll Take My Stand* (New York, 1930); Henry A. Myers, *Are Men Equal* (New York, 1945), pp. 182 ff.; Clinton Rossiter and James Lare, eds., *The Essential Lippmann* (New York, 1963), pp. 143, 392; Wilfrid Parsons, *Which Way Democracy?* (New York, 1939), pp. 287, 288.
65. Louise L. Henricksen, *Anzia Yezierska* (New Brunswick, N.J., 1988), pp. 196, 218; Louis Wirth, *The Ghetto* (Chicago, 1928).
66. June Sochen, *Consecrate Every Day* (Albany, N.Y., 1981); Mark Bowman, "Rabbi Harry H. Epstein," *American Jewish Archives,* 42 (1990): 138 ff.
67. Waldo Frank, *In the American Jungle* (New York, 1937), p. 244.
68. Louis Finkelstein, ed., *Spiritual Autobiographies* (New York, 1952); Marc L. Raphael, *Abba Hillel Silver* (New York, 1989), pp. 86 ff.
69. Smith, *Promise of American Politics,* pp. 221, 222, 227; Rossiter, *Essential Lippmann,* pp. 338, 343; Carroll D. Murphy and Herbert V. Prochnow, *The Next Century Is America's* (New York, 1938), pp. 8, 11, 14; Trout, *Boston, The Great Depression and the New Deal,* p. 19.
70. Anne Morrow Lindbergh, *The Wave of the Future* (New York, 1940), pp. 8 ff., 25; Wallace Stevens, *Collected Poems,* p. 202; Robert Frost, "The Pasture," in *Collected Poems* (New York, 1942), p. 2.
71. Herbert C. Hoover, *American Individualism* (Garden City, N.Y., 1922); Alfred M. Landon, *America at the Crossroads* (New York, 1936), p. 34; Richard Maltby, ed., *Dreams for Sale* (London, 1989), pp. 99, 100; William James Forman, *Our Movie Made Children* (New York, 1933), pp. 161, 163, 168, 281; Sterling, *Best of Will Rogers,* p. 46.

72. Leighton, *Aspirin Age,* pp. 190 ff.; Geoffrey Perrett, *America in the Twenties* (New York, 1982), p. 283; Andre Siegfried, *America Comes of Age,* tr. H. H. Hemming (New York, 1927), pp. 349 ff.; also Zane Grey, *Knights of the Range* (New York, 1939).
73. T. S. Eliot, *The Family Reunion* (1939) and *The Cocktail Party, Collected Poems and Plays* (New York, 1952), pp. 281, 291, 342, 360; Vladimir Nabokov, *Speak Memory* (New York, 1966); Lardner, "Old Folks' Christmas," *Ring Lardner Reader,* pp. 391–400.
74. T. S. Eliot, *The Cocktail Party,* p. 342, and "The Hollow Men" (1925), *Collected Poems and Plays,* p. 59.
75. Thomas Wolfe, *You Can't Go Home Again* (New York, 1939), pp. 412 ff., 742 ff.; Henry A. Wallace, *Whose Constitution?* (New York, 1936), pp. 309, 315 ff.; Nicholas Roosevelt, *A New Birth of Freedom* (New York, 1938), p. 261.
76. Maxwell Anderson, *Winterset* (Washington, D.C., 1935), pp. 133–34; David Sanders, "Ernest Hemingway's Spanish Civil War Experience," *American Quarterly,* 12 (1960): 140 ff.
77. Aiken, *Ushant,* p. 178; William Faulkner, *Light in August* (New York, 1932); Maltby, *Dreams for Sale,* p. 103.
78. Margaret Mead, *And Keep Your Powder Dry* (New York, 1942), pp. 255 ff.; Irwin Shaw, "Act of Faith," *Mixed Company* (New York, 1950); Marianne Moore, "In Distrust of Merits" (1944), in *Collected Poems* (New York, 1955), pp. 135–37; Herman Wouk, *The Caine Mutiny Court-Martial* (Garden City, N.Y., 1954).
79. Sherwood Anderson, *Winesburg, Ohio* (New York, 1919; 1960).
80. Nathanael West, *The Day of the Locust* (New York, 1939), pp. 3, 4, 165; Randall Reid, *The Fiction of Nathanael West* (Chicago, 1967), pp. 144 ff., 156.

CHAPTER 5.

1. Oscar Handlin, ed., *American Principles and Issues* (New York, 1961); Eudora Welty, "The Wanderers," *The Golden Apples* (New York, 1949), pp. 203–44.
2. Isadore Barmash, *The Self-Made Man: Success and Stress American Style* (New York, 1969), pp. 107 ff.; Joseph C. Goulden, *The Best Years of Our Lives* (New York, 1976), p. 137; David Boaz and Edward H. Crane, *Market Liberalism* (Washington, D.C., 1943), p. 364.
3. Thomas R. Dye, ed., *The Political Legitimacy of Markets and Government* (Greenwich, Connecticut, 1990), pp. 21–23; Sidney Verba and Gary R. Orren, *Equality in America: The View from the Top* (Cambridge, Mass., 1985); Charles A. Beard, *The Economic Basis of Politics* (New York, 1960), p. 69; also Scott Nearing, *Freedom: Promise and Menace* (Harkorside, Me., 1961).
4. Robert J. Donovan, *The Second Victory: The Marshall Plan and the Postwar Revival of Europe* (New York, 1987), p. 45; Michael H. Hunt, *Ideology and United States Foreign Policy* (New Haven, Conn., 1987), pp. 151, 152, 159; John Gimbel, *The Origins of the Marshall Plan* (Stanford, Calif., 1976); William O. Douglas, "A World in Revolution" (Tucson, Feb. 14, 1951).
5. Walt W. Rostow, *Eisenhower, Kennedy and Foreign Aid* (Austin, Texas, 1985), pp. 36 ff., 41, 46, 54, 77 ff., 83, 92 ff., 217; David Porter, *United States Foreign Aid* (New York, 1990), pp. 10 ff.; Raymond Aron, *The Industrial Society* (New York, 1967), pp. 8 ff., 51 ff.

6. Edward C. Banfield, *American Foreign Aid Doctrines* (Washington, D.C., 1963), pp. 17, 42 ff.
7. Goulden, *Best Years of Our Lives,* pp. 180 ff.; Stuart Bruchey, *Enterprise* (Cambridge, Mass., 1990), p. 501; Willard W. Cochrane, *The Development of American Agriculture* (Minneapolis, 1979); Wheeler McMillen, *Feeding Multitudes* (Danville, Ill., 1981).
8. Marc Kramer, *Three Farms* (Boston, 1980), pp. 91, 92, 158 ff.; Nicholas Lemann, *The Promised Land* (New York, 1991), p. 5; Gary Paulsen, *Farm: A History and Celebration* (Englewood Cliffs, N.J., 1977); Robert C. Williams, *Fordson, Farmall and Poppin' Johnny: A History of the Farm Tractor* (Urbana, Ill., 1987).
9. Bruchey, *Enterprise,* pp. 501, 506; James Brough, *The Woolworths* (New York, 1982), p. 189; Jean Labatut, ed., *Highways in Our National Life* (Princeton, N.J., 1950).
10. Oscar Handlin, "Second Chance for the South," *Atlantic Monthly* (Dec., 1953): 54 ff.; Bruchey, *Enterprise,* p. 533; Glenna Mathews, *Just a Housewife* (New York, 1987); Ann Oakley, *Woman's Work* (New York, 1975).
11. Bruchey, *Enterprise,* pp. 491–93.
12. J. Paul Getty, *The Golden Age* (New York, 1968), pp. 17, 55 ff.; Peter C. Wensberg, *Land's Polaroid* (Boston, 1987), p. 127; Barmash, *The Self-Made Man,* pp. 12, 22 ff.; Stephen A. Marglin and Juliet B. Schor, eds., *The Golden Age of Capitalism* (Oxford, 1990); William H. Chafe, *The Unfinished Journey* (New York, 1991), p. 114.
13. Steven Mintz and Susan Kellogg, *Domestic Revolutions* (New York, 1988), p. 180; Hillel Schwartz, *Never Satisfied* (New York, 1986), pp. 233, 235, 246 ff.; also Bernard Malamud, *The Assistant* (New York, 1957); Brough, *Woolworths,* pp. 189–90.
14. Alice Teichova *et al.,* eds., *Historical Studies in International Corporate Business* (New York, 1989).
15. Mira Wilkins, ed., *The Growth of Multinationals* (Brookfield, Vt., 1991); Geoffrey Jones, ed., *Transnational Corporations: A Historical Perspective* (London, 1993); Carl H. A. Dassbach, *Global Enterprises and the World Economy* (New York, 1984).
16. Richard Eells, *The Political Crisis of the Enterprise System* (New York, 1980), p. 37.
17. Peter F. Drucker, "Worker and Work in the Metropolis," *Daedalus* (Fall 1968): 1243 ff.; Bruchey, *Enterprise,* p. 534; W. Andrew Achenbaum, *Old Age in the New Land* (Baltimore, 1978), p. 144; Martin Feldstein, ed., *The American Economy in Transition* (Chicago, 1980), pp. 486–92.
18. Leonard S. Silk, *The Research Revolution* (New York, 1960); Henry C. Dethloff, *Americans and Free Enterprise* (Englewood Cliffs, N.J., 1979), pp. 290–91.
19. George A. Smith, Jr., *Managing Geographically Decentralized Companies* (Boston, 1958); Peter Collier and David Horowitz, *The Fords* (New York, 1987); Deborah Shapley, *Promise and Power: The Life and Times of Robert McNamara* (Boston, 1993), pp. 53 ff.; Philip Langman, *Born to Pay* (Boston, 1987), pp. 241–42; also Vance Packard, *The Hidden Persuaders* (New York, 1957).
20. Goulden, *The Best Years of Our Lives,* pp. 112, 113, 122; Mabel Newcomer, *The Big Business Executive* (New York, 1955); Chafe, *Unfinished Journey,* pp. 114–15; Irving S. Shapiro, *America's Third Revolution* (New York, 1984); Courtney C. Brown, *Beyond the Bottom Line* (New York, 1979).
21. William J. Baumol, *et al., Productivity and American Leadership* (Cambridge, Mass., 1989); Bruchey, *Enterprise,* p. 524; Goulden, *Best Years,* pp. 92 ff.; Harold G. Vatter,

The United States Economy in the 1950s (New York, 1963); Dye, *Political Legitimacy of Markets,* pp. 58–59; Dethloff, *Americans and Free Enterprise,* pp. 277–78.

22. Mintz and Kellogg, *Domestic Revolutions,* p. 185; Clinton Rossiter and James A. Lare, eds., *The Essential Lippmann* (New York, 1963), pp. 31, 206.
23. John P. Diggins, *The Proud Decades* (New York, 1988), pp. 235 ff.; John M. Phelan, *Media World* (New York, 1977); Jeffrey Shrank, *Snap, Crackle and Popular Taste* (New York, 1977).
24. *Public Papers of the Presidents, Harry S Truman 1948* (Washington, D.C., 1964), pp. 409 ff.; *Public Papers of the Presidents, Harry S Truman 1949* (Washington, D.C., 1964), pp. 1, 2; Monte M. Poen, *Harry S Truman Versus the Medical Lobby* (Columbia, Mo., 1979), pp. 87 ff., 97, 139, 145 ff., 208.
25. Samuel Lubell, *The Hidden Crisis in American Politics* (New York, 1970), pp. 21, 55 ff., 77; George Comstock, *The Evolution of American Television* (Newbury Park, 1989), pp. 126 ff.
26. Goulden, *Best Years,* pp. 162; Allen Drury, *Advise and Consent* (Garden City, N.Y., 1959); Robert J. Donovan, *Eisenhower* (New York, 1956), pp. 64 ff., 71 ff.
27. Jeffrey M. Berry, *Feeding Hungry People* (Rutgers, N.J., 1982), pp. 3 ff.; Robert A. Caro, *The Power Broker* (New York, 1974), p. 7.
28. David M. Ricci, *The Transformation of American Politics* (New Haven, Conn., 1993).
29. Peter F. Drucker, *The Concept of the Corporation* (New York, 1946); Eugene V. Rostow, *Planning for Freedom* (New Haven, 1959).
30. Max Lerner, *Actions and Passions* (New York, 1949), pp. 224, 289 ff.; James Burnham, *The Managerial Revolution* (New York, 1941); Russell Kirk, *The Conservative Mind* (Chicago, 1953); John K. Galbraith, *The Affluent Society* (Boston, 1958); Laura Thompson, *Toward a Science of Mankind* (New York, 1961), p. vii; Friedrich A. von Hayek, *The Miracle of Social Justice* (Chicago, 1976).
31. Diggins, *The Proud Decades,* p. 228; David M. Potter, *People of Plenty* (Chicago, 1954); Friedrich A. von Hayek, *The Road to Serfdom* (Chicago, 1944).
32. Rowland Evans, *Lyndon B. Johnson* (New York, 1968); Kenneth W. Thompson, ed., *The Johnson Presidency* (Lanham, Md., 1986); Philip R. Rulom, *The Compassionate Samaritan* (Chicago, 1981).
33. U.S. General Accounting Office, *Domestic Energy Resources and Reserve Estimates* (Washington, 1977).
34. Mark H. Rose, *Interstate Express Highway Politics, 1941–1956* (Lawrence, Kansas, 1979), pp. 33 ff., 41 ff., 69 ff.; Caro, *The Power Broker,* pp. 921 ff.
35. Berry, *Feeding Hungry People,* pp. 7, 10 ff.; Robert H. Jackson, "The Task of Maintaining Our Liberties," *American Bar Association Journal,* 29 (November 1953).
36. Richard H. Rovere, *General MacArthur and President Truman* (New Brunswick, N.J., 1992); Clifford J. Durr, *Civil Liberties and World Peace* (New York, 1950); Ronald Radosh, *The Rosenberg File* (New York, 1983); Kevin J. Smant, *How Great the Triumph: James Burnham, Anti-Communism and the Conservative Movement* (Lanham, Md., 1992), p. 43; David Spitz, "Burnham's War on the Soviets," *New Republic,* 22 (March 20, 1950), p. 19; Andrew Sinclair, *Red and Blue: Cambridge, Treason and Intelligence* (Boston, 1986); Stephen Koch, *Double Lives: Spies and Writers in the Secret Soviet War of Ideas against the West* (New York, 1994); Zechariah Chaffee, *Free Speech in the United States* (Cambridge, 1941), pp. 564–65; Alan Barth, *The Loyalty of Free Men* (New York, 1951), p. 231; Francis Biddle,

The Fear of Freedom (Garden City, New York, 1951), pp. 185–96; Ralph S. Brown, *Loyalty and Security* (New Haven, 1958), pp. 3–20.

37. William F. Buckley, Jr., *God and Man at Yale* (Chicago, 1951); Earl Warren, *Address at Washington University* (St. Louis, 1955); John Lord O'Brian, *National Security and Individual Freedom* (Cambridge, Mass., 1955), pp. 14–17.
38. Brian Boyd, *Nabokov: The American Years* (Princeton, N.J., 1991); Steve Nelson, *et al., Steve Nelson, American Radical* (Pittsburgh, 1981), pp. 303, 314 ff., 374; Samuel A. Stauffer, *Communism, Conformity and Civil Liberties* (Garden City, N.J., 1955), p. 234.
39. Ralph L. Roy, *Apostles of Discord* (Boston, 1953), pp. 325 ff.; Charles Higham, *American Swastika* (New York, 1985), pp. 274 ff.; American Business Consultants, *Red Channels* (New York, 1950); Benjamin R. Epstein, *Report on the John Birch Society, 1966* (New York, 1966), pp. 1–2, 59; Biddle, *The Fear of Freedom,* p. 254; Harry and Bonaro Overstreet, *The Strange Tactics of Extremism* (New York, 1964), pp. 141, 157–59, 189–90.
40. Diggins, *Proud Decades,* p. 163; George Nash, *The Conservative Intellectual Movement in America Since 1945* (New York, 1976), pp. 114, 119, 138 ff.; Fred J. Cook, *Maverick* (New York, 1984), pp. 28 ff., 251 ff.; Arthur Miller, *The Crucible* (New York, 1971); Stephen Koch, *Double Lives* (New York, 1992); Ellen W. Schrecker, *No Ivory Tower* (New York, 1986), pp. 126 ff.
41. Donovan, *Eisenhower,* pp. 243 ff.; George D. Aiken, *Senate Diary* (Brattleboro, Vt., 1976).
42. *Flemming* v. *Nestor,* 363 U.S., 603; Mark Landis, *Joseph McCarthy: The Politics of Chaos* (London, 1987), pp. 131–42; Athan Theoharis, *Seeds of Repression: Harry S Truman and the Origins of McCarthyism* (Chicago, 1971); Alan D. Harper, *The Politics of Loyalty: The White House and the Communist Issue* (Westport, Connecticut, 1969).
43. J. D. Salinger, *Catcher in the Rye* (New York, 1951), p. 244.
44. Michael Barone, *Our Country* (New York, 1960), pp. 301–302.
45. John F. Kennedy, *To Turn the Tide* (New York, 1962), pp. 6–11; Seymour E. Harris, *Economics of the Kennedy Years* (New York, 1964); Shapley, *Promise and Power,* p. 102; William S. Leuchtenberg, *In the Shadow of F.D.R.* (Ithaca, N.Y., 1983), pp. 90 ff.; Gerard T. Rice, *The Bold Experiment* (Notre Dame, Ind., 1985); Chafe, *The Unfinished Journey* pp. 186, 190 ff.
46. Leo Fishman, ed., *Poverty Amid Affluence* (New Haven, 1966).
47. Barone, *Our Country,* pp. 367 ff., 378, 397; Chafe, *Unfinished Journey,* pp. 232, 234; Richard Neustadt and Ernest May, *Thinking in Time* (New York, 1986), pp. 411–15.
48. Poen, *Harry S. Truman,* pp. 211, 215 ff.; Ronald L. Numbers, ed., *Compulsory Health Insurance* (Westport, Conn., 1982), pp. 11, 130; Marshall Kaplan and Peggy L. Cuciti, eds., *The Great Society and Its Legacy* (Durham, N.C., 1986), p. 4; James Jones, *Bad Blood,* pp. 188 ff.; David S. Hirschfield, *The Lost Reform* (Cambridge, 1970), p. 35.
49. Marilyn Lashley, *Public Television* (Westport, Conn., 1992), pp. 19 ff., 30 ff.; Joseph A. Califano, Jr., *The Triumph and Tragedy of Lyndon Johnson* (New York, 1993); Livingston Biddle, *Our Government and the Arts* (New York, 1988); Ronald Berman, *Culture and Politics* (Lanham, Md., 1984).
50. Barone, *Our Country,* p. 372.

51. Barmash, *Self-Made Man,* pp. 151 ff.; Jeffrey Hart, *When the Going Was Good* (New York, 1982), pp. 146 ff.; Marynia Marnham and Ferdinand Lundberg, *Modern Women* (New York, 1947); Max Lerner, *America as a Civilization* (New York, 1957), pp. 582, 599 ff.
52. Nathan Silver, *Lost New York* (New York, 1967); Whittaker Chambers, "Cold Friday," *Ghosts on the Roof* (Washington, D.C., 1989); Barone, *Our Country,* p. 412.
53. Gresham M. Sykes, *The Society of Captives* (New York, 1965); Shapley, *Promise and Power,* p. 56; Barbara C. Jordan and Elspeth D. Rostow, eds., *The Great Society* (Austin, Tex., 1986), p. 8; Barone, *Our Country,* p. 395; Chafe, *Unfinished Journey,* p. 243.

CHAPTER 6.

1. Paul R. Spickard, *Mixed Blood* (Madison, Wis., 1989), pp. 52 ff., 67 ff.; Ralph L. Roy, *Apostles of Discord* (Boston, 1953), pp. 30 ff.; Charles Glock and Rodney Stark, *Christian Beliefs and Anti-Semitism* (New York, 1966); Gertrude Selznick and Stephen Steinberg, *The Tenacity of Prejudice* (New York, 1969).
2. Fred J. Cook, *The Corrupted Land* (New York, 1966), pp. 333 ff.; Charles S. Reich, *The Greening of America* (New York, 1970), pp. 98, 285; Michael Barone, *Our Country* (New York, 1990), p. 449.
3. Judith E. Doneson, *The Holocaust in American Film* (Philadelphia, 1987); Ilan Avisar, *Screening the Holocaust* (Bloomington, Ind., 1988).
4. Ashley Montague, *Man's Most Dangerous Myth: The Fallacy of Race,* 4th ed. (Cleveland, 1964); Roy, *Apostles of Discord,* p. 129.
5. Al Santoli, *New Americans* (New York, 1988), pp. 103, 163, 207, 307.
6. Peter De Vries, *The Blood of the Lamb* (Boston, 1961), pp. 231–41; Oscar Handlin, *The American People in the Twentieth Century* (Cambridge, Mass., 1954); Gerhard Lenski, *The Religious Factor* (New York, 1963); Bernard Malamud, *The Assistant* (New York, 1957); Peter De Vries, *Mackerel Plaza* (Boston, 1958); Andrew Greeley, *Ethnicity in the United States* (New York, 1974).
7. *Braunfeld* v. *Brown* (1961); *Sherbit* v. *Verner* (1963); Roy, *Apostles of Discord,* pp. 146 ff., 203 ff.; George Kranzler, *Williamsburg* (New York, 1969), pp. 19 ff., 179 ff.; Terry Eastland, *Religious Liberty in the Supreme Court* (Washington, D.C., 1993).
8. Harvey Swados, *On the Line* (Boston, 1957); Antanas J. Van Reenan, *Lithuanian Diaspora: Königsberg to Chicago* (Latham, Md., 1990), pp. 149 ff.; Kranzler, *Williamsburg,* pp. 213 ff.
9. Andrew Buni, *The Negro in Virginia Politics* (Charlottesville, Va., 1967), p. 207.
10. Le Roi Jones, *Home* (New York, 1961); Bernard Malamud, "Black Is My Favorite Color," *Idiots First* (New York, 1963).
11. Ira H. Freeman, *Out of the Burning* (New York, 1960), pp. 149, 161 ff.; *Autobiography of Malcolm X* (with Alex Haley, New York, 1965); Shane Stevens, *Go Down Dead* (New York, 1966). See also Gresham M. Sykes, *The Society of Captives* (New York, 1965), pp. 84 ff.
12. Roy, *Apostles of Discord,* p. 134; E. Franklin Frazier, *Black Bourgeoisie* (New York, 1957).
13. Roger D. Abrahams, *Deep Down in the Jungle* (Chicago, 1970), pp. 18 ff., 27, 195 ff.; Elliot Liebow, *Tally's Corner* (Boston, 1967).
14. Michael D. Davis and Hunter R. Clark, *Thurgood Marshall: Warrier at the Bar, Rebel*

on the Bench (New York, 1992), pp. 143–44, 175; *Brown* v. *Board of Education* (1954), 347 U.S. 492 ff.; Charles A. Miller, "Constitutional Law and the Rhetoric of Race," in Donald Fleming and Bernard Bailyn, eds., *Law in American History* (Boston, 1971), pp. 180 ff.; Roy, *Apostles of Discord,* pp. 80 ff., 119 ff.; Richard Kluger, *Simple Justice: The History of Brown v. Board of Education* (New York, 1976); William H. Harbaugh, *Lawyer's Lawyer: The Life of John W. Davis* (New York, 1973), pp. 483, 492–510.

15. Davis and Clark, *Thurgood Marshall,* pp. 179, 193; Robert J. Donovan, *Eisenhower* (New York, 1956), p. 154; Buni, *Negro in Virginia Politics,* pp. 190 ff.; see also Jeffrey A. Marx, "Give Me My Childhood Again," *American Jewish Archives,* 43 (1991): 119; Deborah D. Moore, *At Home in America* (New York, 1981), pp. 16, 67, 68.
16. Samuel Lubell, *The Hidden Crisis in American Politics* (New York, 1970), p. 159; Charles Abrams, *Forbidden Neighbors* (New York, 1955), pp. 137 ff., 152, 161, 169 ff., 178, 224 ff., 229 ff.
17. Tony A. Freyer, *The Little Rock Crisis* (Westport, Conn., 1984); Davis and Clark, *Thurgood Marshall,* p. 197.
18. Kugler, *Simple Justice,* p. 546; Ernest Dunbar, ed., *The Black Expatriates* (New York, 1968); Ralph Ellison, *Invisible Man* (New York, 1952); James Baldwin, *Nobody Knows My Name* (New York, 1954); James Baldwin, *The Fire Next Time* (New York, 1963); Imamu Amiri Baraka (Le Roi Jones), *It's Nation Time* (New York, 1970).
19. Peter Goldman, *The Death and Life of Malcolm X* (Urbana, Ill., 1979), pp. 134, 148, 154, 157; "Bayard Rustin Meets Malcolm X," *Freedom Review* (January 1993): 73 ff.; William O'Neill, *Coming Apart* (Chicago, 1971).
20. Charles Murray, *Losing Ground: American Social Policy, 1950–1980* (New York, 1984), p. 33.
21. John Egerton, *A Mind to Stay Here* (New York, 1970), pp. 51 ff.; John Ehle, *The Free Men* (New York, 1965); August Meier and Elliot Rudwick, *Core* (New York, 1973).
22. Mary T. Clark, *Discrimination Today* (New York, 1966); Egerton, *A Mind to Stay Here,* p. 21.
23. Carl M. Bauer, *John F. Kennedy and the Second Reconstruction* (New York, 1972), pp. 89 ff., 101 ff.
24. Davis and Clark, *Thurgood Marshall,* p. 270; H.R. 7152.
25. President Lyndon B. Johnson to Congress, March 15, 1965; *Congressional Record,* Proceedings and Debates of the 89th Congress, 1st Session, Vol. III, No. 4 (Washington, D.C., 1965): 4924–26; Abigail Thernstrom, *Whose Votes Count* (Cambridge, Mass., 1989); Barone, *Our Country,* p. 403; William H. Chafe, *Unfinished Journey* (New York, 1991), pp. 235, 236.
26. Davis and Clark, *Thurgood Marshall,* p. 270; Robert H. Bremner, *et al., American Choices* (Columbus, Ohio, 1986), pp. 58 ff.
27. Peter Skerry, *Mexican Americans the Ambivalent Minority* (New York, 1993), p. 144; Saul D. Alinsky, *Reveille for Radicals* (New York, 1946); Martin Oppenheimer and George Lakey, *A Manual for Direct Action* (Chicago, 1965), pp. viii, xiii, 67, 77, 93, 113; Si Kahn, *How People Get Power* (New York, 1970), pp. x, 33, 106, 109; O'Neill, *Coming Apart,* p. 167; Charles R. Morris, *A Time of Passing* (New York, 1984), p. 117; Egerton, *A Mind to Stay Here,* p. 128; August Meier *et al.,* eds., *Black*

Protest in the 1960s (New York, 1991), p. 126; Bruce Perry, ed., *Malcolm X: The Last Speeches* (New York, 1989), p. 68.

28. Lyndon B. Johnson, *This America* (New York, 1966), pp. 7–8; Martin Luther King, Jr., *I Have A Dream* (New York, 1968).
29. Bruce Perry, *Malcolm X,* pp. 157, 177, 179; Egerton, *A Mind to Stay Here,* pp. 101, 104; Johnson, *This America,* pp. 6–7.
30. Dave Berkman, "The Segregated Medium," *Columbia Journalism Review,* 5 (Fall 1966): 29 ff.
31. Cyrus Colter, *The Rivers of Eros* (Chicago, 1971), p. 77; Robert F. Drinan, *Democracy, Dissent and Disorder* (New York, 1969), p. 53; also, *e.g.,* Ben Caldwell, *The Job* (1968).
32. Marshall Kaplan and Peggy L. Cuciti, eds., *The Great Society* (Durham, N.C., 1986), pp. 213, 214; Ione Malloy, *Southie Won't Go* (Urbana, Ill., 1986); Gary Orfield, *Must We Bus? Segregated Schools and National Policy* (Washington, D.C., 1978), pp. 11, 28, 122–23.
33. See, e.g., a *New York Times* survey of white attitudes, September 21, 1964; Dean Harper, "Aftermath of a Long, Hot Summer," *Trans-Action,* II (1965), 9, 10. See also Harold R. Isaacs, *The New World of Negro Americans* (New York, 1963); and Robert Penn Warren, *Who Speaks for the Negro?* (New York, 1965). For the background, see Richard Bardolph, *The Negro Vanguard* (New York, 1959); August Meier, *Negro Thought in America 1880–1915* (Ann Arbor, 1963). On the extremists, see Irving Howe, "New Styles in 'Leftism,' " *Dissent* (Summer 1965), 12, 14, 18 ff.; Orfield, *Must We Bus,* p. 423; Alan Lupo, *Liberty's Chosen Home* (Boston, 1988); Ronald P. Formisano, *Boston Against Busing* (Chapel Hill, N.C., 1991), pp. 203, 223, 226.
34. Stevens, *Go Down Dead,* p. 169; Abrams, *Forbidden Neighbors,* pp. 103 ff., 120 ff.; Edward C. Banfield, *The Unheavenly City* (Boston, 1970), *passim;* Jerry Cohen and William S. Murphy, *Burn Baby Burn* (New York, 1966); Robert E. Conot, *Rivers of Blood, Years of Darkness* (New York, 1967); Robert M. Fogelson, ed., *The Los Angeles Riots* (New York, 1969); Kaplan and Cuciti, *The Great Society and Its Legacy,* p. 211; Barone, *Our Country,* pp. 384, 387, 418; Marvin E. Gettleman, ed., *The Failure of American Liberalism* (New York, 1971), pp. 522 ff., 538, 549.
35. Stokely Carmichael and Charles R. Hamilton, *Black Power* (New York, 1967); Eldridge Cleaver, *Soul on Ice* (New York, 1968); August Meier *et al.,* eds., *Black Protest in the Sixties* (New York, 1991), pp. 114, 168 ff.; Elaine Brown, *A Taste of Power* (New York, 1992); John A. Williams, *The Man Who Cried I Am* (Boston, 1967); O'Neill, *Coming Apart,* pp. 168 ff., 173 ff.; Barone, *Our Country,* pp. 386, 419; Drinan, *Democracy, Dissent and Disorder,* p. 143; Jean Christie and Leonard Dinnerstein, eds., *Decisions and Revisions* (New York, 1975), p. 339; Gettleman, *Failure of American Liberalism,* pp. 516, 517.
36. Murray, *Losing Ground,* pp. 42 ff.; David J. Bodenhamer and James W. Ely, Jr., *The Bill of Rights in Modern America* (Bloomington, Ind., 1993), pp. 156 ff.
37. Davis and Clark, *Thurgood Marshall,* p. 332; Andrew Hacker, *The End of the American Era* (New York, 1970), p. 111; O'Neill, *Coming Apart,* pp. 186, 192 ff.; Peter Collier and David Horowitz, *Second Thoughts* (Lanham, Md., 1989), pp. 217 ff.; Murray Friedman, *What Went Wrong?* (New York, 1993).
38. Oscar Lewis, *La Vida* (New York, 1965), pp. 264 ff., 444 ff.
39. Kranzler, *Williamsburg,* pp. 206 ff; Oscar Handlin, *The Newcomers* (Cambridge,

Mass., 1959), pp. 93 ff.; Salvatore J. LaGumina, *Vito Marcantonio* (Dubuque, Iowa, 1969); Earl Shorris, *Latinos* (New York, 1992).

40. Claude Brown, *Manchild in the Promised Land* (New York, 1965); James Jennings and Monte Rivers, eds., *Puerto Rican Politics in Urban America* (Westport, Conn., 1984), pp. 92, 140; Peter Matthiessen, *Sal Si Puedes: Cesar Chavez and the New American Revolution* (New York, 1969), p. 359; O'Neill, *Coming Apart,* pp. 295 ff.
41. O'Neill, *Coming Apart,* p. 174.
42. Barone, *Our Country,* p. 437.
43. Robert F. Berkhofer, Jr., *The White Man's Indian* (New York, 1978); Robert L. Dorman, *Revolt of the Provinces* (Chapel Hill, N.C., 1993), pp. 66 ff.; also, e.g., Conrad Richter, *A Country of Strangers* (New York, 1966); Zane Grey, *The Vanishing American* (New York, 1925); Dee A. Brown, *Bury My Heart at Wounded Knee* (New York, 1970); Handlin and Handlin, *Liberty in Peril,* pp. 142 ff.; above, ch. 4 at note 60.
44. Nancy F. Cott, ed., *A Woman Making History* (New Haven, 1991), pp. 277 ff.; Lotte Bailyn, *Breaking the Mold* (New York, 1993).
45. Paul R. McHugh, "Psychiatric Misadventures," *American Scholar,* 61 (Autumn 1992): 497 ff.; Rael J. Isaac and Virginia C. Armat, *Madness in the Streets* (New York, 1992).
46. O'Neill, *Coming Apart,* p. 186 ff.; Barone, *Our Country,* p. 426.
47. Reich, *Greening of America,* pp. 58, 119.

CHAPTER 7.

1. Norman Mailer, "The White Negro: Superficial Reflections on the Hipster," *Dissent* (Summer 1957): 276 ff.; Charles S. Reich, *The Greening of America* (New York, 1970), pp. 288 ff.; Charles Murray, *Losing Ground* (New York, 1984), pp. 18, 19.
2. Eugene O'Neill, *Lazarus Laughed* (1928), *Plays* (New York, 1955).
3. Oscar and Lilian Handlin, *Liberty and Power* (New York, 1986), pp. 17 ff., and *Liberty in Expansion* (New York, 1989), pp. 64 ff.
4. William O'Neill, *Coming Apart* (Chicago, 1971), pp. 292, 298; William Leuchtenberg, *A Troubled Feast* (Boston, 1979); David Chalmers, *And the Crooked Places Made Straight* (Baltimore, Md., 1991), pp. 15 ff.; Reich, *Greening of America,* p. 355; Tom Hayden, *Reunion* (New York, 1988), p. 502; Andrew Hacker, *The End of the American Era* (New York, 1970), p. 25.
5. Elliott J. Gorn, *The Manly Art: Bare-Knuckle Prize Fighting in America* (Ithaca, N.Y., 1986), pp. 248–51, 253; Joyce Carol Oates and Daniel Halperin, *Reading the Fights* (New York, 1988), p. 54; Charles Samuels, *The Magnificent Rube* (New York, 1957); Maxine E. Richard, *Everything Happened to Him* (New York, 1936), pp. 262 ff., 273 ff., 292; Norman Mailer, *The Fight* (Boston, 1975); Michael O'Brien, *Vince* (New York, 1987), pp. 377–82.
6. Mario Puzo, *The Godfather Papers* (New York, 1972); Oates and Halperin, *Reading the Fights,* pp. 47–49, 50; J. H. H. Gaute and Robin Odell, *The Murderers' Who's Who* (London, 1979), pp. 346, 347; Peter Lewis, *Eric Ambler* (New York, 1990).
7. Joseph C. Goulden, *The Best Years* (New York, 1976), p. 361; Howard Zinn, ed., *Justice in Everyday Life* (New York, 1974), pp. 365–66; Saul Alinsky, *Reveille for*

Radicals (New York, 1969), pp. x, xii; Andrew Hacker, *End of the American Era,* pp. 5, 9.

8. Edward Jay Epstein, *News from Nowhere* (New York, 1974), pp. 4, 5; Richard Campbell, *Sixty Minutes and the News* (Urbana, Ill., 1991); O'Neill, *Coming Apart,* p. 294.
9. Reich, *Greening of America,* pp. 9, 11, 301, 302; Ripon Society, *Instead of Revolution* (New York, 1971), p. 11; Thomas H. Marshall, *Class, Citizenship, and Social Development* (Garden City, New York, 1964), pp. 172–73; O'Neill, *Coming Apart,* p. 355; Marion K. Sanders, *The Professional Radical: Conversations with Saul Alinsky* (New York, 1970), pp. 45, 53; Kirkpatrick Sale, *Human Scale* (New York, 1980), p. 48; John P. Diggins, *The Proud Decades* (New York, 1988), pp. 215 ff.; Barone, *Our Country,* pp. 389 ff., 392, 491, 530.
10. Eugene O'Neill, *Long Day's Journey into Night* (New Haven, 1956).
11. Estes Kefauver, *Crime in America,* ed. Sidney Shalett (New York, 1951); Fred J. Cook, *A Two-Dollar Bet Means Murder* (New York, 1961); Thomas F. A. Plant, *Alcohol Problems* (New York, 1967), pp. 189, 197; Harrison M. Trice, *Alcoholism in America* (New York, 1966).
12. Donald W. Goodwin, *Alcohol and the Writer* (Kansas City, 1988); Aldous Huxley, *Doors of Perception* (New York, 1954); John Rublowsky, *The Stoned Age* (New York, 1974), pp. 87, 136, 141, 153, 159, 181; Lester Grinspoon, *Marihuana Reconsidered* (Cambridge, Mass., 1971); Arnold S. Treback, *The Great Drug War* (New York, 1987), pp. 7 ff.; Timothy Leary, *The Politics of Ecstasy* (New York, 1968), pp. 43, 56–57, 65–69, 132–33, 141.
13. Fannie Hurst, *Back Street* (New York, 1931); W. A. Swanberg, *Citizen Hearst* (New York, 1961); David M. Kennedy, *Birth Control in America* (New Haven, 1971).
14. 381 U.S. 479.; G. Egner, *Contraception versus Tradition* (New York, 1966), p. 178; Samuel Walker, *In Defense of American Liberties* (New York, 1990), pp. 300–301.
15. Elizabeth Draper, *Birth Control* (London, 1965); William H. Robertson, *Illustrated History of Contraceptives* (Casterton Hall, Carnforth, 1990), pp. 126 ff., 134 ff.; Charles Rembar, *The End of Obscenity* (New York, 1986); Barone, *Our Country,* p. 468.
16. Hacker, *End of the American Era,* pp. 31 ff.; Barone, *Our Country,* pp. 421 ff.; Abbie Hoffman, *The Best of Abbie Hoffman* (New York, 1989), pp. 100, 147–48; Joel Makower, *Woodstock: The Oral History* (New York, 1989), pp. 297, 298–99; Anthony M. Casale and Philip Lerman, *Where Have All the Flowers Gone* (Kansas City, 1989), p. viii.
17. Lawrence Ferlinghetti, *A Coney Island of the Mind* (Norfolk, Conn., 1958), pp. 44, 45.
18. Mary Cassata and Thomas Skill, *Life on Daytime Television* (Norwood, N.J., 1983), pp. 96 ff.
19. Ithiel de Sola Pool, *The Social Impact of the Telephone* (Cambridge, Mass., 1977), pp. 218 ff.; Hillel Schwartz, *Never Satisfied* (New York, 1986), pp. 252, 253; Erving Goffman, *Gender Advertisements* (Cambridge, Mass., 1979), pp. vii–ix, 84; Hilde Bruch, *Eating Disorders* (New York, 1973); Jill Welbourne and Joan Purgold, *The Eating Sickness* (Brighton, England, 1984); Cherry Boone O'Neill, *Starving for Attention* (New York, 1982); Susie Orbach, *Fat Is a Feminist Issue* (New York, 1978); Susie Orbach, *Hunger Strike* (London, 1986); Harvey A. Levenstein, *Revolu-*

tion at the Table: The Transformation of the American Diet (New York, 1988), pp. 194–211; Herbert I. Landon, *Closing the Circle* (Chicago, 1984), p. 88.

20. Gerold Frank, *The Boston Strangler* (New York, 1966).
21. Merle Miller, *Lyndon* (New York, 1980), pp. 308 ff.; David F. Greenberg, *The Construction of Homosexuality* (Chicago, 1988), pp. 429, 455–56, 458–81; Martin Duberman, *About Time* (New York, 1991), pp. 262–67.
22. Ned Rorem, *Music from the Inside Out* (New York, 1967), p. 30; Landon, *Closing the Circle,* pp. 102–29; David Horowitz *et al.,* eds., *Counterculture and Revolution* (New York, 1972), pp. 112–31.
23. Barone, *Our Country,* p. 463; Chalmers, *And the Crooked Places Made Straight,* p. 89; Peter Collier and David Horowitz, *Second Thoughts* (Lanham, Md., 1989), p. 176.
24. O'Neill, *Coming Apart,* pp. 293 ff.; Robin Morgan, *Going Too Far* (New York, 1977), pp. 82 ff., 123 ff.
25. Jacques Barzun, *Science* (New York, 1964), pp. 77, 120 ff.; also Gordon Welchman, *The Hut Six Story* (New York, 1982).
26. Ernest Gellner, "The Stakes in Anthropology," *American Scholar,* 57 (1988): 19 ff.; Thomas A. Nelson, *Kubrick* (Bloomington, Indiana, 1982), pp. 79–98, 99–132; Martin Duberman, *About Time,* p. 290.
27. Paul Hollander, *The Survival of the Adversary Culture* (New Brunswick, N.J., 1988), p. 155; Alinsky, *Reveille for Radicals,* pp. ix, xiii; Reich, *Greening of America,* pp. 360–61; Lawrence Lader, *Power on the Left* (New York, 1979), pp. 297–99; Horowitz *et al., Counterculture and Revolution,* pp. 190, 204.
28. James B. Conant, *The American High School Today* (New York, 1959).
29. Vincent Sheean, *Personal History* (Boston, 1969), p. xii; Glenn Jeansonne, *Gerald L. K. Smith* (New Haven, 1988), pp. 192 ff.; Jenna Joselit, *New York's Jewish Jews* (Bloomington, Ind., 1991), *passim*; Frank Razelle, *Televangelism* (Carbondale, Ill., 1987), pp. 17, 71; Ralph L. Roy, *Apostles of Discord* (Boston, 1953), pp. 350 ff.; O'Neill, *Coming Apart,* pp. 312 ff.; John P. Diggins, *America in Peace and War* (New York, 1988), p. 258.
30. Landon, *Closing the Circle,* pp. 122–25; Steven Levy, *The Unicorn's Secret* (New York, 1988), pp. 53 ff., 71 ff., 95; Michael A. Bernstein, "Murder and the Utopian Moment," *American Scholar,* 61 (Spring 1992): 213 ff.
31. Charles Manson, *Manson in His Own Words,* ed. Noel Emmons (New York, 1986).
32. Vincent Bugliosi, *Helter Skelter: The True Story of the Manson Murders* (New York, 1974), pp. 55, 64, 85, 132, 220, 456.
33. Mary McCarthy, "Ghostly Father, I Confess," *Harper's Bazaar,* 75 (April 1942): 52 ff.
34. Landon, *Closing the Circle,* p. 110; Sara Evans, *Personal Politics: The Roots of Women's Liberation in the Civil Rights Movement and the New Left* (New York, 1979); O'Neill, *Coming Apart,* pp. 295 ff.
35. Evans, *Personal Politics,* pp. 225 ff.
36. Leonard Wolf, *Voices from the Love Generation* (Boston, 1968), pp. 118, 155; Oscar and Mary Handlin, *Facing Life* (Boston, 1971); Warren G. Bennis and Philip E. Slater, *The Temporary Society* (New York, 1968), p. 128; Nigel Young, *An Infantile Disorder?* (London, 1977), pp. 361–62.
37. Norman Mailer, *Armies of the Night* (New York, 1968), p. 288; Stokely Carmichael, *Stokely Speaks* (New York, 1971), pp. 47, 156, 199–200; Michael Freedland, *Jane*

Fonda (New York, 1988), pp. 154, 158; Reich, *Greening of America,* p. 391; Chalmers, *And the Crooked Places,* pp. 85–87; Todd Gitlin, *The Whole World Is Watching* (Berkeley, 1980).

38. Ferlinghetti, *Coney Island of the Mind,* p. 57; Wolf, *Voices from the Love Generation,* pp. 9, 26 ff., 94, 250, 280; Donald N. Michael, ed., *The Future Society* (n.p., 1970), pp. 64 ff.; Victor Turner, *Dramas, Fields, and Metaphors* (Ithaca, N.Y., 1974), pp. 244, 246, 247, 261.
39. Thomas Jefferson, *Works,* ed. P. L. Ford, 12 vols. (New York, 1905), 11:82.
40. Eugene O'Neill, *Long Day's Journey into Night* (New Haven, 1956); Martin Tropp, *Mary Shelley's Monster* (Boston, 1976), pp. 169 ff.; Michael, *Future Society,* pp. 68 ff.; O'Neill, *Coming Apart,* p. 295.
41. Barone, *Our Country,* pp. 385, 451; O'Neill, *Coming Apart,* pp. 281–87.
42. James W. Trent and Judith L. Craise, "Commitment and Conformity," *The Journal of Social Issues,* 23 (1967): 34 ff.
43. *Washington Post,* May 29, 1969.
44. Chalmers, *And the Crooked Places,* pp. 84 ff.; August Meier *et al.,* eds., *Black Protests in the 1960s* (New York, 1991), p. 121; O'Neill, *Coming Apart,* pp. 282, 291.
45. Ira C. Magaziner, "We Need a Cultural Revolution," *Brown Alumni Monthly* (July 1969): 30 ff.
46. Freedland, *Jane Fonda,* p. 192; Ralph Keyes, *We the Lonely People: Searching for Community* (New York, 1973), pp. 212 ff.; Warren G. Dennis and Philip E. Slater, *The Temporary Society* (New York, 1968), p. 136; Mark Lewisohn, *The Complete Beatles Chronicle* (London, 1992), p. 139; Reginald Major, *A Panther Is a Black Cat* (New York, 1971), pp. 291–92.
47. Fyodor Dostoyevsky, *Notes from the Underground,* trans. Mirra Ginsburg (New York, 1974); Albert Goldman, *The Lives of John Lennon* (New York, 1988), p. 394; Sale, *Human Scale,* p. 45; Landon, *Closed Circle,* pp. 135–37.
48. O'Neill, *Coming Apart,* pp. 182 ff.; Casale and Lerman, *Where Have All the Flowers Gone?* pp. 30, 44, 47, 71.
49. Ferlinghetti, *Coney Island of the Mind,* p. 9; Irwin Shaw, *Two Weeks in Another Town* (New York, 1960); Michael Shnayerson, *Irwin Shaw* (New York, 1989), p. 258; Charles Boer, *Charles Olson in Connecticut* (Chicago, 1975), p. 19.
50. Robert Lowell, *Life Studies* (London, 1959); Marc Eliot, *Death of a Rebel* (Garden City, N.Y., 1979), p. 223; Kevin Duffy, *Children of the Forest* (New York, 1984), pp. 84, 176 ff.
51. O'Neill, *Coming Apart,* p. 288; Lowell, *Life Studies.*
52. Major, *A Panther Is a Black Cat,* p. 282.

EPILOGUE

1. James L. Baughman, *The Republic of Mass Culture* (Baltimore, 1992), p. 221.
2. Thomas B. Edsall, *The New Politics of Inequality* (New York, 1984); Richard E. Morgan, *Disabling America: The Rights Industry in Our Time* (New York, 1984).
3. Michael Barone, *Our Country* (New York, 1990), pp. 441, 566 ff.; Martin P. Wattenberg, *The Decline of American Political Parties* (Cambridge, Mass., 1984), pp. 125–31.
4. Peter Collier and David Horowitz, eds., *Second Thoughts* (Lanham, Md., 1989), pp. 143 ff.

5. See below, note 10; Morgan, *Disabling America,* pp. 138–39.
6. James Bryce, *The American Commonwealth,* 2 vols. (London, 1888), 2:606; John Spargo, *Socialism* (New York, 1906), p. 236.
7. Robert H. Bremner, *et al., American Choices: Social Dilemmas and Public Policy since 1960* (Columbus, Ohio, 1986), p. 29; Charles Murray, "The Coming of Custodial Democracy," *Commentary,* 86 (Sept. 1988): 19 ff.
8. Abigail Thernstrom, *Whose Vote Counts* (Cambridge, Mass., 1989); also Frances Fox Piven and Richard A. Cloward, *Poor People's Movement* and *Why Americans Don't Vote* (New York, 1989).
9. Peter Skerry, *Mexican Americans* (New York, 1993), pp. 36, 48, 49.
10. *E.g.,* Michel Rosenfeld, *Affirmative Action and Justice* (New Haven, 1991), pp. 335 ff.; also Bremner, *American Choices,* p. 54.
11. Bremner, *American Choices,* p. 56; Morgan, *Disabling America,* pp. 176–77; Lewis H. Lapham, *The Imperial Masquerade* (New York, 1990), p. 92.
12. 438 U.S. 407 (1978): 160 ff.; Lee Rainwater and William Yancey, *The Moynihan Report* (Cambridge, Mass., 1967); Thomas Sowell, "Affirmative Action," *Commentary,* 88 (Dec. 1989): 21 ff.; *Civil Rights Update,* March, Apr., 1992; Oscar Handlin, "The Bill of Rights in Its Context," *American Scholar,* 62 (Spring 1993), 177 ff.; Daniel J. Bodenhamer and James W. Ely, Jr., eds., *The Bill of Rights in Modern America* (Bloomington, Ind., 1993), pp. 39ff., 72 ff., 92 ff.
13. Shelby Steele, *The Content of Our Character* (New York, 1990); Stephen L. Carter, *Reflections of an Affirmative Action Baby* (New York, 1992); Morgan, *Disabling America,* pp. 191–97.
14. Bert E. Swanson, *School Integration Controversies in New York City* (Bronxville, N.Y., 1965); Ray C. Rist, *The Invisible Children: School Integration* (Cambridge, 1978).
15. Carter, *Reflections;* Hillel Levine and Lawrence Harmon, *The Death of an American Jewish Community* (New York, 1992).
16. Oscar Handlin, *Truth in History* (Cambridge, Mass., 1979), pp. 380 ff.; *New York Times,* Dec. 21, 1984.
17. *New York Times,* Nov. 13, 1991; *Washington Post,* Dec. 3, 1991; Abigail Thernstrom, "Guinier Miss," *The New Republic,* June 4, 1993, pp. 16 ff.; Barone, *Our Country,* p. 565.
18. Stanley Lieberson and Mary C. Waters, *From Many Strands* (New York, 1988), p. 22.
19. Henry H. Mitchell, *Black Belief* (New York, 1975); also Sandra T. Barnes, ed., *Africa's Ogun* (Bloomington, Ind., 1989).
20. Joel Kotkin, *Tribes* (New York, 1992); Michael Novak, *The Rise of the Unmeltable Ethnics* (New York, 1972).
21. John C. Harles, *Politics in the Lifeboat* (Boulder, Colo., 1993); Edward J. Lincoln, "The Showa Economic Experience," in Carol Gluck and Stephen R. Graubard, eds., *Showa* (New York, 1992), pp. 191–208; Michael Levin, "Response to Race Differences in Crime," *Journal of Social Philosophy,* 23 (1992): 29 ff.
22. Arthur M. Schlesinger, Jr., *The Disuniting of America* (New York, 1992); Rita Kramer, "Are Girls Short-Changed?" *Commentary,* 93 (Dec. 1992): 48 ff.; Allan Bloom, *Closing of the American Mind* (New York, 1987); Martin Anderson, *Imposters in the Temple* (New York, 1992).
23. Edward Bellamy, *Looking Backward* (New York, 1960); J. J. Rousseau, *The First*

and Second Discourses, ed. R. Masters (New York, 1964), p. 101; Murray, "Custodial Democracy," pp. 19 ff.; Charles R. Morris, *A Time of Passion* (Cambridge, 1984), p. 187; Ralf Dahrendorf, *The New Liberty* (London, 1975), pp. 14, 32.

24. Robert Nisbet, *The Present Age* (New York, 1988).
25. John P. Diggins and Mark E. Kann, eds., *The Problems of Authority in America* (Philadelphia, 1982), pp. 9, 60; Kenneth Boulding *et al., From Abundance to Scarcity* (Columbus, Ohio, 1978), pp. 72 ff.; Kirkpatrick Sale, *Human Scale* (New York, 1980); Barone, *Our Country,* pp. 596, 601; Collier and Horowitz, *Second Thoughts,* p. 99; Fred Hirsch, *Social Limits to Growth* (Cambridge, Mass., 1976), pp. 167 ff.; James T. Patterson, *America's Struggle Against Poverty, 1900–1980* (Cambridge, Mass., 1981), pp. 202–204; Bruce A. Ackerman, *Reconstructing American Law* (Cambridge, Mass., 1984), pp. 99 ff.
26. Alan S. Blinder, *Growing Together* (Knoxville, Tenn., 1991); Murray, *Losing Ground,* pp. 49 ff.; Patterson, *America's Struggle Against Poverty,* pp. 200 ff.
27. Gladys Taber, *Still Cove Journal* (New York, 1981), pp. 6, 7; Jack Kugelmass, *The Miracle of Intervale Avenue* (New York, 1986); John A. Howard, ed., *Essays on Freedom* (Greenwich, Conn., 1984), p. 67; Marshall Blonsky, *American Mythologies* (New York, 1992), p. 473; James W. Clarke, *On Being Mad or Merely Angry* (Princeton, N.J., 1990).
28. David Plante, *The Woods* (New York, 1982), p. 122; Charlotte Ryan, *Primetime Activism: Media Strategies for Grass Roots Organizing* (Boston, 1991), pp. 4–5, 236–37.
29. Norman Corwin, *Trivializing America* (Secaucus, N.J., 1983), pp. 16–17, 173; Robert Slater, *Portraits in Silicon* (Cambridge, Mass., 1987); Patterson, *America's Struggle Against Poverty,* pp. 208–209.
30. Murray, *Losing Ground,* pp. 60 ff.
31. Barone, *Our Country,* pp. 563, 564; E. P. Thompson and Ben Thompson, *Star Wars: Self Destruct Incorporated* (London, 1985), pp. 1, 14, 65–67; Union of Concerned Scientists, *The Fallacy of Star Wars* (New York, 1984), p. iii; Kerry L. Hunter, *The Reign of Fantasy: The Political Roots of Reagan's Star Wars Policy* (New York, 1992), pp. 94–95.
32. Paul Fussell, *Bad* (New York, 1993); Peter Schrag, *The End of the American Future* (New York, 1973), p. 115.
33. Craig Lambert, "The Life of the Party," *Harvard Magazine* (October 1993): 44; Lois Swann, *Torn Covenant* (New York, 1981); Barone, *Our Country,* p. 538; Lapham, *Imperial Masquerade,* pp. 274–75; Thomas R. Edwards, *Over Here* (New Brunswick, N.J., 1991), pp. 99–105; Edward Pessen, *Losing Our Souls* (Chicago, 1993); H. W. Brands, *The Devil We Knew: Americans and the Cold War* (New York, 1993).
34. Donald T. Oliver, *Animal Rights* (Washington, D.C., 1993); Richard P. Adler, ed., *All in the Family* (New York, 1979); Marvin E. Gettleman, *The Failure of American Liberalism* (New York, 1971), pp. 510–15; Lapham, *Imperial Masquerade,* p. 275; Timothy Leary, *Changing My Mind* (Englewood CLiffs, N.J., 1982), pp. 256–57; Samuel Walker, *In Defense of American Liberties* (New York, 1990), p. 318; Lee Quinby, *Freedom, Foucault and the Subject of America* (Boston, 1991), pp. 152–72; Joel Spring, *Images of American Life* (Albany, N.Y., 1992), p. 254.
35. Steffan B. Linder, *The Harried Leisure Class* (New York, 1970); Anthony Quinn, *The Original Sin* (Boston, 1972).
36. Maud Ellmann, *The Hunger Artists: Starving, Writing, and Imprisonment* (Cam-

bridge, Mass., 1993), pp. 9–10, 113; Jean Baudrillard, *America,* tr. Chris Turner (New York, 1988), pp. 31, 35.

37. Joseph Monninger, *The Family Man* (New York, 1981); Paul A. Cantor, "Stephen Greenblatt's New Historicist Vision," *Academic Questions,* 6 (Fall 1993): 21–36.
38. Hester Eisenstein, *Contemporary Feminist Thought* (Boston, 1983), pp. 117 ff., 137 ff.; Blonsky, *American Mythologies,* p. 40; Baudrillard, *America,* pp. 38, 47.
39. Charles Murray, "The Legacy of the 1960s," *Commentary,* 94 (July 1992): 23 ff., 25, 26.
40. Gerard Sullivan and Harvey Aronson, *High Hopes: The Amityville Murders* (New York, 1981); Murray, "Legacy of the 1960s," *loc. cit.,* 94:25 ff.; Howard, *Essays on Freedom,* pp. 101, 107; Russell Jacoby, *The Last Intellectuals* (New York, 1987), p. 181; Ruth Wisse, "Living with Women's Lib," *Commentary,* 86 (Aug. 1988): 40 ff.; Jack Whalen and Richard Flacks, *Beyond the Barricades: The Sixties Generation Grows Up* (Philadelphia, 1989), p. 227; also William J Bennett, ed., *The Index of Leading Cultural Indicators* (Washington, D.C., 1993), No. 1.
41. Martin Duberman, *About Time* (New York, 1991), pp. 332, 351–52, 422–23; Springer, *Images,* p. 257.
42. James H. Jones, *Bad Blood: The Tuskegee Syphilis Experiment* (New York, 1993), pp. 220–41.
43. Joseph Monniger, *Family Man* (New York, 1982); Patricia Chute, *Castine* (Garden City, N.Y., 1987); Lucy Honig, *Picking Up* (South Harpswell, Maine, 1986); Dana A. Jennings, *Mosquito Games* (New York, 1989); André Dubus, *We Don't Live Here Anymore* (New York, 1984).
44. Albert Goldman, *The Lives of John Lennon* (New York, 1988), pp. 679 ff.

INDEX